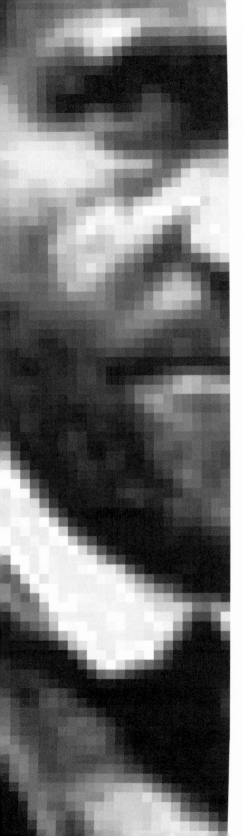

GRANT'S

SECRET SERVICE
The Intelligence War from Belmont to Appomattox

William B. Feis

University of Nebraska Press : Lincoln and London

Library of Congress Cataloging-in-Publication Data

Feis, William B., 1963–
Grant's secret service : the intelligence war from
Belmont to Appomattox / William B. Feis. p. cm.
Includes bibliographical references and index.
ISBN 0-8032-2005-7 (cloth : alkaline paper)
1. United States – History – Civil War, 1861–1865 –
Secret service. 2. United States – History – Civil
War, 1861–1865 – Campaigns. 3. Grant, Ulysses
S. (Ulysses Simpson), 1822–1885 – Military leader-
ship. I. Title.
E608 .F45 2002   973.7'85–dc21   2001037673

Parts of chapter 1 and the epilogue of the present
work appeared in a different version in "'He Don't
Care a Damn for What the Enemy Does out of His
Sight': A Perspective on U. S. Grant and Military
Intelligence" in *North & South* 1 (January 1998): 68–
72, 74–81, and are reprinted with permission of the
publisher. Chapter 3 was previously published as
"Grant and the Belmont Campaign: A Study in
Intelligence and Command" in *The Art of Command
in the Civil War* (Lincoln: University of Nebraska
Press, 1998) and is reprinted with permission by the
University of Nebraska Press. Portions of chapter 10
were previously published in "A Union Military
Intelligence Failure: Jubal Early's Raid, June 12–July
14, 1864" in *Civil War History* 36 (September 1990):
209–25 and "Neutralizing the Valley: The Role of
Military Intelligence in the Defeat of Jubal Early's
Army of the Valley, 1854–1865" in *Civil War History* 39
(September 1993): 199–215. The material from both
of these *Civil War History* articles is reprinted with
the permission of The Kent State University Press.

In memory of La Veta P. Feis (1910–2000) and Edwin C. Fishel (1914–1999)

CONTENTS

ILLUSTRATIONS

ACKNOWLEDGMENTS

Many people helped make this book possible, and though they deserve much credit and gratitude for their patience and advice, I willingly shoulder the blame for all errors. First, my deepest gratitude goes to my two graduate advisors at the University of Nebraska–Lincoln and The Ohio State University. Dr. Peter Maslowski was a model of scholarly professionalism who inspired me during my undergraduate and graduate days at UNL. Together we discovered the uncharted world of Civil War military intelligence and came up with the idea for this project. I believe the findings in this study more than justify our early enthusiasm. I am also thankful for his friendship and sage advice. His faith in me helped transform my love of history from infantile fascination to a profession. It is safe to say that, without Pete and his red pen, I would not be where I am today.

My dissertation advisor, Dr. Allan R. Millett, taught me so much about the Civil War, military history, and the historical profession, but I am most thankful for the wonderful friendship we developed while "campaigning" at Gettysburg, Carnifex Ferry, Franklin and Nashville, the Wilderness, and Shiloh. Without his guidance, vast knowledge of military history, and friendship, I would not be the historian I am. If my professional accomplishments even approached the level of his remarkable and distinguished career, I would consider myself fortunate. A finer scholar and "pard" would be hard to find.

The late Edwin C. Fishel, the dean of Civil War military intelligence, was with me in spirit every step of the way. His groundbreaking study of intelligence in the eastern theater, his experience in the intelligence business, and his mastery of the resources at the National Archives made my research much more profitable and enjoyable. From him I learned what it truly means to be a gentleman *and* a scholar. His willingness to share ideas, research notes, and insights gained from decades of research provided a model of scholarly cooperation and selflessness. Most of all, my long research trips to Washington were always brightened by the many dinners shared with Ed and his wife, Gladys, at the Cosmos Club. Those who study the "late unpleasantness" for a living as well as for fun owe a great debt to Ed Fishel.

I am also indebted to Michael Musick and Michael T. Meier of the

Military Reference Branch at the National Archives. Their knowledge of the records and their help in identifying other places to search paid off handsomely. Their devotion to public service and to history is inspirational; I raise my BVU coffee mug to both of them. Bradley E. Gernand, senior archivist at the Library of Congress, was also tremendously helpful in locating possible sources. The staffs at the Indiana Historical Society, the Indiana State Library, the Illinois State Historical Library, and the State Historical Society of Iowa all provided excellent suggestions and invaluable assistance. The University of Nebraska Press showed early interest in this project and provided much encouragement and valuable advice along the way. Also, my copyeditor, Kevin Brock, used his eye for detail and knowledge of the Civil War to improve the manuscript in significant ways.

I would also like to thank the men of the Forty-ninth Ohio Volunteer Infantry for allowing me to join their ranks once a year for my annual campaign. They are an outstanding group of reenactors whose love of the Civil War is an inspiration.

Two of my students, Grant Nulle and Daniel Rheingans, helped with the maps and during the copyediting phase. I am grateful for their hard work and for their good-natured approach to some onerous tasks. Both are gifted individuals who will go far. Also, my gratitude goes to Rick Shafer in BVU's Teaching and Learning with Technology Center for helping me navigate the complex and dangerous world of disk translation.

I could never repay the enormous debt of gratitude I owe my parents, Gil and Polly Feis; my sister Mary Karczewski; and my grandparents Bill and Anne Doering for their steadfast support and endless faith in me. I only wish my grandmother La Veta Feis, who passed away before the manuscript went to press, could see what her love and support helped make possible. I am also grateful to Sharon and Dick Bartholomew for not only sharing their daughter but also making West Virginia my second home. My dear friends John Stull, Greg Keller, Steven Helm, Beth Russell, Joyce Grimes, and Suzanne Studer were always there for me. The sunshine they bring to my life means more than they could ever know.

Finally, to my wife, colleague, best friend, and soul mate, Dixee Bartholomew-Feis, I owe everything. Her love, patience, understanding, and the example she sets as a gifted teacher, not to mention her exceptional editing skills, made this book possible.

Grant's Secret Service

INTRODUCTION

"He Don't Care a Damn
for What the Enemy Does
out of His Sight"

"There are no more important duties which an officer may be called upon to perform," asserted West Point professor Dennis Hart Mahan, "than those of collecting and arranging the information upon which either the general or daily operations of a campaign must be based." With this passage, the foremost military thinker in America before the Civil War stressed the importance of military intelligence, or the collection and use of information, to generalship. Insights into an enemy's organization, movements, strength, capabilities, and intentions provide a foundation upon which a commander formulates his own plans. After all, asked French theorist Antoine Henri Jomini, "how can any man say what he should do himself, if he is ignorant [of] what his adversary is about?" In nineteenth-century warfare, however, finding reliable and timely information was a Herculean task, especially since slow communications could render even good intelligence useless. In addition, both Federal and Confederate armies lacked formal intelligence organizations, operational guidelines, and personnel experienced in the secret side of war. Most Civil War officers learned about the intelligence "business" on the job. But generals are measured by their successes and failures, and these outcomes hinge upon decisions made at crucial times. To rephrase Jomini, how can historians judge their choices if we are ignorant of the information upon which their decisions were based? Determining what a commander knew, when he knew it, and how he used what he knew offers a valuable—and perhaps more evenhanded—perspective from which to view the nature of command in the Civil War. This book focuses on Ulysses S. Grant's collection and use of military intelligence from his early command assignments in Missouri in 1861 to his final campaigns in Virginia in 1864–65. Analyzing the information and interpretations that shaped his decisions can provide deeper insights into Grant as a military leader and perhaps shed more light on how he became one of the war's most successful generals.[1]

To examine Grant's campaigns from this perspective, however, requires a brief examination of the nature of Union intelligence operations—or what contemporaries called "secret service"—during the Civil War. In the modern military definition, "information" is merely raw, undigested news on the enemy that has yet to be analyzed and shaped into a coherent form. "Intelligence," though, refers to the product of the evaluation and interpretation of the information streaming in to headquarters. During the Civil War, however, the terms were synonymous and used interchangeably (a practice that will be followed in this study). Typically, if an officer claimed to have received intelligence, he meant only that bits of unprocessed information had reached his desk. Analysis and interpretation of this evidence was usually done in his head and not, like today, by professional intelligence analysts. In the mid-nineteenth century, no military or civilian personnel had any formal training in this specialty. As a result, professional and volunteer officers entered the war with little exposure to this facet of command. Accordingly, intelligence operations were mostly ad hoc affairs, as varied in their scope and effectiveness as the personalities and experience of the individuals directing them. With no permanent armywide intelligence apparatus at their disposal, neither side ensured a consistent emphasis on systematic and ongoing collection and analysis at any level of command.

Most commanders recognized the importance of possessing information on the enemy, but finding it remained a complex task. Generals on both sides utilized various collection methods and received information from a multiplicity of human sources (called HUMINT in modern terminology).[2] These can be further classified as either "passive" sources (prisoners of war, deserters, refugees, local civilians, and slaves) or "active" sources (spies, scouts, cavalry reconnaissances, visual observations, intercepted correspondence, and enemy newspapers). The terms "scout" and "spy" were also used interchangeably, though scouts were typically enlisted men or noncommissioned officers who prowled the no man's land between the lines, while spies resided in enemy territory and reported via secret messenger.

In his classic *On War*, Prussian military theorist Carl von Clausewitz complained that "Many intelligence reports in war are contradictory; even more are false, and most are uncertain." Civil War officers generally would have seconded this observation as they struggled to determine the veracity of sources, a constant and important variable in all calculations. For Union military leaders, the quest for information from behind Confederate lines depended upon operatives who were familiar with "rebeldom." In addition to the more glamorous scouts and spies, other sources proved valuable because of their unique knowledge of the enemy. Deserters, prisoners, refugees, and Southern slaves were potential wellsprings of information if utilized carefully. Since most of these individuals were untrained observers, their reliability varied greatly. Some exaggerated reports to secure favorable treatment or to receive increased pay, while others simply misinterpreted what they had seen or heard. A commander fought a relentless battle of wits as he tried to extract useful news from those coming into his lines. But possessing accurate information was not enough; to be useful it had to reach the decision maker before the press of time rendered it moot. Reliant upon horses or their own feet for transportation, operatives struggled mightily to transmit their news quickly. Dodging enemy patrols and guerrillas, wandering at night across unfamiliar and sometimes forbidding terrain at the mercy of the elements, avoiding suspicion from a hostile citizenry, and hoping friendly pickets would hold their fire as one returned to the lines all delayed the transmission of intelligence. Moreover, once behind Union lines, convincing local commanders of one's credentials (especially since an operative dared not carry any incriminating identification) also cost precious time. After a scout negotiated these obstacles and reached his employer, chances were good the information he brought would be stale. Even if an informant brought in accurate and timely news, one final hurdle remained: convincing the decision maker to believe it. As a result of all the difficulties associated with wartime intelligence work, pervasive and paralyzing uncertainty hung like a pall over the decision-making process. Clausewitz noted that the difficulty of "accurate recognition," or the ability to penetrate the fog of war and glimpse the truth, constituted "one of the most serious sources of friction in war." Many Civil War officers would have agreed.[3]

Though commanders faced daunting obstacles in their search for information, the operatives they sent on secret service missions confronted an even worse fate. Both sides wasted little time in incarcerating or killing those suspected of spying for the enemy. Not a few individuals ended their careers in irons or at the end of a noose. After the war, stories of executions excited and touched the reading public. Who could forget the loyalty of Sam Davis or the stoic demeanor of Timothy Webster as they faced the hangman? But for every Davis or Webster, there were a handful of operatives like scout Oliver Smith Rankin of the Tenth Indiana who died unheralded and unreported. Arrested while on a secret mission in Tennessee, his captors dragged Rankin into some nearby woods and executed him with a shotgun, leaving his body to the wolves.[4]

Whether frustrated by a dearth of information or befuddled by a flood of contradictory reports, Civil War commanders had basically three ways to deal with uncertainty: (1) ignore intelligence altogether and forge ahead, trusting in luck, intuition, and enemy miscues to achieve success or avoid disaster; (2) view intelligence as a panacea and intensify collection efforts in the belief that *more* information will eventually erase all doubts and lead to the right decision; or (3) pursue intelligence and utilize what is collected, accepting uncertainty as a constant and managing it by finding other ways to compensate for imperfect knowledge. The character, intellect, and experience of individual officers determined which perspective—or combinations thereof—would be chosen at the moment of decision. Clausewitz believed what he called "military genius" to be a crucial factor in the process. This rare quality allowed an officer, even in the midst of chaos and impending disaster, to see "glimmerings of the inner light which leads to truth," an attribute the French called *coup d'oeil* and what Clausewitz described as an "inward eye" allowing a commander to make "sound decision[s] . . . in the midst of action." But these qualities alone did not promise success. The essential component of military genius, concluded Clausewitz, was "the courage to follow this faint light wherever it may lead." As scholar Michael I. Handel observed, however, even the most pronounced military genius could not overcome basic human nature. "In the final analysis," he wrote, "intelligence problems are human problems—problems of perception, subjectivity, and wishful thinking—and thus are not likely to disappear." Regardless of the era, the war, or the technological advances in collection methods and communications, the decision maker—burdened by fears, overconfidence, paranoia, physical and mental exhaustion, uncertainty, and self-delusion—will always take center stage.[5]

The options Ulysses S. Grant chose while in the spotlight of command, how he overcame or succumbed to uncertainty and human nature, and the overall impact the "information war" had upon his campaigns reveals much about his success as a military leader. But to understand the influences that shaped his approach to intelligence, it is necessary to examine the formative experiences from his pre–Civil War military career.[6]

After graduating from West Point in 1843, where he had received very limited exposure to intelligence matters in the classroom, Grant accepted a commission as a brevet second lieutenant in the Fourth Infantry. The growing threat of war with Mexico brought him to Corpus Christi,

Texas, in the late summer of 1845 as part of Maj. Gen. Zachary Taylor's "Army of Observation" monitoring the disputed territory along the Mexican-American frontier. In the spring of 1846 and in later campaigns, Taylor utilized a local network of informants in Corpus Christi but relied heavily upon the reconnaissance and mapmaking skills of topographical engineers on his staff, including Lt. George G. Meade. During the battle of Palo Alto (May 8, 1846), one of his "topogs," Lt. Jacob E. Blake, rode in front of the Mexican lines within musket range, stopping periodically to count the number of enemy soldiers in formation. Prior to the battle of Monterey (September 19–20, 1846), Taylor used information provided by his topographers to devise his attack plan. But "Old Rough and Ready's" martial reputation rested upon his penchant for fighting, not on his ability to collect information. Meade criticized Taylor for his "perfect inability to make any use of the information" he received. Even after success at Monterey, Taylor made minimal efforts to collect and analyze intelligence. Col. Ethan Allen Hitchcock, who would become Winfield Scott's inspector general, alluded to Taylor's perpetual lack of intelligence during a visit to his camps early in the war. After being briefed on the enemy's situation, Hitchcock complained that Taylor was still "quite in the dark" with regard to the Mexican army's movements and intentions. "The General may have information which he keeps to himself," he noted, "but I know him too well to believe he has any."[7]

Despite his shortcomings, Grant deeply admired Taylor and strove to emulate his hero's leadership style. "No other man," claimed historian Grady McWhiney, "so profoundly influenced Grant's pre–Civil War military education." His description of Taylor's leadership style seemed a mirror image of his own, especially in the ability to convey orders clearly and succinctly. Though he did not share Taylor's ambivalence toward intelligence, Grant apparently learned one lesson from his hero about the relationship between decisions and military information. In his memoirs, Grant criticized Scott for seeing "more through the eyes of his staff officers than through his own" and admired Taylor because he "saw for himself." Though he sometimes relied upon the interpretations of others, during the Civil War Grant preferred to "see for himself," meaning he made decisions based upon his own perceptions of the situation. For better or worse, this desire sometimes colored his interpretation of the intelligence he received.[8]

Although critical of his overreliance on others to inform decisions, the true beginning of Grant's intelligence education came under the tutelage of Winfield Scott in central Mexico. After joining the general's overland campaign to Mexico City in the spring of 1847, Grant, the quartermaster of the Fourth Infantry, participated in intelligence operations and witnessed how the effective use of information and maintaining the initiative could secure victory. As Scott's army moved inland from its base at Veracruz, Grant observed two battles in particular that revealed the value of reliable intelligence. Scott had a penchant for detailed planning and, as a result, routinely dispatched patrols to gain information on enemy dispositions and terrain before committing to battle. At Cerro Gordo, the Mexican commander, Gen. Antonio Lopez de Santa Anna, planned to blunt the American inland advance in a mountain defile along the National Road leading from Veracruz to Mexico City. Halting Scott's forces there would trap the Americans in the coastal lowlands during the season for deadly yellow fever, a disease more dreaded than Mexican bullets. Santa Anna believed he held an impregnable position. But Grant noted that Lt. P. G. T. Beauregard, Capt. Robert E. Lee, and other army engineers proved him wrong when they discovered a way to turn the left flank of the Mexican line "over ground where [Santa Anna] supposed impossible." On April 17 Scott's forces, led by the engineers, did just that and sent Santa Anna and his troops fleeing toward Mexico City.[9]

Grant received his first hands-on experience with intelligence just before American forces marched into the Valley of Mexico. After Cerro Gordo, Scott concentrated his forces at the town of Puebla, about seventy miles east of Mexico City. The division under Brig. Gen. William J. Worth, including the Fourth Infantry, entered the town on May 15, followed later by Scott and the rest of the army. The Americans remained in Puebla until early August while Scott, anxious to move on Mexico City, awaited reinforcements and searched the countryside for supplies to support his troops now isolated from their base at Veracruz. "Old Fuss and Feathers" also seized the opportunity to gather information on Santa Anna's forces, the defenses of Mexico City, and the condition of the roads and terrain approaching the capital. Stalled in the middle of enemy territory and separated from his base by miles of rugged country controlled by unfriendly Mexican guerrilla units, Scott needed reliable information now more than ever.[10]

Col. Ethan Allen Hitchcock, recently transferred from Taylor's army and in charge of Scott's secret service, wasted little time in addressing the situation. In June he hired Manuel Dominguez, an established highway-man and resident of Puebla, as a courier. Incarcerated in the Puebla jail when Hitchcock found him, Dominguez accepted the colonel's offer and before long had brought his entire band of two hundred men on board as spies, guides, couriers, and guerrillas. Known as the "Mexican Spy Company," Dominguez's men scouted the roads to Veracruz and Mexico City, collected information from contacts among the population, ha-rassed guerrillas, and penetrated the Mexican capital to learn more about its defenses.[11]

While Scott prepared for the coming offensive, the Mexican Spy Com-pany and reconnaissance patrols headed by engineers searched for the best approach to the capital city. Scott saw several possible routes to Mexico City, including a northern route around Lake Texcoco aimed at Santa Anna's northwestern defenses and another route along the south-ern shore of Lake Chalco toward San Augustín and the fortifications south and west of the city. The swampy nature of the terrain around the fortified city, accessed primarily by causeways, limited American options. Engineers on Scott's staff and army topographers pored over the avail-able maps of the area, penciling in information gleaned from their own reconnaissances and from spies and local inhabitants. After learning about the impracticability of the northern route, Scott opted for the ad-vance along the southern shore of Lake Chalco.[12]

Grant played a minor role in the intelligence-gathering operations at Puebla. Probably because of his contacts among the population gained while procuring supplies for the regiment, Grant queried local citizens about the roads between Puebla and Mexico City and about the latter's defenses. He also examined the "Mexican scouts in our camp," un-doubtedly a reference to Dominguez's operatives, and kept track of the intelligence gained on what he called an "information map." Not only was Grant involved with collecting information, he also analyzed and used what he learned to formulate a plan to assail the Mexican capital. Scott's decision in early September to attack the city from the west and southwest had resulted in the battles of Contreras, Churubusco, and Molino del Rey. But as of September 12, the stout fortress of Chapultepec still stood between the Americans and Mexico City. At that time Grant issued his first "intelligence report": "My observations convince me that we have other strong works to reduce before we can enter the city. . . . From my map and all the information I acquired while the army was halted at Puebla, I was then, and am now more than ever, convinced that the army could have approached the city by passing around north of it, and reached the northwest side, and avoided all the fortified positions, until we reached the gates of the city at their weakest and most indefensible, as well as most approachable points." He forwarded the assessment to his superiors but never learned whether it reached Scott's headquarters. Though confident in his conclusions and disappointed in Scott's choices, Grant assumed that "the commanding General had possessed himself of all the facts" before making his decision. Nearly four decades later Grant remained convinced his assessment and course of action were correct. "It has always seemed to me," he wrote, "that this northern route . . . would have been the better one to have taken." [13]

During the Mexican War, Grant observed two very different approaches to intelligence and decision making. He admired Taylor's reliance upon his own perceptions of the situation when crafting a battle plan instead of depending too heavily upon the views of informants and staff officers. But Scott's avid pursuit of information and skillful use of engineers for reconnaissance showed the advantages of ascertaining "all the facts" before committing to a course of action and the value of a competent intelligence staff. But which approach would Grant adopt in the next war? After the Civil War, fellow officer and trusted friend William Tecumseh Sherman provided one possible answer. While discussing the qualities that made Grant a victorious commander, he indicated that it was not his friend's relentless quest for intelligence but rather his ambivalence toward it that played a key role in Grant's successful campaigns. "I'll tell you where he beats me and where he beats the world," he proclaimed. "He don't care a damn for what the enemy does out of his sight, but it scares me like hell!" [14] Determining whether Sherman was right composes the essence of this study.

"My Means of Information Are Certainly Better Than . . . Most"

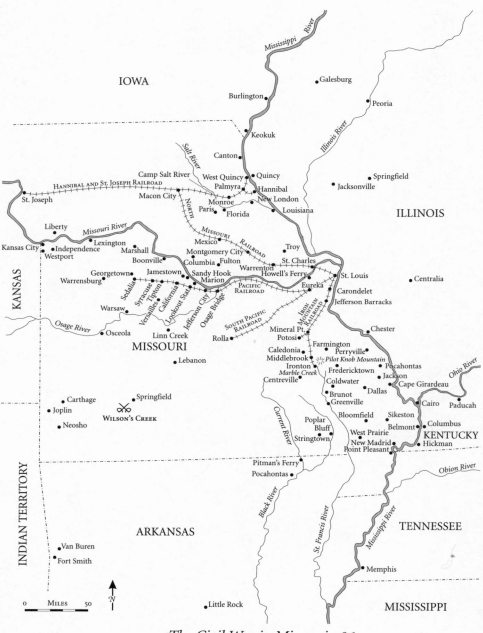

The Civil War in Missouri, 1861

As Col. Ulysses S. Grant led the Twenty-first Illinois into northern Missouri in the summer of 1861, the responsibilities of command pressed hard upon him. That an entire regiment depended upon him to make the right decisions had a chilling effect. He recalled later that the "sensations" he experienced while marching into the war zone "were anything but agreeable," especially since his earlier military career had not prepared him psychologically for this moment. "I had been in all the engagements in Mexico that it was possible for one person to be in," he wrote later, "but not in command." [1] His time in Missouri would constitute his first real exposure to the complexities of leadership in war. And what he learned he discovered on the job. Among other things, he had to learn the "business" of collecting, collating, analyzing, and using intelligence. As with many of his fellow officers, Grant would learn that intelligence in the Civil War was an ad hoc affair demanding improvisation and, more importantly, the ability to manage uncertainty.

On July 11 Grant and his men arrived in Missouri, a state torn by internal divisions. Pro- and anti-secession forces as well as mere criminals and opportunistic marauders roamed the countryside, preying upon enemy soldiers, innocent civilians, and each other. Tasked with protecting the army's railroad supply lines in the northern part of the state from guerrillas and mounted raiders, Union troops soon found themselves in the midst of this hostile environment. A few days after their arrival, Brig. Gen. John Pope, in charge of Union-held territory north of the Missouri River, sent Grant to Monroe, Missouri, to rescue a Federal regiment besieged by forces under Brig. Gen. Thomas Harris of the pro-Confederate Missouri State Guard. Harris retreated before Grant's troops arrived, and the Twenty-first Illinois was stationed along the Hannibal and St. Joseph Railroad to protect it from further Confederate raids. [2]

Grant soon received orders to lead an expedition against Harris, who was supposedly camped near Florida, Missouri, twenty miles away on the Salt River. Though a relatively minor episode in the war, Grant later claimed this mission forever changed his view of warfare. As his men approached Harris's reported bivouac site, he again struggled with the burden of command. All the drilling, the discipline, the headaches, and the anticipation had come down to this moment. The loneliness and fear

nearly overwhelmed him. His prior combat experience in Mexico involved risking only his own life. Now the lives of many depended upon
him, a realization that caused his anxiety to swell with each step. He
described the scene: "As we approached the brow of the hill from which
it was expected we would see Harris' camp, and possibly his men already
formed to meet us, my heart kept getting higher and higher until it felt
to me as though it was in my throat. I would have given anything then
to have been back in Illinois, but I had not the moral courage to halt and
consider what to do; I kept right on." At the crest of the hill, the valley
unfolded beneath him. Much to his relief, only a deserted campsite
loomed in the distance. Harris had retreated. This experience, Grant recalled, had taught him a valuable lesson about war: "From that event to
the close of the war," he wrote, "I never forgot that [the enemy] had as
much reason to fear my forces as I had his." [3]

In Grant's memory the expedition marked a positive turning point
in his thinking on war. But on the surface, the episode does not reflect
well upon Grant from an intelligence standpoint. The apprehension he
felt as he neared his objective suggests that he possessed little up-to-date
information on Harris's whereabouts. The evidence reveals, however,
that Grant knew more about the enemy than he admitted in his memoirs. The day before the expedition commenced, he expressed doubt
that his troops would encounter any Confederates. "From the best evidence that can be obtained here," he wrote, "Harris' command is not
likely to be found at Florida nor at any other point where a regiment of
Federal troops are together." [4] Contrary to his postwar recollections,
Grant *never* expected to find Harris on the other side of that hill. This is
not to say that he did not have his famous revelation about fear, for even
the best intelligence does not eliminate all the doubt and anxiety atten-
dant with leading men in combat. But Grant did not pursue his quarry
blindly; he possessed information from which he concluded that his
column would not find Harris at Florida. As he reached the brow of the
hill, that assessment proved correct. In addition to his martial epiphany
about fear, perhaps he learned another lesson that day. The failed pursuit of Harris was the first instance during the war where Grant collected
and used intelligence. The fact that he reached the right conclusion undoubtedly increased his confidence in his ability to handle this essential
facet of command. As the summer wore on, that feeling would continue
to grow.

Shortly after the Harris expedition, Maj. Gen. John C. Fremont assigned Grant, now a brigadier general, to command the military district headquartered at Ironton, Missouri. A topographical engineer, famed explorer, and now head of the Western Department, Fremont—nicknamed "The Pathfinder"—was an avid consumer of information. To meet his needs, he employed fellow explorer Edward M. Kern as his secret service chief and created the "Jessie Scouts," an intelligence unit named in honor of his wife. To ensure that his subordinate followed his lead, he instructed Grant to "scour the country" and keep informed of the enemy's intended movements "by employing reliable spies." As Grant settled into his new command, he began constructing his first rudimentary intelligence system. But locating reliable scouts and spies proved a difficult task. Ideally, these operatives were recruited from the ranks of Southern Unionists because they knew the terrain and understood the "movements, feelings, [and] habits" of the people. "We must use men who have been in rebeldom," observed one Federal officer, "to do our work effectively." But this goal often proved difficult to achieve. Col. C. Carroll Marsh at Cape Girardeau found that Missouri Unionists were, for the most part, untrustworthy. Part of the problem, Marsh observed, was that their sympathies to the old flag were well known to their neighbors, which compromised their effectiveness and sometimes shortened their life expectancy. To find men whose loyalties were unknown to the local population, Marsh had to comb southern Illinois for secret-service recruits.[5]

In Missouri, Grant utilized scouts and spies but also obtained intelligence from less sensational passive sources. Local civilians, slaves and free blacks, and refugees fresh from enemy territory could provide news of recent troop movements and dispositions, furnish information on the location and condition of the roads, and comment on terrain. Prisoners of war and enemy deserters, if questioned properly, could also supply insights into the Confederate order of battle, an important asset for tracking movements and formulating strength estimates. Experience dictated, however, that information derived from these sources be evaluated with care. Col. Lew Wallace, a future general and author of *Ben Hur*, commented upon the dangers of relying too heavily upon these individuals for information. "Now I may be listening to a story of the advance of the enemy," he observed, "an hour hence I shall be as reliably told that Columbus [Kentucky] is evacuated and the Confederates gone to New Orleans." Those with Confederate sympathies rarely told the truth and might even become a source of information for the enemy. Unionists could be intimidated into silence or compelled to lie by their pro-secessionist neighbors. "[T]hose who tell us know nothing," Wallace concluded, "those who do know will not tell." As a result, lamented another Union officer in Missouri, "we rarely know the movements of the enemy until too late." For these reasons, Grant remained wary of reports from local citizens and advised subordinates to exercise caution when procuring information from them.[6]

Despite these impediments, Grant worked tirelessly to keep himself informed and soon experienced success in collecting and interpreting intelligence. When rumors emerged purporting that a Confederate force under Brig. Gen. William J. Hardee was at Greenville, Missouri, preparing to attack Ironton, Grant dispatched cavalry reconnaissances and had at least four spies operating behind enemy lines. One of these, Lt. Henry Houts of the Sixth Missouri Infantry (U.S.), successfully infiltrated Hardee's camps at Greenville. Unfortunately, the Confederates captured and executed Houts for espionage, a testament to the dangers of spying.[7]

This intelligence sweep paid off, and by August 10 Grant had enough information to refute the rumors. According to "spies, and loyally disposed citizens," he wrote, "no force within thirty miles of us . . . entertain[s] the least idea of attacking this position." But persistent rumors predicted the immanent capture of Ironton by a large Southern force. Grant knew that Hardee had three thousand men at or near Greenville (in reality he had four thousand), but as before, "no information has been received to lead to the supposition that this place is in danger of an immediate attack." Grant ignored the grim tales of impending disaster circulating in the town and relied instead upon his own intelligence, which led him to a different conclusion.[8]

Though Hardee had indeed planned to capture Ironton as part of a major offensive against St. Louis, the operation never commenced. Success hinged upon the cooperation of Brig. Gen. Gideon J. Pillow's forces at New Madrid and Brig. Gen. M. Jeff Thompson's Missouri State Guard units roaming the southeastern section of the state. But on August 8, the offensive hit a snag when Pillow refused to join the Ironton expedition and pursued his own plan to attack Cape Girardeau. Unable to muster enough forces for his operation, on August 9 Hardee retreated from Greenville toward Pitman's Ferry, Arkansas. Although Grant had no idea why Hardee withdrew, by this time he had concluded from intelligence that Ironton remained safe, at least for the moment.[9]

Despite Grant's successful assessment, the threat of attack still remained. Maj. Gen. Leonidas Polk, commander of Confederate Department Number Two, ordered Pillow to cooperate with Hardee in a new offensive against Ironton. On August 12 Hardee's four thousand troops began retracing their steps toward Greenville. Grant detected this move the next day, noting, "it is very reliable that 5000 well armed men, under Gen. Hardee are advancing upon this place." With Hardee on the move, the Union commander strengthened his defenses. But the Confederate offensive unraveled once again due to command infighting. Convinced that the opportunity to seize St. Louis had passed, on August 21 Hardee, whose advance had stalled at Greenville as a result of the internal squabbles, jettisoned the Ironton scheme entirely.[10]

By then Grant had been reassigned to Jefferson City in time to deal with the next crisis. On August 10, forces under Missouri major general Sterling Price and Confederate brigadier general Ben McCulloch had defeated a Federal army at Wilson's Creek and forced it to retreat, a move that exposed the rest of the state to a possible Confederate invasion. Wasting little time, Price occupied Springfield and then advanced west toward Fort Scott, Kansas, with the ultimate goal of turning north toward the Missouri River. McCulloch occupied Springfield and pondered his next move. Confederate forces did not yet threaten Jefferson City when Grant arrived on August 21. Determining their location and movements posed difficulties, however, especially since Grant had to create a "secret service" from scratch every time he assumed a new post. But at Jefferson City he wasted little time recruiting and dispatching scouts and spies into enemy territory. In fact, within a few days of his arrival he had placed operatives in Lebanon and Springfield. On August 26 Grant concluded from the latest news that the "Springfield army" (McCulloch), numbering around three thousand men, remained stationary, an assessment correct in every detail. However, more rumors soon emerged that cast doubt upon that appraisal. Grant noted that the local citizenry had given life to this gossip and had worked themselves into a frenzy as a result. "There is considerable apprehension of an attack soon," Grant observed, but he remained confident in his earlier evaluation. "My impression," he concluded, "is that there is no force sufficiently strong enough to attempt" an assault on Jefferson City. Trusting in his own sources and refusing to be stampeded by rumor, Grant again made a correct assessment; at that moment, Price was advancing *away* from Jefferson City while McCulloch thought only of retreating back to Arkansas.[11]

After a month of campaigning, Grant's experiences with intelligence had been overwhelmingly positive. Twice he had heard rumors predicting an attack by large Confederate forces and both times he relied upon information gathered by his own scouts and spies to form a correct conclusion. The ability to glean the truth from contradictory reports had prevented Grant from being stampeded by unsubstantiated rumors. And these successes only increased his confidence in his intelligence system. "[M]y means of information," he bragged at the time, "are certainly better than . . . most."[12] The next test, however, would be one of the most critical. Intelligence alone cannot determine a course of action; only commanders can do that. Though demonstrating proficiency at gathering and assessing intelligence, Grant had yet to use this information to make a major command decision. That was about to change.

On September 1 Grant again moved to a new assignment, this time to command the newly formed District of Southeast Missouri, which included the area bordering neutral Kentucky along the Mississippi River on the east and abutting Confederate Arkansas to the south. All of Missouri south and east of Ironton as well as southern Illinois fell within the district's boundaries, including several key garrisons at Bird's Point and Cape Girardeau. Overseeing around thirteen thousand men, Grant now commanded more troops, outposts, and territory than in any of his previous postings. Because of its strategic location at the confluence of the Mississippi and Ohio Rivers, Grant established his headquarters at Cairo, Illinois, on September 4.[13]

Current information on the Confederates operating in southeastern Missouri remained a primary concern, especially the activities of Jeff Thompson's Missouri State Guard units. Fifteen hundred strong and self-styled the "Swamp Rats" because they often hid out in Missouri bogs, Thompson's force troubled Federal commanders in the area. "Everyone gives me credit of having at least 7,000 men," Thompson boasted, "and I have them frightened nearly to death." His statement contained much truth, and Fremont hoped Grant could exterminate the "Swamp Rats" before they caused too much trouble. The department commander also instructed his subordinate to patrol the Missouri side of the Mississippi River toward New Madrid and occupy Belmont, a river landing located opposite Columbus, Kentucky, only eighteen miles south of Cairo. All this was in preparation for achieving Fremont's immediate goal of occupying Columbus, a crucial step in his bid to win control of the entire Mississippi Valley.[14]

By the beginning of September, however, the Confederates had also turned their gaze toward neutral Kentucky. From New Madrid, Pillow urged Confederate authorities to seize and fortify Columbus as the best way to protect the "gateway into Tennessee" and maintain control of the Mississippi River to Memphis. Whoever occupied the town first, he argued, would gain the upper hand in the region. He correctly estimated that Fremont had also cast a covetous eye upon Columbus, warning, "If he gets possession of it once, you can never dislodge him." Better to disregard Kentucky neutrality and capture Columbus while it was unoccupied, Pillow argued, than to expend blood and treasure taking it from the Federals later on. When Grant's troops occupied Belmont on September 2, Polk became convinced that this move was but a first step toward a general Union advance into eastern Kentucky. Believing that the slightest hesitation might lose the Bluegrass State for the Confederacy, the next day Polk ordered Southern forces in Missouri to enter Kentucky and seize Hickman, Columbus, and Paducah.[15]

As Polk positioned his forces to invade Kentucky, Grant heard reports of a Confederate withdrawal in Missouri but did not interpret it as a prelude to an invasion. Capt. William S. Hillyer, one of Grant's staff officers, notified Fremont on September 1 that Jeff Thompson, who had been in Benton, had retreated toward New Madrid. "[T]his information is derived from several sources," he reported, "each corroborating the others." In addition, news arrived that Hardee's army had departed Greenville for the Arkansas line.[16] Taken together, these reports convinced Grant that the enemy had abandoned their forward positions and marched south. As before, his information and his assessment proved accurate. What remained unclear, however, was what it all meant.

To uncover their intentions, Grant dispatched an expedition under

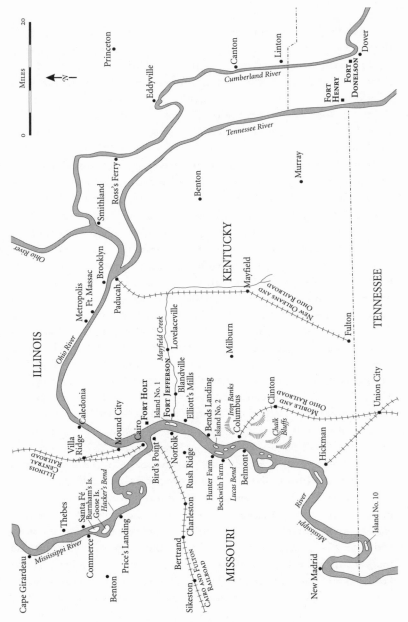

Cairo and Vicinity, 1861

Col. Gustav Waagner down the west bank of the river. Charged with monitoring activity on the opposite shore, Waagner's column arrived in Belmont on September 2, a move that triggered Polk's decision to advance into Kentucky. The following day, Waagner notified Grant of "an important movement of cavalry and infantry on the Heights in and near Columbus." More ominously, he observed, a "new secession flag" floated above the town. Unsure of how to respond to the events unfolding before his eyes, Waagner implored: "What shall I do with Kentucky?" The same day, Commander John Rodgers, in charge of the Union gunboats *Tyler* and *Lexington* supporting the Belmont expedition, reported that small arms fire rained down from heights on the Kentucky side when he passed Columbus. He also reported that the Southern force occupying Hickman appeared to be "considerable." Combined with news of the precipitate withdrawal of Southern forces in Missouri, Grant had concluded by September 4 that the enemy had indeed invaded the Bluegrass State. "I regret to inform you," he wrote in a letter to the Kentucky state government, "that Confederate forces in Considerable numbers have invaded the territory of Kentucky and are occupying & fortifying strong positions at Hickman & Chalk Bluffs [Columbus]." Grant's immediate reaction was to fight the Confederates for possession of Columbus. Since Polk had already settled the neutrality issue, he hinted to Fremont his willingness to cross the Mississippi and seize the town and the heights, a movement the department commander himself had endorsed as part of his grand strategy. Hopeful, Grant was awaiting instructions from St. Louis when an exhausted, dust-covered figure suddenly appeared in Cairo.[17]

Employed as a "military expert" on Fremont's staff, Charles De Arnaud, a former officer in the Russian army, arrived at Grant's headquarters on September 5. The Pathfinder had sent his favorite operative to "go down and see what General Pillow is doing" and to visit strategic points behind enemy lines as far south as Louisiana. This information would be valuable in planning Fremont's Mississippi Valley campaign. While returning to St. Louis, however, De Arnaud stumbled upon the Confederate invasion of Kentucky and hurried to warn Grant. This news corroborated Waagner's observations, but the remainder of his report left the district commander facing a very difficult decision.[18]

After receiving confirmation from St. Louis of the spy's credentials, Grant listened attentively to his story. In addition to seizing Hickman and Columbus, the Russian stated, "The enemy is marching in large force to take Paducah, on the Ohio River, to invade Southern Illinois." De Arnaud then impressed upon Grant the necessity of seizing Paducah before the Confederates arrived. Located on the Kentucky shore at the confluence of the Ohio and Tennessee Rivers, the loss of Paducah, he warned, would "endanger all the positions that we were at that time occupying." Moreover, capturing the town also offered the Federals certain advantages, for it would "flank [the enemy] in their movements in southeast Missouri" and "threaten their rear [at Columbus]." After conferring with Grant, De Arnaud telegraphed the same information to Fremont, advising him that the Union occupation of Paducah would "frustrate the enemy's plans and secure for us the Tennessee River." He ended his report with the plea "No time to lose." [19]

Before that moment, attacking Columbus had been foremost on Grant's mind. Realizing the significance of this new development, however, Grant wired Fremont: "I am getting ready to go to Paducah." Although receiving no official authorization to do so, he forged ahead on the conviction that further delay would cost the Federals an important foothold in Kentucky. On the morning of September 6, Grant's troops landed at Paducah and, without firing a shot, claimed the town for the Union. The fact that he found "numerous secession flags flying over the city" and heard rumors of Confederate troops only sixteen miles away was all the justification he needed for the unsanctioned invasion. According to De Arnaud, Grant had arrived none too soon, coming "within a few hours of the large [enemy] force that was already at Mayfield" twenty-three miles away. Leaving a subordinate in command of the town, Grant returned to Cairo and found a message from Fremont belatedly authorizing his movements.[20]

The occupation of Paducah remains one of Grant's more monumental decisions during the Civil War. If the Confederates had captured the town, they could have denied Union forces access to the Tennessee River, an important Union invasion corridor slicing through Kentucky and Tennessee, and would have threatened Grant's left flank and southern Illinois. From an intelligence perspective, however, his decision to capture Paducah remains troubling. He made this critical decision, which carried tremendous political and military implications, based upon the word of a single spy whom he had never met and without any effort to obtain corroboration. "I took possession of Paducah," he later wrote to De Arnaud, "solely on information given by yourself."[21]

As it turned out, Grant based his decision upon flawed information. Despite his contention that Confederate flags fluttering from windows in town proved he had barely beaten his foe to the punch, the evidence indicates otherwise. Polk had originally targeted Paducah for occupation, but the Confederate advance sputtered at Hickman and Columbus. He did send two brigades to Mayfield but only *after* learning of Grant's advance into Kentucky and only to protect his right flank, not to launch an offensive. Contrary to De Arnaud's report, no Confederate forces were moving toward Paducah when Federal troops entered the town.[22]

Why would Grant base such a momentous decision on the word of a single source without first obtaining corroboration? The answer lies in the situation at the moment the spy appeared on September 5. By then, Grant had been in district command only one day and in Cairo barely three. In the past he had managed to construct a rudimentary intelligence network fairly quickly, but the rapid pace of his transfers between Jefferson City and Cairo, not to mention his inadequate staff, worked against him on this count. When De Arnaud presented his information, Grant had neither the means nor the time to corroborate the report. But he did know from earlier reports that the enemy had occupied Hickman and Columbus, although he heard nothing about a move on Paducah. At that moment, moreover, he remained focused upon a possible advance on Columbus. Whether prodded by De Arnaud or realizing it on his own, Grant understood that Paducah's strategic value made it a logical Confederate objective. The scenario depicted by the spy was not beyond the realm of possibility. Realizing that trusting Fremont's operative posed fewer risks than dismissing his report or wasting precious time awaiting independent confirmation, Grant chose to act despite the substantial risks involved. Since the South had already trampled upon Kentucky's neutrality, if he seized the town before the enemy, whether or not De Arnaud spoke the truth would be irrelevant; Paducah would be in Union hands. However, if the spy was correct, the delay caused by disbelief or the search for confirmation might forfeit the town to the enemy, a much too heavy price for absolute certainty. In this instance, the potential benefits of seizing the initiative, even if based on bad intelligence, outweighed the hazards of inaction. As Clausewitz observed, on some occasions "timidity will do a thousand times more damage in war than audacity." When the dust settled, Grant's decision proved to be the right one.[23]

In the final analysis, Grant acted upon his perception of what the enemy—and perhaps what he himself—would likely do in that situation. A Confederate move on Paducah was a distinct possibility; De Arnaud's information made it a certainty in Grant's mind. Given this view, he needed no corroboration of the spy's report because it fit his mental picture of the unfolding situation. More importantly, it provided an opportunity to advance, something he had longed to do anyway.

In combination with his earlier intelligence successes, this episode greatly enhanced Grant's conviction that he could quickly and accurately read an unfolding military situation. But this emerging faith contained certain risks if taken too far. An overreliance upon perceptions, which might amount to nothing more than wishful thinking, could lead to a fixation on only those reports that harmonize with one's own expectations. Napoleon called this "making pictures," or forming a fixed image of the enemy, which could cloud judgment and impair the ability to see the true situation. But the French general also realized that this was unavoidable. "In war," he intoned, "everything is perception." In such an environment, "It is upon a just comparison and consideration of the weight due to different impressions that the power of reasoning and of right judgment depends." [24] At Paducah, Grant weighed the evidence and made his choice, hoping all along that the initiative would compensate for any shortcomings in his intelligence.

Taken together, the Harris expedition, the tracking of Hardee, and the Paducah occupation reveal much about the early evolution of Grant's thinking on intelligence operations. The fact that he actively sought information on the enemy from the very beginning attests to his keen appreciation of its necessity. Repeated success in intelligence operations also enhanced his confidence in undertaking them. At Paducah, however, two other factors emerged that would influence his views. First, Grant began to recognize the advantages of seizing and maintaining the initiative. Forcing the enemy to react to his own moves shifted the burden of uncertainty to the Confederates, leaving them to ponder, to speculate, and to make mistakes. In essence, the initiative could be a handy substitute for intelligence or at least compensate for its shortcomings, an important insight that also fit with Grant's aggressive nature. Second, he seemed to display what the French termed *coup d'oeil*, which allowed him to make the correct decision at the right moment without wasting time waiting for absolute certainty. Sherman put it more succinctly: "He uses such information as he has according to his best judgment." Just how much these nascent characteristics and Grant's intelligence experience in Missouri would influence future campaigns remained to be seen.[25]

"I Always Try to Keep Myself Posted"

Upon learning that Confederate forces had invaded Kentucky on September 4, Grant penned a quick message to Western Department headquarters. "Troops . . . can be spared from here," he wrote, "to take possession of Columbus heights." Once this was accomplished, he predicted, "New Madrid will fall within five days."[1] But success hinged upon avoiding delay, and Grant recommended that this operation commence the following day. Although department commander John Fremont frustrated his ambitious plans, from this moment the capture of Columbus, Kentucky, with its commanding view of the Mississippi River and its importance in the Confederate defensive scheme in the West, became Grant's primary objective. Until Federals occupied the town and its adjacent heights, the enemy controlled the river and could thwart any Union offensives against strategic points farther south. Grant's fixation would culminate in the battle of Belmont on November 7, 1861, the first major engagement of his command. How he arrived at that point, however, was the product of many factors, not the least of which was two months worth of intelligence work and his willingness, as demonstrated by his unauthorized seizure of Paducah, to act "on his own hook" should the need arise.

Just as Grant appreciated the strategic significance of Columbus, so did the Southern high command. Maj. Gen. Leonidas Polk, commander of Confederate Department Number Two and now headquartered in Columbus, and Richmond officials recognized the town's value and assigned it a prominent role in their defensive strategy in the West. "Its possession," Brig. Gen. Gideon Pillow asserted, "is a military necessity involving the ultimate safety of Tennessee." Once in possession of the town and its adjacent heights, the Confederates invested significant resources to defend it. Before long, Polk had transformed Columbus, nestled among high bluffs that overlooked a substantial stretch of the river, into a bastion that became known as the "Gibraltar of the West," anchoring the left flank of the main Confederate defensive line in the western theater. Stout fortifications on the heights, appropriately named the "Iron Banks," bristled with a vast array of artillery that commanded river traffic like silent sentinels. The Mobile and Ohio Railroad, which ran south out of Columbus to Mobile, Alabama, added to the town's strategic importance.[2]

Across the river and in the shadow of the Columbus guns lay Camp Johnston, a small Confederate outpost established near Belmont, Missouri, to protect a ferry landing and a key communication line between Kentucky and Rebel commands in southeastern Missouri. This Southern toehold on the western bank also offered a convenient portal into southeast Missouri and a staging area for advances against Cairo, Cape Girardeau, and St. Louis. Confederate forces in Columbus and Belmont not only posed a formidable impediment to Federal operations on the Mississippi but also threatened the Union presence in southeast Missouri, a region already menaced by guerrillas, M. Jeff Thompson's Missouri troops, and Brig. Gen. William Hardee's army in northern Arkansas.[3]

Both Grant and Fremont respected Columbus's strength and realized that the Belmont outpost represented a dangerous breach in their Missouri defenses. Believing that Columbus should be taken before Polk had time to strengthen the position, Grant pressed his superior to advance immediately. Fremont initially concurred with Grant's appraisal and on September 8 unveiled a grand plan to expel the enemy from southeastern Missouri and then capture Columbus. He proposed dispatching troops from Paducah under the command of Brig. Gen. Charles F. Smith toward "the rear and flank of Columbus" while Grant drove Thompson and any other Confederate forces out of Missouri. Once this phase was complete, Fremont envisioned a combined assault by Smith and Grant on Columbus from different directions. After capturing the Confederate stronghold, the department commander hoped to seize Hickman and eventually move on Memphis, predicting that his grand offensive would produce "glorious" results for Union arms in the West.[4]

Even before this pronouncement, Fremont had indicated to Grant the importance of clearing the western bank. On August 28 he envisioned a converging attack on Thompson using Grant's troops. Although this maneuver never got underway, Fremont's instructions revealed that crushing Thompson and occupying Belmont were essential precursors to operations against Columbus. After ordering Col. Gustav Waagner and the gunboats to seize Belmont and "keep possession of that place," Fremont added, "It is intended in connection with all these movements to occupy Columbus in Kentucky as soon as possible."[5] Though frustrated by the results of Waagner's expedition, on September 8 Fremont presented to Lincoln his ambitious plan to topple the Confederate Gibraltar.

Unfortunately for Fremont, Sterling Price forced "The Pathfinder" down a more conservative trail. The Confederate victory at Wilson's Creek on August 10 and the subsequent Union withdrawal toward St. Louis left the rest of Missouri open to invasion. By early September, Price appeared on the Missouri River at Lexington. Mindful of this rapidly deteriorating situation and unwilling to risk a reverse on the Mississippi until he had subdued Price, Fremont shelved his grand offensive indefinitely and turned his attention westward. On September 10 he ordered Grant to remain on the defensive and limit his activities to chasing guerrillas.[6]

While waiting for Fremont to bag Price and return his attention to the Mississippi, Grant prepared his troops and used his secret service to monitor Polk's activities downriver. Considerable intelligence came from passive sources, including prisoners of war, enemy deserters, local residents, and refugees, who furnished information on Confederate forces in the area and on the local road networks. Active sources tapped by Grant included spies operating in Columbus, scouts prowling near enemy lines, and reconnaissance patrols, both land-based and waterborne. The former commander at Cairo, Col. Richard J. Oglesby, had recruited a stable of scouts and spies but found that the news "gathered from my (not always so) confidential men" was "not always reliable and true," compelling him to discharge several operatives. Though Grant retained some of Oglesby's secret service employees, he undoubtedly recruited others and increased their activity.[7]

Composed primarily of infantry units due to a shortage of mounted patrols, land-based reconnaissance expeditions originated from Grant's outposts closest to enemy territory. Patrols from Bird's Point in Missouri, led by Oglesby and Col. W. H. L. Wallace, monitored the Charleston-Belmont vicinity, while in Kentucky patrols sent from the Union outposts at Fort Holt and Fort Jefferson watched for enemy activity north of Columbus. Land-based reconnaissance patrols often received assistance from the Union navy plying the Mississippi above Columbus. The gunboats *Tyler, Lexington,* and *Conestoga,* under the overall direction of Capt. Andrew Hull Foote, performed many duties for the army. They supported amphibious landings and protected scouting parties on land by distracting the Columbus river batteries. The navy also reconnoitered above Columbus and Belmont, supplying information on the number and types of guns in Columbus and on the size of the military encamp-

ments surrounding the city. Foote's gunboats also performed "recon-
naissance-by-fire" missions to locate Confederate forces concealed in the
woods along the western bank. The explosion of an 8-inch shell in the
middle of camp "was not a very pleasant introduction to the Gun Boats,"
remarked one Confederate whose bivouac the navy discovered in this
manner. Besides causing Polk's men some anxious moments, the Federal
navy played an important intelligence-gathering role.[8]

On September 10 it seemed as if Grant might have to shift from thinking about an offensive against Columbus to defending his command.
From a gunboat commander, Grant learned that transports laden with
Southern troops had crossed to Belmont and that as many as three thousand troops now occupied Camp Johnston. Though concerned, the general doubted that Polk would embark on an offensive in Missouri so soon
after invading Kentucky. "[M]y impression," he wrote, "is that they want
time to prepare for defense" of their recent acquisitions before risking
an advance. This assessment of Confederate intentions came mostly
from a captured copy of Polk's General Order Number Nineteen, dated
September 7, which one of Grant's spies brought in the following day.
This document indicated to Grant that Polk was too preoccupied with
organizing, supplying, and resting his command to embark upon a major offensive at the moment. As Grant knew well from his recent experience at Paducah, transitioning from invasion to occupation was no
easy task, and Polk, attempting to fortify and hold both Columbus and
Hickman, had his hands full. In Grant's mind the Confederates at Columbus were focused on defensive preparations and had neither the time
nor the resources to initiate an advance into Missouri. This interpretation became a dominant thread woven throughout Grant's later assessments of enemy intentions.[9]

Even if the Confederates planned to maintain the initiative, Grant felt
that the most likely target would be Paducah since that position, now in
Union hands, posed the most serious threat to Columbus. Nevertheless,
in his mind neither Cairo nor Paducah were in immediate danger. Believing that the Confederates had temporarily relinquished the initiative,
he saw an opportunity to put Fremont's suspended plan into action. On
September 10 he made another request for permission to advance downriver instead of waiting on Polk to make up his mind. "If it was discre-
tionary with me," he prodded Fremont, "I would take Columbus."[10]

The knowledge that Polk and Pillow were the principal officers in Columbus also contributed to Grant's pacific picture of the enemy. Polk's military reputation had suffered as a result of his hasty and, to some, ill-conceived invasion of Kentucky that placed the onus of violating that state's neutrality squarely on the South. Once characterized as a "vain cadet," the Episcopal bishop had few admirers wearing either the blue or the gray, with the notable exception of his most powerful supporter, Jefferson Davis. Similarly, his subordinate, Gideon Pillow, inspired more ridicule than fear. Like many officers familiar with Pillow's background, Grant openly despised the haughty Tennessean. His incompetence in military affairs, revealed during the Mexican War when he placed the ditch on the wrong side of his fortifications, earned him the derision of West Pointers, while his arrogance merited the contempt of most everyone else. One officer claimed that Pillow was "as consum[m]ate an ass, as any army, modern or ancient, has ever been inflicted with." When he heard that Pillow had earned a command in southeastern Missouri, Grant predicted he "would not be a formidable enemy." This rather unflattering view of his opponents would have a significant effect on Grant's future decisions. "Knowing Polk's caution and believing Pillow to be a fool," argued one historian, led Grant to take risks he might not have attempted if faced with more competent adversaries.[11]

Information soon arrived, however, that contradicted Grant's view that his lackluster opponents were pursuing a purely defensive strategy. On September 11 he questioned a Confederate deserter who stated that five thousand troops had recently crossed to Belmont and that officers in Columbus spoke confidently of forthcoming attacks on Bird's Point and Cairo. To verify this, Grant immediately dispatched a patrol under Oglesby and a gunboat toward Belmont. Oglesby returned on September 16 and reported that the Camp Johnston garrison had not received any reinforcements and still numbered around three thousand men. More importantly, while observing the camp he saw no telltale preparations being made for a forthcoming offensive.[12]

Grant believed so fervently that his adversary thought only in terms of defense, however, that before the reconnaissance patrols could even report, his thoughts had already returned toward his own future offensive. On September 12 Grant offered Fremont a two-pronged plan aimed at clearing the Confederates out of Missouri and ultimately turning Columbus. First, he proposed that Charles Smith's Paducah forces turn the Confederate left flank by attacking Union City, Tennessee, a key supply depot twenty miles south of Columbus, and severing Polk's communications. Second, another flanking force in Missouri, presumably under Grant's command, would march on Belmont under the protection of the gunboats. With his supply lines cut and threatened on both flanks, Polk "would be forced to leave Columbus." [13] Although reminiscent of his own earlier plan to capture the Confederate stronghold, Fremont filed his subordinate's plan without comment.

After hearing more news of Confederate activity on September 15, though, Grant's attention turned toward matters of defense. The latest rumors claimed that Polk had evacuated Columbus, but whether the Rebels were "marching upon Paducah or leaving Kentucky altogether" remained a mystery. Although doubtful that his adversary had any offensive inclinations, Grant needed the services of his scouts and spies now more than ever. Unfortunately, he faced a crisis on that front. Earlier that month he had requested more money for intelligence operations and had also asked permission to maintain and control his own secret service budget. However, department headquarters issued no reply. When these latest rumors surfaced, Grant again contacted St. Louis, this time using the seriousness of the present crisis as a pretext. "It is highly necessary to get information which cannot be obtained from our own reconnoitering parties," he complained, "[but] without money to pay, the services of citizens cannot much longer be obtained." He feared that, without proper compensation for the risks they incurred, particularly those who resided behind enemy lines, his sources would likely return home in silence. Fremont finally granted his request, but three days—and the motivating crisis—had passed before Grant received the needed funds for his secret service. [14]

Despite these monetary troubles, Grant searched diligently for any information that would shed light upon the reported evacuation of the Columbus garrison and their possible destination. Finally, he learned from both a deserter and from a spy known as "Mr. L.," most likely John Lellyett, a resident of Nashville, political crony of Andrew Johnson, and itinerant Union spy in Kentucky from 1861 to 1862, that on September 14, ten thousand troops under Gen. Albert Sidney Johnston, the new commander of the Confederacy's Department Number Two, had left Columbus and marched toward Mayfield, Kentucky. According to both sources, Johnston's ultimate objective was to capture Paducah. Combined with the unconfirmed reports of the evacuation of Columbus, Grant should have been duly alarmed at these ominous developments. But he remained suspicious of these corroborating reports, stating, "I do not think this movement [on Paducah] has been made." Nevertheless, he accelerated defensive preparations. On September 20 Grant's intelligence brought welcome news that the Confederates at Mayfield had returned to Columbus.[15]

In reality, Southern forces had indeed occupied Mayfield, just as Grant's sources had claimed, but in nowhere near the strength reported. The force depicted by intelligence as an army led by Johnston was actually only two regiments under Brig. Gen. Benjamin F. Cheatham sent to secure Polk's right flank. Similarly, what Grant saw as the termination of an offensive against Paducah was in reality the retreat of Cheatham's column toward Columbus, a move prompted by the lack of fresh water and supplies in Mayfield. In any event, Polk had little desire to launch an offensive. At that time the bishop-general feared that Union forces in Paducah were poised to attack the Confederates, not the reverse, which led to Cheatham's foray to Mayfield. The Confederate withdrawal only strengthened Grant's perception that the enemy remained in a defensive mode.[16]

On September 23 a spy in Columbus challenged that view, warning that Polk had dispatched more troops to Belmont, which prompted Grant once again to send Oglesby toward Camp Johnston. But the patrol found that only twenty-five hundred of Thompson's men now occupied Belmont, indicating that no infusion of troops from Columbus had occurred. In addition, Oglesby also observed no preparations being made for an impending departure. The results of the reconnaissance once again confirmed Grant's suspicions that the enemy remained "confined to their encampments at Columbus and Belmont."[17]

Despite the district commander's assessment and the confidence he placed in Oglesby's judgment, the latest rumor of Confederate forces crossing into Missouri had caused great trepidation in St. Louis, especially in light of events in western Missouri. In late September, Sterling Price's state troops had reached the Missouri River and captured the Union garrison at Lexington, a loss that reverberated throughout the Western Department. With the fate of his command as well as that of the Union cause in Missouri at stake, Fremont feared the worst. In response to the crisis, he left for western Missouri on September 24 to personally direct operations against Price. Fearful that recent events

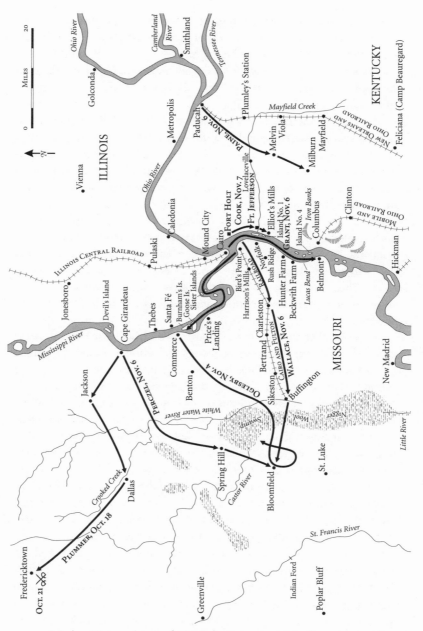

Major Operations of Grant's Command in Late 1861

might encourage Polk to reinforce Price or perhaps attempt to expel Union forces from Paducah and southeastern Missouri, Fremont directed Grant and Smith to remain on the defensive and work together to "control" any Confederate aggression. Although he afforded them some latitude to attack if the chance arose, Fremont was adamant that they avoid taking risks. "[A]t present," instructed Fremont, "I am not in favor of incurring any hazard of defeat." Suspending all offensive operations along the Mississippi River, "The Pathfinder" embarked on a mission to salvage western Missouri and his own embattled reputation.[18]

At the time, Grant concurred with his superior's decision to delay an assault on Columbus, though for different reasons. While the department commander feared a simultaneous advance against Cairo and Paducah in support of Price's operations, Grant believed Polk had no intention of attacking, thereby surrendering the initiative to the Federals. But acute manpower and supply shortages dampened Grant's ardor for an advance. He possessed sufficient forces to defend Cairo, he complained, but not enough for "an aggressive movement against the large force now occupying Columbus." In a letter to his wife, Grant reflected upon the frustrating situation. "All is quiet here now," he remarked, but just "How long it will remain so is impossible to tell." One thing was certain, he added, "If I had troops enough[,] not long." The prospects for an advance in the near future, however, depended upon Fremont's success against Price. Until these two forces locked horns in western Missouri, Columbus would have to wait. Frustrated by the inertia gripping the District of Southeast Missouri, Grant fixed his gaze upon Columbus, confident that only the want of men and supplies and Fremont's obsession with Price prevented him from reducing the Gibraltar of the West to rubble.[19]

Even though Fremont's priorities remained focused on western Missouri, the possibility that Polk might send reinforcements to Price's invading army kept him glancing nervously toward the east. On September 28 Fremont warned Grant that the Confederates had evacuated Columbus and crossed to Belmont to support Price's operations. The Cairo commander replied with an air of confidence that, on the contrary, "Everything here is quiet [with] no rumors to disturb it." A few days later he completely dismissed Fremont's report as idle gossip. "There is no enemy on the Missouri side of the river," Grant concluded, "except Jeff Thompsons force at Belmont." But even this contingent posed a minimal threat since a small Union force could "easily drive them from [the] vicinity." [20]

Grant had barely dismissed this latest rumor when news of increased Confederate activity in Kentucky riveted his attention. On September 30 a wounded Confederate prisoner let slip that a large column under Pillow had departed Columbus for Paducah. Lacking any contradictory evidence, a wary Grant traveled to Paducah to assist Smith with defensive preparations. Once again, the Confederate attack failed to materialize. When Grant returned to Cairo, he received another report of Southern troops crossing to Belmont intent upon capturing Cape Girardeau. But Grant's operatives and Smith's scouts unearthed no corroborative evidence of Confederate movements in any direction. Once again, Grant's intelligence had supported his belief that Polk remained on the defensive. As a result, on October 4 he wrote that the enemy had "no concerted plan to attack [Cairo], Cape Girardeau or Paducah." [21]

Despite Grant's recent assurances, the tide of rumors refused to ebb. On October 6 he again received news from department headquarters that Albert Sidney Johnston was at Belmont with a large force preparing to attack Cape Girardeau. These latest reports caused Grant some stressful moments because he had yet to receive any reliable information from his regular sources. "I always try to keep myself posted as to [the enemy's] movements," he complained, "but I [have been] at a loss for the last few days." All of the gunboats were out of service, his scouts had returned empty-handed, and one of his spies, from whom he expected a "full & accurate report," had not been heard from. Facing a critical information shortage, Grant dispatched an infantry patrol toward Belmont and sent Johnston Brown, a Union scout, to "ascertain the position . . . of the enemy." Until more evidence arrived, though, Grant held to his original views that "the enemy have no present intention of moving on Cape Girardeau" and that if the Confederates planned to attack anywhere, Paducah would likely top their list. [22]

The next day Grant received word that an attack on Paducah was precisely what Polk had in mind. His source was a priest whose flock included some Confederate officers and enlisted men in Columbus. When Smith, who questioned the clergyman, relayed this information to Grant, he seemed reluctant to place much credence in it. And he was not alone. Other officers in his command also doubted the possibility of an attack on Paducah. Col. Lew Wallace may have summed up the prevalent feeling among the Paducah garrison at the time. "[W]hile we don't remit our vigilance," he observed, "we are not greatly concerned." Grant also doubted the priest's report but, at the same time, had received news that reinforcements had reached Columbus, swelling its garrison to forty-five thousand men. But even this information, which Grant felt "disposed to look upon as reliable," failed to alter his view of the enemy. "My own impression," he explained to Fremont, "is that they are fortifying strongly and preparing to resist a formidable attack and have but little idea of risking anything upon a forward movement."[23]

While watching for signs of movement from Columbus, Grant also monitored the activities of Thompson and Hardee. Throughout September, Federal intelligence had kept an eye on Thompson, whose force of around twenty-five hundred men had not ventured far from Belmont. But on October 1, Thompson's brigade departed for New Madrid to obtain supplies for a proposed advance on Cape Girardeau. The "Swamp Rats" had a well-earned reputation for being elusive, especially among footsore Union infantrymen tasked with chasing them. After a failed attempt to bag Thompson, one tired soldier complained, "there seems to be nothing reliable about any of the reports we have of him." But this time the Missourian fooled no one. The same day that he departed for New Madrid, a deserter told Grant of the move and subsequent information gleaned from prisoners and civilians in the area corroborated the story.[24]

Unaware that the Federals were on his trail, Thompson resupplied his troops at New Madrid and then headed for Cape Girardeau, reaching Sikeston on October 4. Thirty miles shy of his objective, the campaign was postponed due to inadequate manpower, and the column headed west toward the safety of the swamps. Grant knew the Thompson had reached Sikeston and was then delighted to learn of the Rebels' hasty retreat west. With the "Swamp Rats" out of the picture, the Cairo commander concluded once and for all that "There is [now] no force . . . threatening Cape Girardeau."[25]

But Thompson was not finished. Finding retreat distasteful, he attempted to salvage his aborted mission and turned north toward Fredericktown, about twenty-five miles east of Ironton. After skirmishing with Union forces on October 17, Thompson occupied the town. With fewer than two thousand men and new recruits scarce, however, he planned to remain only "until the enemy discovers my weakness." But

Grant already knew this. Intelligence sources had numbered Thompson's brigade at less than three thousand men. Hoping to remove this irritant from the region, Grant sent Col. Joseph Plummer and forty-five hundred men to destroy Thompson's command. Plummer's men routed the "Swamp Rats" on October 21 and forced them to retreat southward toward Greenville. Claiming that the victory at Fredericktown had "crushed out the Rebellion in South East Missouri," after October Grant believed he had neutralized Thompson and the last vestige of Confederate resistance in southeastern Missouri.[26]

During September and October, Grant also kept a close watch on Hardee's activities in northeastern Arkansas. Busy recruiting, training, and supplying his brigade, Hardee had remained ensconced in his Pitman's Ferry camps since late August. That changed on September 17, 1861, when Polk ordered Hardee to Columbus. After several delays, "Old Reliable" Hardee and his four-thousand-man brigade finally trudged out of their camps, crossed the Mississippi, and on October 6 reached Columbus. Unfortunately for Polk, Johnston had decided that central Kentucky needed Hardee's troops more than Columbus and ordered the brigade to join Brig. Gen. Simon Bolivar Buckner's army at Bowling Green. With little rest in-between, Hardee's footsore column reached central Kentucky around October 13.[27]

Grant first learned of Hardee's departure from Pitman's Ferry on September 28, but initially he was skeptical of the report, probably doubting that the Confederates would leave northern Arkansas undefended. On October 16 Brig. Gen. William T. Sherman, whose forces faced Buckner in central Kentucky, confirmed that Hardee had reached Bowling Green. Two days later, one of Grant's spies from Columbus and New Madrid corroborated this news. Although Hardee's transfer relieved Grant, it caused headaches for his fellow Ohioan. Sherman already believed that Buckner possessed superior numbers and intended to attack Louisville; the news of Hardee's arrival further convinced him of impending disaster. From his perspective, the Confederate legions gathering to the south appeared formidable, although Buckner's forces numbered far fewer than the Union commander believed. Moreover, the Confederates were just as fearful of Sherman as he was of them and entertained few thoughts of an advance to the Ohio River. Nevertheless, Sherman's paranoia reached fever pitch, and feeling cut off and doomed, he implored Grant to rattle the gates of Columbus and relieve the pressure on him.[28]

In response, the Cairo commander told Smith: "If you have any plan to propose I am ready to cooperate to the extent of my limited means." But Fremont nipped these preparations in the bud, which led a frustrated Grant to give up hope of advancing on Columbus anytime soon. "[T]he fates," he moaned, "seem to be against any such thing." With Hardee gone, Thompson neutralized, and Polk on the defensive, Grant's desire to seize the initiative burned ever hotter. "What I want," he declared, "is to advance." [29]

A report on October 25 indicating that Johnston had gone east to inspect the defenses at Cumberland Gap raised Grant's hopes. Combined with intelligence showing that only 10,000–15,000 troops remained in Columbus (Polk actually had 17,230 men left), Grant discerned an emerging pattern in Confederate behavior. Specifically, he observed their tendency to weaken the left flank on the Mississippi to shore up the center and the right at Bowling Green and Cumberland Gap. Convinced now more than ever that the Confederates in Columbus had neither the will nor the manpower for an offensive campaign, Grant once again lobbied headquarters for permission to advance. "Such [drafts] have been made upon the force at Columbus for the Green River country [central Kentucky] and possibly other parts of Kentucky," Grant told Fremont, "that if Genl Smith and my command were prepared [Columbus] might now be taken." Although Grant then promptly retreated from his proposal, citing inadequate supplies, arms, and transportation as the chief impediments to success, he had put Fremont on notice that an opportunity was at hand, and only headquarters could provide the logistical support required to capitalize on it. Had Fremont authorized an advance that day, the Cairo commander would undoubtedly have overlooked his shortages and forged ahead. But this request, like those before it, elicited a negative response from St. Louis. [30]

By the end of October, a certain view of the military situation in southeastern Missouri and Kentucky had taken shape in Grant's mind. First, he believed that Thompson represented only a minimal threat after his thrashing at Fredericktown and that the "Swamp Fox" had put considerable distance between himself and Union forces in the region. He also knew that Hardee's forces had been transferred from northern Arkansas to central Kentucky. Only Belmont and New Madrid remained as symbols of Confederate resolve to hold southeastern Missouri. As for western Kentucky, Grant suspected that Columbus had suffered serious manpower losses to reinforce Buckner's command, sapping what little enthusiasm the bishop-general had for an offensive. The ever-cautious Polk, he believed, would wait for the Federals to assail his Gibraltar.

The first evidence that Grant leaned toward this perception came on September 9 when he interpreted Polk's General Order Number Nineteen as a defensive manifesto. Whether prescience or wishful thinking on Grant's part, the resulting picture of a defensive-minded foe persisted and became a common denominator in later intelligence analyses. Thus, the more Grant assumed that Polk had eschewed the offensive option, the more this judgment shaped his ongoing assessment of the overall situation. Using another example, when he learned on October 6 of the supposed Confederate advance on Paducah, Grant held firm to his impression that the enemy had no such designs. Despite having information that contradicted this view, he maintained, "My beleif is that the attack will not be made for the present." When he heard on another occasion that Johnston had occupied Belmont with a large force, he again deferred to this perception, despite possessing "no reliable intelligence" to support it. By October, his assessments were based heavily upon a perception of the enemy that had become imbedded in his mind. In so doing, he had violated Napoleon's rule against "making pictures," or fixating upon a certain view of one's foe. But Grant's conception of the enemy's intentions, buttressed by the bulk of his intelligence, proved correct. By early November, detaching troops from Columbus had become anathema to Polk, who warned of "the serious consequences" resulting from such a policy. More importantly, the Confederate commander was thinking only in terms of defense, just as Grant had surmised. But until Fremont authorized an attack, his subordinate's prescient assessments mattered little.[31]

On November 1, Fremont finally lurched into action, instructing Grant to make "demonstrations" toward Charleston and Norfolk, Missouri, and also against Blandville, Kentucky. Since the object of the movement was to occupy the enemy's attention at these places, Fremont specifically forbade him from attacking any point. In conjunction with Grant's demonstration, Charles Smith received instructions to move aggressively toward Columbus but was also prohibited from engaging the enemy "without special orders." Unlike the directive sent Grant, the orders Smith received explained the rationale behind the movements on both sides of the river. According to Fremont, the plan was designed to "occupy the enemy in the Mississippi Valley" in case Polk attempted to reinforce Sterling Price.[32]

The next day, Fremont added to Grant's mission after learning that Thompson had resurfaced near the St. Francis River, sixty-two miles southwest of Cairo. Fearful that the Southern cavalryman might work in concert with Polk to screen reinforcements heading to Price, the department commander instructed forces in southeastern Missouri to drive him into Arkansas. Even though Grant by this time viewed the "Swamp Rats" as a minor threat, he dispatched Oglesby with four thousand men and Plummer with another three thousand in pursuit. Instead of merely pushing the Rebels out of the state, however, he told Oglesby to find and destroy Thompson's command. With these columns underway, Grant returned to his preparations for the demonstration.[33]

On November 5 Grant indicated his intention to do more than mere saber rattling during the upcoming maneuvers. On that day he informed Smith of his intention to "menace Belmont," a position well south of the objectives stipulated in Fremont's directive of November 1. The next evening two Union brigades, nearly three thousand men, boarded transports at Cairo, steamed downriver, dropped anchor along the Kentucky shore a few miles above Columbus, and under the watchful eyes of the gunboats, waited silently for the dawn.[34]

Early on November 7, Grant's men disembarked three miles above Belmont and began their march toward the Confederate camp. Occupied by one infantry regiment, a battalion of cavalry, and an artillery battery and commanded by Col. James C. Tappan, Camp Johnston came alive at the news of the Federals' approach. When word of the attack reached Polk's headquarters, however, the Confederate commander convinced himself that the ruckus on the opposite shore was merely a diversion masking an assault upon Columbus. Until he determined otherwise, Polk kept his troops concentrated on the Kentucky side of the Mississippi. He did send four of Pillow's Tennessee regiments, about twenty-five hundred men, to support Tappan. These troops received the order to reinforce Camp Johnston just as they were departing Columbus for Clarksville, Tennessee. In a move to strengthen the defenses farther east, Johnston had ordered Pillow's entire division (five thousand men) to northern Tennessee, causing a further drain on the ranks in Columbus. The gunfire across the river interrupted their journey, and the Tennesseans crossed to meet the Federal onslaught. As this force arrived to even the odds, Grant pressed his attack.

After heavy fighting in a cornfield northwest of the camp, the Confederate line collapsed. Though orderly at first, their retreat soon lapsed into chaos as panic gripped Pillow's men. The Federals continued to drive them toward the river and finally captured Camp Johnston. With victory in their grasp and exhilarated by their first taste of combat, many of the pursuing Union soldiers, ignoring the pleas of their officers to press the pursuit, began looting the camp. As Pillow's men huddled along the bank or fled upriver, Grant's attack sputtered.

On the opposite bank, Smith's demonstration from Paducah failed to convince Polk for very long that the Belmont attack was only a diversion for a main strike against Columbus. Once Polk concluded that Smith was not a threat, he dispatched more reinforcements under Cheatham to rescue the beleaguered Pillow. Glimpsing transports loaded with Southern soldiers heading his way, Grant ordered his men back to the boats, but it took time to get them reorganized and underway. Meanwhile, the Confederates, buttressed by Cheatham's arrival, began a dogged and deadly pursuit of the retreating columns. Some Federal units had to cut their way out and Grant himself barely escaped capture. Under fire from the shoreline, the Union transports finally slipped away and returned to Cairo. The retreat from Belmont resulted in the withdrawal of all Federal troops operating in southeastern Missouri and western Kentucky.[35]

After the battle Grant crowed about his "complete" victory and claimed that he had "accomplished all that we went for, and even more," somehow forgetting about his panic-stricken retreat that had left the enemy in possession of the field. His triumphant rhetoric failed to quell a storm of criticism that met him the moment he stepped off the *Belle Memphis* in Cairo. "[W]e have met the enemy and they are not ours," trumpeted one newspaper correspondent, echoing the sentiments of many in the North. Others berated the general for fighting a battle that had "cost many good lives and resulted in very little, or nothing." A soldier in Oglesby's command spoke for many when he proclaimed, "Grant got whipped at Belmont."[36]

Over time, historians joined this debate and raised serious questions concerning Grant's actions that day. Ranging from commendation to condemnation, scholars have attempted to unravel the mysteries of Belmont and extract something meaningful from the sacrifice. While one author viewed the battle as a "folly" defying military logic because it "was so ludicrous and its outcome so disastrous," another declared that Belmont illustrated "a few of the qualities which carried Grant to eventual victory" (that is, initiative, aggressiveness, and determination) and established him as a fighting general. One historian claimed that Grant's day at Belmont "was rounded out in such a way that gives it a good place in military history." The author of the only monographic treatment of the battle asserted that Grant learned valuable lessons about command and leadership that day, noting, "He had done well; he would do better." [37]

At some point in their treatises, these historians have grappled with Grant's after-action reports containing the justifications and objectives behind the attack. On November 10 Grant sent Fremont the first brief account of the battle, which included his reasons for attacking Belmont. First, preventing Polk from sending troops to reinforce Price's army in Missouri had been a primary motivation. Second, he hoped to intercept an enemy force supposedly sent from Columbus to strike Oglesby and Plummer, who were still hunting for Thompson west of Belmont. Apparently, Grant deemed this report unsatisfactory and later submitted a more detailed sketch, complete with official correspondence and certain insights absent from the initial summary. The revised report, dated November 17, 1861, became the general's official rendition of the campaign. Consistent with the first, he again stressed that preventing troops in Columbus from reinforcing Price and protecting Oglesby and Plummer were the key motivations behind the attack. But unlike his earlier report, this time he explained how and why these objectives became paramount and, ultimately, why he attacked Belmont. [38]

With regard to the reinforcements heading for Price, a movement that never occurred, Grant stated that he first learned of it from a telegram dated November 5 from Fremont, which he also claimed authorized him to proceed with the demonstration ordered on November 1. But Grant failed to provide a verbatim copy of this telegram, an unusual oversight considering its importance to his case. Not only has the telegram itself failed to materialize, neither Grant's headquarters correspondence nor Fremont's letterbooks contain any record of it. More importantly, two days after the battle, Capt. Chauncey McKeever, who handled all of Fremont's correspondence, stated that no order to attack Belmont was ever issued. Finally, on November 5, Grant told Smith that he was still acting under Fremont's original orders dated November 1 and 2. The absence of this key telegram, McKeever's testimony, and the complete lack of corroborating documentation leave little doubt that the message never existed. But even if the mysterious telegram had reached Grant, it is doubtful that he would have accepted it without question given his strong belief that Polk, already weakened by detachments sent east, had neither the desire nor the manpower to reinforce Price.[39]

Grant's prebattle correspondence, particularly those dispatches where he discussed his plans, contains no mention of Polk sending a force after Oglesby and Plummer or of interrupting reinforcements from reaching Price as the main reasons behind his attack. Not until the day after the battle—and in his second telegram to Fremont—did Grant refer to Price or to the enemy's efforts to reinforce him. In this dispatch, Grant first provided an estimate of Federal casualties and the number of Confederate prisoners in his possession. He then told of how both he and McClernand had lost their horses to enemy fire. After this piece of trivia, Grant noted as an afterthought that "Prisoners taken report that a large force [was] prepared to . . . join Price." The attack on Belmont, he claimed, "will no doubt defeat this move." Curiously, Grant did not seem to be in any hurry to relay the above news to Fremont who, given his fixation upon Price's army and the thrust of his alleged directive of November 5, would have wanted to know *immediately* about this ominous development. More important, however, is that nowhere in his correspondence—either before or immediately after the battle—did Grant indicate that the *prevention* of this supposed movement had been the primary motivation behind his decision to assail Belmont.[40]

Somehow, this postbattle discovery that Confederate troops were supposedly on the way to Price became in Grant's final account a major justification for his attack on the Confederate camp, even though he had never mentioned this rationale before leaving Cairo. Writing to his father on the evening of November 8, he stated *for the first time* that a primary goal behind the Belmont expedition was to *prevent* reinforcements from joining Price, but the general made no mention of any orders directing him to do so.[41] Basically, Grant had stumbled upon this information *after* the battle (from Confederate prisoners), but the belief that he had indeed disrupted the flow of reinforcements going to Price gave his attack, so far devoid of any tangible results and coming under increased criticism, a nobler purpose and the appearance of success. From then on, Grant let this post-Belmont discovery stand as an essential factor in his decision to assail the outpost.

Grant's second stated objective—the protection of the columns under Oglesby and Plummer sent in pursuit of Thompson—appears dubious as well. On November 6, troops from Cairo boarded the transports and steamed downriver, stopping for the night along the Kentucky shore. According to Grant, at 2 A.M. the next morning, a messenger from Col. W. H. L. Wallace arrived in the general's cabin aboard the *Belle Memphis* and relayed news from a "reliable Union man" in Charleston that Confederate troops had recently crossed to Belmont to hunt down the Union columns chasing the "Swamp Rats." "This move," wrote Grant in his official report, "seemed to me more than probable" and ultimately drove him "to attack vigorously at Belmont." Unfortunately, like the telegram of November 5, no other evidence has surfaced to verify that Grant ever received this message.[42]

Wallace's role as the purveyor of the information also casts doubt upon the existence of the message. Although his command stopped in Charleston that night while en route to join Oglesby, Wallace's post-Belmont correspondence discredits Grant's claim about his involvement in sending the message. On November 14, Wallace blasted his superior for engaging in such a foolish and costly engagement and rendered perhaps the most stinging indictment of his conduct. He maintained that Grant "had not the courage to refuse to fight" even though the "advantages were all against him & any permanent or substantial good [was] an utter impossibility." Though the battle "demonstrated the courage and fighting qualities of our men," he continued, "it cost too much." These statements appear rather odd coming from the officer who supposedly provided the information that initiated the very attack he now condemned. Also, Wallace gave no indication that he knew of the alleged Confederate move to Belmont or that he had transmitted this important news to Grant that night. In fact, had he known that Confederate troops were moving west from Belmont, he neglected to impart this news even to Oglesby, the one officer who truly needed to know. Moreover, given that, in Grant's version, the Belmont attack *saved* the two columns from being attacked from the rear, Wallace had an odd way of showing his appreciation. But even if Wallace had supplied the information, the news would have had little impact. Grant had already determined to attack Belmont before the transports departed Cairo.[43]

Finally, the fact that the November 5 telegram and the 2 A.M. intelligence report first appeared in Grant's official report, which was not composed until May 1864 and backdated to correspond with the battle, also makes these references suspect. Grant's chief-of-staff John A. Rawlins and Lt. Col. Theodore S. Bowers, the authors of the report, relied upon memory and an assortment of documents to reconstruct what had transpired nearly three years earlier, thereby subjecting their interpretation to the whims of clouded recollections, the absence of key actors (W. H. L. Wallace was killed at Shiloh in April 1862), and the taint of hindsight. Judging from the rough treatment given Grant over Belmont, their account was possibly an effort to deflect further criticism from their boss, now commander of all Union armies. Unfortunately, in their attempt to set the record straight, Rawlins and Bowers only confused the issue further by offering unsubstantiated evidence to demonstrate that their chief had exhibited wisdom and prudence, not reckless insubordination. Perhaps Grant scholar John Y. Simon offered the best advice on how to deal with the November 5 telegram, the 2 A.M. intelligence report, and the justifications that supposedly emerged from them. "Recognizing their questionable origins," he cautioned, "we can better understand the battle by ignoring both." [44]

Following that advice remains unsatisfying, however, unless another explanation for Grant's decision can be found. Put another way, if the general's postbattle rationale for assaulting Belmont is discarded, why did he risk lives and his career on a venture that had no perceivable purpose? Surely his desire to "bloody" his men cannot by itself account for his decision. Why, then, did U. S. Grant fight at Belmont? Consulting Professor Simon on this question, he once again offers wise counsel: "The answer must be found in [Grant] himself, and no simple answer will do." [45]

Factoring Grant's prebattle perceptions into his decision-making calculus produces a compelling alternative to the general's explanation for the attack. As examined earlier, his interpretation of Confederate intentions, based upon a mixture of intelligence, assumptions, and intuition, had remained fundamentally unchanged since September. Combined with other factors, this mental image influenced Grant's final decision and propelled him toward Belmont. On November 5 the Cairo commander outlined his plans for the upcoming operation and, in the process, revealed that he intended to do more than merely amuse the

Columbus garrison with a pointless demonstration. Unaware that Smith was already under orders to demonstrate against Columbus, Grant asked the Paducah commander to support his operations in Missouri by sending a reconnaissance-in-force toward the Confederate stronghold. Grant hoped Smith's move would divert Polk's attention and prevent him from "throwing over the river much more force than they now have" at Belmont, thereby allowing the troops from Cairo time "to drive those [forces] they now have [there] out of Missouri." To accomplish this part of the plan, Grant assembled an expeditionary force to "menace Belmont." Saying nothing about reinforcements heading for Price but recognizing the vulnerability of the contingent pursuing Thompson, Grant informed Smith that the primary objective of this dual movement was "to prevent the enemy from sending a force to fall in the rear of those now out from this command." [46]

The next day, however, Grant had changed his mind. Instead of protecting Oglesby and Plummer, he moved toward diverting these troops for use in his operations against Belmont. Later that day, he went even further. The latest intelligence showing a depletion of the Columbus garrison by transfers to central Kentucky combined with two months of false alarms had vindicated Grant's long-held view that Polk had neither the forces nor the desire to venture into Missouri. Seeing an opportunity to seize the initiative along the Mississippi, Grant ordered W. H. L. Wallace to intercept Oglesby and instruct him to break off his pursuit of Thompson (Plummer would continue the chase) and turn southeast toward Confederate-held New Madrid, roughly twenty-five miles southwest of Belmont. His instructions suggest that he expected the combined Oglesby-Wallace column to be in the field for several days, perhaps anticipating extended operations beyond the Belmont engagement. [47] Once underway toward New Madrid, Grant told Oglesby to contact him at Belmont, indicating that he intended to be in control of the town by that time.

Thus, instead of mindlessly chasing Thompson, whom he saw as a minor threat anyway, or exhausting his men by marching them about the countryside in harmless demonstrations, Grant saw an opportunity to drive the enemy from southeastern Missouri, which both he and Fremont believed was a necessary prelude to a campaign against Columbus. When Oglesby, after receiving his new orders from Wallace, boasted that his command "could march to Memphis," he undoubtedly understood that Grant had in mind more than mere saber rattling. Restless from months of inactivity and perhaps fearing that another chance might not come along, Grant forged ahead—just as he did at Paducah in September—believing the results would justify the risks. Perhaps Charles W. Wills, a soldier in Oglesby's brigade, came closest to deciphering Grant's true intentions: "I think the Paducah forces were to take Columbus, Grant was going to swallow Belmont, we were to drive all the guerrillas before us to New Madrid, and then with [the] Paducah forces and Grant's we were to take Madrid and probably go to Memphis or maybe join Fremont." This drive to seize the initiative and the willingness to "try conclusions" became hallmarks of Grant's generalship.[48]

The plan to capture Belmont and New Madrid and to force the Southerners out of southeast Missouri, however, had not originated with Grant. In early September, Fremont had indicated his desire to expel pro-Confederate forces from southeastern Missouri when he ordered Grant to capture Charleston, Sikeston, and Belmont and to "follow the retreating Rebels to New Madrid." In his grand offensive unveiled three days later, Fremont declared that Grant's primary objectives were to control the west bank of the Mississippi opposite Columbus, capture New Madrid, and dislodge the enemy from the region while forces from Paducah outflanked Columbus. Once this phase was complete, the department commander hoped to launch a combined attack on Columbus and Hickman as part of a drive down the Mississippi Valley toward Memphis. Although his fixation on southwestern Missouri checked the plan in mid-September, Fremont fully intended to "move on Memphis" after defeating Price.[49] Grant's actions on November 6–7 must be viewed within this context. He was not moving blindly downriver "looking for a fight" anywhere he could find it but following a general course plotted by "The Pathfinder" in early September. With Thompson neutralized, Polk locked into the defensive, and Confederate leadership fixated on central Kentucky, Grant saw in early November an opportunity to set in motion Fremont's original plan in hopes of regaining the initiative in the Mississippi Valley.

Grant considered his attack on Belmont as the opening salvo of Fremont's grand offensive. After the battle the departmental commander indicated that he was indeed thinking about initiating this offensive too. The situation in central and western Missouri, however, delayed its implementation.[50] As a result, instead of unleashing a general offensive on

November 1, Fremont called only for a demonstration to distract Polk. Anxious to advance since September, Grant jumped the gun, disobeying a direct order against initiating an attack. But this sort of behavior was nothing new. Two months earlier he took Paducah without authorization, a move fraught with far more political and military risks than the assault on Camp Johnston. And since Fremont had belatedly endorsed and had even tried to take credit for that earlier gambit, Grant may not have feared official sanction if he stretched his orders again, especially if he achieved success.

The Cairo commander's hunger for the initiative also factored in to events on November 7. When two opponents fielded armies of inexperienced volunteers, he once reasoned, to delay an offensive for the sake of more preparation gained nothing since the enemy would use the time for similar purposes. The army that first seized the initiative ultimately gained an important advantage. And since the Union carried the burden of forcing open the Mississippi, in Grant's mind an offensive became a question of when, not if. From the day he assumed command at Cairo, he had waited anxiously for Fremont to unleash his forces. Moreover, Grant's intelligence-driven perception that the Confederates in Columbus posed only a minimal offensive threat heightened his awareness of the opportunity presented to him in early November.[51]

The assault on Belmont also made sense for other reasons. First, the mere presence of this Confederate outpost represented a dangerous chink in the Federal armor in southeastern Missouri. Second, the troops occupying the camp also presented an inviting target for Grant, especially since a sizable expanse of water stood between the garrison and support from Columbus. Union intelligence had also shown that only a small force, typically no more than three thousand troops, occupied Belmont at any one time. By November 7 the odds were even better as Grant knew that Thompson, the last known occupant at Camp Johnston, had evacuated the area. Third, in order for the New Madrid phase of the plan to succeed, Grant had to protect Oglesby's flank as he moved south toward his objective, and neutralizing the Belmont garrison would attain that end. And fourth, from the earlier Union occupation of Belmont and numerous reconnaissances in that direction, essentially dress rehearsals for the actual advance, he had gained a working knowledge of the roads and terrain in the area. Although commanded by the Columbus batteries, Belmont remained a vulnerable and inviting target.[52]

By November, Grant had also gleaned from his intelligence that the Confederate high command had thinned the ranks at Columbus, leading him to conclude that their main worry would be ensuring the safety of the post. If threatened on both sides of the river, Polk would most likely remain behind his defenses, conserve his manpower, and leave Camp Johnston to its own fate, especially if he believed the scuffle across the river might be a diversion masking a main thrust against Columbus. In the final analysis, the odds were good that Polk would not risk the Gibraltar of the West to save a minor outpost, which might allow Grant's forces to seize the western bank with little interference from across the river. Although Polk did send troops to rescue Belmont, his initial hesitation revealed the merit of Grant's assumptions.[53] Finally, with Belmont and New Madrid in Union hands, and with Smith keeping Polk's forces close to home, the combined offensive might turn Columbus and force its abandonment, a scenario that Grant had envisioned as early as September 12.

Overall, the Belmont campaign further increased Grant's confidence in intelligence and in his ability to use it. Contrary to the perception that bad information precipitated the battle of Belmont, Grant based his decision to assault the outpost on good intelligence tempered by a perceptive reading of the enemy's situation and the likely behavior of their leaders. In essence, Belmont was his bid to initiate the long-awaited campaign to claim the Mississippi Valley and, in his view, to start winning the war before it became too costly. Instead of a fruitless battle brought about by flawed information, as some have argued, Belmont was actually a potentially profitable engagement born of two months of secret service work, Grant's reading of enemy intentions, and his growing belief in the initiative as a decisive element in war.

"You Will Soon Hear if My Presentiment Is Realized"

Time only magnified the importance of the Belmont campaign in Grant's mind. The expedition, he wrote, was "a greater success than . . . first thought." [1] Though many disagreed with this assessment, perhaps Grant spoke more of the intangible benefits that resulted from his first fight. From his perspective it had emboldened Union forces while striking fear among the Columbus garrison, who now worked feverishly to strengthen their works in preparation for the inevitable Federal on-slaught. But Belmont had only stoked his desire for a major offensive. Although Fremont had been transferred east, effectively burying his grand campaign idea, Grant continued to concentrate on Columbus and western Kentucky. But his fixation on capturing the Confederate Gibral-tar would not last. Before long, his attention would shift toward Forts Henry and Donelson, two important enemy installations being built on the Tennessee and Cumberland Rivers.

Until then, Grant doubled his efforts to gather intelligence on Colum-bus. Luckily, during the remainder of 1861, his concerns over the security of southeast Missouri had all but disappeared. The threat from Thomp-son ebbed as desertions and lagging reenlistments eroded his strength (a fact duly noted by Grant), leaving by December only a handful of "wretched, ragged, dispirited looking set of men" in the ranks. With the "Swamp Rats" neutralized, between mid-November 1861 and Janu-ary 1862, Grant received only one report of threatening activity in the area. Polk's unwillingness to leave his works and the Union's apparent control of the western bank of the Mississippi River convinced many in blue that Columbus was ripe for the plucking, a conclusion reached by a soldier in the Thirteenth Wisconsin who wrote: "We really want a turn with them at Columbus." [2]

In the meantime, Grant reorganized his headquarters, delegating some intelligence duties to staff members. A topographical engineer during the Mexican War, Col. Joseph D. Webster was Grant's chief of staff, aiding the general in analyzing information and placing it on maps. Capt. Wil-liam S. Hillyer, one of Grant's aides, was responsible for sending out scouts and spies and coordinating their activities.[3] Admiral Foote also had his headquarters at Cairo and shared with Grant the results of naval patrols down the Mississippi, Cumberland, and Tennessee Rivers. Post commanders on both sides of the Mississippi also reported regularly any information they acquired. By years' end, Grant's headquarters was becoming an intelligence clearinghouse with reports arriving from various sources and locations. For example, within one three-week period, Grant heard news from a Memphis refugee, two Confederate deserters, and four spies posted in Columbus.[4] One of these spies, a former "Jessie Scout" named Charles C. Carpenter, spent a week in the town sketching Polk's fortifications while disguised in a Confederate uniform. When Carpenter returned, Grant proclaimed the sketch "to be as accurate as it is possible to get it before [Columbus] falls into our possession." So confident in his system was Grant that he boasted in early December that he possessed "full means of keeping posted as to what is going on South of this point" and promised to keep his superiors "fully informed."[5]

While Grant could feel confident that he possessed the means to gain accurate information, his own security remained vulnerable. Believing that Cairo was "one of the most exposed Posts, in the Army," Grant attempted to limit the number of people passing through his lines to the south. On November 20 he issued an order prohibiting citizens coming from Missouri or Kentucky from entering Cairo without written authorization. The only exceptions were people "of known loyalty" and those who "do not expect to return South again." Any suspicious characters found roaming Union camps would be arrested as spies.[6]

Grant also initiated more preemptive counterintelligence measures. Exchanged Confederate prisoners posed a real security problem as they departed Union lines, unescorted, heading south. These men, Grant complained, kept the enemy "well informed of all [our] movements." To prevent further leaks, he barred any individuals not in Federal service from crossing his lines without a pass. Allowances had to be made for Unionists attempting to escape Southern control, even though this move might allow an enemy agent to penetrate his security. Believing "it is better that ninety-nine guilty persons should escape than that one innocent person should suffer," Grant expected that at times "we may be deceived."[7]

These counterintelligence measures, which also included a ban on transmitting sensitive information over the telegraph, most likely had some impact on plugging leaks. Regardless of the best efforts, however, Southern operatives still passed information out of Union lines. For example, pro-Confederate general Daniel M. Frost, captured at Camp Jackson in May 1861 and detained in St. Louis until his exchange, managed to transmit a report to Brig. Gen. Gideon Pillow in Columbus regarding the strength and intentions of Union forces in the area. Although everyone coming through Federal lines needed a pass, these were apparently not hard to find, as the case of John D. Weld reveals. A frustrated Union officer noted that Weld, who was under arrest on suspicion of espionage, possessed a provost marshal's pass but then, the officer quipped, "who has not?" Lapses in security troubled other Union commanders as well. Albert Sidney Johnston procured a copy of Maj. Gen. Don Carlos Buell's order of battle from that commander's own records! Grant knew that his counterintelligence efforts were reaping results but could only guess at how much was missed.[8]

Changes in the Union high command and new department boundaries also posed difficulties for Grant's future operations. On November 19 Maj. Gen. Henry W. Halleck assumed command of the new Department of the Missouri, a new administrative entity supplanting Fremont's Western Department. A graduate of West Point, class of 1846, and the author of a textbook on military affairs, Halleck's reputation as an intellectual had earned him the sobriquet "Old Brains." The Confederate high command believed his appointment spelled trouble for Southern fortunes in the West. When word of Halleck's promotion reached Richmond, Jefferson Davis warned, "Federal forces [in the West] are not hereafter, as heretofore, to be commanded by Pathfinders and holiday soldiers, but by men of military education and experience in war." With a command stretching across seven states (Missouri, Iowa, Minnesota, Wisconsin, Illinois, Arkansas, and Kentucky west of the Cumberland River) and under pressure to achieve results, "Old Brains" faced a daunting challenge. The strain showed in January 1862 when he complained to Lincoln that he felt like a carpenter forced to build a bridge using a "dull axe, a broken saw, and rotten timber."[9]

As Halleck settled into command, one of his first priorities was to organize an intelligence system at his own headquarters. He retained some of Fremont's Jessie Scouts, who had remained behind after his predecessor's departure, including Charles C. Carpenter, the detachment's leader. According to a staff officer, Carpenter was "admirably adapted for the dangerous services in which he engages" and possessed both "great shrewdness" and "reckless courage." But the Jessie Scouts also enjoyed confiscating private property for their own use and selling it for profit, a habit that landed Carpenter in jail under Grant's orders. Before his arrest, he had made several trips into southeastern Missouri and western Kentucky, accompanied at times by another Jessie Scout, L. F. Scott, to spy on the garrisons at New Madrid and Columbus. Later, Carpenter would provide valuable service to Brig. Gen. John McClernand during the campaign against Forts Henry and Donelson.[10]

Halleck also reorganized his department, extending Grant's command to include Kentucky west of the Cumberland River (including Paducah) and renaming it the District of Cairo. The region east of the Cumberland fell within the boundaries of Buell's Department of the Ohio. Operating from Louisville, Buell's forces faced Confederate opposition in eastern Tennessee and a large army under Albert Sidney Johnston at Bowling Green. As for Forts Henry and Donelson, both in northwestern Tennessee, neither Halleck nor Buell knew under whose operational authority these positions fell. This division of departments along the Cumberland would pose certain problems for future events in that area, especially with regard to Grant's access to intelligence during the Henry-Donelson campaign. Once the Cumberland and Tennessee Rivers became the focus of offensive operations, cooperation between Halleck and Buell, including the sharing of information, became paramount. Like Halleck, Buell employed his own scouts and spies, one of whom, John Lellyett, traveled in Grant's district and on occasion shared information with Cairo headquarters. But the burning desire of both department commanders to gain overall command of the western theater seriously inhibited productive collaboration. Buell's friendship with Maj. Gen. George B. McClellan, who commanded all Union armies at the time, only complicated matters. Occasionally, these sour relations prevented interdepartmental cooperation and hampered the timely transmission of intelligence to Grant's army in the field.[11]

As Halleck and Buell feuded, Grant continued to gather information about Columbus. From several Unionists he learned that forty-seven regiments of infantry and cavalry, ten light artillery companies, and over one hundred heavy guns defended the town, while another eight thousand men occupied Camp Beauregard, an outpost twenty miles to the southeast. Later in the month, Grant read in a captured issue of the *Memphis Appeal* that the governor of Mississippi had called for ten thousand volunteers to defend Columbus. These reports indicated that the Confederates were expending great energy "to make Columbus impregnable." On December 8 a spy in Columbus corroborated the earlier estimate of regiments and supported Grant's assertion that the Confederates were completely absorbed with defensive preparations. Altogether, this information indicated that the Belmont action had only increased Polk's insecurity and his concern for the safety of the fortress.[12] An offensive against Cairo or Paducah, believed Grant, was the last thing on his mind.

Information arriving in mid-December indicated that Polk's defenses were once again being thinned by detachments sent to protect other positions. A local civilian reported to Grant that four infantry regiments and three gunboats had departed Columbus for New Orleans. Three days later a spy and a Confederate naval deserter brought similar news, claiming, "A great many of the troops are gone." Though believing the enemy still had an advantage in strength, Grant saw clear indications that Polk's command was daily losing strength. Other reports described the conditions within Columbus and the garrison's morale. Rumors circulated purporting that recent recruitment efforts had netted mostly young boys with no training and that shortages of clothing, shoes, and provisions had dampened the ardor to defend the town. According to one deserter, the paucity of supplies had sown discontent within the garrison and among the new arrivals, which were mostly militia units from Tennessee, Mississippi, and Louisiana. "If salt can be kept out," Grant stated with obvious double meaning, "they will have some difficulty saving their bacon."[13]

According to intelligence, the Confederate high command continued to deplete the Columbus garrison to defend other threatened points. For example, on Christmas Eve, Polk detached five thousand troops stationed at Camp Beauregard to Bowling Green. Grant learned of this move within five days, although he estimated the detachment's strength at seven thousand. One of his Columbus spies also reported that Polk was sending away his most seasoned troops, leaving only untrained militia in their place. Indeed, the Confederate commander had been forced to part with experienced soldiers and had only a brigade of untrained Mississippi militia as replacements. These men, Polk complained, "cannot be expected to be very effective." Unwilling to detach additional seasoned troops, he warned Southern authorities that further reductions would "sacrifice this command and throw open the valley of the Mississippi." As his garrison dwindled, Polk's fear of an attack reached new heights. By the end of December, he lapsed into a siege mentality, believing that at any moment fifty thousand Federals might descend upon Columbus. Convinced that his command had lost its offensive punch and concerned about his ability to even defend the fortress, he hunkered down in Columbus and absolved himself of responsibility for protecting the rest of his district, which included Forts Henry and Donelson on the Tennessee and Cumberland Rivers.[14]

Convinced that Polk had lost nearly one-third of his command, Grant again concluded that he faced a weakened foe that had every intention of remaining on the defensive. With this in mind, the district commander requested permission to meet with Halleck in St. Louis to discuss future operations. In his postwar memoirs, Grant claimed that by this time he had already concluded that the "true line of operations . . . was up the Tennessee and Cumberland rivers" against Forts Henry and Donelson and that his trip to St. Louis was to "lay this plan of campaign" before his superior. Nowhere in his previous correspondence, however, did he indicate that he had reached this conclusion. Contrary to his postwar recollections, at the time he requested the first meeting in St. Louis, Grant's focus remained on capturing Columbus, and his letter to Halleck reflected that fact, especially since he spent most of his ink imparting news about conditions in the fortress. And at that moment, the Confederate Gibraltar appeared extremely vulnerable. Instead of going to St. Louis that January to propose a campaign against Forts Henry and Donelson, it is more probable that Grant hoped to convince Halleck that the time had come to eliminate Columbus. Before he could reach St. Louis, however, orders to commence a reconnaissance in force into western Kentucky reached Cairo. By the time Grant finally met with his superior, the Kentucky reconnaissance had decisively shifted his attention toward the forts on the Tennessee and Cumberland.[15]

On January 3, 1862, General in Chief George B. McClellan called for a demonstration against Columbus to prevent the reinforcement of Bowling Green. While Grant's forces kept Polk busy, an expedition would be sent up the Cumberland and Tennessee Rivers to freeze troops at Fort Donelson, Fort Henry, and Clarksville. McClellan also told Halleck that if Columbus appeared vulnerable, "the place should be taken." To accomplish this mission, Halleck ordered Grant to march east of Columbus toward Mayfield and Murray and advised him to deceive the enemy by leaking the news that "Dover [Fort Donelson] is the object of your attack." Even his own troops were to be fed false information. "Make a great fuss about moving all your forces toward Nashville," Halleck instructed, "and let it be so reported by the newspapers." Accordingly, the Cairo commander leaked this information to Northern papers and ensured that copies reached enemy hands. Fearing that Grant's well-known aggressiveness might result in another Belmont, Halleck cautioned against engaging the enemy and conveniently neglected to mention McClellan's instructions to take Columbus if the opportunity arose. Though Grant obeyed orders, he saw the operation as more than just a means to temporarily prevent detachments from leaving the fortress. The reconnaissance was also an opportunity to familiarize himself with the terrain and road networks and, more importantly, to "awaken apprehension for the safety" of Columbus in order to observe Polk's reactions.[16]

Grant's Kentucky demonstration began on January 10, 1862, with Charles F. Smith's Paducah forces marching on Mayfield, Camp Beauregard, and Murray while an infantry detachment and several gunboats moved up the Tennessee to threaten Fort Henry. The expedition ended eleven days later, netting much useful information. From a refugee and articles in the *Memphis Appeal*, Grant learned that seven additional regiments had recently departed Columbus for Bowling Green. According to his calculations, Polk had now lost twenty-four of forty-seven regiments—over half his infantry—since October. "[T]he Garrison of Columbus," Grant proclaimed on January 12, "is now weaker than it has been for several months." Not only that, he added, "it is probable that the best armed and best drilled troops have been taken." As Union troops neared Columbus during the operation, McClernand interpreted the "non-appearance" of any significant Confederate resistance to mean the enemy was "closely collected around camp fires within their entrenchments, and indisposed to take the field." That moment, he later wrote, was perhaps the most "favorable time . . . for [a] successful attack and the capture of Columbus." After observing the disappointment evinced by his men when the demonstration ended without an attempt to storm the stronghold, McClernand urged Halleck to launch an immediate attack while the enemy remained vulnerable.[17]

Grant also lamented the lost opportunity. "My orders were such and the force with me also so small," he complained, "that no attack [upon Columbus] was allowable." On the bright side, however, he had made a "splendid reconnoissance of the country over which an army may have to move," personally riding over thirty miles and acquainting himself with the region surrounding Columbus. During his travels, Grant witnessed the poor road conditions in the vicinity and, like McClernand, noted the curious lack of opposition, even when Union columns edged to within a mile and a half of Columbus. Grant's statements and the fact that he proclaimed the Kentucky demonstration a success *before* Smith had reported the results of his foray up the Tennessee River indicate that Columbus—not Forts Henry and Donelson—remained foremost in his mind. In fact, his presence with McClernand's column instead of with the forces sent toward Fort Henry, in addition to the personal effort he expended to survey the terrain around Columbus, support that conclusion. The Kentucky expedition was, in essence, a dress rehearsal for his hoped-for advance against Polk. Contrary to his postwar memory, therefore, during the demonstration Grant remained fixated upon Columbus and had not yet changed his course toward Forts Henry and Donelson.[18]

Satisfied with the results of the demonstration, on January 20 Grant again requested an audience with Halleck. According to his memoirs, he went to St. Louis to suggest that future Union efforts be directed toward the Tennessee and Cumberland Rivers. However, Smith's report of his foray into Kentucky and up the Tennessee, which would prove critical in shifting the focus from Columbus toward Fort Henry, had not yet reached headquarters when Grant called for the meeting. This fact, along with Grant's longstanding fixation on Columbus, the lack of attention paid to the rivers before January, and his personal participation in the Kentucky demonstration, all cast doubt upon the claim that he requested the conference for the sole purpose of convincing Halleck that Fort Henry was the "true line of operations." It is more likely that he planned instead to press Halleck for an advance on Columbus. Before he departed for St. Louis on January 23, however, some new intelligence arrived and changed his thinking.

That day Smith's report of his expedition toward Mayfield arrived and, according the Grant's memoirs, "confirmed views I had previously held" that the next objective should be the forts on the Tennessee and Cumberland Rivers. Despite the contention that he had entertained this view for some time, it was the combination of Smith's report and the news that Polk had recalled reinforcements that finally led Grant to view Fort Henry as a possible objective. Smith's summary provided four key pieces of information that, combined with reported increases in Columbus's strength, persuaded Grant that operations along the Tennessee River offered the most profitable results. First, Smith complained that the roads south of Paducah were "something horrible" and that he consumed an entire day moving a single brigade three miles. Coupled with McClernand's unfavorable report of the road conditions around Columbus, Grant knew that any reinforcements sent east from Columbus to aid Fort Henry would be unable to get there very fast. Next, he noted that the Tennessee had risen fourteen feet in one week, thus providing enough clearance for both gunboats and transports to navigate the waters above the fort. Third, Smith argued that "two iron-clad gunboats would make short work of Fort Henry," a belief based upon the lack of Confederate naval opposition and personal observations of the position during a reconnaissance that sailed to within three miles of the fortification. A naval officer supported Smith's contentions, observing that the fort was "apparently ill-calculated [in its construction] for defense against bombshells" launched from the gunboats. Finally, and perhaps most important, Smith estimated that perhaps as few as three thousand troops occupied the position.[19]

To Grant, the decision to campaign up the Tennessee River developed from several factors. Though vulnerable and tempting, Columbus was still a well-fortified bastion defended by at least twenty-three regiments. To strike the Confederate Gibraltar also meant marching and receiving supplies over unpredictable roads. Any attack would also have to proceed without the aid of gunboats because the Columbus batteries would prevent them from getting within range. Comparatively, Fort Henry was a less dangerous but a potentially more profitable option. Grant could assail this unfinished, undermanned post with an overwhelming force using Foote's flotilla in support. This expedition would require fewer men than the attack on Columbus, allowing him to leave enough behind to secure Cairo. And since the Confederates reportedly had but one operational gunboat, troops could use river transports to make an amphibious landing above the fort. Both the Columbus and Fort Henry options involved risks, but the latter alternative, if successful, promised the same results—puncturing the Confederate defensive line and turning Columbus—at potentially lower cost. Eliminating both Fort Henry and Fort Donelson, moreover, would cause the fall of Nashville and open two water invasion routes into the heart of the South.[20]

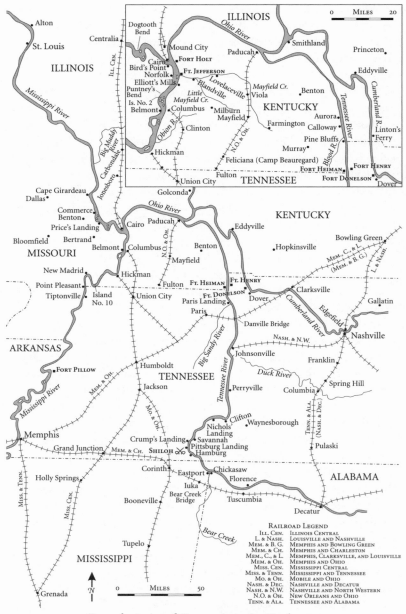

Grant's Area of Operations in Early 1862

Armed with this information, Grant finally went to St. Louis and revealed his plan for an advance upon Fort Henry. The meeting went badly and he left without securing approval. "I was received with so little cordiality," he explained in his memoirs, "that I perhaps stated the object of my visit with less clearness than I might have done." Sensing that Halleck viewed his plan as unworkable, Grant returned to Cairo on January 28 "very much crestfallen." But he refused to capitulate and immediately wired St. Louis for permission to "take Fort McHenry [*sic*] on the Tennessee." This time, however, Foote also announced his support for the plan. Hearing nothing and fearing that inaction ceded the advantage to Polk and those manning the river forts, Grant repeated his request the following day.[21]

Though hesitant, Halleck finally approved the campaign on January 30. But Grant's pleas had not swayed him; a telegram from McClellan had forced Halleck's hand. On January 29 the general in chief telegraphed news from a deserter that Confederate general P. G. T. Beauregard and fifteen regiments had orders to join Southern forces in Kentucky. The specter of Beauregard, who at that time had a solid military reputation, and a large force marching toward the Bluegrass State alarmed "Old Brains." Fearful that these reinforcements would give the enemy an advantage, Halleck wired Grant to "take and hold" Fort Henry. In his written instructions sent later the same day, the department commander warned that Polk would probably try to reinforce Fort Henry and that the arrival of Beauregard's regiments might tip the balance. "It is therefore of the greatest importance," urged Halleck, "that we cut that line before he arrives."[22] Unknown to these Union commanders was that McClellan's information was inaccurate. Beauregard was indeed heading to Kentucky but without any reinforcements.

When the Army of the District of Cairo embarked for the Tennessee River on February 2, Grant had concluded that the Kentucky demonstration had scared Confederate officials into reinforcing Fort Henry, boosting its strength to six thousand men. However, the fort had actually received no new troops and the garrison remained at around three thousand, consistent with earlier Union estimates. But even if double that number manned the works, Grant believed he outnumbered his foe two to one. Other reports had also shed some much-needed light on Fort Henry, a position the Federals still knew very little about. For example, back in December, Daniel K. Boswell, a Unionist from Mississippi, told authorities in Paducah of Fort Henry's "inability to sustain itself" but warned that the fort's strength would be enhanced once the Confederates finished building several new ironclads. Observing that capturing Fort Henry would not only halt the construction of these warships (which it did), Boswell also believed it would bring Union forces a step closer to severing the Memphis and Charleston Railroad, a main east-west artery for the South. Though he carried this same news to Washington and urged a "speedy" advance on Fort Henry, by January no immediate action resulted from his pleas. The none-too-modest Boswell, however, even suggested that the victory at Fort Henry, followed by the capture of Fort Donelson, Bowling Green, and Nashville, would not have occurred if not for the information he provided. Several individuals also claimed they supplied information on Fort Henry, including John Lellyett, steamboat captain Charles M. Scott, Charles De Arnaud, and Anna Ella Carroll, but no evidence suggests that Grant knew about any of these reports.[23]

As Union forces headed up the Tennessee, Grant had already formed in his mind an impression of the enemy. The Confederates in Fort Henry, he believed, were "well fortified and have a strong force." He still knew little about the area where he was about to commit his army and even less about other nearby positions such as Fort Heiman, a small Confederate outpost in Kentucky opposite Fort Henry, and Fort Donelson, a more substantial fortification twelve miles east on the Cumberland. This intelligence gap occurred in part because Grant had never sent any of his own scouts or spies in that direction, indicating the extent to which he had remained focused upon Columbus until late January. The dearth of information translated into serious problems for the Union command, including locating a safe point for disembarkation above the fort. To find a suitable spot, Grant boarded the gunboat *Essex* on a mission to gauge the range and accuracy of the fort's river batteries. Smith, who had taken the *Lexington* to within two and a half miles of Henry in January, reported that the enemy fired only one shell, which fell short by half a mile. Hopeful that their batteries had not improved, Grant brought the *Essex* to within two miles of the fort. Two Confederate shells, one sailing over the boat and the other smashing into the deck—nearly killing Grant—revealed that a landing must occur farther downriver. Based on this information, on February 4 McClernand's men disembarked at Bailey's Ferry, three miles below the fort.[24]

McClernand spent the next two days preparing defenses around the landing and probing the Confederate position. Although he lacked cavalry, he dispatched what he had toward the fort and personally surveyed the terrain. He also enlisted the services of the Jessie Scout Charles Carpenter, who "closely approached [the] defenses and reported to me correctly with regard to them, and the preparations of the enemy." From this information McClernand concluded that Fort Henry had received reinforcements, though how many remained unclear. Remarkably, he estimated that the reinforcements had swelled the fort's garrison to between six and twenty thousand. Another reconnaissance by his scouts on February 5 revealed "a considerable encampment just above and outside" the fort, which seemed to corroborate earlier reports of troops flooding into the region.[25]

Grant had also heard about more troops reaching the fort, but he too had no clear idea how many. "What the strength of Fort Henry is I do not know accurately," he wrote, but predicted that at least ten thousand men now manned the works. Although that many Confederates poised behind strong fortifications might have deterred another commander, Grant allowed neither this intelligence nor the lack of certainty regarding these numbers to alter his course. In fact, by February 5, Grant hoped that the presence of Union forces near the fort would shift some of that uncertainty to the enemy's minds. Not only were the Federal campfires dotting the countryside a beautiful sight to behold, the spectacle "no doubt inspires the enemy, who is in full view of them, with the idea that we have full [forty thousand] men." He also noted that a skirmish between pickets and McClernand's reconnaissance patrols had "badly frightened" the Rebels. But the possibility of more reinforcements reaching the fort led him to commence the attack before the odds shifted. Though uncertainty nipped at the edges of his confidence, Grant prepared to assault Fort Henry but remained steadfast in his prediction of ultimate victory. "You will soon hear," he told his wife on the eve of battle, "if my presentiment is realized."[26]

Meanwhile, Halleck experienced enough anxiety for both officers. In a dispatch dated February 3, which Halleck received two days later, Buell casually mentioned that, in addition to Beauregard's troops reportedly coming from Virginia, another ten thousand Confederates were en route to the forts under the command of Generals John Bell Floyd and Simon Bolivar Buckner. These troops had reportedly departed Bowling Green on January 22 and had already reached Russellville on the Memphis, Louisville, and Clarksville Railroad. In an example of the breakdown of intelligence cooperation between the two departments, Buell had learned of this movement on January 23 but waited nearly two weeks before passing it on to Halleck. Realizing that Grant's fifteen thousand men might soon face the combined forces of Beauregard, Buckner, and Floyd, "Old Brains" urged McClellan to send more troops. By February 6, Halleck's anxiety reached new heights when news arrived that more troops from Bowling Green and Columbus had gone to Fort Henry. "They intend to make a stand [at Fort Henry]," he warned McClellan. "Unless I get more forces, I may fail to take it." Halleck's report seemed to corroborate McClernand's information about Southern reinforcements reaching the area. But Grant was undisturbed by this news and, based upon what he learned during the Kentucky demonstration, remained confident that Polk would not budge from his works even if Fort Henry came under attack.[27]

But before Grant could initiate a land assault against Fort Henry, Foote's gunboats battered it into submission. Since McClernand's troops were unable to prevent most of the garrison from escaping to Fort Donelson, the Federals captured only eighty officers and men. Had Grant maintained his earlier intelligence estimates, he would not have been shocked to learn that the force at Fort Henry had numbered only about three thousand Southerners. The ease of the victory raised his confidence, especially in his ability to correctly assess the enemy and by rapid, forward movements defeat him. Moreover, Fort Henry's fall emboldened him to take more chances. "I intend to keep the ball moving as lively as possible," he wrote, adding that his recent victory had rattled his opponent. And in what would become a fixed perception in his mind for the rest of the war, he noted, "The scare and fright of the rebels up here is beyond conception."[28] In Grant's mind, the balance of uncertainty was shifting. The enemy was beginning to fear him more than he feared them.

After the surrender of Fort Henry, Grant focused on his next objective, and one he knew even less about. Situated on the Cumberland River twelve miles to the east, Fort Donelson remained an enigma to Federal leadership. Such ignorance might have led another commander to await more complete information before plunging into the unknown. But imperfect knowledge did not deter Grant. "I was very impatient to get to

Fort Donelson," he wrote later, "because I knew the importance of the place to the enemy and supposed he would reinforce it rapidly." He reasoned that maintaining the initiative and sending 15,000 Federal soldiers to assail the fort immediately—with or without adequate intelligence—"would be more effective than [sending] 50,000 a month later." [29]

The fact remained, though, that Grant still knew little about Donelson's river and land defenses. Information on the river batteries remained imprecise even though Foote's gunboats had ascended the Cumberland several times to assess them. Lt. S. Ledyard Phelps and the *Conestoga* twice approached Fort Donelson in early December 1861 and returned with only limited information. In late January 1862, an exasperated Phelps complained about his inability to learn much about the fort. "I have been to the bend where a boat's length would have placed us in sight [of Fort Donelson]," he wrote, but the fort's guns forced a withdrawal because "their [target] practice has all been precisely at that point." [30] As a result, he grumbled, "I wholly rely upon others for information." Grant faced the same situation with regard to the rest of Fort Donelson.

Confident in his army and secure in his belief that the Fort Henry operation had scared and demoralized the enemy, Grant presented Halleck with a plan to "take and destroy" Fort Donelson and predicted that it would fall in one day. But muddy roads and high water delayed the advance eastward until February 12. Though frustrating, the setback provided more time for Grant to learn a little more about the regional terrain and road system, an important task given that the Federals had no accurate maps of the area. [31]

Between February 7 and 12, Grant's cavalry, scouts, and engineers surveyed the roads and ground between Forts Henry and Donelson, at times edging to within a mile of the latter's works. From these investigations, Grant learned that two serviceable roads could be used as avenues of approach. The Telegraph Road ran directly toward the fort while the Ridge Road dipped toward Dover, a small town southeast of Donelson. These scouting details, however, shed little light on the ground fronting the fort or on the nature of its defenses. As a result, Col. Joseph D. Webster testified, "Our army approached the place with very little knowledge of its topography." The strength of the garrison also remained a mystery. [32]

When Grant went after Fort Henry, he thought he knew the size of its garrison. Before the move on Fort Donelson, however, he possessed no such information. This state of affairs was not lost upon some junior officers. Before departing Fort Henry, Col. Lew Wallace marveled at "how little we know in advance of the condition of the enemy." His remark accurately reflected the fog that enshrouded the Union command at that moment. On February 8 Grant admitted knowing nothing definite about the size of the enemy's forces before him but understood that "if any reinforcements were on the way for this place no doubt they have, or will, go [to Fort Donelson]." On the eve of the advance three days later, the uncertainty remained. In his orders for the movement, Grant declined to provide explicit directions because the "force of the enemy being so variously reported" made it "impossible to give exact details of attack." Despite the uncertainty, he remained confident of success. According to one story, a correspondent asked the general if he knew the size of Fort Donelson's garrison. Though admitting he did not, this fact did not appear to disturb him much. Instead of fixating upon what he did not know, Grant focused upon making the effort to seize the position and hoping it turned out right. Confident that maintaining the initiative would shift the burden of uncertainty upon the enemy, he brushed aside his own doubts and forged ahead.[33]

The first substantive news on the strength of the Confederate army came from prisoners captured during the advance on February 12. They reported that nearly twenty-five thousand men manned Fort Donelson under the combined command of Pillow, Buckner, Floyd, and Bushrod Rust Johnson. If this figure proved accurate, the enemy outnumbered the Union expedition by ten thousand men. Undeterred, Grant pressed on. By the evening of February 12, the Federals came within sight of Donelson, having encountered only light resistance to that point. It seemed as if the Confederates planned to let Grant smash his army against the fort's defenses instead of taking the initiative and driving the Federals away. Traveling the Telegraph Road, Smith's division deployed on the left directly in front of the fort to cut off an escape to the north. McClernand's First Division followed the Ridge Road and sidled to the right below Dover to block a retreat to Nashville along the southern bank of the Cumberland. As his army tightened the noose, Grant assessed the situation. Neither the unknown strength of the garrison nor the ease with which they could be reinforced from Clarksville or Nashville dampened his enthusiasm. Instead, he boasted that news of the fort's capture would be telegraphed the following day.[34]

Grant later claimed that his confidence was bolstered by the knowledge that Gideon Pillow was in command, a fact he learned on February 9, the very day the Tennessean arrived. Familiar with Pillow's history of incompetence, Grant believed his army "could march up to within gunshot of any intrenchment's [Pillow] was given to hold." Even when he learned that John Bell Floyd, a former secretary of war, was appointed as the senior commander, Grant dismissed him as a mere pawn to "Pillow's pretensions." In fact, after Donelson fell, he claimed that both Pillow and Floyd were "as dead as if they were in their graves for any harm they can do." Grant later admitted that had Buckner been in charge, he would have changed his plans. "I had relied very much," he wrote, "upon their commander [Pillow] to allow me to come safely up the outside of their works." During this operation, therefore, Grant staked much on his perceptions of Confederate leadership.[35]

On February 13, the day Smith and McClernand assaulted the fort without success, Grant remained in the dark regarding Confederate strength. He knew that Floyd had arrived at Donelson with four thousand men but had little else to go on. Nevertheless, the following day Grant estimate that the garrison numbered as high as thirty thousand (a wild overestimate) but noted, "All statements places [*sic*] their numbers much higher." Though supposedly outnumbered and facing stout defenses, he observed that, despite the Southerners' strength, "they do not seem inclined to come out," a factor he viewed as giving him the advantage.[36]

As his subordinate approached Fort Donelson, Halleck continued monitoring Confederate activity in central Kentucky, and with each day he became more convinced that Grant's army was in great danger. In fact, he had provided Buell with his estimate of Confederate troop strength in the area (forty thousand) before Grant himself had even settled on a figure. On February 15 "Old Brains" concluded that Johnston had evacuated Bowling Green to fall upon Grant's rear and that Beauregard had arrived in Columbus and planned to attack Cairo. In a panic, Halleck told McClellan that this was "the crisis of the war in the West" and that he could "do no more for Grant at present." He then halted all reinforcements heading for the Cumberland in order to protect Cairo. Halleck was not the only one anxious about the fate of the expedition. Buell felt certain that the Confederates would attempt to retake Fort Henry, while Assistant Secretary of War Thomas A. Scott feared Grant was in "extreme danger of being cut off by Beauregard." Even McClellan remained pessimistic. For some reason, however, Halleck failed to apprise Grant of the rumored developments and the concerns for his safety. Not until Sherman wrote Grant from Paducah on February 15 did Grant learn of the reported evacuation of Bowling Green and Johnston's rumored reinforcement of Fort Donelson. But Sherman's letter reached the front long after events had rendered its contents moot.[37]

Unaware of the rumors and the anxiety in official circles, Grant continued pressing Fort Donelson. On February 14, Foote's gunboats attempted to repeat their Fort Henry performance but found Donelson's river batteries more than a match. Before the engagement, Foote's intelligence on these guns had been scarce; that day, however, he learned far more than he had wanted to know. Early the next morning, Confederate troops marched silently through the darkness toward their left near Dover in preparation for an attack aimed at punching a hole in the Union right to use as an escape route to Nashville. Leaving the trenches on their right manned with only a skeleton force, the Confederates bet everything on this roll of the dice. Fortunately for them, Union pickets never discovered the movement, probably due to the snowy weather that kept many of them near their fires overnight. Even if they had detected the shift, given Grant's perception of Pillow he might not have believed such reports anyway. Confident that Pillow would remain in place, he left his headquarters to confer with Foote, fully expecting no battle "unless I brought it on myself" since the conditions "were much more favorable to us" than for the enemy. Demonstrating a dangerous tendency that would haunt him on future battlefields, Grant failed to appreciate that his enemy might try the unexpected. As Helmuth von Moltke once observed, just when a commander believed an adversary had only three choices remaining, his opponent would inevitably find and pursue a fourth.[38]

Just before dawn on February 15, the Confederates proved Von Moltke right. Following a plan authored by Pillow, Southern forces smashed through the Union right flank. Despite a determined resistance by the Federals along Wynn's Ferry Road and a counterattack by Smith's troops on the Confederate's weakened right, both of which helped stabilize the Federal line, the Southerners had pried opened an escape route. As both exhausted armies regrouped that night, Grant remained ignorant of the gap in his line and the open road to Nashville. Fortunately for the

Union commander, the breach also remained unknown to the Confederate high command when they met that night. The presence of numerous campfires in the area (later determined to have been started by the wounded) convinced Floyd, who was supported by Buckner and Bushrod Johnson, that the Federals had sealed the gap and made escape impossible. Surrender remained the only viable alternative. In a move that would have surprised Grant, Pillow argued for continuing the fight. But the meeting turned into comic opera when Pillow caved in and, along with Floyd, passed the responsibility for surrendering the garrison to Buckner, after which Floyd and Pillow slipped away. Though some other Confederates escaped overnight, the next day Fort Donelson capitulated.[39]

The loss of the river forts shattered Albert Sidney Johnston's defensive perimeter west of the Appalachians and forced the evacuation of Bowling Green and Nashville. The Union victory would also cause the abandonment of Columbus, Grant's primary objective since his arrival in Cairo. But Johnston formed a new line farther south and again dared the Federals to come test it. Sporting another star for his role in the recent victories and given command of the newly formed District of West Tennessee, Major General Grant felt equal to the challenge.

Prior to Forts Henry and Donelson, Grant had concentrated his efforts and his intelligence resources on hastening the fall of Columbus and opening the Mississippi River above Memphis. By early January he believed that Confederate authorities had substantially weakened Polk's command, making an attack on the fortress plausible. The January demonstration in western Kentucky, in which Grant and McClernand carefully reconnoitered possible approaches to the city without encountering much resistance, further convinced him that Polk's cautious attitude would allow Federal forces to turn the position with little opposition. Only the poor condition of the roads militated against an immediate advance. But the expedition also netted the crucial information that turned Grant's attention toward the Tennessee River. Smith had discovered that only three thousand troops occupied Fort Henry and that the roads that had worked against a Federal advance would also slow reinforcements sent from Columbus to the fort. Moreover, due to its poor construction and location, he believed the gunboats could pound Henry into submission. All these factors helped convince Grant to abandon Columbus and concentrate on Fort Henry, the weak link in the Confederate defenses. The move down the Tennessee River was a dangerous gamble, but one he felt outweighed the risks of doing nothing.

The advance on Fort Donelson was a different matter. Grant knew little about its strength, the layout of its defenses, the terrain between the Tennessee and the Cumberland, or the size of the garrison. He did learn that Gideon Pillow was inside the works, which further emboldened him to take risks. The fact that his forces marched to within range of Donelson's defenses with minimal resistance seemed to validate his unflattering assessment of the Tennessee general. Grant also possessed inadequate knowledge of the battlefield once he arrived, and this became brutally evident after the Confederate counteroffensive on February 15 crumpled his right flank and, unbeknownst to him, opened an escape route for the garrison. Overall, Grant's belief that he was the attacker and that he alone would decide when and where a battle would occur reduced his vigilance. Luckily for him, the blunders committed by the Confederate high command prevented them from capitalizing on his mistake.

To ignore the enemy's strength and position is to court disaster. But Grant's unbending faith in the initiative, echoing Clausewitz's dictum that "the offensive offers much more scope for positive action," affected the intelligence balance between the Federals and Confederates. Before his advance on Donelson, Grant lacked adequate knowledge of the enemy. But he hoped bold moves would thrust the balance of uncertainty upon the enemy, which might lead to timidity and indecisiveness and perhaps reveal opportunities to exploit. Grant's attack on Fort Henry and the subsequent advance against Fort Donelson had precisely this effect. Polk paced nervously behind the Columbus earthworks, Johnston vacillated in Bowling Green, and Pillow and Floyd scrambled to strengthen their defenses while allowing Grant to approach and invest each fort unopposed.[40]

Grant had achieved remarkable success at Forts Henry and Donelson, helped in no small measure by Confederate miscues. But the campaign left indelible impressions upon him. The victories further convinced him that holding the initiative could be decisive. Even stout fortifications like those at Donelson (which he claimed were so formidable that the Confederates "had nothing to do but stand in their places to hold them") with a large garrison (which two spies later estimated to have numbered around forty thousand) were no match for a relentless army willing to take risks.[41] The campaign also revealed that maintaining the initiative reduced Grant's own uncertainty by forcing the enemy to react to *his* movements, not the reverse. Not even the Confederate counterattack at Donelson disabused him of the notion that he alone controlled the course of events.

Perhaps the most important influence upon Grant was that, once again, he demonstrated remarkable prescience when it came to assessing enemy intentions from what intelligence he did possess. He had come to realize that uncertainty does not automatically lead to disaster and, conversely, it might even provide opportunities for an able officer unafraid of taking a calculated risk. During times where information eluded him, Grant refused to let uncertainty paralyze him. Instead, he filled the information vacuum with his own perceptions of the current situation, past experience, intuition, and faith in the initiative. But a fine line separates prescience from wishful thinking. For Grant, the next campaign would reveal the disastrous consequences of confusing the two and of taking the lessons of Forts Henry and Donelson too far.

Chapter 4

"There Will Be No Fight
at Pittsburg Landing"

Just as Grant sat down for breakfast on April 6, the unmistakable roar of gunfire shattered the quiet morning air. Forgetting his hunger, he boarded a steamboat and hastened toward Pittsburg Landing, site of the main Union encampment along the Tennessee River. As he steamed up-river, the firing became heavier and Grant grew more anxious. Was this just another enemy reconnaissance or an all-out attack? Unsure of what lay ahead, he finally reached the landing and found the answer to his troubling question. Though Grant's Federals would prevail in the end, a Confederate army under Albert Sidney Johnston had pulled off one of the war's most dramatic surprise attacks against a commander confident in his ability to remain thoroughly "posted" on the enemy. How this happened has been the subject of much debate. Since surprise attacks often result from intelligence failures, to understand how and why this one succeeded leads to an assessment of the information Grant possessed, and more importantly, the conclusions he derived from it.

After Forts Henry and Donelson, a self-assured Grant looked toward a promising future. "I shall have one hard battle more to fight," he predicted, "[but we] will find smooth sailing after that." To hasten the demise of the Confederacy, he promoted what was becoming a theme of his generalship: always maintain the initiative and "push forward as vigorously as possible." Recent events had already proven the wisdom of this course. After the fall of Forts Henry and Donelson, the Confederates evacuated Bowling Green, Nashville, and Columbus. Johnston's vaunted defensive line had crumbled and, in Grant's estimation, so had Southern morale. "Defeat, disastrous defeat, is admitted," he crowed, leading him to conclude that the rebellion was "on its last legs in Tennessee."[1]

This view, however, conflicted with those of his more studious superior in St. Louis. "We must strike no blow," warned the ever-cautious Henry Halleck, "till we are strong enough to admit no doubt of the result." But in Grant's experience, hesitation favored the enemy. He had sat idly by as the Confederates strengthened Columbus. Delaying gave the Southern armies more time to dig in and increased the difficulty—and the cost—of driving them out. Undoubtedly, Grant would have agreed with Clausewitz, who wrote that "time allowed to pass unused accumulates to the credit of the defender. He reaps where he did not sow."[2] But for now he was forced to follow Halleck's more cautious approach.

While awaiting orders, Grant spent the remainder of February 1862 at Fort Donelson resupplying his army and organizing the new regiments daily swelling its ranks. He also kept abreast of the latest news regarding the enemy. Unfortunately, several possible objectives ran through his mind after the victory along the Cumberland, but as of yet he had no orders to help focus his planning and illuminate his intelligence needs. After the evacuation of Nashville on February 17, Grant concentrated upon Johnston's activities. Now in overall Confederate command in the West, Johnston led a collection of troops from Bowling Green, Nashville, eastern Kentucky, and central Tennessee, and on February 23 Grant learned that this army had retreated to Murfreesboro, some thirty-five miles southeast of Nashville. Two days later, however, new information placed the Rebels in Chattanooga in southeastern Tennessee.[3]

Hoping to learn more about Johnston's and other Confederate forces, Grant ventured to Nashville, now under Federal occupation, to confer with Don Carlos Buell. But the meeting had an inauspicious beginning as Buell, perhaps a bit jealous of the victor of Forts Henry and Donelson, kept Grant waiting for some time. Once he appeared, the two Union generals failed to reach a consensus on the location of Johnston's forces. While Grant remained adamant that Johnston was in Chattanooga, Buell insisted that the Confederates had retreated to Decatur, Alabama, a major depot along the Memphis and Charleston Railroad. And he was right. As it turned out, Grant had fallen prey to a Southern ruse. To befuddle the Federals, Johnston had first marched toward Murfreesboro and forwarded ordnance and quartermaster stores, as well as mail for his troops, to Chattanooga. In reality, he had decided to abandon Middle Tennessee and sent his troops to Decatur with the ultimate destination of Corinth, Mississippi, where forces under P. G. T. Beauregard, Leonidas Polk, Braxton Bragg, and John C. Breckinridge were concentrating to defend the Mississippi Valley.[4]

In addition to being fooled by Johnston's deception, Grant experienced some difficulties in accessing intelligence due to the lack of personnel and resources. After his departure from Cairo in early February, reports from spies operating behind enemy lines dwindled markedly. One possible explanation for this was that, in his haste to get to Fort Henry, Grant left behind what few spies he had. Moreover, the lack of secret service funds prevented him from actively recruiting new operatives, a difficult task anyway given the sparse population in the vicinity of the forts. On February 25 two of Charles F. Smith's spies, returning from a mission to Nashville, Decatur, and Memphis, visited Grant's headquarters. But their report, which contained little news of importance, would be the last from covert operatives to reach him for some time.[5]

On March 1 Halleck ordered Grant to campaign up the Tennessee River to capture Corinth, Mississippi, a vital rail junction twenty miles west of the river. He also planned to seize the railroad depots at Jackson, Humboldt, and Paris in West Tennessee. Halleck warned his subordinate to "avoid any general engagement," noting that retreat remained preferable to battle.[6] Finally able to advance, Grant's Army of the Tennessee boarded transports and, leaving their recent conquests behind, steamed upriver toward what promised to be their next victory.

By March 15 the lead elements had occupied positions on the Tennessee's west bank north of the Mississippi state line. Sherman's Fifth Division, formed at Paducah in late February, occupied Pittsburg Landing, while Lew Wallace's veteran Third Division bivouacked at Crump's Landing several miles downriver. These two divisions represented the vanguard of what would become a major Federal thrust against the new Confederate defensive line that stretched from Island No. 10 on the Mississippi River north of Memphis to Decatur, Alabama. Viewing the Tennessee River as "the great strategic line of the Western campaign," Halleck and Grant hoped to puncture the center at Corinth.[7]

Grant left Fort Henry on March 16 to lead the offensive, confident that he had "such an inside track of the enemy that by following up our success we can go anywhere." The following day he reached his new headquarters at Savannah, Tennessee, on the east bank of the Tennessee nine miles downstream from the rest of the army at Pittsburg Landing. When he arrived, Grant possessed only vague information on the enemy. On March 5 he had heard that twenty thousand Southerners were fortifying Corinth and Eastport, Alabama, on the Tennessee. Sherman corroborated this news the following day. But not until nine days later did Grant receive another estimate of Confederate forces gathering in northern Mississippi. From his sources, Smith reported that the enemy had as many as sixty thousand troops spread out along the railroads from Jackson to Eastport, with the bulk stationed at Corinth, only twenty-two miles southwest of Pittsburg Landing. Though Smith noted that he had yet to find "any thing like the desired information, as to the strength of the enemy," Grant accepted this figure and passed it on to Halleck the next day. Meanwhile, Sherman had also searched for news on Confederate numbers. Although frustrated by "indistinct" information extracted from Confederate prisoners, he estimated that thirty thousand Southerners occupied Corinth while five regiments were stationed at Purdy, a small village a short distance west of Wallace's Crump's Landing position. More importantly, Sherman observed, "Every road and path is occupied by the Enemy's cavalry" and that two Southern regiments were reported at Pea Ridge and Monterey, approximately thirteen miles southwest of Pittsburg Landing. The presence of these forces at Pea Ridge and Monterey would have a profound impact upon Sherman's future interpretations of enemy intentions. Now, however, Grant saw hints that the enemy was indeed concentrating at Corinth to defend northern Mississippi.[8]

On March 17 Grant visited Pittsburg Landing to review Union deployments, a task delegated to Sherman after an accident incapacitated Smith. The Federal encampment stretched from Sherman's division near Shiloh Church toward the landing nearly three miles to the northeast. The front stretched for three and half miles (although not in an unbroken line) between two rain-swollen creeks (Owl and Lick), which refused both flanks, while the rear rested on the Tennessee River. This narrow avenue of approach helped secure that camp against attack since the enemy could only advance from the southwest. Numerous ravines, dense forests, and tangled underbrush, interrupted by an occasional open meadow, made the approach even more difficult. Although earlier instructed by Smith to construct fortifications for "temporary defense," Sherman decided to forego earthworks, claiming the terrain alone "admits of easy defense by a small command." Besides, he admitted later, "I always acted on the supposition that we were the invading army" and, therefore, erecting earthworks "would have made our raw men timid." Also thinking in offensive terms, Grant sustained Sherman's deployments and his decision not fortify.[9]

By the end of March, five Union divisions, nearly thirty thousand men, occupied the woods and meadows around Pittsburg Landing while Wallace's men guarded the supply depot downriver at Crump's Landing. Two of Grant's divisions, Sherman's and another organized on March 26 under Brig. Gen. Benjamin M. Prentiss, were new to the field and lacked adequate arms, training, and discipline. These "green" commands also

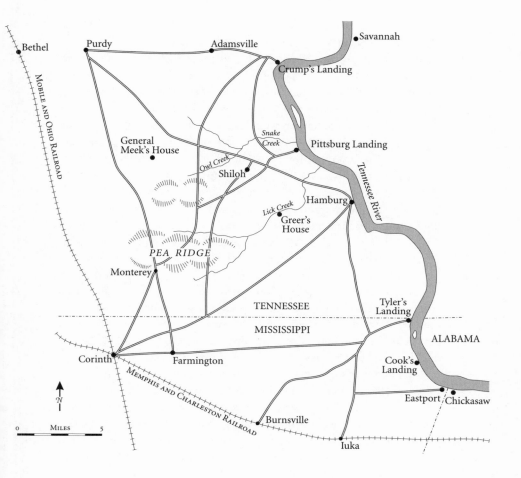

Area around Shiloh

occupied the most advanced positions between Owl and Lick Creeks. Moreover, gaps between regiments and brigades further compromised the defensibility of their camps. Thus, raw troops with little field experience and no fortifications made up the first line of defense for the entire Union encampment. Neither Grant nor Sherman, however, felt the Confederates had any intention of testing these arrangements.[10]

On March 17 one of Smith's scouts reported that nearly 150,000 enemy troops had arrived in northern Mississippi, with 50,000 occupying Corinth alone. The arrival of Johnston's Bowling Green army, he stated, accounted for the increase. But Grant promptly discounted the scout's estimate as "very much exaggerated" because Johnston's arrival in Corinth "was very much against my expectation," indicating he still believed the Southern general and his army remained in Chattanooga. Though acknowledging that the enemy was indeed gathering a large force at Corinth, he felt satisfied that their numbers did not exceed 40,000. The next day he revised this estimate downward after one of Sherman's informants reported that only 20,000 Confederates occupied Corinth. This same source also noted that the enemy had made little effort to fortify their position, an encouraging sign to many Federals who had assumed that their inactivity had given the South, as Lew Wallace noted, "abundant time to build up new Donelsons and Columbuses."[11]

From Sherman's informant Grant also learned that the enemy had detected Buell's approach and estimated his force at 150,000 men. Buell's Army of the Ohio, only comprising 35,000 men, had indeed departed Nashville bound for Pittsburg Landing, but muddy roads and rain-swollen rivers had slowed their approach to a crawl. By mid-March Buell's column was still over one hundred miles away and moving at glacial speed. The Army of the Ohio was the final ingredient in Halleck's grand plan and, to prevent any mishaps from ruining it, he reminded Grant periodically that the order against engaging the enemy remained in effect until Buell reached the Tennessee River. Anxious to determine when he should expect the reinforcement, Grant dispatched two scouts, Irving Carson, a former engineer on the Illinois Central Railroad, and another named Breckinridge to find Buell. Always thinking offensively, he did not give the enemy's awareness of Buell's impending arrival a second thought. Consumed with plans for his own advance, the possibility that the enemy might feel compelled to attack before these additional troops arrived did not concern him.[12]

As more Union troops arrived, Grant grew more confident in the in-evitability of Confederate defeat. In fact, on March 20 an opportunity for a decisive victory appeared close at hand. That day Halleck heard that enemy troops had departed Corinth to attack Federal transports below Savannah and disrupt Union communications. "If so," he told Grant, "General Smith should immediately destroy [the] railroad connection at Corinth." With Smith still bedridden from his earlier accident, Grant directed the operation in person. Bad roads and late-winter storms de-layed the advance, and a report of thirteen trainloads of armed Confed-erates arriving in Corinth finally led to its cancellation. This influx of troops, Grant informed Halleck, "would indicate that Corinth cannot be taken without a general engagement, which from your instructions is to be avoided." Halleck canceled the operation and ordered Grant to re-main in camp, continue fortifying, and wait for Buell.[13]

During his preparations, Grant revealed more about his developing perception of the enemy. Even though the Confederates had supposedly received substantial reinforcements, Grant maintained that their morale was rapidly disintegrating, and as a result, Corinth would fall "much more easily than Donelson did." Southern deserters asserted that a gen-eral feeling of "panic" had spread throughout the army and that many soldiers were reluctant to fight. "All accounts agree," Grant surmised, "that the great mass of the Rank and file are heartily tired." Other Union officers heard the same from their own interrogations of deserters. Ac-cording to Lew Wallace, most indicated that their comrades in Corinth were "demoralized to the last degree" and would not put up much of a fight.[14] These reports convinced him that the enemy's flagging morale meant they lacked the sufficient vigor and zeal required to conduct of-fensive operations. However, though deserters provided valuable intelli-gence throughout the war, accepting their testimony uncritically posed certain risks, as Grant would soon learn. For example, given the stigma attached to abandoning one's comrades, a deserter might lie and tell his captors that his regiment—and perhaps his whole army—was terribly dispirited and ready to desert, all in an attempt to ease his own con-science and excuse his cowardly act. Nevertheless, Grant placed great credence in deserters' reports, especially those that told of ebbing Con-federate resolve, because they confirmed what he *wanted* to believe.

While Grant watched for Buell, his subordinates monitored Confed-erate activities beyond Union lines. Ever since his arrival at Shiloh, Sherman had heard numerous reports of Southern troops lurking near Pea Ridge and Monterey, about ten miles southwest of his camps. An encounter with Confederate cavalry in that vicinity on March 20 and reports of enemy scouts prowling outside his lines convinced Sherman that the Rebels were making "desperate efforts to penetrate our lines to ascertain our approximate force." He had already tightened security in his camps by prohibiting both soldiers and civilians from passing his picket posts, a measure he claimed had left the enemy "utterly at a loss" as to Federal dispositions. Sherman then led a reconnaissance toward Monterey and Pea Ridge to disperse Confederate scouts and cavalry patrols and prevent them from getting too close to his lines. With orders to occupy and "partially" fortify Pea Ridge, Sherman moved out on March 24. Seeing this movement as primarily a counterintelligence operation, he ignored Grant's instructions to hold the position and returned to camp when no enemy troops appeared. Confederate units would reoccupy the Pea Ridge–Monterey area, but Sherman continued to view them as only reconnaissance patrols sent to spy on his position.[15]

The day before Sherman's reconnaissance, Smith reported that, according to a Memphis newspaper, Brig. Gen. Daniel Ruggles, whom he referred to as "a weak vessel," commanded the forces gathering at Corinth. "[T]he enemy are gathering strength at Corinth quite as rapidly as we are here," Grant replied, "and the sooner we attack, the easier will be the task of taking the place." In words reminiscent of his less-than-favorable appraisals of Pillow, he then added: "If Ruggles is in command it would assuredly be a good time to attack."[16] Despite what he saw as a chance to strike another weak Southern commander, Grant had to restrain himself again, having no choice but to wait for Buell to appear at Savannah.

The Army of the Ohio departed Nashville on March 16, but high water on the Duck River near Columbia delayed its progress. Thirteen days later the army finally began crossing and then continued toward the rendezvous on the Tennessee, still nearly seventy-five miles away. During the interim, Buell kept an eye on Johnston, who at last report was heading toward either Decatur or Chattanooga. By March 23 he had a better fix on him, telling Halleck that Johnston's army had marched for Tuscumbia, Alabama, fifty miles southeast of Corinth. That day scouts Carson and Breckinridge reached Buell's headquarters bearing Grant's message of March 19. Buell promptly sent them back to Savannah, which they reached on March 26, with the news of Johnston's move to Tuscumbia. The last information Grant had heard, though, placed Johnston in Chattanooga. Skeptical of Buell's information, he maintained that a weak commander (Ruggles) was in charge at Corinth, which meant that an opportunity was at hand.[17]

Unknown to Grant, Johnston had already arrived in Corinth and assumed overall command. After the loss of the river forts, the Southern high command concentrated all available forces in the West to defend the Mississippi Valley. The key rail junction at Corinth became the focal point, and regiments from all over the Deep South flocked to northern Mississippi, including Bragg's ten thousand troops from the Department of Alabama and West Florida, a brigade of Louisiana infantry from the Gulf Coast led by Ruggles, and the bulk of Polk's former Columbus garrison. Finally, with the addition of Johnston's thirteen thousand men, the forces encamped about the town soon numbered over forty thousand men, which matched Grant's latest estimate. Johnston divided the so-called Army of the Mississippi into three corps commanded by Polk, Bragg, and Hardee with a reserve corps under John C. Breckinridge. With this force, much of it as raw and untrained as Grant's command, he planned to launch a bold counterstroke to turn the tide in the West before Buell could join Grant and together plunge deeper into the heart of the Confederacy. With Kentucky and most of Tennessee already in enemy hands, Johnston saw few alternatives. As one western Confederate concluded, "We have retreated as far South as we can go and if we don't fight now we might as well give up."[18]

Grant knew the enemy was gathering at Corinth but more reports of shattered Southern morale led him to a different conclusion with regard to their intentions. First, he believed that the recent defeats had sent the enemy reeling, leaving him little choice but to dig in and hope for the best. Moreover, their declining vigor and élan lessened the chances that they might attempt to recoup their losses through an all-out offensive. Thus far, Grant's intelligence—mostly from deserters—supported this view. And he shared a majority opinion. Information acquired by Buell and Halleck also pointed to a similar conclusion. On March 24 Buell intercepted some enemy correspondence indicating that forty thousand troops had reached the rail junction and that they "Expect[ed] a battle at Corinth." Two days later Halleck asserted, "the enemy will make his stand at or near Corinth."[19]

Other information also sustained Grant's appraisal of the enemy's intentions. On March 28 the post commander at Fort Henry wrote that a Memphis refugee claimed that the Confederates planned a "desperate stand" at the rail junction. Moreover, the informant added that Richmond had dispatched troops from Virginia to defend northern Mississippi and sent the hero of Manassas, P. G. T. Beauregard, to replace Ruggles. Staff officer Capt. William Rowley indicated that this report led Grant to increase the enemy strength estimate from twenty thousand to as high as seventy-five thousand men. Halleck agreed, affirming that Beauregard had replaced Ruggles and that "a large part of the Manassas army" now confronted the Army of the Tennessee. Despite the serious implications of facing a competent Southern commander reinforced by confident veterans from the Virginia theater, Grant remained unmoved by this development, which later proved false, and saw only Buell's absence delaying the inevitable Union capture of Corinth.[20]

By late March, Grant's belief that the enemy—demoralized and losing cohesion—braced for a final showdown at Corinth had hardened into fact, especially as more intelligence arrived to support it. From a group of deserters, he heard that nearly eighty thousand Southerners shouldered muskets at Corinth but that their withering morale negated their numerical advantage. According to these informants, wrote Grant, "Many men will desert if an opportunity occurs." Halleck remained skeptical, complaining that his subordinate needed to provide "better information as to the enemy's strength in the vicinity of Corinth." He urged Grant to develop a more concrete picture of the enemy situation in northern Mississippi and, in a condescending tone, reminded him, "Your scouts and spies ought by this time to have given you something approximating to the facts of the case."[21]

Grant, however, felt confident that he already knew "the facts of the case" and therefore saw little need to vigorously pursue additional intelligence. The observations of Confederate deserters, which comprised the bulk of Grant's information, had apparently told him all he needed to know. No reports from active sources reached his headquarters between March 17 and April 6 because he never sent out any scouts or spies during that time. The Army of the Tennessee had ample cavalry for reconnaissance, but neither he nor his subordinates employed them aggressively. More importantly, Grant reorganized his cavalry on April 2, transferring various regiments to new divisions and placing many units *hors de combat* as they moved to their new assignments and familiarized themselves with new surroundings. For example, on April 5 portions of Sherman's veteran Fifth Ohio Cavalry, which had spent the past two weeks patrolling the region between Shiloh Church and Monterey, the most likely avenue for an enemy advance, moved to Maj. Gen. Stephen Hurlbut's division. Their replacements, two battalions of the Fourth Illinois Cavalry, were new to the area and had little time to become acquainted with the roads and terrain, leaving the Fifth Division without effective reconnaissance capability during the daylight hours of April 5. Historian Stephen Z. Starr commented that the preoccupation of the cavalry with the reorganization, combined with Grant's desire "to leave well enough alone" and not dispatch patrols toward Corinth, meant that Union troopers had "no time for what they should have been doing in the near proximity of a large enemy force." This redistribution of horsemen, as later events would reveal, could not have come at a worse time.[22]

As mentioned earlier, reports from scouts and spies employed at Grant's headquarters were noticeably absent during this period. Although scouts Carson and Breckenridge were available, Grant apparently utilized their services primarily to track Buell's progress, not to watch the enemy. Before April 6, not a single spy from Corinth or elsewhere reported to Savannah.[23] One reason for this was that the rapid pace of events since February had left little time for secret service recruitment. An acute shortage of money also contributed to the atrophy of his intelligence arm. Wrestling with financial difficulties resulting from Fremont's extravagant spending, Halleck had reined in departmental outlays, including expenditures for secret service. In December 1861 he informed one commander that his spies would be paid for past services, but that the "number and expense of such persons should be diminished as much as possible." Although no record exists showing that Grant received similar advice, money was in short supply throughout the department and intelligence operations undoubtedly suffered as a result.[24] But given his earlier success by relying upon the initiative in the absence of intelligence, thus shifting the burden of uncertainty upon the enemy, Grant probably lost little sleep over the matter.

Scouts and spies employed by the six division commanders also maintained a low profile, if they ventured out at all. For example, Charles Carpenter and L. F. Scott of the Jessie Scouts had provided valuable service during the Henry-Donelson campaign, and Maj. Gen. John McClernand had retained them during March. However, their penchant for "stealing and plundering" brought an end to their service with the army. Calling them an "intolerable nuisance," Grant had both men arrested on March 25 and shipped under guard to St. Louis, leaving McClernand without two of his most reliable scouts at a critical juncture.[25]

Sherman, whose command occupied the most forward position, also failed to dispatch operatives, relying instead upon pickets and an occasional cavalry patrol for information and early warning. He had utilized scouts and spies before but for some reason saw little need for their services at Pittsburg Landing, in part because he had already determined that the enemy would not dare attack the Federals at their base. But he also distrusted spies, scouts, and especially "secesh" sources, complaining later that the information derived from them was "always unsatisfactory." The divisions of Hurlbut and W. H. L. Wallace, both officers new to the myriad responsibilities of such large commands, relied upon Sherman—because of his advanced position and experience—to gather pertinent intelligence. Prentiss, whose brigades occupied the Union left, deployed his pickets only three hundred yards from his camps and, as with Hurlbut and Wallace, left the task of detecting an enemy buildup to Sherman. Even when deployed, however, the raw troops of these divisions had received little instruction in the finer points of picketing and reconnaissance. Only Lew Wallace had dispatched scouts, but they were sent primarily to alert him of Confederate movements toward Crump's Landing.[26]

Why Grant refrained from recruiting scouts and spies at Savannah remains unclear. One historian has argued that the Federal command experienced an information drought at Pittsburg Landing due in part to demographics. Few people resided in the area, so the argument runs, and those who did were reticent, either from fear of retribution or out of prosecession sympathies, to work for the Federals. Moreover, most Unionists in the region, the most natural candidates for espionage behind enemy lines, lived on the east bank of the Tennessee. This state of affairs supposedly limited the number of civilian candidates for secret service. Curiously, however, Grant claimed that "union sentiment seems to be strong in the south part of the state," boasting that over five hundred loyal Tennesseans had joined his army, while dozens more had come in to escape Confederate conscription. On the west bank, an area supposedly devoid of loyalists, Lew Wallace "colonized" around one hundred refugees in his camps for military service, leading him to believe that "there is Unionism still left in Tennessee." In fact, Wallace received good topographical intelligence from these men. Though Grant harbored the Unionists who reached his lines, he left largely untapped this potential pool of informants.[27]

A key reason for the deficiencies of Grant's secret service was that, by April 1, his mental picture of the enemy had already crystallized. From information acquired since early March, he had concluded that the enemy had concentrated a large force at Corinth to repel a Union attack. And since Fort Donelson, his intelligence had also depicted a Southern army prostrated by low morale and on the verge of disintegration. Depression, discouragement, and fatalism, which can spread like cancer in an unsuccessful army, had the potential to offset their reported numerical superiority if, as Grant expected, mass desertions ensued once the shooting started outside Corinth. This growing malaise would also discourage new and untrained soldiers from leaving the safety of their fortifications. In this case, the baleful influence of entrenchments that, according to Sherman and Grant, "made . . . raw men timid," applied to the enemy as well.[28]

Another major influence upon Grant's assessment was the enemy's past behavior. The Southern commanders he faced had reacted fairly consistently, opting to dig in, use interior lines to reinforce threatened points, and await an attack rather than seek the offensive. Only in emergencies, for example at Belmont and Fort Donelson, did they venture out of their earthworks. By April the Confederates had followed this script closely and, from all indications, planned an encore at Corinth. Beauregard, in fact, had advocated just such a strategy. Viewing the terrain between Corinth and Pittsburg Landing as unsuitable for "purely offensive" operations, he proposed to wait for the Federal advance and then strike them away from their base. Albert Sidney Johnston, however, had no intention of playing the role assigned him by his adversary.[29]

Finally, Grant believed fervently that by seizing and maintaining the initiative, he had shifted the burden of uncertainty—and the need for intelligence—to Southern leaders, who now had to anticipate and react to his movements. "I regarded the campaign . . . as an offensive one," Grant wrote later, "and [I] had no idea that the enemy would leave strong intrenchments to take the initiative when he knew he would be attacked where he was if he remained." Perhaps Sherman summed up best the prevailing sentiment during that time. "We were supposed to be a vast aggressive force sent . . . to invade the South," he recalled, "and for us to have been nervous on the Subject of attack would have indicated weakness." Given the above assessment, by April 1 the only unknown for Grant and his lieutenants remained Buell's itinerary.[30]

Unlike Johnston, Sherman waited anxiously for the upcoming Union advance. But during the first days of April, his command spent more time observing and, at times, tangling with Confederate units lurking about his front than preparing for offensive operations. Still concerned with Southern attempts to discover his strength and deployments, Sherman dispatched a mixed force of infantry and cavalry on April 3 to clear his front of enemy pickets, scouts, and cavalry patrols and to capture prisoners for interrogation. Col. W. H. H. Taylor of the Fifth Ohio Cavalry received orders to "[b]ring in every suspicious person" but avoid molesting civilians engaged in "legitimate" pursuits. This restriction resulted from Grant's disgust over a rash of recent arbitrary arrests of citizens by overzealous Federal officers. Aside from the embarrassment caused by detaining innocent civilians, Grant understood that they also posed a potential information hemorrhage. Since these uncharged civilian prisoners had to be released, he observed, Union officers were essentially "admitting spies [sic] within our lines." Taylor observed these restrictions, bagging a private in the First Alabama Cavalry, whom Sherman believed was "pretty intelligent," and "Dr. Parker," a civilian arrested for alerting enemy pickets of the Union approach. Both were sent to Savannah for questioning.[31]

During the operation, Taylor learned, either from the Alabama cavalryman or a woman "living near the [Confederate] picket post" who exposed Dr. Parker's deed, that the Southerners had three regiments of infantry, one of cavalry, and an artillery battery stationed near Pea Ridge and Monterey. The presence of these units in this area, however, came as no surprise to Sherman. Earlier in March he knew that Confederate troops had occupied that area as a base for sending out patrols toward the Union camps. Since Sherman chose not to seize the ridge in March and Grant had failed to press the issue, nothing prevented the enemy from using Pea Ridge and Monterey as a forward observation post—and a tripwire—along the road to Corinth. The enemy, Sherman noted on April 4, sent pickets and cavalry "almost to our very camps," but these men always "fall back whenever we show ourselves, [since they were] designed simply to carry notice of an advance in force on our part." Thus, with the Fifth Division camps only ten miles from the Rebel post, the appearance of Confederate pickets and cavalry near Sherman's front was neither unexpected nor unusual. For these reasons, he remained sanguine that the Confederates would "await our coming at Corinth" and that the enemy's Pea Ridge–Monterey outpost posed no threat.[32]

Grant received Sherman's and Taylor's reports on April 3 and possibly even interrogated the Alabama cavalryman and Dr. Parker, although no record of these sessions has been found. If he questioned the prisoners, apparently nothing they imparted persuaded the general to alter his perspective.[33] That same day, Grant told Halleck that his view of the situation remained fundamentally unchanged. "Deserters occationally come in," he wrote, "but all that can be learned from them that is reliable is that the force [in Corinth] is large and increasing." They also described the hopelessness that permeated the enemy's ranks, confirming his belief that "many would desert if they could." Even in the face of Halleck's demand for more precise information, he held fast to his earlier assessment. To Grant, deserters had already revealed all that he needed to know.[34]

By late March, however, Johnston had decided upon a far more aggressive course. On the evening of April 2, he ordered an advance on Pittsburg Landing to drive the invaders into the Tennessee before Buell could render assistance. For the Confederates to abandon their fortifications and march an army—supposedly composed of undisciplined and demoralized troops—to assail a victorious Federal force at their base was to Grant a remote possibility at best. Though he later claimed—erroneously—that "every effort [was] made to keep advised of all movements of the enemy," in truth, he did no such thing. Similar to Pillow's attack at Fort Donelson, Grant was surprised when Johnston chose von Moltke's "fourth option." The Confederate leader hoped to catch Grant napping by doing something his Federal counterpart would not expect. After considerable delays and miscues on the march—an inevitability given the imperfect knowledge of the road system, misinterpreted or missed orders, and the inexperience of both soldiers and officers—Johnston's army reached its attack position the evening of April 5, two days behind schedule. The green Confederates had all but announced their arrival with beating drums, intermittent shouts, and scattered gunfire as troops tested their weapons for damp powder. Despite the opposition of the esteemed Beauregard, who argued that the racket had surely tipped their hand, Johnston did not flinch. "I would fight them if they were a million," he proclaimed and slated the attack for daybreak of April 6. That night nearly forty thousand Southern troops bedded down near the Union lines, some within earshot of Sherman's and Prentiss's camps, and awaited the dawn. They would find out soon enough if the Union army had discovered their approach.[35]

As Johnston's columns snaked their way toward the Tennessee, Grant remained blissfully unaware of the approaching danger. Enemy activity west of Crump's Landing, however, raised some concerns. On April 2, Confederates under Benjamin F. Cheatham established an outpost at Purdy, ostensibly to monitor Lew Wallace's division guarding the supply depot. Wallace interpreted Cheatham's movement as an attack on Crump's Landing and formed his division to meet it. Grant instructed Sherman to watch for enemy troops moving across his front and placed W. H. L. Wallace and Hurlbut on alert but downplayed the possibility of an assault on Crump's Landing. Ironically, Cheatham thought the sudden appearance of Lew Wallace's brigades meant an attack on Purdy, and his urgent dispatches to that effect prompted Johnston, who viewed the Union activity as an indication of Buell's impending arrival, to hasten the planned movement toward Pittsburg Landing. Grant knew nothing of what transpired in Corinth, but he now entertained the possibility that the Confederates might make small-scale attacks on vulnerable points along the Union line, especially Lew Wallace's isolated position. "I feared it was possible that he might make a rapid dash upon Crump's and destroy our transports and stores . . . before Wallace could be reinforced."[36] This prospect remained at the forefront of his mind until early April 6.

Lew Wallace also took the threat seriously. The Confederates could easily transport troops by rail from Corinth to Bethel Station, a stop along the Memphis and Ohio Railroad only a few miles west of Crump's Landing. Shortly after his arrival at the landing, Wallace, aware of the remote nature of his position, took measures to protect his command from surprise attacks, including hiring three scouts—Horace Bell, formerly of the Sixth Indiana Infantry; John C. Carpenter of the Fifth Ohio Cavalry; and W. C. Sanders, a local civilian.[37] Carpenter and Bell scouted the roads toward Corinth, though rarely venturing past Monterey, while Sanders, masquerading as a secessionist, visited Purdy regularly. With these scouts on patrol, Wallace boasted, "not even a squad of bush-rangers" could elude his surveillance net.

On the evening of April 4, as Wallace fretted about Cheatham, Horace Bell returned with ominous news. He had traveled several miles south of Monterey on the main Corinth road and found the entire Confederate army, commanded by Johnston, advancing toward Pittsburg Landing. Estimating their force at fifty thousand men, Bell predicted they would reach the Federal encampment by nightfall of April 5. According to Wallace, just as Bell finished his report, Carpenter returned with similar information. The division commander claimed he immediately forwarded a dispatch to Grant and instructed the courier to deliver it in person at Pittsburg Landing. If the general had retired to Savannah, the messenger was to order the postmaster to deliver it without delay. But Grant never acknowledged receiving such information, nor has a copy of this correspondence surfaced.[38]

In a letter to Wallace written over forty years later, however, Horace Bell corroborated the general's story, though his version differed on a few points, stating that Wallace indeed possessed "full, reliable, and correct information" on the enemy and told him that "if the battle of Shiloh was a surprise, it was not such to yourself." Thus, Lew Wallace *did* receive information on April 4 indicating a large-scale Confederate advance upon Pittsburg Landing. Yet, despite professing his belief in the accuracy of Bell's information, Wallace relayed the news in a manner inconsistent with its supposed importance and failed to even ensure its receipt. This apparent neglect, he later claimed, resulted from his fear of appearing too overbearing and pretentious in the eyes of his superior. He also assumed, moreover, that the commanding general's intelligence sources had probably already alerted him to this development. "[W]hat right," he asked, "had I to suppose General Grant was not on the watch, with more facilities at his command than belonged to me?" He never dreamed, he admitted, "that a force from Corinth meaning battle . . . could close in upon our divisions . . . without full knowledge of it at headquarters."[39]

But Wallace's excuses seem unconvincing when compared to the potentially disastrous consequences for the army if Grant was somehow unaware of the movement. Perhaps the true reason why Wallace failed to forward Bell's intelligence with more alacrity was that he placed little stock in it. On April 5, the day Bell predicted the Confederate army would appear on the Union front, Wallace appeared unmoved by the possibility of an attack on the main Union encampment and, instead, worried about the safety of his own position. That day, he asked W. H. L. Wallace, commander of the division closest to Crump's Landing, to have his cavalry familiarize themselves with the road between their respective commands in case the Third Division needed reinforcements to repel an attack on the depot. But Lew Wallace apparently saw little need for haste since he slated this reconnaissance mission for April 6, the day *after* Bell expected the Confederates to arrive. The scout's report failed to impress Wallace as much as he later claimed.[40]

Lew Wallace's skepticism may have also prevented him from forwarding Bell's report to other division commanders, particularly Sherman and Prentiss. Nor did he mention the episode in his official report. Not even his brigade commanders, whom he supposedly informed immediately, viewed the news as significant enough to merit inclusion in their own official accounts. In fact, the first printed reference to this incident came in Wallace's autobiography published in 1906, twenty-one years after Grant's death had ended a bitter feud between them over Wallace's tardiness in supporting the main Union army on the first day. This controversy tarnished Wallace's reputation and spilled over into the postwar era, when he endeavored, somewhat unsuccessfully, to defend himself against Grant's criticisms. This is not to imply that Wallace imagined the whole event, especially since Bell verified it in 1901, but rather to argue that his doubts concerning the accuracy of the intelligence affected his actions. Overall, Bell's report apparently had less influence upon Wallace than he later confessed, and if Grant indeed received the news, it failed to change his view that the enemy remained in Corinth awaiting a Federal advance.[41]

In the meantime, increased Confederate activity on Sherman's front raised concern. Early on April 4, a Union picket stationed near Seay Field and the main to Corinth road less than a mile south of Sherman's most advanced brigade reported seeing Southern soldiers eating breakfast in the nearby woods. From this observation, the picket believed the enemy was "in full force." Later that day the First Alabama Cavalry bagged one of Sherman's outposts. The Seventy-second Ohio Infantry, an inexperienced regiment drilling nearby, and a battalion of the Fifth Ohio Cavalry under Maj. Elbridge G. Ricker gave chase and engaged the enemy horsemen in a sharp skirmish. Ricker's Ohioans eventually scattered the Alabamians and pursued them for nearly a quarter-mile. But as the Union troopers crested a hill, they ran headlong into two Confederate infantry regiments and artillery arrayed in line of battle. Ricker finally extracted his men, bringing away ten prisoners from the First Alabama Cavalry.[42] At division headquarters, Sherman attached no special significance to the skirmish, even though Ricker emphasized that both enemy infantry and cavalry lurked nearby.

Sherman has received ample criticism for apparently ignoring these ominous signs pointing to an attack on his Shiloh camps, an oversight that one historian believed "cannot be explained or excused." But there is a rational explanation for Sherman's behavior. Enemy cavalry stalking the roads between Corinth and Shiloh and the presence of infantry and artillery supports in the vicinity of Pea Ridge and Monterey was simply old news. Although he acknowledged that the enemy had a "considerable force" south of his camps, none of this worried him. "We all knew the enemy was in our front," he wrote after the battle, "but [I] had to guess at his purpose." Sherman's best guess, however, proved dreadfully wrong. As evidenced by a letter written to Thomas Ewing on April 4, Sherman remained convinced that the Confederates encountered by his patrols were merely advanced guards and reconnaissance forces posted near Pea Ridge and Monterey assigned to probe Union defenses and alert Corinth of an advance, which explained their continual presence outside his lines. "The enemy is at Corinth," he observed, "with strong Cavalry and Infantry pickets toward us." But their presence never bothered him because their only purpose, he believed, was to alert Corinth when Grant's army lurched into action. "When we move forward," Sherman predicted confidently, "the first collision will occur at Monterey or Pea Ridge and from there all the way to Corinth." And he was not alone in his prediction of a running fight once the Union advance clashed with the Confederate outposts close of Pittsburg Landing. "It is thought the Rebels will not make much of a stand at Purdy," wrote a soldier in the ranks, "but will fall back to Corinth as we advance." Sherman realized too late, however, that on April 4 his troops had bumped into the advance units of the entire Confederate army creeping north from Corinth.[43]

Reveling in his minor victory of the previous day, Sherman reported on April 5 that quiet prevailed near Shiloh and that, while enemy cavalry remained on his front, the infantry and artillery had retreated nearly six miles. But the division commander had few means of verifying this information because his cavalry units were in the midst of the reorganization ordered by Grant. Nevertheless, he felt comfortable with his interpretation that the remaining Southern troops on his front were merely probing for information. So confident was he that they were but a token force, that on the evening of April 5 he talked casually of sending cavalry to "drive away or capture" these annoying units. The strength of Sherman's belief in his assessment helps explain why he grew impatient with several of his subordinates when they reported with growing alarm an increase in enemy activity in the woods and fields south of Shiloh Church.[44]

Meanwhile, Grant displayed even less concern for the possible intent behind recent Confederate activity. Perhaps fearing that Sherman might drag the army into an engagement against Halleck's orders, on April 4 Grant rushed to see his subordinate and survey the situation in person. While en route he met Col. James B. McPherson and W. H. L. Wallace, who informed him that the skirmish that day had amounted to little and that Sherman expected no more trouble. Caught in a rainstorm and trusting in Sherman's judgment, Grant canceled his rendezvous and returned to Pittsburg Landing.[45]

The next day Sherman gave his appraisal of the situation along the Union front. "The enemy . . . got the worst of it yesterday," he stated, "and will not press our pickets far" for fear of risking another defeat. Though conceding the possibility of more Confederate probes, he believed they posed no major threat. Sherman reiterated this view in his report after the battle: "On Saturday [April 4] the enemy's cavalry was again very bold, yet I did not believe that he designed anything but a demonstration." Confident in his assessment, on April 5 he wrote the words that would haunt him the remainder of his career: "I do not apprehend anything like an attack on our position." His superior concurred, later admitting that the enemy sortie on April 4 was viewed as a mere reconnaissance-in-force and in no way portended a major Confederate offensive. By the evening of April 5, Grant's army prepared for a fight, but one most believed would happen some twenty miles south at Corinth.[46]

Along with his report of the recent skirmish, Sherman also sent Grant the ten prisoners captured from the First Alabama, who bragged unabashedly that their comrades were poised to drive the Union army into the Tennessee River. Although transported to Savannah late on April 5, Grant either neglected to interrogate them or found their stories unconvincing. Even if they continued to boast about thousands of Rebels bearing down upon the Shiloh camps, why would Grant believe them when most of the evidence he had contradicted their stories? Other Union officers dismissed the chattering cavalrymen's stories as "a hoax," and Grant probably reached the same conclusion. Long before this moment, he had ruled out the possibility of an attack on Pittsburg Landing based upon intelligence and his own instincts, intuition, and experience. For the most part, these had not failed him in the past. In a subsequent telegram to department headquarters, Grant echoed Sherman's appraisal, stating that he had "scarsely the faintest idea of an attack, (general one,) being made upon us." He anticipated that the Confederates might attempt more small-scale raids similar to the one on Sherman's outposts, but that was all. "There will be no fight at Pittsburg Landing," he predicted on April 5, "we will have to go to Corinth, where the rebels are fortified."[47]

Even as Confederate troops filed into position opposite Union lines on April 5, Grant remained content that the enemy's main body remained at Corinth with small contingents posted along the railroads. He estimated Corinth's strength, including those units within supporting distance, at eighty thousand men, the same number as reported six days earlier. In addition, he believed Beauregard, not Johnston, commanded the Confederate army, a belief held by Halleck as well.[48] Unknown to Grant, his earlier assessment that Johnston was in Tennessee or Georgia was about be corrected. Though he complained about the unreliability of some of his intelligence on the evening of April 5, he remained confident that a demoralized enemy remained entrenched at Corinth. And he was not alone in this view. "The forty or fifty thousand traitors have been . . . living miserably," observed Lew Wallace, and the situation in Corinth was so desperate that soldiers stole food from each other in order to survive. Johnston's army, he concluded, "is stinging itself to death." The thousands of Confederates lurking in the dark woods just beyond the Union camps would soon prove otherwise.[49]

Early the next morning, Johnston's Army of the Mississippi crashed through the woods and pounced upon the unsuspecting Federals, some of whom had to form battle lines along their company streets. Elements of the Twenty-fifth Missouri patrolling near Fraley Field had provided some warning after they collided with the Confederate advance at around 3 A.M. But not until Sherman saw the glistening bayonets of Bragg's infantry bearing down on his camps at about 8 A.M. did he realize that this was more than a mere demonstration. As he later admitted, "I did not think Beauregard would abandon his railroads to attack us on our base." This mistaken belief, which helped Sherman explain away Confederate activity on his front in the days preceding the battle, led to the surprise that morning.[50]

Grant first heard the heavy firing around 7 A.M. Before heading toward the sounds of the guns, he notified Buell of the latest development, claiming rather curiously that he had been "looking for this," although not before "Monday or Teusday." This statement, written before Grant had even determined where the firing came from, did not mean that he expected a major assault against Pittsburg Landing but rather reflected his expectation that the enemy might attack his supply base at Crump's Landing or demonstrate against Sherman's perimeter south of Shiloh Church. Buell confirmed this interpretation when he noted that, at first, Grant viewed the firing upriver as merely "an affair of outposts" since "the same thing . . . [had] occurred for the two or three previous days." Not until he neared Crump's Landing did he realize that the sounds of battle emanated from the main Federal encampment farther upstream. Clearly, Grant did not foresee a large-scale Confederate assault upon Pittsburg Landing on that peaceful Sunday morning.[51]

Though shocked by the sudden onslaught, some Union brigades fought tenaciously. Others disintegrated. By noon, Sherman's and Prentiss's camps lay behind enemy lines and the Federals scrambled to save their right flank. Scattered remnants of Prentiss's, W. H. L. Wallace's, and Hurlbut's divisions formed for a desperate stand along a sunken road soon to be christened the "Hornet's Nest." By 5:30 P.M. the Federal right and the Hornet's Nest position had collapsed, but they had bought Grant enough time to rally his troops and establish a new defensive line near the landing. As night and a torrential downpour settled in, Buell's troops arrived and, with the addition of Lew Wallace's division, gave Grant an additional twenty-four thousand men. Realizing that the Confederates were probably as disorganized as his own units, Grant believed the Union army would prevail "if we could only take the initiative."[52]

Without reconnoitering the enemy's position, the next morning Grant and Buell struck the Confederates all along the front and eventually drove them back through the shattered Union camps. Astonished that the Union army remained intact after the beating they took on Sunday, the Southerners were unprepared for this grand assault. The Federal counterattack proved too much for their tired and depleted ranks. Beauregard, now in command after Johnston's death on Sunday, ordered a general retreat back to Corinth. Over the next few days, his weary army limped into town, thus ending the South's major bid to reclaim the initiative in the Mississippi Valley. The remarkable turnabout from defeat to victory on April 7 had revealed the iron will and steady nerve of U. S. Grant. Even though his army was surprised and hit hard, he demonstrated what one intelligence expert called a "tolerance for disaster," somehow maintaining his composure and a blind faith in ultimate victory. Unfortunately, the shoestring save of the Army of the Tennessee came at a cost of 13,047 Federal casualties, including over 1,700 dead.[53]

Despite Grant's triumph, there remains little doubt that the Confederate attack came as a complete surprise. Some of his men certainly thought so. "I think Gen. Grant fell short in his duty," claimed one soldier, while another complained that, despite omens like the boasts of the Confederate prisoners captured on April 4, the Union high command expected "as much to see the devil himself as to see the rebels come and attack us in our own camp." John Rawlins conceded this point after the war, admitting, "we did not expect to be attacked in force that morning, and were surprised that we were."[54]

Although Grant certainly bears the responsibility for being caught off-guard, the prebattle assessment of enemy intentions that led to the surprise was, given the circumstances, a logical and understandable conclusion. As the Confederates gathered at Corinth, Grant faced two plausible explanations for the concentration. On the one hand, Southern forces might be converging upon Corinth to establish another defensive barrier, this time to protect the Mississippi Valley and the important rail connections with the rest of the Confederacy. On the other, they might be assembling a strike force at the rail junction in preparation for a major counteroffensive to expel the invading Federal army and regain the initiative. Both interpretations were equally credible, but Grant's assessment of Confederate morale (based on deserter reports), his earlier intelligence analyses, and past experience pointed to an enemy locked into a defensive posture. "To turn a retreat into a counteroffensive is considered one of the most difficult feats in warfare," noted one historian, and "neither Grant nor Sherman dreamed that Johnston could do it."⁵⁵

Although deserters and other passive sources composed the foundation of Grant's strategic perspective, their reports corroborated each other in two important respects. They agreed, first, that the Confederates intended to make a stand at Corinth and, second, that sinking morale and growing despondency permeated the Rebel ranks so deeply that, when the Federals finally moved, many of those green Southern soldiers would throw down their arms and head for home. Grant's correspondence, moreover, provides no indication that he received any reports contradicting this picture, much less news predicting a massive Confederate counterstroke. If he indeed received such information, he probably dismissed it, failing as it did to mesh with his "picture" of the situation. Furthermore, if his division commanders feared such a possibility, none expressed concern save Lew Wallace, though even he doubted the likelihood of such an occurrence. Sherman stood the best chance of divining enemy intentions since he had more opportunities to capture prisoners and scout the roads to the south. Contrary to a popular argument, however, Sherman did not reject information that contradicted his views out of fear that crying wolf, a practice that had cost him his command in Kentucky in 1861, might once again raise questions about his mental stability. Far from dismissing information because of such a selfish motive, Sherman had a rational explanation for the enemy's presence on his front and for what he described as their "saucy" behavior.⁵⁶

Like Grant, neither Halleck nor Buell seemed worried about an attack on Pittsburg Landing either. Thus, the evidence sustained the view that the Confederates would make their stand at Corinth. In his biography of Sherman, John Marszalek maintained that the Union leadership at Shiloh, having dismissed the possibility of attack, "simply ignored all information to the contrary." Michael Fellman recently echoed this sentiment, arguing that Sherman "ignored the evidence brought to him."⁵⁷ On the contrary, neither Grant nor Sherman purposely disregarded contradictory intelligence; they simply misinterpreted it.

In her classic study of U.S. intelligence and Japan's surprise attack on Pearl Harbor in 1941, Roberta Wohlstetter discussed the concepts of "signals" and "noise" in intelligence analysis. A signal is a "piece of evidence that tells about a particular . . . enemy move or intention." Noise, on the other hand, is comprised of "competing or contradictory signals." Before Pearl Harbor, she argued, "there was a good deal of evidence available to support all the wrong interpretations." However, these various readings "appeared wrong only *after* the event." Similarly, prior to the Shiloh surprise, Grant had received "signals" that, after the fact, seemed obvious indicators of an attack. But at the time, the "noise" generated by an equally plausible—yet completely erroneous—interpretation, namely that a demoralized enemy waited at Corinth, drowned out a more accurate rendering of those signals. This occurrence is natural and perhaps unavoidable as long as human nature, which is susceptible to wishful thinking, subjectivity, and self-confirming beliefs, remains the crucial factor in intelligence analysis and decision making. Once this noise-mistaken-as-truth became imbedded in Grant's mind, any fears of an attack—and thus the need for heightened security or entrenchments—declined precipitously. He simply believed the enemy would not dare attack such a strong army at its base. Any information indicating otherwise was dismissed. "If no one is listening for signals of an attack against a highly improbably target," argued Wohlstetter, "then it is very difficult for the signals to be heard." [58]

In addition to the noise generated by a competing interpretation, what Wohlstetter called a "local background of noise" created by one's past military successes also deafened Grant to the approach of the enemy. The Union victory (at least in his estimation) at Belmont; the surrender of Forts Henry and Donelson, which he claimed were "easy"; and the subsequent abandonment of Kentucky and most of Tennessee merely solidified Grant's growing sense that the South lacked the morale and the will needed to prevail. In his view, the enemy was far too dispirited and fearful to attempt a counteroffensive and therefore would retreat, entrench, and react to Union movements. Reinforced by intelligence from deserters, this view became etched in his mind. But these past victories and the perceived advantages offered by the initiative concealed the inadequacies of Grant's information. As a result, both veteran and green Union officers leaned toward explanations of Confederate behavior that conformed to a popular view at headquarters. Wohlstetter ascribed this phenomenon to "the very human tendency to pay attention to the signals that support current interpretations." As a result, the Federals at Pittsburg Landing became, as one officer noted, "too easy going and less careful." [59]

In the final analysis, Grant violated a central tenet of intelligence by basing his overall assessment on assumptions about the enemy's intentions rather than knowledge of his capabilities.[60] Instead of a large army preparing to defend its homeland, Grant saw only a beaten army teetering on the brink of disintegration. This perception, supported by intelligence *he chose to believe*, diminished his vigilance before Shiloh. He failed to realize that desperation could breed boldness as well as hopelessness. But his rendering of Confederate intentions, based upon their past behavior and the results of his intelligence analysis, was a rational and logical assessment *at that time*. Although guilty of letting down his guard in close proximity to the enemy and allowing wishful thinking to adversely influence his views, Grant cannot be faulted for his shortcomings as a clairvoyant. For not even the finest intelligence can predict with absolute certainty what the enemy *will* do; it can only supply indications of what he *can* and *might* do. "At its best, intelligence can provide the bounds for strategic calculation," argued one scholar, "but it is asking too much to expect it to look into the future."[61] Grant had only his perceptions, instincts, experience, and imperfect military intelligence to guide him, not a crystal ball.

The surprise at Shiloh, therefore, resulted from Grant's fundamental misreading of the information available to him. During World War II, Allied forces in the Ardennes in December 1944 suffered from a similar malady. Like Grant, Allied commanders assumed the Germans "could no longer win the war" and that any offensive action they took "could only delay the inevitable." Also like Grant, they failed to allow for enemy opportunism and that, out of desperation, a foe might still "envisage the possibility, no matter how remote, for a substantial, though not decisive . . . victory." It took the Germans then and Albert Sidney Johnston over eighty years earlier to reveal the enormous chasm between reality and wishful thinking in their opponent's optimistic assessments. Both Grant and the Allied high command failed to heed Napoleon's warning that maintaining a fixed image of the enemy was "the worst thing of all."[62]

The Shiloh experience forced Grant to revisit a lesson learned in the early days of the war in Missouri. Back in August 1861, Grant led troops into hostile territory for the first time. As his column neared the site of a reported enemy encampment, he found himself overcome with fear and trepidation. Much to his relief, however, the foe had fled upon hearing of his approach. Looking over the deserted camp, Grant experienced an epiphany. At that moment he realized the enemy feared *him* as much as he feared the enemy.[63] As a result of his recent successes, however, Grant's rendering of that lesson had undergone a subtle yet dangerous evolution. By April 1862 he had convinced himself that the Confederates feared him *more*. The long gray battle lines rolling through Union camps in the early dawn of April 6 revealed the horrible depth of his self-deception.

Chapter 5

"With All the Vigilance
I Can Bring to Bear I Cannot
Determine the Objects
of the Enemy"

For several weeks after Shiloh, both sides tended their wounded, buried the dead, and prepared for the next bout. Henry W. Halleck arrived at Pittsburg Landing and took charge of the upcoming offensive against Corinth. As punishment for the recent near-disaster, Grant watched from the sidelines as Halleck directed the next campaign. Fearing another surprise and anxious to fight war according to the book, "Old Brains" advanced south cautiously and at glacial speed, entrenching at every stop. At this ponderous pace, it took nearly a month to traverse the twenty-two miles to Corinth. On May 30 the Confederates evacuated the rail junction without a fight and retreated south to Tupelo, which caused the abandonment of Memphis. Elevated to the post of general in chief of all Union armies, in mid-July Halleck hurried to Washington, once again leaving Grant in overall command of operations in the Mississippi Valley.

Before his departure, however, Halleck had dispersed his combined armies in northern Mississippi and western Tennessee to safeguard the Union's recent gains. To make matters worse, in mid-June, Don Carlos Buell's Army of the Ohio departed on a mission to seize Chattanooga and East Tennessee. When Grant arrived in Corinth on July 17, his scattered force, consisting of 63,709 men in the Army of the Tennessee and the Army of the Mississippi, guarded a front 115 miles long and protected over 360 miles of track. In addition to chasing ubiquitous guerrillas, rebuilding railroad bridges, replacing torn-up track, and managing an overtly hostile population, Grant had to monitor enemy forces fifty miles farther south at Tupelo. The loss of the initiative after the Corinth campaign, sealed by Halleck's decision to disperse the army, not only forced Grant to defend a far-flung command but also placed the burden of uncertainty back on his shoulders. Forced into a situation he despised, he had little choice but to determine and react to the enemy's moves as best he could. "In this he was only manifesting one of his chief military characteristics," wrote staff officer Horace Porter, "an inborn dislike to be thrown upon the defensive." Until he consolidated his armies for an offensive, the Confederates could strangle his logistical lines and pounce on isolated garrisons. In this situation, intelligence would become a critical necessity in protecting his scattered forces.[1]

From the beginning of his tenure, however, Grant encountered difficulties meeting his intelligence needs. First, communications between posts remained tenuous; guerrillas and Confederate cavalry severed telegraph wires, interrupted rail traffic, and captured Union couriers.[2] Second, the lack of a centralized armywide intelligence service left this task in the hands of individual field commanders, whose efforts depended heavily upon their attitude toward the "business" and their own past experiences.[3] Fortunately for Grant, several subordinates understood the importance of gathering information on the enemy and worked tirelessly to procure it. Sherman, now head of the District of Memphis, had learned a lesson at Shiloh and began dispatching scouts and spies regularly. Brig. Gen. William S. Rosecrans, commanding the Federal Army of the Mississippi, brought his keen organizational skill to bear upon secret service operations, which would profoundly influence future operations in the region. Rosecrans received permission from Halleck to "arrange his scouts and cavalry movements" completely independent of direction from headquarters, an arrangement Grant honored.[4]

When Grant assumed command, he not only needed intelligence on the enemy but also had to prevent the Confederates from getting information on him. Counterintelligence problems had vexed him during his brief stay in Memphis in June 1862 when the activities of prosecession civilians made life difficult for Union occupiers. At the time, he complained, "spies and members of the southern army are constantly finding their way in and out of the city in spite of all vigilance." This frustration led him to take the drastic measure of expelling all families of soldiers and officials in Confederate service from the city. The problem followed Grant to his new headquarters in Corinth. According to Rosecrans, the enemy apparently believed "our guards about Corinth are badly posted" and took advantage of it. As a result, he warned, "their spies go where they please." On the defensive and widely spread out, Grant vowed to staunch this potential information hemorrhage. On July 28 he issued General Orders Number Sixty-five, declaring: "Hereafter no Passes will be given to Citizens of States in Rebellion, to pass into our lines . . . except to persons employed on secret service." In addition, passes issued to Union operatives had to come from division commanders. Though primarily a measure to weed out enemy agents and prevent unauthorized individuals from slipping back and forth across the lines, the directive impacted positive intelligence operations as well. It instructed Union pickets to send all Confederate deserters and prisoners of war to the nearest commanding officer for a "thorough examination." As Grant had learned, the information provided by these men could be either very important or decidedly useless. Nevertheless, their testimony was not expendable. Mandating that officers interrogate deserters and prisoners meant that, for the first time under his command, these sources would be mined on a more systematic basis.[5]

Despite indications that Grant had learned from his intelligence mistakes at Shiloh, not everyone was convinced. Several weeks before Halleck received his summons to Washington, Grant had advised him that thirty thousand Confederates were prepared to attack LaGrange, Tennessee. Perhaps afraid that Shiloh had scared his subordinate into believing every rumor of an attack, Halleck chided Grant for confusing gossip with the truth. "Why not sen[d] out [a] strong reconnaissance," he suggested, "& ascertain *facts?*" The present situation "looks very much like a mere stampede," he observed, warning, "Floating rumors are never to be received as facts." Annoyed, Grant replied coolly: "I heed as little of the floating rumors about the City as any one" and flatly denied being panicked by hearsay. "Stampeding," he asserted, "is not my weakness." Despite Halleck's rebuke, Grant was pursuing intelligence more aggressively. Having yielded the initiative to the enemy, he realized that information upon which to mount a defense was essential.[6]

Though demoralized by recent defeats, Confederate forces at Tupelo remained potent adversaries worthy of respect. The new Confederate commander, Braxton Bragg, knew that the Federals had relinquished the initiative in Mississippi and perhaps provided an opportunity to avenge earlier losses. But reports of Buell's Army of the Ohio heading back to Tennessee prevented him from seizing the moment. Instead, on June 27, Bragg detached Maj. Gen. John P. McCown's division toward Chattanooga to help Maj. Gen. Edmund Kirby Smith defend East Tennessee against Buell. The remainder of his army—thirty-five thousand men—followed on July 23. Initially sent to reinforce Smith's command for defensive purposes, by fall Bragg's mission had evolved into a major offensive designed to liberate Tennessee and Kentucky. Though taking a circuitous route through Mobile, Montgomery, and Atlanta, his army still reached Chattanooga before Buell. With Bragg's army gone, only sixteen thousand men under Maj. Gen. Earl Van Dorn, whose primary duty was the defense of Vicksburg, and another sixteen thousand led by Maj. Gen. Sterling Price remained behind to deal with Grant. Their main objective was to keep him from reinforcing Buell and parry any thrusts toward the interior of Mississippi.[7]

As Bragg prepared his army for the move, Grant received a series of confusing reports regarding his adversary's possible objectives. On July 19 a railroad employee from Mobile asserted that Bragg intended to retake Corinth. The next day, however, an escapee from the Tupelo jail claimed that Bragg's army had already departed for Chattanooga. To add to the confusion, a deserter overheard Price promise his Missourians that they would soon return, after a short detour through Kentucky, to their home state. This assorted information revealed only that a move from Tupelo was afoot but shed little light on the enemy's real intentions. Grant even suspected that the reports concerning Bragg might have been planted "with the view of having the information reach us" in order to sow confusion. By month's end, these conflicting reports and rumors were all he possessed. The day Bragg's Army of the Mississippi (later renamed the Army of Tennessee) boarded trains for Chattanooga, Grant admitted, "nothing absolutely certain of the movements of the enemy have been learned." Concerned for the safety of Corinth, the Federal commander continued to monitor events in Mississippi. Luckily, he had some experienced subordinates who aided in this endeavor.[8]

As commander of the Army of the Mississippi (U.S.), Rosecrans brought an engineer's sense of organization and detail to intelligence collection. Shortly after arriving at Jacinto in late June, he assembled a corps of scouts and spies under the immediate command of Brig. Gen. Charles S. Hamilton. Rosecrans also focused on becoming familiar with the terrain and road systems as well as with enemy positions and movements. Drawing upon his experience in the U.S. Army Topographical Engineers, he formalized the use of "information maps," or detailed sketches constantly updated with the latest intelligence derived from all sources. Copies were made and distributed to field commanders with instructions to send revisions and new information to headquarters in order to keep the master map updated. To ensure accuracy in this process, Rosecrans assigned each brigade a topographical engineer whose primary responsibility was to amend the maps and send changes to Jacinto. Impressed by Rosecrans "most excellent map" because it showed "all the roads and streams in the surrounding country," Grant "deferred very much" to his subordinate's judgment on intelligence matters in that vicinity.[9]

Rosecrans' army also contained talented officers who instinctively and aggressively pursued information on the enemy. One of his cavalry commanders, Col. Philip H. Sheridan, possessed an intense appreciation for intelligence, what he called "that great essential of success." Stationed at Booneville, Mississippi, about thirty miles north of Tupelo, Sheridan was "expected to furnish, by scouting and all other means available, information as to what was going on within the Confederate lines." On July 27 a patrol from his brigade drove Confederates out of Ripley and captured a bundle of private correspondence, the contents of which provided ample evidence of Bragg's departure to East Tennessee. This news, corroborated by Sherman a few days later, led Grant to conclude that Bragg was gone, leaving "but a small force in front of us." [10]

True to his nature, Grant now saw an opportunity to destroy these remnants. Ever cautious, Halleck preferred that he remain on the defensive as a reserve for Buell's army, which was still slogging its way toward Chattanooga, until events in Tennessee dictated another course. Frustrated, Grant downplayed the threat to Buell. Based upon information contained in some intercepted letters from Confederate soldiers, he argued that Bragg was leading "the mass of [his] disciplined troops" to Richmond, Virginia, not to East Tennessee, leaving behind mostly untrained and undisciplined regiments. Though possessing "no positive evidence of this," he stood by this conclusion, adding only that "the conviction is strong with me." Discontent with being Buell's reserve, perhaps Grant hoped that Bragg's entry into Virginia would end his supporting role and free Union forces in Mississippi for offensive operations. Though driven more by his own desires than hard facts, Grant remained adamant that the Confederate Army of the Mississippi had gone to Richmond. Even Buell's impassioned argument that the Confederates proposed to concentrate in East Tennessee and attempt to "regain what they have lost" failed to change his mind. [11]

Grant's concerns over Bragg's destination were soon eclipsed by the activities of enemy forces in northern Mississippi. On August 12 a spy from Mobile claimed that Price planned a demonstration from Tupelo to "cover a flank movement on the rail road" toward Tennessee. In other words, Price hoped to divert Grant's attention while his Army of the West slipped around the Union left into Tennessee. News from Buell's front made this move seem more likely. Bragg had beaten Buell into Chattanooga and was now preparing to launch a major counteroffensive in

Tennessee and Kentucky. On August 14 Grant dispatched two of Rose-crans' divisions to the Army of the Ohio. With this reduction, and having to defend so many points, he grew more anxious that the Mississippi Confederates might discover and exploit his weakness. But until the Federals defused the situation in Tennessee, a large-scale offensive in Mississippi was out of the question. "I am now in a situation," Grant complained, "where it is impossible for me to do more than to protect my long lines of defense." He had surrendered the initiative and could only wait to see if Price and Van Dorn would seize it.[12]

In late August, Grant fretted about the depletion of his army and speculated on the enemy's next move. Before this time, he thought Price's main role was to freeze Union forces along the Tennessee-Mississippi border while Bragg stirred things up in Tennessee. But the loss of more of his own troops to Buell changed his mind. Grant now believed that Price and Van Dorn would take advantage of his weakened and scattered condition to regain earlier losses in northern Mississippi. By the end of August, rumors that Price was advancing toward Corinth and that enemy cavalry had disrupted communications in West Tennessee seemed to confirm this assessment. And just when he needed all the forces he could muster, Grant had to send another division to Buell.[13] With enemy activity escalating and his own strength dwindling, he now faced two serious problems. First, in order to maintain an adequate defense and eventually shift to the offensive, he needed either reinforcements or a reduction of his commitments in West Tennessee and northern Mississippi. Before releasing another division for service with Buell, Grant convinced Halleck to abandon the Memphis and Charleston Railroad east of Corinth. To facilitate a speedy concentration upon any threatened point, he also shuffled troops until over half of his remaining forty-five thousand troops were clustered near the front.

The second problem was finding intelligence on Price. On the defensive and tied to fixed positions, this function became essential for successfully resisting any Confederate advance. In anticipating and responding to Price's movements, he could not afford to weaken one area to strengthen another until reasonably certain of the Missourian's location and intentions. In early September, Grant reviewed the options open to his adversary. Price could pass around Rosecrans' flank at Corinth, covering the move with a demonstration elsewhere, cross the Tennessee, and descend upon Buell's rear. Alternatively, he might remain in

the area to immobilize Grant and prevent him from detaching more reinforcements. If he discovered the weakened and dispersed condition of
the Federal forces, Price had another option: he might roll the dice and
go after Corinth. His cavalry and the Mississippi Partisan Rangers under
Col. William C. Falkner had already made supplying the town difficult.
A coordinated offensive might reclaim the vital rail junction, loosen the
Union's grip on the region, and perhaps revive Confederate fortunes in
the West. Watching and waiting for Price to make his move, Grant remarked that, for him, this was the "most anxious period of the war."[14]

Meanwhile, Sterling Price had also pondered his options and decided
upon his next move. Under orders from Bragg to prevent Grant from
sending reinforcements to Buell, Price looked to Van Dorn for assistance. Although offering to help immobilize Grant, Van Dorn, coequal
to Price in the confusing world of the Confederate command structure
in the West, had in mind a much more ambitious objective—the libera-
tion of West Tennessee. Until his plan received the blessing of Confederate authorities, Van Dorn balked at aiding Price. The situation changed
when Bragg reported that the Federals had evacuated Alabama and were
"rapidly falling back from all points in Middle Tennessee to Nashville."
Believing that northern Mississippi would also be evacuated and that the
remainder of the Rosecrans' Army of the Mississippi would be sent to
Tennessee, he ordered the Army of the West to march on Nashville and
prevent a junction between Rosecrans and Buell. Price left Tupelo on
September 7 and marched north along the Mobile and Ohio to Guntown, thirty-five miles south of Corinth. While there he learned that
Rosecrans occupied Iuka, twenty miles southeast of Corinth on the
Memphis and Charleston. Interpreting this to mean that the Federals
were indeed en route to join Buell, he began his pursuit. Leaving Van
Dorn on his own, Price headed toward Iuka.

By that time, however, Rosecrans had abandoned Iuka and retreated
toward Corinth. Only a rearguard of fifteen hundred men remained to
oversee the removal of army stores. On September 13 Price's cavalry
appeared south of the town. The Federals fended off the Confederate
troopers, but upon learning from prisoners that Price's infantry was not
far behind, the garrison evacuated the town, leaving behind a mountain
of supplies. Price entered Iuka at sunrise on September 14. Informed
that Rosecrans had retreated to the west and was not headed for Tennessee, Price saw an opportunity and wrote Van Dorn pledging his

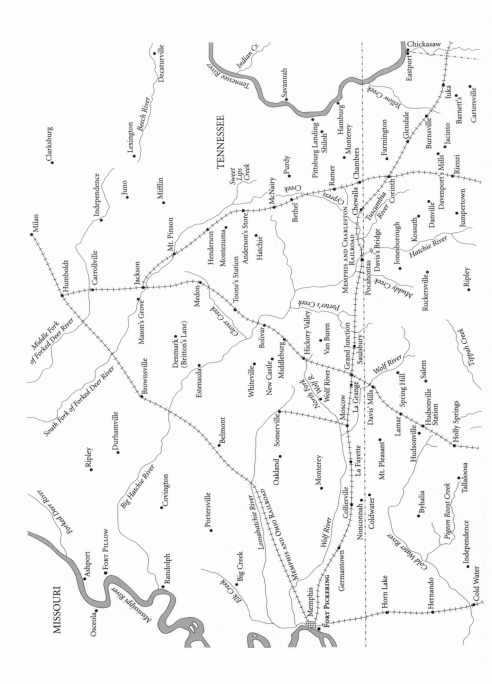

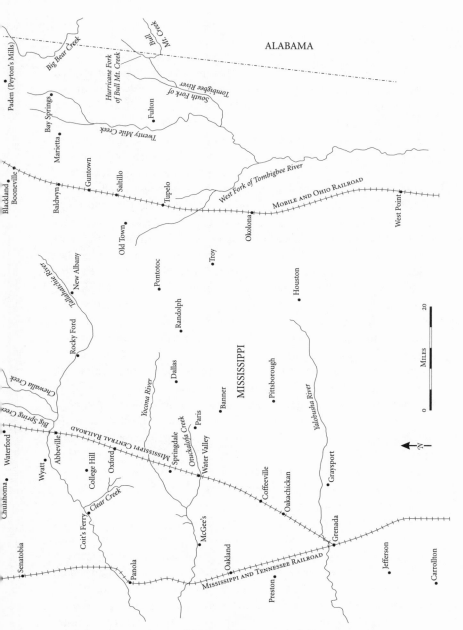

ALABAMA

Paden (Peyton's Mills)

Big Bear Creek

Bull Mt. Creek

Hurricane Fork of Bull Mt. Creek

South Fork of Tombigbee River

Bay Springs

Fulton

Twenty Mile Creek

Marietta

Blackland

Booneville

Guntown

Baldwyn

Saltillo

Tupelo

West Fork of Tombigbee River

MOBILE AND OHIO RAILROAD

Okolona

West Point

Old Town

New Albany

Pontotoc

Troy

Randolph

Houston

MISSISSIPPI

Rocky Ford

Tallahatchie River

Dallas

Pittsborough

Chewalla Creek

Yocona River

Banner

Yalobusha River

Big Spring Creek

Waterford

Springdale

Paris

Abbeville

MISSISSIPPI CENTRAL RAILROAD

Onuckalofa Creek

Wyatt

College Hill

Oxford

Water Valley

Grayport

Chulahoma

Clear Creek

Coffeeville

Coit's Ferry

Oakachickan

Senatobia

McGee's

Grenada

Jefferson

Oakland

Carrollton

Panola

Preston

MISSISSIPPI AND TENNESSEE RAILROAD

MILES

0   20

N

Major Operations of Grant's Command in Late 1862

support for a combined offensive against the prize of northern Mississippi: Corinth.[15]

Sketchy reports of Price's movements and possible intentions trickled in to Grant's Corinth headquarters. On September 7, scouts employed by Hamilton stated that Price's army—estimated to be thirty-six thousand strong—had left Tupelo and reached Twenty Mile Creek. Later the same day, Hamilton claimed that new information revealed that Price and Van Dorn had united but as of yet had no plans to attack. The following day, he again changed his mind, believing now that this combined force intended to attack Corinth. Rosecrans disagreed. From his perspective, the enemy had two choices: slip past the Union left into Tennessee or "attempt to disloge [sic] us" from Corinth. To him, the report of a large Confederate encampment at Twenty Mile Creek indicated that Price and Van Dorn had chosen the first option. A reconnaissance sent by Rosecrans also found the nearest enemy concentration to be near Baldwyn, thirty miles south of Corinth on the Mobile and Ohio. But this force contained only a few regiments and showed "no particular signs of movement." Certain in his assessment, Rosecrans concluded that "the rebels are playing a game of bluff" and that the troops at Baldwyn were there only to "cover up a movement on Buells right and rear" through northern Alabama.[16]

Unlike Rosecrans, Grant puzzled over these conflicting reports with little success. "With all the vigilance I can bring to bear," he wrote on September 9, "I cannot determine the objects of the Enemy." Although some evidence pointed toward an attack on Corinth, he also saw merit in Rosecrans' interpretation. Although Grant downplayed the possibility of an attack on either Corinth or Bolivar, Tennessee, and despite Halleck's reassurance that "[t]here can be no very large force to attack you," he continued concentrating his forces to act as a ready reserve for any threatened point along the left and center.[17]

As Price's troops closed on Iuka, Rosecrans tried to persuade Grant that the enemy's movements were designed to shield a larger advance across the Tennessee. As evidence, he submitted that the unusual amount of noise generated by the enemy belied their true mission as a diversion. Moreover, he believed the Confederates had intended to send Price to Tennessee all along. And looking at the situation from Bragg's perspective, he argued, "it is in their interest to do this." Hamilton, on the other hand, still viewed things differently, especially after a deserter told him that Price and an army of forty thousand were at that moment only thirty miles from Corinth preparing to seize the town. By September 11, Hamilton had finally convinced Grant that Corinth was in danger. That day, Grant wired Halleck: "Everything indicates that we will be attacked here [Corinth] in the next 48 hours." Before long, more intelligence arrived to challenge this assessment.[18]

The following day, Sherman reported that a sizeable enemy force occupied Holly Springs, about fifty miles southwest of Corinth, with plans to either attack the Union center at Bolivar or "hold us in check while Bragg pushes on to Kentucky." Rosecrans heard rumors about the fall of Iuka the same day it occurred but insisted that Price was still headed away from Corinth toward Buell's rear. Hamilton provided support for Rosecrans' assessment the next day when prisoners confirmed that Price was then twenty miles south of Iuka at Peyton's Mills. This report, according to Hamilton, confirmed "a movement east of the Rebel Army." Other prisoners and local citizens provided more support when they claimed that the Missourian's objective was "some point on the Tenn[essee] River." At that moment, however, the Army of the West was only a day's march from Corinth and preparing to join Van Dorn.[19]

After reviewing the evidence, Grant predicted on September 15 that Van Dorn's army, now resting at Holly Springs, would soon advance on Corinth to divert attention away from Price's passage into Tennessee. Grant placed Price's main army at Bay Springs, at least a day's march south of his actual position, and believed he was heading northeast toward the Tennessee River. Hoping to prevent his escape, the Federal commander proposed striking this force before it reached Bear Creek in northwestern Alabama. The plan rested upon Grant's belief that Van Dorn could not possibly reach Corinth until September 19, four days hence. If he could smash Price before that time, he could deny Bragg needed reinforcements and prevent Price and Van Dorn from uniting to threaten Corinth. Little did he know that the two generals were already discussing a union for that very purpose.[20]

A report from a Union patrol along with statements from prisoners revealed that by September 17—nearly three days late—Iuka had fallen. Despite the news, Rosecrans remained confident that Price still aimed for Tennessee. Believing wrongly that the fires in Iuka the previous evening indicated that the enemy had abandoned the town, he predicted that Price had already "crossed the Defiles of Bear Creek & will pass the

Tennessee before it rises." Later the same day, however, a deserter told Rosecrans that the Confederates still occupied Iuka, hoping to lure Grant out of Corinth. Once the Federals went after Price, he warned, Van Dorn planned to "leap in on Corinth from the west." Grant dismissed this assessment and remained confident that Van Dorn remained too far south to threaten Corinth. The next day additional information seemed to confirm this opinion. One of Rosecrans' spies reported witnessing "a continuous movement . . . of forces Eastward" toward the river since September 12. He then noted that Van Dorn and Price were acting independently and pursued different objectives. Neither commander, he asserted, planned to assail Corinth. Confident that "there is but little force south of Corinth for a long distance," Grant moved to catch Price before he disappeared across the river. "[U]nless the approach of a large force on [Corinth] should call us back," he informed the War Department, a Federal attack on Iuka would render it "impossible for Price to get into Tennessee." [21]

On September 19 Grant recaptured Iuka after a sharp fight. Price escaped to Baldwyn, hoping to join Van Dorn at Holly Springs. Though Price had earlier abandoned the plan to cross the Tennessee in favor of uniting with Van Dorn, Grant felt certain his victory had prevented the Army of the West from escaping Mississippi. But he was also lucky. For almost three days, he was unaware that Price's army had reached Iuka. Had the Confederate commander pressed onward into Tennessee (at this point he was within easy reach of the Tennessee River crossings in northwestern Alabama) or moved to join Van Dorn against Corinth, he might have stolen a march on Grant. Though successful, the Iuka campaign revealed the difficulties of tracking enemy forces. Price had already shown how easy it was to march undetected through the Mississippi countryside. Without possessing the initiative and forced to rely heavily upon imperfect and scarce intelligence, Grant faced a difficult test as the leaves began to turn in northern Mississippi. [22]

After moving his headquarters to Jackson, Tennessee, Grant received some hints as to the enemy's future objectives on September 22. Rosecrans relayed information brought in by a scout named Levi H. Naron (also known as "Chickasaw") who had infiltrated Price's camps the night of the Iuka fight. According to Naron, the two Southern armies had not yet united. Moreover, he overheard some Confederate officers claim that if Van Dorn failed to move immediately upon Memphis, they would "throw up their commissions." [23] Utilizing additional reports brought in by other scouts, Grant soon believed that Bolivar or Corinth—not Memphis—were the most likely targets.[24]

About this time, Van Dorn left his camp at Davis' Mill and joined Price at Ripley on September 28. Under Van Dorn's overall command and renamed the Army of West Tennessee, this combined force numbered around twenty-two thousand men. The army's main objectives were to seize Corinth, drive Grant out of Mississippi, and use the liberated town as a base for future operations into West Tennessee. On September 29 Van Dorn's force departed Ripley and, to preserve the mystery of their ultimate objective, bivouacked at Pocahontas, a point equidistant between Bolivar and Corinth. They then marched to Chewalla, just north of the Mississippi state line, and on October 3 appeared north of Corinth facing the old Confederate works now manned by Rosecrans' men. That day and the next morning, Van Dorn hammered at the Union entrenchments but was forced to withdraw toward the Hatchie River.[25]

As the enemy force inched toward Corinth in early October, Grant completely misjudged their actual whereabouts. Buffeted by conflicting reports, one of which claimed that Price and Van Dorn "had effected a junction & [planned to] go to Tennessee," he finally determined on September 30 that Price remained in Ripley and Van Dorn was near Somerville, Tennessee, heading east to "effect a lodgement on the Mississippi above Memphis." By this time, however, the Army of West Tennessee was only twenty miles northwest of Corinth. By October 1, he had a firmer grasp on the truth. Rosecrans relayed a remarkably accurate report from a civilian that twenty thousand Confederates were just then advancing on Pocahontas. Prisoners captured near Corinth claimed that a Confederate force was on the Pocahontas-Corinth road, a report later confirmed by another source. From this intelligence, Grant finally concluded that Price and Van Dorn had indeed joined (though he warned Maj. Gen. Stephen Hurlbut, commanding the Federal garrison at Memphis, that the latter might still be west of Bolivar) for an attack on the Union left. "It is now clear," he wired Halleck, "that Corinth is the point."[26]

But Rosecrans had different ideas about the enemy's true objective. He learned from cavalry patrols that a large enemy force had reached Pocahontas on October 1. Although he recalled his outposts and other detachments as a precaution, persistent rumors purporting that the main blow would fall upon either Jackson or Bolivar in Tennessee colored his view of the situation. When Union cavalry encountered Van Dorn's column near Chewalla, Rosecrans dismissed it as a diversion. On October 3 an "unusually reliable" scout reported seeing thirty thousand enemy troops near Chewalla but assured his commander that they intended "to make their main move on Bolivar." Rosecrans later complained that the lack of accurate maps of the area northwest of town, a strange complaint coming from the officer who prided himself on his system of "information maps," prevented him from determining "whether to expect a strong demonstration here . . . while the blow was struck elsewhere or vice-versa." But to the Joint Committee on the Conduct of War, Rosecrans testified that he "thought it was in their interest to move at once on Bolivar and Jackson" and, therefore, "expected only a demonstration on Corinth." In what was certainly an unintentional but nevertheless stinging indictment of his own intelligence, Rosecrans admitted that his troops waited in their works "wholly ignorant of what Van Dorn was doing at Chewalla." [27]

So convinced was Rosecrans that the enemy would attack somewhere else, on October 2 he considered moving his *entire* command across the Hatchie River, leaving Corinth uncovered, and pursuing the enemy. Though believing that Corinth was the main enemy objective, nagging doubts led Grant to allow Rosecrans to proceed with his plan "if practicable," urging him to "inform yourself as well as possible of the strength and position of the enemy" before embarking. Clearly, Rosecrans believed until fairly late that the enemy determined to attack elsewhere. Not until Van Dorn's infantry rolled over his outer defenses did he realize his mistake. [28]

After severe fighting that lasted until midday of October 4, Rosecrans repulsed Van Dorn and forced him to retreat toward the Hatchie River. At Davis's Bridge, Union forces dispatched to relieve Corinth seized the span and blocked Van Dorn's retreat as Rosecrans closed on his rear. Finding another place to cross, the Army of West Tennessee escaped, reaching Holly Springs on October 13. Disgusted with Rosecrans for letting the enemy elude his grasp, Grant ordered him back to Corinth on October 7. [29] Grant claimed later that Corinth had alleviated "any further anxiety for the safety of the territory within my jurisdiction," but the record tells a different story. Reports of massive reinforcements arriving in Mississippi and rumors of renewed Confederate aggression continued to reach his headquarters. In fact, this news so worried Grant that he again feared for the safety of Corinth. And he was anything but confident in the ability of his intelligence to track enemy movements. Although Iuka and Corinth had worked out well, the difficulties experienced in finding and tracking Confederate forces risked the safety of Corinth and possibly even West Tennessee. This experience only strengthened Grant's resolve to regain the initiative and put the shoe on the other foot.[30]

By the end of the month, the situation had changed in several important ways. On October 25 Grant assumed command of the newly formed Department of the Tennessee, which encompassed northern Mississippi and all of Kentucky and Tennessee west of the Tennessee River. Rosecrans left for Tennessee to command the Army of the Cumberland, formerly Buell's Army of the Ohio. General Hamilton assumed command over the District of Corinth, including Rosecrans' former troops. Although it is unclear how many individuals from Rosecrans' secret service accompanied him to Nashville, Hamilton's scouting corps, as well as some spies from the old Army of the Mississippi, remained behind at Corinth. These agents formed the nucleus of what would become the first systematic intelligence organization used by Grant during the war.[31]

The reverse at Corinth and Bragg's subsequent defeat at Perryville, Kentucky, on October 8 dashed Southern hopes of reclaiming their losses in the West. With the Confederate tide receding, the initiative passed to the Federals. Always seeking opportunities, Grant once again looked forward to carrying the war into the Deep South. More importantly, the enemy withdrawal freed a number of troops—both veterans and new levies—for duty in Mississippi. With more men, Grant could think seriously about an offensive against Vicksburg, the next obstacle to Union control of the Mississippi River. Within twenty-four hours of assuming his new command, Grant sent Halleck a plan for a campaign against the river citadel. Realizing that his current strength limited him to defensive operations, Grant suggested tearing up the railroads "to all points of the compass from Corinth" and concentrating his forces, now freed from guarding these lines, for an advance southward down the Mississippi Central Railroad toward Grenada. This turning movement would sever the Yazoo Delta region from the remainder of the state and "cause the evacuation of Vicksburg." Grant understood that pushing toward Vicksburg would put the enemy on the defensive and compel them to abandon further attempts on Corinth. In addition, remaining on the static defensive had magnified his intelligence shortcomings, but regaining the initiative stood to minimize those inadequacies. Yet even as he put his army in motion, Grant could not afford to ignore an enemy who had a knack for appearing out of nowhere.[32]

After Corinth, Grant learned that Van Dorn's army had retreated to Holly Springs and was then placed under the command of Lt. Gen. John C. Pemberton, who oversaw the new Department of Mississippi and East Louisiana. By month's end, some reports stated that Pemberton intended to resume offensive operations, possibly with help from Gen. Joseph E. Johnston and a large force rumored to be at Columbus, Mississippi. As a result, Grant warned Halleck, "Everything now indicates an early attack on Bolivar or Corinth." On November 1, however, new rumors predicting the evacuation of Holly Springs replaced these earlier reports. Despite the caveat that he was "at a loss to divine their plans from any reliable facts in my possession," Sherman noted that several sources had witnessed Pemberton's artillery on railroad cars heading south, a sure sign of an impending evacuation. This bit of news also indicated something else. "They would hardly venture to attack you or Corinth," Sherman wrote John A. Rawlins, "if it be true they sent off their artillery." Hamilton agreed, adding, "is it not likely the Rebels are evacuating Holly Springs and covering it by a feint on Bolivar[?]" Grant concluded that, in the absence of concrete evidence, the best defense he could muster was to advance into Mississippi and drive the enemy from his front, eliminating all the guesswork. "Corinth," he reasoned, "will then be covered." By November 4, he had ordered Hamilton and Brig. Gen. James B. McPherson to take their commands to Grand Junction, Tennessee. Designated as the left (Hamilton) and right (McPherson) wings, these combined forces, numbering around thirty-one thousand men, prepared to advance toward Holly Springs along the Mississippi Central, using the rail line to connect them to supply bases farther north.[33]

By November 6, Grant had concluded that Pemberton remained in Holly Springs with around thirty thousand men, although these troops were reportedly "in rather a disorganized condition." These reports only increased his confidence and his eagerness to advance. "I can now move from here with a force sufficient to handle that number without gloves." The next day two deserters from a Confederate Kentucky regiment revealed that the Union buildup at Grand Junction had caused the evacuation of Holly Springs. Attempting to verify this report, McPherson interrogated Confederate prisoners but found their testimony less than helpful. "Some say the infantry has all gone," he reported, while "others [say] that they are there in strong force." He did learn that an evacuation order had been issued, but "some General came up and put a stop to it." An escaped Union prisoner confirmed this last report. Sherman afterward relayed intelligence that Holly Springs was either evacuated or so reduced as to no longer pose a threat. To find the truth, Grant dispatched McPherson on a reconnaissance toward the town, hoping Pemberton would still be there. "If the enemy will remain at Holly Springs," he proclaimed, "it will satisfy me."[34]

McPherson's reconnaissance reached the Cold Water River just north of Holly Springs on November 9 and found the enemy in battle lines on the southern bank. Heeding Grant's instructions to avoid a general engagement, McPherson retreated to LaGrange, Tennessee. Based on this probe and intelligence obtained from citizens, deserters, and prisoners, Grant deduced that Pemberton had not abandoned Holly Springs. He also constructed his first order of battle for Pemberton's army, which was accurate with regard to the number of divisions, the identity of their commanders, and the size of the overall force. But McPherson had encountered Pemberton's rear guard above Holly Springs, not his main body. The Confederate commander had evacuated the area on November 9, and within twenty-four hours the Army of Mississippi had successfully retired to a second line south of the Tallahatchie River at Abbeville, eighteen miles from Holly Springs. Not until November 13 did Grant learn of this development. By then, however, the opportunity to assail Pemberton before he attained more defensible ground had vanished.[35]

After Pemberton reached the Tallahatchie, Grant received Halleck's blessing to advance and on November 28 embarked upon his first major offensive since Shiloh. In addition to McPherson's and Hamilton's troops, Sherman joined the campaign from Memphis. In the midst of this grand thrust, Grant received alarming reports that Bragg's army, at last report facing Rosecrans outside Nashville, had departed Middle Tennessee for Mississippi. Unwilling to abort his offensive, he relied upon the new commander at Corinth to remain vigilant and warn him if these reports proved true. The job of securing the department's left flank and watching for reinforcements coming from Tennessee fell to Brig. Gen. Grenville M. Dodge.[36]

Formerly colonel of the Fourth Iowa Infantry, Dodge had been a division commander in Brig. Gen. Samuel R. Curtis's Army of the Southwest and had participated in the battle of Pea Ridge in March 1862 before being transferred to Halleck's department. Before coming to Corinth, Dodge supervised railroad-rebuilding projects in West Tennessee. The months spent on this duty had stoked his desire to return to the battlefield. At one point he informed his wife, "I prefer to go to Grant, take a fighting division, and take my chances." Once in command at Corinth, a crucial rail junction, supply center, and staging area for future campaigns, Dodge's wish had apparently come true. And since Grant was preparing his first campaign against Vicksburg, the next battles promised to be decisive. Dodge was now close to the action and longed to take part. "I ache to get in this fight," he wrote. In the end, he would play an important role in the coming campaigns against Vicksburg, but one far different from what he had imagined.[37]

Shortly after Hamilton departed, Dodge heard that Maj. Gen. Lew Wallace was on the way to relieve him so that he could join the army in the field. A change in Wallace's orders scuttled those plans and Dodge remained in Corinth. As he waited for his replacement, the arrival of several unexpected visitors at his headquarters altered the course of his career under Grant's command. On November 12, 1862, three spies formerly employed by Rosecrans arrived with startling news that Bragg had detached forces to Mississippi. Sensing the importance of this intelligence, Dodge forwarded a summary to Grant's headquarters. The report seemed to confirm one of the Federal commander's major concerns: that Bragg would dispatch reinforcements either to defend Vicksburg or to fall upon his rear. To ensure that attempts to transfer troops to Mississippi would be detected, Grant wired Dodge on November 18 asking for help: "Can you get information from the East, say as far as Florence [Alabama]? I want to hear from along the Tennessee [River] from Tuscumbia eastward to know if any rebel troops are crossing there." A few days later, Rawlins instructed him to "send out spies and scouts [to the] east and obtain all information possible." Interpreting these instructions to mean he had "carte blanche to take care of that front," Dodge created a secret service organization more elaborate and extensive than Grant probably imagined. Although he would send spies and scouts as far as Mobile and Atlanta, his primary responsibility was to watch the eastern flank of Grant's department, especially the Tennessee River crossings, for Confederate reinforcements coming from Middle Tennessee.[38]

Although no evidence suggests Grant was aware of it, Dodge had prior experience with intelligence operations. While stationed at Rolla, Missouri, in late 1861, he became involved—somewhat by accident—in secret service activities. Maj. Gen. John C. Fremont, then in command of the Western Department, had repeatedly sent the Iowan reports about enemy movements near Rolla and ordered him to verify them. For several weeks, Dodge's cavalry wore itself out chasing these rumors, which were often proved false. Finally, a cavalry officer approached him with an idea. "I have plenty of men in my company," stated the officer, "[that] I can send out to everyone [*sic*] of these places and keep them there, . . . or they can go from here and ascertain the truth." Intrigued by the idea and also under orders from Fremont to dispatch "special spies or scouts," Dodge began recruiting Unionists who lived outside his lines to monitor Confederate movements deep in enemy territory and sent Union soldiers recruited from the ranks into or near the opposing lines to gather information. "Their reports soon came in, and were forwarded to head-quarters," he later wrote, "where it became know that the reports received from me were accurate." At the battle of Pea Ridge, Dodge's intelligence system paid off. The day before the battle, one of his scouts informed Maj. Gen. Samuel R. Curtis, who did not expect a Confederate attack and whose forces were not yet concentrated, that the enemy was approaching and intended to fight. This news, corroborated by other sources, gave Curtis time to prepare for the onslaught. Pea Ridge resulted in a Union victory, and according to Dodge, "this information saved us." Though he claims too much for his scout, who brought in only one of several reports indicating the Confederates' rapid advance, Dodge had proven that he knew how to get information on the enemy.[39]

In late November, as Grant embarked upon his first attempt to capture Vicksburg, Dodge remained behind but knew his commander needed him where he was. Another officer told him that, during a recent conversation with Grant, the general remarked that Dodge was "a good man for any place but he could not be spared from Corinth." Grant later confessed that the Iowan was "peculiarly fitted" for his new command due to his prewar experience on the frontier. He knew how to improvise in emergencies and always "acted promptly without waiting for orders," both of which would be essential qualities for Dodge's unique mission.[40]

Dodge began constructing an intelligence organization that would eventually stretch from Corinth to Atlanta and into the interiors of Mississippi, Alabama, and Tennessee. From a nucleus of eleven operatives, mostly the remnants of Rosecrans' old secret service, Dodge's corps of scouts and spies burgeoned to over 130 operatives by late 1863, although only two dozen or so were on his payroll during any one month. Scouts regularly ventured toward the Tennessee River and into enemy lines to monitor troop movements, while spies stayed in Vicksburg, Meridian, Selma, Mobile, Chattanooga, and Atlanta and sent periodic reports to Corinth by secret messenger. The First Alabama Cavalry (U.S.), formed by Dodge in the fall of 1862 from Unionists in northern Alabama and commanded by his chief of staff, Col. George E. Spencer, became a source for operatives, producing at least twenty-two secret service recruits. "These mountain men were fearless and would take all chances," claimed Dodge, making them perfect candidates for espionage duty. Their families still living behind Confederate lines also provided valuable information. From November 1862 through July 1863, Dodge's men completed over two hundred missions and logged thousands of miles.[41]

As it grew, Grant placed great value upon Dodge's intelligence system and defended his subordinate against attempts to compromise it. In early January 1863, for example, Dodge learned his quartermaster could no longer cover his secret service costs. Moreover, the quartermaster, citing army regulations, also refused to remunerate any personnel who failed to sign a voucher, which contained the name, the nature of the service, and the amount each spy or scout received in compensation. Dodge refused to allow this, arguing, "There are citizens living in the South who give me the most valuable information [who] will not sign a voucher for fear of consequences in the future." If a person residing in the Confederacy spied for the Federal army and then signed a voucher—a far from confidential document—he or she risked having the nature of their service revealed, which could lead to threats and violent retribution from their fellow Southerners both during and after the war. Alabama Unionist William Hugh Smith, who escaped to Union lines in 1862 and then spied for Dodge, is one example of the past coming back to haunt a former secret service employee. Before becoming a "scalawag" governor of Alabama during Reconstruction, Smith served as a circuit-court judge. However, his judicial career took a nasty turn when lawyers arguing cases before him uttered "insulting phrases concerning his war record." The abuse became unbearable and Smith resigned. Knowing that secret service recruitment, not to mention the effectiveness of his current operatives, would suffer if word spread that the army would not protect their anonymity, Dodge seized control over the money and disbursements from his quartermaster. He kept vouchers but refused to send duplicates to headquarters as required by regulations. To hide their identity after the war, Dodge retained all copies of secret service vouchers instead of sending them to the War Department; they remain filed in his personal documents. For those who vehemently objected to leaving any paper trail, Dodge kept a record of "Vouchers Not Filled Out" to track expenditures. Furthermore, he often used a letter or a symbol in place of an operative's name when writing in his intelligence diary and never referred to them by name in his official correspondence. When complaints reached his desk, Grant supported his subordinate's action.[42]

Paying secret service personnel also presented a vexing problem, especially since scouts and spies took enormous risks and expected to be well compensated in return. "I have collected a corps of rather efficient men," Dodge wrote in January, "[but] unless I can have funds to use I cannot hold them together." To raise money independent of the army, he began selling confiscated cotton and using the proceeds for the secret service. For his part, Grant ordered that the revenue generated from the sale of trade permits, which allowed the buyer to traffic in cotton within the department for a fee of one hundred dollars, be collected by the department provost marshal, Col. William S. Hillyer, and deposited in a "secret service" account in Memphis. Following Dodge's lead, he later expanded the sources of revenue to include money procured from the sale of cotton and other property confiscated from secessionists. Grant even went so far as to allow another commander to supplement his secret service budget with an eight-thousand-dollar "assessment" levied on Southern civilians who had the misfortune of living near a Union depot raided by the enemy. As Dodge's network grew to meet Grant's intelligence needs, he needed every penny he could find; in March alone, he required nearly five thousand dollars to cover his secret service expenses.[43]

Not everyone, however, approved of this unconventional arrangement. The first objection came from Dodge's immediate superior in Memphis, Maj. Gen. Stephen Hurlbut. In early March 1863, Dodge had emptied his secret service coffers and asked Hillyer for five thousand dollars from the account in Memphis. As Grant was busy preparing for his next campaign against Vicksburg, Hillyer forwarded the request to Hurlbut. Seeing that Dodge had recently received a large amount from the Memphis secret service fund, the general grew suspicious. He instructed Hillyer to suspend payment until Dodge could justify to whom and for what purposes he had disbursed his previous allotment. The Iowan refused, claiming that not even the commanding general possessed that sort of information and had never asked for it. When the matter reached Grant, he immediately sided with Dodge to protect the anonymity of operatives and maintain the effectiveness of his network.[44]

The second objection came from Washington. In June 1863, Hillyer let slip before a military commission investigating cotton sales on the Mississippi that Dodge possessed large amounts of money for secret service. When asked to whom he reported his disbursements, he replied that he did not know. Hillyer later warned Grant, "The court seemed to put some stress on this point" and advised him to require all officers receiving secret service funds to "report to you what they have done with it." Grant managed to avoid further inquiries from the commission without taking such a step, trusting in Dodge to be honest in his use of government money. And this trust was no small matter. Between November 1862 and July 1863, Dodge expended over twenty-one thousand dollars on the secret service, and his commander never knew where one penny of it went. Although Grant probably never knew the true extent of these operations, his defense of Dodge's practices indicates that he understood not only the essential role of intelligence but also that in Dodge he had found the right man to oversee its collection, especially in that difficult winter of 1862. Perhaps Grant's comment in late 1862 best captures the essence of the Iowan's contributions over the next ten months. "You have a much more important command than that of a division in the field."[45]

As Dodge watched the left flank and the Tennessee River crossings, Grant looked toward the Tallahatchie and Pemberton's newest line of defense. On November 28 he advanced down the Mississippi Central with nearly forty thousand men, secure in the knowledge—provided by Dodge—that Bragg remained in Middle Tennessee. As for reliable information on Pemberton, Grant possessed very little. As the army advanced, an escaped slave claimed that Pemberton's men were cooking rations in preparation for an evacuation of the Tallahatchie line. Contradicting that testimony, however, was a captured Confederate spy who, after being "pumped by one of Hamilton's scouts" who was disguised in a Confederate uniform and placed in his jail cell, insisted that Pemberton intended to fight along the Tallahatchie. Hamilton also found more evidence to support this latter story. The following day, however, a former manservant in Pemberton's army alleged that orders had been issued to strike tents and pack three-days' rations in preparation for a withdrawal. This conflicting evidence led Grant to report on November 29 that he possessed "no reliable information from the enemy." [46]

On December 1 a Union cavalry patrol verified the manservant's story. "The Enemy deserted their fortifications yesterday," Grant informed Halleck. Compelled to withdraw "for the defense of Vicksburg," Pemberton and his army of twenty-one thousand had abandoned the Tallahatchie line and reached the south bank of the Yalobusha River at Grenada, a distance of about fifty miles, by December 5. Grant's advance down the Mississippi Central had certainly played a role in this withdrawal, but the cooperation of another Union column from Helena, Arkansas, proved decisive. The news of this force streaking across the Yazoo Delta toward Grenada prompted Pemberton's decision.[47]

As Union cavalry pursued the enemy toward the Yalobusha, rumors that Confederate authorities had dispatched reinforcements to Pemberton again reached Grant's headquarters. This time, however, with Pemberton in trouble and Vicksburg at stake, the odds appeared better that these rumors might contain a shred of truth. On December 3 Joseph Palmer, one of Rosecrans' former scouts now working for Dodge, came from Alabama with news that a substantial portion of Bragg's cavalry and some infantry were en route to Mississippi. Another spy, sent on an extended mission by Rosecrans in October, finally returned and reported that the enemy had evacuated Arkansas in order to "concentrate their whole force East of the Miss." [48]

To get at the truth, Grant turned to his man at Corinth. "I get news from Bragg daily," replied Dodge, "but for the past week it has been very conflicting." He was certain, however, that no enemy troops had crossed the Tennessee east of Decatur, Alabama. By December 10, Grant felt relatively certain that "Bragg intends to stay where he is." Unknown to Dodge or Grant, Bragg had indeed detached an infantry brigade in late November for service with Pemberton, and these regiments reached Grenada via the Mobile and Meridian Railroad on December 17. Although Grant heard rumors of infantry moving to Pemberton through Meridian on December 14, he was skeptical because "it does not agree with what [I] have heretofore heard." As long as reinforcements traveled by this circuitous route while Dodge looked for them to cross the Tennessee, it would not be the last time Bragg reinforced the Mississippi line right under Grant's nose.[49]

Meantime, Grant established his headquarters at Oxford and his principal supply depot at Holly Springs, where tons of supplies had already begun accumulating to support the offensive deeper into Mississippi. As he waited for crews to repair the railroad reaching Oxford, he changed his plans. On December 8 Sherman returned to Memphis with instructions to assemble an expedition to attack the Vicksburg fortifications along the Yazoo River northeast of the town. At the same time, Grant planned to hold Pemberton at Grenada and wait for Sherman to dislodge the Vicksburg garrison. If Pemberton withdrew, Grant intended to "follow him even to the gates of Vicksburg."[50]

On December 11 Grant's lead elements crossed the Yocona River and occupied Water Valley, about thirty miles northeast of Grenada. Once again, rumors of troop transfers between Tennessee and Mississippi began to emerge. Though earlier rumors of this sort had proven false, Grant advised Dodge to "[k]eep a sharp lookout for Bragg's forces." Over the next few days, conflicting reports trickled in, some indicating that Bragg himself was on the way to Mississippi with a large force while others purported that he was preparing his army for a stand against Rosecrans. After analyzing these reports, Grant concluded on December 16 that Bragg's entire army was headed toward the Tennessee River and requested, as he would do many times in the future, that Rosecrans pursue them.[51]

When he received this request a day later, Rosecrans disputed his former commander's assessment because, he wrote, "Bragg was in Murfreesboro this morning." Not only that, he continued, during a recent visit to the newly christened Army of Tennessee, Jefferson Davis had reportedly proclaimed that Middle Tennessee "must, could & should be held." Rosecrans' appraisal of the situation proved correct. By early December, Bragg felt that sending more troops to Mississippi jeopardized the security of Tennessee and therefore rebuffed Pemberton's requests for assistance. "Cannot move infantry across the Tennessee," he wrote on November 21, promising instead to send Nathan Bedford Forrest to disrupt Grant's communications in West Tennessee. By December 15, Forrest's command—about twenty-one hundred strong—had reached the

Tennessee River at Clifton and prepared to stir up trouble in the Federal rear.[52]

Rosecrans discovered Forrest's departure on December 11 and promptly warned Grant. Dodge picked up the trail the following day when a scout reported that Forrest's troopers were heading toward the river. Although estimated to number nearly ten thousand men, Grant noted that "Dodge . . . had a scout among [Forrest's command] before they commenced crossing" who estimated their strength at half that number.[53] Arguably the most feared Confederate in the West, Forrest crossed into West Tennessee and demonstrated just how vulnerable Grant's outposts were to mounted raids. His expedition absorbed the attention not only of the post commanders in the region but also kept Dodge and Grant busy chasing the Confederate troopers. In fact, the Corinth commander cobbled together a force to pursue Forrest and on December 18 headed to Jackson, Tennessee. With Dodge absent from his post, his intelligence operations all but ceased until Christmas Eve. In the end, Forrest's West Tennessee raid, in conjunction with other events, helped deal a mortal blow to Grant's overland advance on Vicksburg and had disastrous consequences for Sherman's attack against Chickasaw Bluffs northeast of the town.

As Forrest wreaked havoc deep in the Union rear, another Confederate cavalry column departed Grenada bound for Holly Springs, the key supply depot forty miles behind Grant's headquarters at Oxford. Pemberton hoped a raid on Holly Springs and the destruction of portions of the Mississippi Central and the Memphis and Charleston rail lines might compel Grant to abandon his offensive. Earl Van Dorn, now in command of Pemberton's cavalry, left Grenada on December 17 with a force of thirty-five hundred men and reached Pontotoc later that day. Purposely avoiding any roads leading to Holly Springs, Van Dorn made it to the Tallahatchie River at New Albany the following evening. The next day the column arrived at Ripley and, after learning from a scout that the Holly Springs garrison remained unaware of their approach, turned due west and raced toward the town. Early on September 20, Van Dorn's troopers descended upon Holly Springs, routed the unsuspecting garrison, and captured or destroyed vast amounts of material meant to supply Grant's army. The Confederate raiders then left the smoking ruins of Holly Springs behind and headed north to dismantle the railroads.[54]

Not until late on December 19 did Grant learn about Van Dorn's column snaking its way northward. That day, he received news that three thousand Confederate cavalrymen were galloping north to sever his communications. He wired Corinth for help, but Dodge was still pursuing Forrest in West Tennessee and was unable to provide assistance. Grant also warned Col. Robert C. Murphy, the commander at Holly Springs, and instructed him to watch for enemy movements. He also told Murphy that, based on the latest intelligence, the raiders would not reach the Tallahatchie at Rocky Ford—about twenty miles southeast of Holly Springs—until the evening of December 19. Murphy replied that, due to a lack of reliable maps, he had no idea where Rocky Ford was but affirmed that his cavalry was ready for duty. Confident that the raiders would only reach the crossing that night and then resume their journey on December 20, Grant told Murphy at 11 P.M. that there was no hurry. "In the morning [December 20] will be early enough for your cavalry to start," he advised. Van Dorn's raiders, however, were a full day's march ahead of Grant's intelligence and descended upon Holly Springs before Murphy could dispatch his patrols or cobble together an adequate defense. Not until a Union officer, who had barely escaped Holly Springs before the onslaught, brought news of the disaster did Grant know the full extent of his intelligence error. Furious, Grant blasted Murphy for being a coward and a traitor.[55]

But Grant should also shoulder some of the blame because he possessed enough information to have avoided this disaster. Returning to Oxford from a raid on the Mobile and Ohio near Tupelo, Union cavalry under Col. T. Lyle Dickey encountered Van Dorn's column as it moved north from Pontotoc in the early afternoon of December 18. This meant that the Confederates were farther north than Grant had estimated and would likely reach the Tallahatchie *that night* (December 18), not the next day. Had Grant known this, he might have placed Holly Springs on alert sooner and urged Murphy to send out cavalry patrols immediately, perhaps increasing the chances that the Confederate's approach might have been detected in time. In warfare, however, "friction" often interferes to make even the best situations turn sour. Realizing that news of a large body of enemy cavalry advancing north would be of interest to Grant, Dickey sent several couriers to speed this important news to Oxford. That evening, the colonel discovered to his horror that the messengers had misunderstood their orders and, instead of rushing to Grant, had remained with the column. He dispatched new messengers, but as luck would have it, they became lost and failed to reach Grant's headquarters until the morning of Van Dorn's attack.[56]

But even if these couriers had reached Grant in time, it would have made little difference. Dickey reached Oxford at 5:30 P.M. on December 19, ahead of his couriers who were still wandering about the countryside. The cavalry commander reported to Grant what he had seen at Pontotoc the previous day. According to Dickey, "notice was at once telegraphed to every point on the railroad north." He even bragged that his timely news had "saved every station . . . except Holly Springs" and that it should have spared that post as well, alluding to Murphy's alleged incompetence.[57] However, the only message that apparently went over the lines that night said nothing of the enemy's last known location nor did it provide any estimates of Van Dorn's current position. Moreover, Grant's telegram of December 19 to Murphy, which contained the news that the enemy would only reach Rocky Ford that evening and that he could delay sending his cavalry out until morning, was sent at 11 P.M., long after Dickey had made his report. Thus, Grant had in his possession intelligence that placed the Confederates farther north than previously believed. This news obviously failed to change his mind, and this misjudgment cost him his main supply depot. Consumed with his own offensive operations, and perhaps believing that having the initiative obviated the need for vigilance, the general disregarded new evidence that might have saved Holly Springs. Though blaming Murphy, it is clear that Grant also had a hand in the events that led to disaster.[58]

The surprising success of Van Dorn's sweep through Holly Springs and Forrest's West Tennessee raid convinced Grant that his logistical connections were far too vulnerable to sustain an overland campaign against Vicksburg. As long as he depended upon ever-lengthening supply lines, the danger of raids loomed large, especially since his intelligence had enough gaps—both in collection and analysis—for an enterprising foe to slip through. Reluctantly, Grant withdrew slowly toward West Tennessee. Though one avenue to Vicksburg had closed, he would find another.[59]

The news of the Holly Springs debacle and Grant's subsequent retreat did not reach Sherman, who was then advancing for an attack on Vicksburg from the northeast, until too late. The success of Sherman's assault on Chickasaw Bluffs along the banks of the Yazoo River depended heavily upon Grant's ability to keep Pemberton at Grenada and prevent

the Confederate commander from shuttling reinforcements to Vicksburg. Van Dorn's success allowed Pemberton to transfer troops from the
Yalobusha and elsewhere to help the small Vicksburg garrison (only fifty-
five hundred men) deal with Sherman. When he learned that Sherman's
troops had landed on December 26, Pemberton rushed two brigades
from Grenada toward the scene. During December 27–29, the Federals
launched several unsuccessful yet bloody assaults against the defenses at
Chickasaw Bayou. On January 2, 1863, Sherman retreated, having demonstrated the futility of attacking Vicksburg from the northeast. The reinforcements sent by Pemberton made the difference for the Southerners. "It is doubtful," noted one historian of the battle, "whether the
Vicksburg Confederates could have held off Sherman's legions without
these troops." [60]

Unknown to Grant, more units in addition to the Grenada forces had
been dispatched to Vicksburg. Feeling the pressure of Union forces upon
his native state, Jefferson Davis authorized the transfer to Mississippi
of Maj. Gen. Carter L. Stevenson's nine-thousand-man division from
Bragg's army on December 14. After a long journey by way of Atlanta,
Mobile, Meridian, and Jackson, two of Stevenson's brigades filed into the
works on December 29 in time to help parry Sherman's final assaults. [61]
Not until January 1, 1863, did Grant discover the arrival of this division
in Vicksburg. But Rosecrans must share part of the blame for Grant's
ignorance, for he knew on December 24 that about ten thousand troops
had departed for Mississippi but failed to share this knowledge with his
fellow officer.

In addition, Dodge also failed to detect this movement. He focused
his attention on the Tennessee River crossings in West Tennessee and
northern Alabama, the shortest route between Bragg's army and Mississippi. Stevenson traveled another line, coming by rail from Chattanooga
through Mobile. As of yet, Dodge did not have these avenues under surveillance. At one point he did hear from an escaped Union prisoner
named Loran W. Pierce that a large force from Tennessee had passed
through Mobile headed for Vicksburg. But since Dodge believed it more
likely that Bragg would send reinforcements directly across the Tennessee, especially given the immediate danger posed by Sherman, he placed
more stock in the views of the scouts watching the river crossings. And,
of course, these men were confident that none of Bragg's army had gone
west. On December 31, 1862, a refugee from Chattanooga reported wit-

nessing "trains loaded with Kirby Smiths & Stephensons troops going to Jackson Miss." Though the man told a "straight story," Dodge cautioned Grant against accepting it at face value. "I have heard such rumors as this before but placed no reliance in them." By New Years' Day, however, Grant had heard enough to convince him that reinforcements had indeed come from Tennessee. By that time, however, this revelation meant little to Sherman's men who had already experienced the Rebel arrival firsthand. This episode also had implications for the future. The inability of Union intelligence to sniff out the transfer of Stevenson's division prompted Dodge to focus more attention on this southern route, an expensive and dangerous venture requiring the use of spies living deep within enemy territory. More importantly, the ease with which Bragg utilized interior lines to secretly shuttle a large force (Stevenson's division alone represented nearly one-fourth of his infantry) to Mississippi, compounded by Rosecrans' reluctance to do anything to prevent Bragg from detaching reinforcements, presaged a problem that Grant would again face during his second campaign against Vicksburg.[62]

The events of the past few months had tested Grant's intelligence capabilities like never before. Tasked with defending a large area with few men, he relied upon all of his division commanders to watch their fronts. The addition of Dodge's nascent intelligence network vastly improved his ability to monitor traffic between Tennessee and Mississippi. But dispersal of collection efforts sometimes led to the production of too much information, which obscured the truth as much as not possessing enough. Moreover, much of the information Grant received was contradictory, which sometimes left him in as much in the dark as if he had received no reports at all.

During the fall of 1862, Price and Van Dorn had successfully eluded Grant's intelligence network. Having yielded the initiative before Iuka and Corinth, inaccurate information on the whereabouts of the enemy could have been disastrous. But Grant had prevailed. Holly Springs, however, revealed that bad intelligence or the disregard of new information, even when one possessed the initiative, could be devastating. The inability to protect his supply lines forced Grant to abandon the overland approach to Vicksburg. Though primarily a logistical problem, his predicament during December 1862 was compounded by his inability to accurately track enemy forces. The security of his supply lines depended heavily upon being able to identify and meet threats to them.

The enemy's use of interior lines to shift troops from one theater to another without detection was also a serious challenge, one he hoped Grenville Dodge would master. In the final analysis, Grant's logistical problems and the unsatisfying end to his first campaign against Vicksburg stemmed in part from his intelligence woes. Only time would tell whether these same problems would hamper his next campaign against the Confederacy's last and most imposing fortress on the Mississippi.

Chapter 6

"I Have Reliable Information from the Entire Interior of the South"

Following the Holly Springs and Chickasaw Bluffs disasters, Grant determined the Mississippi River would be the axis of advance for his next attempt at Vicksburg. This avenue promised to reduce reliance upon overland logistical lines that presented easy targets for mounted raiders who, as Van Dorn demonstrated, were difficult to track in hostile territory. But this new campaign posed significant challenges of its own, especially with regard to intelligence procurement. Part of his campaign preparation focused on finding the best avenue of approach once ashore. Sherman's experience in January had revealed the difficulty of overcoming the Confederate defenses northeast of the city. Vicksburg's river defenses consisted of powerful batteries perched along the steep hills running northeast to Haynes' Bluff and southward past the town to Warrenton. To sail past these defenses, Federal vessels had to first negotiate a hairpin curve, all the while under fire from the river batteries, then run a gauntlet of shot and shell for several miles. Vicksburg's guns also commanded the opposite bank and could blast attempts to cross the river or harass troop movements on the Louisiana shore. Enhanced by rugged terrain east of town, the land defenses added to the stout nature of the position, which was described as "frightful" by one observer. With over twenty thousand troops (a number that would grow with time) manning this fortress, Lt. Gen. John C. Pemberton seemed poised to dash Union hopes of gaining control of the Mississippi. During the next few months of 1863, finding a way to crack these defenses and capture Vicksburg became Grant's primary goal.[1]

From January through March, he explored several different ways to turn the Confederate position and avoid the teeth of their defenses. "The problem," Grant wrote later, "was to secure a foothold upon dry ground on the east side of the river." But this proved to be an onerous task. Grant experimented with several different water routes, including carving his own canals and using Lake Providence, Yazoo Pass, or Steele's Bayou to circumvent Pemberton's defenses. None of these enterprises bore much fruit. Another option was to march his forces down the Louisiana side to a suitable crossing place below Vicksburg. But above-average water levels on the west bank delayed that operation. By April 1, however, the roads had improved and Grant scrapped the other projects in favor of marching the Army of the Tennessee to a point midway between Warrenton and Grand Gulf and ferrying it across the river. Once on the other side, he could turn north toward Warrenton and Vicksburg or head south to aid Maj. Gen. Nathaniel Banks in his effort to capture Port Hudson. Regardless of which way he turned, Grant believed that once he crossed the Mississippi, Vicksburg was doomed.[2]

Intelligence on Vicksburg and its defenders would undoubtedly be a valuable asset in making decisions about where to cross and in identifying the position's strengths and weaknesses. Finding information from the Mississippi side proved difficult, and much of what arrived at Grant's headquarters at Young's Point, Louisiana, only muddied already murky water. By late February, many rumors predicted that Pemberton planned to hold Vicksburg at all costs, but other reports claimed that the Confederates would evacuate the city without a fight. To confuse matters even more, other sources suggested that the Confederates hoped the Federals would land below Vicksburg and leave West Tennessee open to invasion. These contradictory reports and the difficulty in verifying them led to frustration. "It is impossible to get information from [Vicksburg]," Grant complained. "Even deserters who come can tell nothing except of their own regiments or Brigade at furthest." A month later, he still grumbled that he possessed "no means of learning anything from below except what is occationally learned through Southern papers." As a result, wrote Charles A. Dana, a War Department official attached to Grant's staff, "This is not so well informed a place as I hoped to find it."[3]

Several reasons account for the dearth of reliable intelligence at Young's Point. First, Grant had reduced his commitments in West Tennessee, stripped the region of available Union troops, and left the defense of the department primarily to Maj. Gen. Stephen A. Hurlbut in Memphis. Since Corinth was under Hurlbut's command, Grenville Dodge reported to Charles S. Hamilton—later replaced by Maj. Gen. Richard J. Oglesby—who then relayed his intelligence reports to Memphis. The responsibility for forwarding news from Corinth to Young's Point fell to Hurlbut, who according to one officer did not always follow through.[4] Since no telegraph line yet connected Grant with Memphis, news from Dodge sometimes took a week to ten days to reach field headquarters. Second, Dodge's information was useful primarily for determining if reinforcements were coming from Tennessee and not for providing insights into Vicksburg and its environs. His scouts and spies roamed West

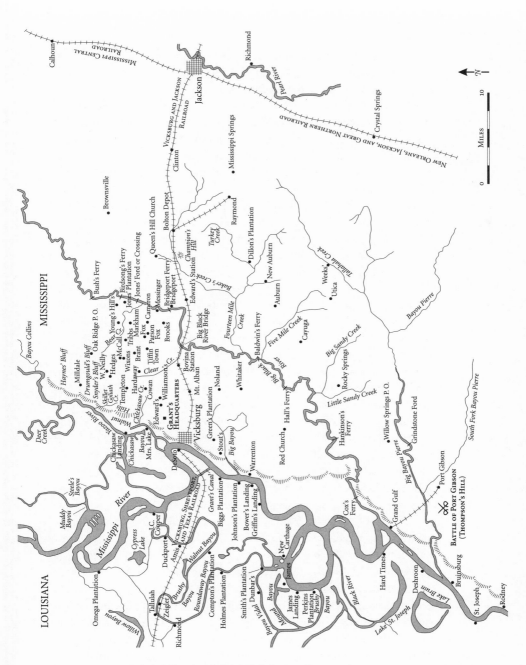

Later Phase of the Vicksburg Campaign

Tennessee, northern Mississippi, and Alabama and were too far removed to provide information from behind Pemberton's lines. Moreover, their primary mission—early detection of Confederate reinforcements from Braxton Bragg's Army of Tennessee—now took on added importance since both Rosecrans and Hurlbut desperately needed information of that sort as well. Dodge attempted to infiltrate Vicksburg, but watching Tennessee consumed most of his time and resources, which left Grant on his own with regard to intelligence about his operational area.[5] Though experienced in these matters, Grant neither established a formal secret service at his field headquarters nor pursued information with the same zeal that had marked his efforts outside Columbus in 1861. To him, holding the initiative was not only more advantageous in a campaign, it also promised to decrease the amount of information required to conduct operations, especially compared to what was needed for a successful defense.

Grant proceeded with the plan to get below Vicksburg. Fixed in his mind was the belief that "Vicksburg could only be successfully turned from the South side of the City." In early April, Maj. Gen. John McClernand's corps traveled downriver to New Carthage, Louisiana, midway between Warrenton and Grand Gulf. Once the expedition was underway, keeping the enemy in the dark became paramount. It did not take long, however, for Northern correspondents to uncover the story and wire it to their newspapers. Dana noted on April 10 that several Northern newspapers had reported McClernand's movement and revealed the plans for the campaign. Dana claimed that the enemy would probably view the account as a deceptive ploy "to cover other designs," especially since Grant still believed that Pemberton expected the Federals to launch another attack against the bluffs above the city. Plagued by the inability to get reliable intelligence from Vicksburg, however, Grant could only guess at what the enemy truly believed. Just in case, though, Grant sent Maj. Gen. Frederick Steele toward Greenville, about one hundred miles upriver from Vicksburg, to divert attention from McClernand and persuade Pemberton that the Federals remained focused on the northeastern fortifications. The Greenville expedition (April 2–25), in conjunction with the withdrawal of the Yazoo Pass expedition and reports that transports loaded with Union troops had headed upriver, succeeded in fooling the enemy more than even Grant could have hoped. From all this activity, Pemberton concluded that the Federals had abandoned their campaign and were withdrawing to Memphis, probably to reinforce Rosecrans in Tennessee. As a result, when the Confederate commander heard rumors about McClernand's advance downriver on April 9, he ignored them. Grant's deceptions worked so well that a confident Pemberton, usually reluctant to detach troops for service outside Mississippi, returned two brigades (about eight thousand men) from Carter Stevenson's division to Bragg.[6]

The same day this column departed, a spy from Vicksburg named W. I. Morris reached Corinth and reported that eight thousand troops had left for Tennessee. One of Dodge's operatives, Morris had gone to Vicksburg on March 21 and, besides learning about the detachment, discovered that the enemy faced serious supply shortages and that the garrison of twenty-five thousand men was stretched from Grand Gulf on the Mississippi north to Greenwood on the Yazoo River. More importantly, he stated that Pemberton had constructed defenses three miles east of town comprising fortifications that, in some places, were several lines deep. "Every Hill and ridge has a work upon it," he claimed. But Morris then added that, despite their preparations, the Confederates "do not fear an attack from that direction."[7] This news seemed to confirm that the Steele's Bayou and Yazoo Pass expeditions had "tended to confuse and mislead" the enemy as to the true plan. More importantly, Morris's intelligence revealed that Grant was poised to strike where the enemy might least expect it.[8]

Other than Morris's report, though, Grant possessed little intelligence on Pemberton's defenses or the disposition of his army. By April 14, Dana noted that the prevailing sentiment at headquarters was that the enemy remained ignorant of McClernand's movement and looked "for an assault on Hayne's Bluff or Vicksburg direct" from the north. Grant had faced other Confederate fortresses, and he undoubtedly drew upon those experiences to guide him in the absence of information. He likely assumed that Pemberton, like his predecessors at Columbus and Fort Donelson, planned to wait for the Federals to attack his fortifications northeast of town, just as Sherman had done at Chickasaw Bluffs. Based upon his own experience and buttressed by Morris's intelligence, Grant prepared to cross the river below the town and gain a beachhead on the east bank "before the enemy could offer any great resistance."[9]

On the night of April 16, Union gunboats and transports passed the Vicksburg batteries without serious damage. Six days later, another flotilla survived the gauntlet and moved into position to ferry Grant's infantry across the river. Flooding on the Louisiana side, however, delayed the arrival of his columns. If running the batteries had not revealed his real objective to the Confederates, Grant feared this last delay might give Pemberton time to figure it out. To prevent this, he ordered Col. Benjamin H. Grierson and fifteen hundred cavalrymen to sweep through central Mississippi, sever Pemberton's communications, and divert his attention away from the operations west of the river. Grierson's command departed LaGrange on April 17 and reached Baton Rouge on May 2. During their ride, the raiders torched supplies, smashed Confederate communications, and distracted Pemberton's attention from Grant's activities. At the same time as this raid, a force under Dodge advanced into the Tuscumbia Valley in northern Alabama while cavalry under Col. Abel D. Streight from Rosecrans' army slashed across that state to sever the Western and Atlantic Railroad. Unaware of the full impact of these expeditions and possessing no reliable way of finding out, Grant only hoped Pemberton had been distracted long enough.[10]

During this phase, news from inside Vicksburg remained scarce due, in part, to Grant's failure to pursue it in a systematic fashion. According to provost marshal records, after Morris returned on April 13, he sent no more scouts or spies into the Vicksburg vicinity. Two other operatives, Lorain Ruggles and Solomon Woolworth, had earlier made trips into the town, but none of these men were on Grant's payroll by early May.[11] Though Grant could have borrowed a few of Dodge's men, no such request has been found. But even if he had, Dodge could not have obliged—during most of April and early May, his corps of scouts were in northern Alabama participating in a raid on the Tuscumbia Valley.[12] Regardless, the uncertainty failed to bother Grant. By now he was convinced that Pemberton expected the Federals to attack the bluffs northeast of town, a situation that played perfectly into his plans.

Based on this assessment, Grant moved quickly to "obtain a foothold on the east bank of the Mississippi River," instructing McClernand's corps to seize Grand Gulf. To conceal the concentration on the west bank, Grant planned another diversion. While Rear Adm. David Porter's gunboats bombarded Grand Gulf in preparation for the real landing, transports loaded with Sherman's men steamed toward Snyder's Bluff and then feigned an attack on the Confederate fortifications along Walnut Hills. This movement, he hoped, would reinforce Pemberton's sense

1. Ulysses S. Grant (Courtesy of U.S. Army Military History Institute)

2. Maj. Gen. William S. Rosecrans brought an engineer's sense of detail and organization to secret service operations under his command. His intelligence network formed the foundation of a system later utilized by Grant. (Courtesy of Library of Congress, Prints and Photographs Division)

3. Brig. Gen. Grenville M. Dodge created the largest and most extensive intelligence network of the war. From their base at Corinth, Mississippi, his secret operatives—numbering over 130 men and women—roamed as far as Mobile, Chattanooga, and Atlanta. When army bureaucracy threatened the anonymity of Dodge's agents, Grant supported him in preserving the secrecy of his personnel. (Courtesy of U.S. Army Military History Institute)

4. Maj. Gen. George G. Meade inherited the Army of the Potomac's Bureau of Military Information when he took command in 1863. Though skeptical of the bureau's value as an intelligence arm, especially after its poor performance during Jubal Early's raid in 1864, he later became an avid consumer of the information it provided. (Courtesy of Library of Congress, Prints and Photographs Division)

5. Col. George H. Sharpe, deputy marshal and former attorney from New York, organized and led the Army of the Potomac's Bureau of Military Information, which was the most sophisticated and efficient all-source intelligence system created during the war. Though nearly disbanded in 1864, the bureau became a key asset in Grant's bid to deny Robert E. Lee strategic mobility and the use of interior lines in Virginia. (Courtesy of Roger D. Hunt Collection, U.S. Army Military History Institute)

6. Capt. John McEntee established branch offices of the Bureau of Military Information with other Union commands in Virginia and was a seasoned interrogator. (Courtesy of U.S. Army Military History Institute)

7. Scouts and guides of the Army of the Potomac, March 1864. This motley group of soldiers and civilians worked secretly and silently—always in danger of being captured and executed for espionage—to hasten the fall of Richmond and Petersburg. Though often forgotten in the din of battle, these men provided distinguished service on the front lines of the intelligence war. (Courtesy of Library of Congress, Prints and Photographs Division)

8. The Bureau of Military Information staff, Army of the Potomac, in northern Virginia in 1864. *Left to right:* Col. George H. Sharpe, John C. Babcock, Capt. Paul Oliver, and Capt. John McEntee (Courtesy of Library of Congress, Prints and Photographs Division)

9. Lt. Gen. Ulysses S. Grant at Cold Harbor, Virginia, 1864. The campaign in Virginia severely tested Grant's views on military intelligence but ultimately led to the development of the war's most sophisticated all-source secret service operation. (Courtesy of National Archives)

155

10. Grant and his staff at City Point, Virginia. Brig. Gen. Marsena R. Patrick, provost marshal general of the "Armies Operating against Richmond" and staunch advocate of the Bureau of Military Information, is on Grant's left. (Courtesy of National Archives)

11. Elizabeth Van Lew led one of three spy rings in Richmond and provided valuable information on living conditions and military movements within the city. (Courtesy of Cook Collection, Valentine Museum, Richmond, Virginia)

of where the main attack would likely fall. And it worked. Even after hearing reports of an "immense force" collecting across from Grand Gulf, Pemberton—fixated on Sherman's diversion—hesitated to send reinforcements downriver.[13]

Again, Grant had no sure way of knowing whether the diversion would fool Pemberton long enough to allow McClernand to cross safely. Initially, it appeared as if the deception had failed. A local preacher interviewed by Admiral Porter claimed that Pemberton had seen through the feint and was prepared to smash the landing near Grand Gulf. "They have been preparing this place six weeks," he warned, "and have known all about this move." A concerned Grant personally surveyed the Grand Gulf position on April 24 but came to the opposite conclusion. Not only was it weaker than Porter indicated, Grant believed that, if attacked soon, "the place will fall easily."[14] Indications that Sherman had indeed fooled the enemy also emerged during interrogations of Confederate prisoners. As a result, the navy proceeded with a preliminary bombardment, but five hours of shelling failed to reduce the position. Since the Grand Gulf batteries posed a major threat to any landing in the vicinity, Grant moved the operation farther downriver—and to a landing site he knew even less about.[15]

Although he lacked intelligence on enemy troop deployments below Vicksburg as well as Pemberton's movements, Grant transferred his army to a position opposite Rodney, Mississippi. His maps showed a good road stretching from Rodney to Port Gibson, a key position in the rear of Grand Gulf where the roads to Vicksburg and the state capital at Jackson converged. Capturing Port Gibson would force the evacuation of Grand Gulf and open the roads to both key towns. On the evening of April 29, however, a man familiar with the opposite shore arrived at army headquarters and revealed that a good road not found on any maps connected Bruinsburg, ten miles above Rodney, with Port Gibson. Without reconnoitering the area to verify the report or to ascertain if Confederate troops had arrived in the area, Grant—intent upon reaping the benefits of the initiative—decided to push on and cross to Bruinsburg.

Although the information proved correct, this episode underlines Grant's lack of foreknowledge about his operational area. No Union scouts, spies, or patrols had combed the east bank south of Vicksburg for possible landing sites or to locate enemy forces, although Grant later admitted that he fully expected the Grand Gulf garrison to "come out to meet us." Regardless, due to the lack of reconnaissance and operatives on the opposite bank, he found himself relying upon the word of a single civilian source as a foundation for this important decision. As this episode shows, Grant was not afraid to grasp opportunities and take risks even when faced with overwhelming uncertainty. At that moment, his faith in the initiative and in his *coup d'oeil* proved critical in defying doubts and providing the courage to press on.[16]

On April 30 McClernand's corps rushed ashore at Bruinsburg unopposed, secured the bluffs above town, and moved east toward Port Gibson. As Maj. Gen. John B. McPherson's corps landed the next day, McClernand's troops marched on Port Gibson and engaged the enemy in a fierce fight amidst rough terrain marked by heavily wooded ridges and cut by ravines carpeted with nearly impenetrable underbrush. Grant described this part of Mississippi as the "most broken and difficult to operate in I ever saw." Like his superior, McClernand possessed only fragmentary information as to the whereabouts of the enemy's main force. In fact, after attaining the bluffs above Bruinsburg, McClernand hoped to "surprise the enemy *if* he should be found in the neighborhood of Port Gibson." Confederate major general John S. Bowen did not disappoint his adversary and mounted a stubborn defense of the town. On May 2, however, the smaller Confederate force relinquished its position and retreated north across Big Bayou Pierre. The capture of Port Gibson neutralized Grand Gulf, leading to its evacuation a day later. Grant wired the happy news to Henry Halleck in Washington, boasting that the Bruinsburg crossing "undoubtedly took them much by surprise."[17]

Luckily for Grant, the deficiency of information on the enemy during the initial phases of the campaign was counterbalanced by his counterpart's mistakes and misjudgments. Pemberton's wishful thinking—that Grant would hammer away at the bluffs northeast of the city—colored his perceptions and slowed his reactions to seemingly obvious indications that the enemy had other plans. Not until May 1 did he fully comprehend the magnitude of his miscalculations and frantically recalled troops from as far away as Grenada, Meridian, and Port Hudson. By this time, however, it was too late to stem the tide of Union troops flowing across the river.[18]

After the battle at Port Gibson, Grant began his inland thrust. Instead of advancing directly upon Vicksburg, he chose an indirect approach. Realizing that bagging Pemberton's army meant more than capturing the town, he planned to cut his communications with Jackson, which connected Vicksburg with the rest of the Confederacy, and then prevent the garrison's escape. Cutting the Southern Railroad, destroying supplies at Jackson, and dispersing any relief forces gathering to the east would isolate Pemberton and leave him twisting in the wind. McClernand's and Sherman's corps moved toward Edward's Depot, a key stop on the Southern Railroad, while McPherson marched on Jackson. From the outset, Grant designed his movements to sow uncertainty in Pemberton's mind as to the true Federal objective. The key to success, especially deep in Confederate territory, was to maintain the initiative and make the enemy guess at his objectives. But the farther he moved inland, the more removed he became from Dodge's intelligence network and news about reinforcements coming from Tennessee. Disconcerting rumors of that nature already pressed on the army's timetable. On May 6, reports indicated that Bragg had sent reinforcements to Mississippi. This news, compounded by the inability to detect the whereabouts of these detachments, bedeviled the Federal commander, forcing him to faithfully rely upon the Army of the Cumberland in Nashville to keep Bragg occupied and prevent him from sending aid. "Should not Gen Rosecrans," he urged Halleck, "at least make a demonstration of advancing?" [19]

Procurement of intelligence on Pemberton's movements also proved difficult. Grant had sent most of the cavalry in with his advance, but the rugged terrain severely restricted their usefulness as a reconnaissance force.[20] In fact, many troopers spent the campaign delivering dispatches instead of gathering information. Nevertheless, Grant improvised. Robbed of their primary mission because the numerous hills and ravines impeded visual communications, the chief signal officer, Capt. J. W. DeFord, divided his men into four detachments, one for each corps and Grant's headquarters, and sent them on scouting missions. As a result, boasted DeFord, "each corps commander was kept well informed as to his own command and General Grant as to the whole army." Cavalry and Signal Corps scouts accounted for only a small portion of information received by Grant during the campaign, though. Judging from the journal kept by Lt. Col. James H. Wilson, the staff officer tasked with recording all the news arriving at headquarters, information gleaned from deserters, escaped slaves, civilians, newspapers, and intercepted mail accounted for most of the intelligence.[21]

By May 12, Grant's army occupied a line from Fourteen Mile Creek eastward toward Raymond, south of and parallel to the Vicksburg and Jackson Railroad. That day, McPherson's troops defeated a Confederate force at Raymond and sent it reeling toward Jackson. News of the victory reached Grant's headquarters later that night and, in conjunction with other information, helped him determine his next move. First, he concluded from several earlier reports that Pemberton had fortified and reinforced Edward's Depot, a key position east of the Big Black River along the Vicksburg and Jackson Railroad. According to one source, that was the point where "the rebels intend to make their big stand." [22] Convinced that Edward's Depot was "the point on the railroad the enemy have most prepared for receiving us," on May 13, Grant ordered McClernand to "keep up appearances of moving on that place" by advancing toward it. While McClernand kept Pemberton occupied, Grant hoped "to get possession of less guarded points first." Second, a local citizen claimed that Jefferson Davis told Pemberton "to hold the [Mississippi] river at all hazards and that re-enforcements would be sent from the East." Daily reports of Southern troops gravitating toward Mississippi seemingly verified this statement. On May 9 McPherson reported that reinforcements gathered from all over the South had reached Jackson. Two days later a captured letter from Edward's Depot boasted that a large contingent of troops from South Carolina, commanded by P. G. T. Beauregard, had reached the Big Black. [23]

Aware that Pemberton waited at Edward's Depot and fearful that thousands of Southern troops were en route to Mississippi, Grant quickly turned his army toward Jackson to smash the garrison there before it became too strong and to drive away any reinforcements lurking nearby. He then would turn toward Vicksburg. The night before the assault on the capital, a strange visitor arrived at headquarters. Charles S. Bell, formerly of the Nineteenth Illinois Infantry and now a spy for General Hurlbut, had just come from Jackson disguised as a Rebel staff officer. He told Grant that Gen. Joseph E. Johnston and two brigades had arrived to reinforce the town, with more on the way. At that moment, though, the garrison remained weak. If Grant attacked in the morning, Bell proclaimed, the Federals would meet with little opposition since only six thousand men occupied the defenses. The prospect of more reinforcements and Bell's extremely accurate estimate was what Grant needed to confirm his decision to strike on May 14. Although this move would expose his rear to the enemy posted at Edward's Depot, he gambled that

concerns for the safety of Vicksburg would keep Pemberton locked behind his fortifications.[24] Situated between two enemy armies and far
from his supply base, Grant's inland thrust had placed him in a dangerous position. If ever he needed luck or *coup d'oeil*, this was the moment.

After a sharp fight on May 14, Union troops captured Jackson, forcing
Johnston, who upon his arrival had assumed overall command of the
Mississippi Valley region, to evacuate the six-thousand-man garrison
and retreat north toward Canton. The night before the capital fell, Johnston had requested that Pemberton move east from Vicksburg in order
to "re-establish communications, that you may be re-enforced." He also
instructed his subordinate to attack the Union rear if practicable. To ensure its receipt, he sent the message by three separate couriers. One of
the dispatch bearers, probably Charles S. Bell, delivered Johnston's note
to McPherson, who promptly relayed it to headquarters.[25] When Grant
received the intercept on the evening of May 14, his fears of what Johnston would do outweighed his concerns about an attack from the rear.
Reflecting his belief that the Vicksburg garrison would not risk defeat
outside its Edward's Depot fortifications, a notion supported by a report
that Pemberton had abandoned Edward's Depot and retreated toward
Vicksburg, Grant focused on preventing Johnston from uniting with his
comrade. After surveying the situation, he concluded that Johnston intended to cross the Big Black farther upstream, connect with Pemberton's
command, and "beat us into Vicksburg." With Richmond undoubtedly
pressuring both generals to hold the Mississippi fortress at all costs,
Grant assumed that, once together, Pemberton and Johnston would retreat within Vicksburg's defenses and await a Federal attack, just as their
predecessors had done at Columbus and Fort Donelson. To ruin their
plans required swift action. "The enemy [Johnston] retreated north, evidently with the design of joining the Vicksburg forces," Grant wrote Halleck on May 15. "I am concentrating my forces at Bolton to cut them off
if possible."[26]

By nightfall of May 15, the Federals had seven divisions on three different roads converging against Edward's Depot. But new information
forced Grant to rethink his current assessment of enemy intentions.
From Bolton, McClernand informed Grant that "reports were rife that
the enemy were moving in strong force upon me" from the direction of
Edward's Depot. But not until early on May 16, when two railroad employees appeared, did Grant receive the evidence he needed. William

Hennessey and Peter McCardle had departed Vicksburg a few days earlier, and both had passed through Pemberton's army before entering Union lines. They claimed that most of the Vicksburg garrison, estimated at between twenty thousand and twenty-five thousand men, was advancing east from Edward's Depot to give battle. According to Fred Grant, who was with his father at the time, the general "seemed surprised at the news he received." Indeed, before Hennessey and McCardle arrived, Grant was focused upon preventing Pemberton and Johnston from uniting and then retreating into Vicksburg, not on receiving an attack. Besides, to believe Pemberton would attack in the open when he had strong works at Edward's Depot and Vicksburg went against Grant's expectations and previous experience. But instead of the two Confederate armies uniting west of the Big Black to defend the city, it now appeared as if Pemberton indeed planned to assail Grant's army east of the river. "I have just received information that the enemy has crossed Big Black with the entire Vicksburg force," Grant wrote to McPherson. "He was at Edward's Depot [Station] last night and still advancing." Armed with this information, which he acquired purely by luck, Grant recalled Sherman, who was scheduled to remain in Jackson one more day, and pushed west to meet the threat.[27]

Meanwhile, instead of marching to join Johnston or attack Grant's main force, Pemberton had marched south from Edward's Depot to attack Grant's communications with Grand Gulf. If successful, he reasoned, this expedition would seriously disrupt or even defeat the Union offensive. But Pemberton's southward march, when combined with Johnston's simultaneous northward retreat from Jackson, meant the two Confederate armies were moving in *opposite* directions. Johnston realized this on May 15 and ordered Pemberton to reverse course and move to Clinton, where he hoped his own Jackson army would be waiting. The order reached the Vicksburg commander, who had marched only six miles south of Edward's Depot, at 6:30 A.M. on May 16. Pemberton changed course and marched north toward the railroad. Once there, he would turn east toward Clinton. However, Johnston based his directive on the false belief that the bulk of Grant's army remained in Jackson; in fact, he worried that, if left alone for long, the Federals would erect fortifications and hold the town. By the time Pemberton received the order, though, Grant's lead elements had passed Bolton.[28]

Driven by the information brought by the two railroad employees,

Grant pushed on toward Edward's Depot to engage Pemberton, seemingly oblivious that this move exposed his rear to Johnston. According to Dodge, however, Grant knew much more about Johnston than he revealed. The same morning that Hennessey and McCardle arrived, a man named Sanburn, one of Dodge's scouts who had just left Johnston's army, arrived at headquarters. From Sanburn's description of the position and strength of Johnston's force, Grant concluded that the so-called Army of Relief remained too far away to help Pemberton. This meant that the Federals could either drive Pemberton back to Vicksburg and cut him off from Johnston or smash the garrison and take the river citadel before Johnston arrived. In that one critical morning, Grant acquired timely intelligence on both enemy armies, which led directly to Pemberton's defeat at Champion's Hill later that same day. After suffering another defeat at the Big Black River Bridge the following morning, Pemberton's army, minus Brig. Gen. William W. Loring's division, which had been cut off from the main body at Champion Hill and eventually joined Johnston, limped into the Vicksburg defenses with the Federals close behind. In the final analysis, Grant's arrival at the gates of this second "Gibraltar of the West" was the product of luck, initiative, and believing in the right intelligence at the right time.[29]

"The enemy have been so terribly beaten," Grant beamed on May 17, "that I cannot believe that a stand will be made unless the troops are relying on Johnstone [sic] arriving with large reinforcements." He dismissed this last possibility, however, believing instead that Johnston would not sacrifice his own command on such a venture, especially "if he was atal [sic] informed of the present condition of things." After chasing Pemberton into the defenses ringing Vicksburg and consequently brimming with confidence, Grant determined to take the city by force. On May 19 and 22, claiming that his men "believed they could carry the works in their front," Grant assaulted the Confederate works. Pemberton's men, proving that from behind stout fortifications even demoralized troops could mount a stubborn defense, repulsed both Union attacks and inflicted heavy casualties. Failing to capture the city by storm, Grant opted to starve the Vicksburg garrison into submission.[30]

With siege operations underway, the Federal commander turned his attention toward Johnston's army still lurking somewhere east of the Big Black. Relying upon Dodge and his own intelligence assets, Grant hoped to track that army's movements, detect any increases in its strength, and prevent it from relieving Vicksburg. By May 23, Union intelligence placed Johnston's force, estimated at eight thousand men, north of Jackson with reinforcements from throughout the South arriving daily. Though it posed a significant threat to Federal operations against Vicksburg, at this early stage of the siege Grant remained confident that the garrison would succumb within a few days, leading him to worry less about a rescue attempt. The Federals had also erected a logistical barrier between Johnston and Pemberton. With the countryside between Jackson and Vicksburg denuded of forage and supplies, the Confederates would find the distance difficult to traverse without encumbering themselves with a large wagon train. Sensing time was on his side, Grant expected Pemberton to concede before Johnston could find a way to save him. They might attempt a rescue mission, Grant mused, "but I do not see how they can do it." Nevertheless, he added, "I will keep a close watch on the enemy."[31]

As the siege continued, however, fears that Johnston and his Army of Relief might charge against the Federal rear whittled away at Grant's optimism, especially as more reports arrived about reinforcements pouring into Confederate camps at Canton. An attempt to raise the siege, Grant came to realize, was now the "greatest danger." Complaining of the lack of cavalry to "guard properly against this," he cast about for mounted units to perform reconnaissance duty, including a fruitless plea for the return of Grierson's command still with Banks at Port Hudson. The campaign had already worn down the small cavalry force at Grant's disposal, especially once siege operations commenced. Troopers spent much of their time carrying messages between officers along the extensive lines, a duty that exhausted both horses and men. This function absorbed so much of their time that Sherman called his cavalrymen "mounted orderlies." Grant's appeals for more cavalry went unanswered until three regiments arrived in mid-June. In the meantime, reconnaissance duty fell to the infantry.[32]

On May 26 Grant ordered Maj. Gen. Francis P. Blair with six brigades to drive out enemy troops and strip bare the peninsula between the Yazoo and Big Black Rivers, a natural avenue of approach to Vicksburg from the northeast known as the "Mechanicsburg Corridor." When Blair reached Mechanicsburg three days later, he reported encountering no enemy troops west of the Big Black and noted that all his sources agreed that Johnston remained at Canton collecting and organizing a force, which was predicted to reach forty-five thousand.[33] A force that size could cause Grant many headaches, and it became clear that he needed to be vigilant in watching for troops coming from Tennessee and elsewhere. Once again, primary responsibility for this mission fell to Grenville Dodge in Corinth.

As the Army of Relief kept Grant on edge, Dodge tried to ease his anxiety with information. In the month of June, he sent more operatives (twenty-six) into the field and spent more money ($5,110) on secret service than during any other month. In addition to sending men to watch the major Tennessee River crossings at Savannah and Hamburg in Tennessee and at Eastport in Alabama, Dodge instructed some operatives to monitor troop movements along the major railroads and roads in Mississippi, especially near Enterprise, Meridian, Jackson, Jacinto, and Rienzi. According to Dodge, this intelligence network provided enough coverage to spot Confederate reinforcements once they crossed into Mississippi. "[W]e kept a large number of spies in the rear of Vicksburg," his chief of staff recalled later, "and daily furnished General Grant with information concerning the movement of troops in Mississippi." [34]

Dodge realized the sooner he detected these transfers the better. To accomplish this, he assembled a corps of spies—known as his "principal outside scouts"—to watch the major railroads and roads used by Bragg to transfer reinforcements to Mississippi. Dodge posted these spies as far away as Georgia (Atlanta and Dalton), Alabama (Florence, Selma, Decatur, and Mobile), and Tennessee (Chattanooga and Columbia). These operatives, mostly Southern Unionists, sometimes reported in person, but many remained behind enemy lines and communicated through secret couriers. Once they reported, Dodge sent a summary to Maj. Gen. Richard Oglesby, who then forwarded it to Memphis. From there, Hurlbut relayed the substance to Grant via mail. In all, this process took five to ten days. Due to the urgent nature of some information, however, Dodge gave some spies the discretion to "go right in and try to get to General Grant at Vicksburg instead of coming to me." This was a very dangerous undertaking, as evidenced by the fact that at least two spies were killed making the attempt.[35]

Typically, Dodge paid scouts $50 for their services, but due to the long-term and more hazardous nature of their duties, spies earned between $250 and $500, depending upon the importance of the information they provided. One spy, for example, earned $500 for accompanying a Confederate division from Chattanooga to Selma and then scurrying to Corinth with the news. Though Dodge often referred to the spies as "his boys," several of them were in fact women. During the Vicksburg campaign, Mississippians Jane Featherstone and Mary Malone brought important intelligence from Jackson and Selma. Dodge valued the information provided be these—and other—women in his employ and felt a fatherly duty to protect them in this dangerous line of work. For example, when Confederate officials arrested Mary Mainard, another of his female operatives, Dodge implored Oglesby to let him rescue her. "She is an old hand [in] the business," he wrote, "and I am anxious to do something for her." Incredibly, he then suggested abducting a Confederate officer's wife and holding her hostage until the enemy released his spy. "I do not suppose," he wrote, "it is in exact accordance with the laws of war to take hostages . . . but I am willing to bring it on." No records indicate that Dodge pursued this course, and Mainard remained in jail until war's end. However, the episode reveals Dodge's willingness to undertake extreme measures to protect his operatives.[36]

But as Dodge's network grew to support Grant's intelligence needs, maintaining secrecy and protecting identities posed tremendous problems. In exasperation, he sent one scout back to Cairo "for fear of his betraying other scouts" because "he gets drunk & tells all he knows." The general also sidelined another operative because the enemy had captured him so many times that he had become "well known south of me." Dodge could only hope that his operatives followed the advice he gave his chief of scouts back in December: "All reports that they bring in will be immediately reported to me, and when sent on duty they will inform no person of the nature of the service. They will also keep as far as practicable aloof from anyone not connected with them and will not inform anyone of the nature of their employment. To be efficient they must keep their identity and business to themselves. They are too apt to retail their news to unauthorized persons and thereby become known, not only to our command, but to the enemy." Despite these warnings, Dodge struggled throughout his tenure at Corinth to plug potential leaks, protect the anonymity of his operatives, and maintain the integrity of his network.[37]

As Dodge spread his intelligence net across the South, his operatives began producing evidence that enemy troops were indeed en route to Johnston. Hurlbut reported on May 29 and 30 that, in addition to troops arriving from Port Hudson and Mobile, Bragg was sending 20,000 men—at least three divisions—to Mississippi. The following day Grant summarized his intelligence, much of which came from a civilian in Yazoo County interrogated by a Union patrol. Pemberton, Grant believed, had 18,000 in his command, an estimate that exceeded the true number by only 644. He also calculated Johnston's present strength to be between 20,000 and 25,000 men, of which he could identify only his original force at Jackson (8,000), Loring's division (3,000), a brigade from South Carolina (6,000), stragglers from Pemberton (2,000), and a force of unknown size from Mobile. Though small at present, Grant warned, Johnston would work tirelessly to raise at least 40,000 troops. "The enemy," he observed, "clearly perceive the importance of dislodging me at all hazards." What troubled him most, however, was the report of three divisions coming from Tennessee, especially since Rosecrans had given no sign of advancing against Bragg and forcing him to keep his army intact. Undoubtedly, this sizeable force, combined with troops already present in Canton and Vicksburg, would have a tremendous impact on Federal operations.[38]

Intelligence already in Grant's hands, had he known of it, might have eased his mind. On May 30, Union pickets captured several civilians attempting to smuggle two hundred thousand percussion caps and some official correspondence into Vicksburg, including a dispatch from Johnston discussing the size of the reinforcements from Bragg. But the message meant nothing to Grant because it was written in code and he had no cipher clerk on his staff. Annoyed, he sent it to the War Department for deciphering and not until mid-June did he finally see the plaintext message.[39]

Unable to read Johnston's mail, Grant turned to Corinth. On May 31 three of Dodge's spies—two of them women—returned from trips to Selma, Meridian, Jackson, and Mobile and reported that Johnston was "receiving reinforcement hourly" from Tennessee, Georgia, and South Carolina. Moreover, they estimated that Johnston commanded twenty thousand men and that only two divisions had left Bragg. As he telegraphed this information, Dodge added, "I think you can rely upon the above as correct [since they] all agree in main though coming from different directions."[40] Though Dodge's spies proved correct—Bragg had sent only two divisions to Johnston—as late as June 8, Grant still worried that one more was en route. Perhaps he remained wedded to this conclusion because much of his intelligence indicated that troops from across the South were arriving daily in Canton and that Johnston planned to move when he had enough. One such report came from a Union cavalry patrol that had reconnoitered the roads toward Jackson disguised as Confederates. From interviews with civilians along the way, they determined that Johnston had thus far collected eighteen thousand men at Canton and expected more every day. A talkative Confederate officer had volunteered that Johnston would not attack Grant until he had forty thousand men, a number he expected to attain in about ten days. As the siege wore on into June, Grant anxiously awaited that moment, calling for his own reinforcements that soon increased his own strength to seventy-seven thousand.[41]

Reports received during the first week of June revealed that the Army of Relief remained at Canton. But when the Rebel force moved, Grant predicted that it would probably come down the Mechanicsburg Corridor and attempt to "compel me to abandon the investment of the city." When news arrived on June 4 that enemy troops occupied Yazoo City, it appeared as if the Confederate had read his mind. A day earlier, Grant had dispatched an expedition under Brig. Gen. Nathan Kimball toward Mechanicsburg to collect "all possible information" on Johnston's forces at Canton. After receiving this new intelligence, he turned to Kimball for verification. Local residents informed the expedition commander that thirteen thousand Southern troops had indeed reached Yazoo City and that Johnston had at least forty thousand men under his command. All signs indicated that the Army of Relief was on the move, leading Kimball to retreat to Haynes' Bluff. At the same time, a deserter informed Grant that Johnston was "advancing from Canton to the Big Black with a large force." To check this story, he dispatched a cavalry patrol toward Mechanicsburg. Charles A. Dana, Secretary of War Edwin M. Stanton's representative at Army of the Tennessee headquarters, accompanied the reconnaissance and on June 8 reported that they had found "no signs of any considerable force of the enemy." Dana then concluded, "No doubt Johnston had moved some of his troops this side of the Big Black but his main force yet stays at Canton." Relieved, Grant accepted this assessment.[42]

Dodge's operatives had also produced important intelligence, including the discovery of the arrival of two divisions of Bragg's army in Canton; before this time, Grant feared that *three* divisions had left Tennessee. With the help of Dodge's scouts, he was now certain that only the two under John P. McCown and John C. Breckinridge had reached Mississippi. The discovery of these divisions illuminates the efficiency Dodge's network and why Grant trusted it. McCown's division (actually only two brigades) arrived in Canton on May 21. The day before, however, a spy just in from Chattanooga reported that a division had passed through "bound to Vicksburg" and that empty cars were en route to Tennessee, indicating that more detachments were on the way. On May 24 Breckinridge departed Bragg's army with about 5,200 men and arrived in Canton eight days later. On May 30 Dodge's scouts reported that a division had passed through Selma, noting that one of Breckinridge's staff members accompanied the troops. Spy J. T. Evans had actually tagged along with Breckinridge's column as far as Selma before slipping away to Corinth. Dodge's staff forwarded a summary of these reports to Memphis, along with other evidence collected by another scout named James H. Elkton, the day before Breckinridge reached Canton. As a result, Dodge stated that he was now "of the opinion that Breckinridge has joined [Johnston]." By June 11, Grant had correctly identified both divisions and estimated their size at 9,000 (the spies said 10,000) soldiers, which proved to be only 700 over the actual number. From the numbers provided in his June 11 summary, however, he apparently believed Johnston's force numbered around 35,000. But Dodge's men would have disagreed with this estimate; they had consistently placed the strength of the Army of Relief between 20,000 and 30,000 effectives. At that time, Johnston's rolls contained only 24,100 men. Impressed with the wide reach of the Corinth network, Grant proclaimed proudly that, because of Dodge, he now possessed "reliable information from the entire interior of the South."[43]

In the coming days, Grant would again learn that identifying the enemy's order of battle was far easier than speculating on his intentions. The same day that Grant issued his intelligence summary, Maj. Gen. Cadwallader C. Washburn, commanding at Haynes' Bluff, warned that most of Johnston's army had reportedly crossed the Big Black near Mechanicsburg. Over the next few days, other Union commanders from different sectors corroborated Washburn's report. After hearing this intelligence, as well as rumors that the Vicksburg garrison pinned all their hopes on Johnston, Grant sent Washburn to investigate on June 13.[44]

Two days later Washburn sent a spy known as "Mr. McBirney" to Grant's headquarters. Having just left Yazoo City, McBirney reported that two infantry divisions occupied Yazoo City. Though concerned, Grant concluded from this news that recent enemy movements did not indicate "an intention to attack Haines Bluff, immediately." Later in the day, however, Grant rushed troops to that area after hearing that Johnston had ordered the force at Yazoo City to advance while another division crossed the Big Black from Jackson. Though no attack transpired, by June 18 Grant still believed the Confederates were concentrating between the Yazoo and the Big Black to attack Haynes' Bluff. Only when more intelligence arrived purporting that Johnston had withdrawn his forces back across the Big Black did Grant breathe easier. Not until June 20 did he realize that he had been looking for an attack in the wrong direction. When Washburn reported on June 11 that a portion of Johnston's army had crossed the Big Black, he was partially correct. Confederate troops had indeed crossed the river but in the opposite direction. That day Johnston had withdrawn an infantry brigade from the corridor and was concentrating at Vernon for an attack on Grant using the lower crossings of the Big Black east of Vicksburg. By the time Grant learned of this shift on June 20, Johnston had changed his mind. News of large Federal reinforcements and strong Union defenses along the river led the Confederate general to abandon his attack and shelve his plans for future offensive action. Shortly thereafter, Johnston wrote Pemberton, "I am too weak to save Vicksburg." Save for some reconnaissances, the Army of Relief remained idle for the next two weeks, effectively sealing the fate of the Vicksburg garrison.[45]

At Federal headquarters, though, no one knew that Johnston had all but abandoned Pemberton. Grant believed that the enemy's withdrawal from the Mechanicsburg Corridor meant only that Johnston had determined to cross the Big Black from Jackson to either attack the siege lines or march to Port Hudson. On June 22 Dana announced that "Joe Johnston's plan is at last developed" after a large Confederate cavalry force drove away a Union patrol west of the Big Black at Bush's and Birdsong's Ferries, which indicated to many that Johnston was clearing the area in preparation for a crossing. Giving more weight to this interpretation was the operative Charles S. Bell. Upon his return from spying on Johnston's army, and after providing the general with the correct password ("rifle ranger") to authenticate his secret service credentials, Bell reported that the enemy troops in the Mechanicsburg Corridor had withdrawn to Canton and that at least three divisions were moving south from Vernon, indicating that a general advance was underway.[46] From this evidence Grant concluded, "There is now every probability of an attack from 'Johnston' within 48 hours" and predicted the enemy would cross the Big Black "above Bridgeport," probably at Bush's and Birdsong's Ferries. With the Army of Relief apparently on the move, he dispatched five brigades under Sherman to form a defensive line along Bear Creek while the remainder of the Army of the Tennessee continued the siege. In all, he redeployed nearly thirty-four thousand troops to halt this supposed advance. "His movements are mysterious," admitted Grant, but promised to "use every effort to learn any move Johnston may make."[47]

To learn more, Grant told Sherman to scour the area near the Big Black River for information. By June 27, Sherman had found "[n]ot a sound, syllable, or sign to indicate a purpose of crossing Big Black River toward us." Although cognizant that the enemy possessed "[e]very possible motive" to relieve Pemberton, the evidence convinced Sherman that Johnston was not even trying. Dana reached the same conclusion based on the evidence collected at Grant's headquarters. "The report [of June 22] that Joe Johnston had crossed the Big Black, . . . was erroneous," he wrote Stanton. "The siege goes on as usual."[48]

The day Sherman reported his findings, however, a Union spy fresh from Canton stated that Johnston was ready to move with thirty-five thousand men and planned to advance once some final reinforcements arrived from Bragg. Alarmed, Grant now concluded that the Army of Relief might attack his rear as early as July 1. Unknown to him, however, events in Tennessee had dramatically altered Johnston's situation in Mississippi. Rosecrans had finally lurched into action on June 23 and flanked Bragg's Tullahoma position, sending the Army of Tennessee retreating toward Chattanooga. Fleeing for his army's existence, Bragg had no troops to spare. Though unaware of these developments, when no attack came on July 1, Grant changed his tune. "Whether he will attack or not," he concluded, "I look upon now as doubtful." By that time, Union scouts had reported that Johnston's army remained in its camps at Canton, Vernon, Brownsville, and Bolton.[49]

The scouts, however, had missed something. On June 29 Johnston had marched his army toward the Big Black River crossings in a last ditch effort to divert Grant's attention and allow the Vicksburg garrison to escape. By July 5 he still lingered on the east bank pondering whether to cross north or south of the railroad. Before he could make up his mind, however, Pemberton surrendered; the Army of Relief had no one left to save.[50]

As Grant kept a careful eye on Johnston, he also monitored conditions behind the siege lines in Vicksburg. Deserters came in on a regular basis and provided insights into the state of the garrison's morale and estimates of when supplies would be exhausted. Those who reached Union lines between May 22 and July 4 consistently told of decreasing rations and gruesome tales of men reduced to eating pea-flour bread, rats, and mules. A spy employed by Admiral Porter left Vicksburg in mid-June and observed that insufficient food and hard labor had nearly exhausted both soldiers and civilians.[51] Others spoke of hospitals full of sick and malnourished soldiers and of low morale and near mutiny in the ranks. As early as June 28, some deserters predicted that food shortages and crumbling spirits would force a capitulation by July 4. Even as they ate rats and cursed the endless shells lobbed into the city by Grant's guns, many soldiers and civilians still pinned their hopes on their comrades across the Big Black. "Their principle faith," Grant observed in late June, "seems to be in Providence & Jo Johnston."[52] Unfortunately for the Confederacy, neither one showed up to save the beleaguered city. On Independence Day, Pemberton surrendered the river bastion and his army. After the fall of Port Hudson five days later, the Federals had at last reclaimed the Mississippi.

When Grant crossed to Bruinsburg on April 30, he knew little about the enemy or the terrain he would encounter. Nevertheless, he seized the initiative and shifted the burden of uncertainty to the Confederates by forcing them to react blindly to Union thrusts, increasing the likelihood that they might commit fatal errors. Well-executed deceptions also helped in this process. The character and judgment of his opponents, as well as Grant's experience in dealing with Confederates and their fortresses, also influenced his decisions. He refused to let gaps in intelligence enervate his campaign and instead concentrated upon moving ahead, letting the initiative span the breach. Once the siege of Vicksburg commenced, however, intelligence procurement became far more important, much as it had during the summer and fall when Union forces remained on the defensive in northern Mississippi. During the campaign, Grant showed that success was possible even without adequate intelligence as long as a commander maintained the offensive and refused to let inevitable uncertainty lead to paralysis. But he also demonstrated at times that there was no substitute for competent collection and use of information.

Despite winning the most important victory of his career thus far, Grant had little time to celebrate; Johnston's army still lurked across the Big Black River. Immediately following the surrender of Pemberton, Sherman went after this force in the hopes of bagging another trophy. Aware that Grant's entire army was now free to concentrate against him, Johnston scurried back to Jackson with Sherman close behind. After a week of inconclusive skirmishing, on July 16 the Virginian evacuated Jackson for the second time that season and retreated thirty-five miles east to Morton. Johnston's small army was now all that stood between the Federals and the resources of Alabama. And with the Mississippi in their grasp, Union forces in the West could now concentrate on capturing Chattanooga, the gateway to Atlanta. Now a major general in the U.S. Army as a result of his success, Grant looked forward to his next campaign, sensing that he would play a major role once again. As long as the war continued, he wrote at the time, "I do not expect to be still."[53]

"What Force the Enemy Have . . . I Have No Means of Judging Accurately"

After the fall of Vicksburg, Grant looked ahead to new challenges and toward ending the rebellion as quickly as possible. After solidifying the Union hold on the Mississippi Valley, Grant looked southeast toward Mobile, Alabama, as his next objective. Planning for that campaign ended abruptly, however, as events in Tennessee demanded his attention. In early July, Rosecrans had maneuvered Braxton Bragg's army out of Middle Tennessee and sent it reeling toward Chattanooga. Forced to evacuate that railroad town, Bragg retreated into northern Georgia while Rosecrans claimed the "Gateway of the Confederacy." On September 19–20, however, the Confederate Army of Tennessee, with help from Lt. Gen. James Longstreet's corps on loan from the Army of Northern Virginia, exacted revenge when it smashed Federal forces at Chickamauga and drove them back to Chattanooga. Occupying the heights overlooking the town, Bragg besieged Chattanooga and nearly severed the Army of the Cumberland's supply lines. With food stockpiles dwindling and both men and animals on reduced rations, the army faced starvation unless help arrived soon. Described by Lincoln as acting "confused and stunned like a duck hit on the head," Rosecrans appeared incapable of solving the logistical problem or dealing with Bragg. On October 18 Grant met Secretary of War Edwin Stanton in Louisville and accepted command of the newly created Military Division of the Mississippi, a vast geographic command comprised of the departments and armies of the Ohio, the Cumberland, and the Tennessee. Grant replaced Rosecrans with Maj. Gen. George H. Thomas and elevated William T. Sherman to head the Army of the Tennessee. And instead of only sending men and arms, Grant planned to direct the relief of Chattanooga in person. Not only did he hope to end the siege but he also foresaw an opportunity to accomplish much more. Atlanta, the biggest prize in the West, beckoned.[1]

Before reaching Chattanooga, Grant met with Rosecrans, and despite the animus between them dating back to the battle of Corinth, he recalled that his subordinate had made "some excellent suggestions" as to the next course of action. Apparently, however, Rosecrans failed to share the latest intelligence on the enemy. A few days after the meeting, Grant complained that he still knew little about the forces ringing Chattanooga. His only information came from deserters, whose knowledge was "limited to their own brigades or Divisions at furthest." This problem appears strange given the emphasis Rosecrans' had always placed on intelligence procurement. He had committed tremendous time, energy, and resources in creating an effective network. Rosecrans laid the foundation for Grenville Dodge's organization in Corinth, and in Nashville he had established the so-called Army Police, a comprehensive intelligence outfit under Col. William Truesdail, whose duties included information collection, counterintelligence, and investigations of disloyalty in the city. The information gathered by this organization, as well as from a myriad of other sources, formed the basis of Rosecrans' brilliant deception of Bragg during the Tullahoma campaign. Just two weeks before briefing Grant, Rosecrans' intelligence had also formulated an order of battle for the Army of Tennessee, which was fairly accurate and provided an estimate (although highly inflated) of its strength. Apparently, Grant never received such details.[2] Rosecrans' reticence led Grant to complain, "What force the enemy have . . . I have no means of judging accurately." Their recent movements also remained a mystery. "[F]or the last few days there seems to have been some moving of troops," he observed, "But where to I cannot tell." Without Dodge, who was still in Corinth and would soon be employed rebuilding the rail system between Nashville and Chattanooga, Grant was on his own.[3]

Having survived a harrowing journey over Walden's Ridge, traversing the same roads used to move supplies into Chattanooga, the new commander arrived on October 23, 1863. His recent passage left little doubt of the need for a more reliable means of supplying Thomas's army. After witnessing firsthand the ragged and starving condition of the Army of the Cumberland, Grant worked to relieve the suffering in preparation for commencing offensive operations. As one officer noted at that time, the army had but three options: "open the river, retreat, or starve." But Grant refused to abandon the town or to let his men starve. "Since Vicksburg fell this has become really the vital point of the rebellion," he asserted, and therefore "requires all the care and watchfulness that can be bestowed upon it."[4]

A plan to open a better supply line using the Tennessee River had already been approved by Rosecrans when Grant arrived. Brig. Gen. William F. "Baldy" Smith had devised a scheme for opening a "cracker line" by seizing Brown's Ferry, a crossing on the Tennessee two miles west of

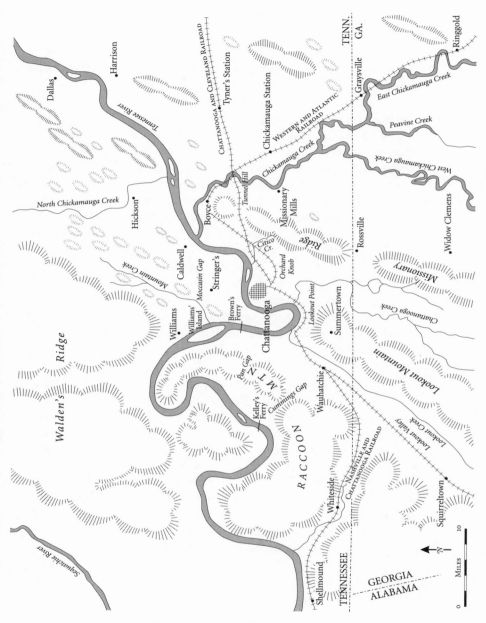

Harrison

Dallas

Tennessee River

Ringgold

TENN.
GA.

Graysville

East Chickamauga Creek

Peavine Creek

CHATTANOOGA AND CLEVELAND RAILROAD

Tyner's Station

Chickamauga Station

WESTERN AND ATLANTIC RAILROAD

Chickamauga Creek

West Chickamauga Creek

North Chickamauga Creek

Hickson

Tunnel Hill

Boyce

Missionary Mills

Rossville

Widow Clemens

Mountain Creek

Caldwell

Moccasin Gap

Stringer's

Citico Cr.

Orchard Knob

Missionary Ridge

Williams

Williams' Island

Brown's Ferry

Chattanooga

Lookout Point

Summertown

Chattanooga Creek

Walden's Ridge

Pen Gap

MTN.

Kelley's Ferry

Cummings Gap

Wauhatchie

Lookout Mountain

RACCOON

Lookout Valley Creek

NASHVILLE AND CHATTANOOGA RAILROAD

Whiteside

Squirreltown

Sequatchie River

Shellmound

TENNESSEE

GEORGIA

ALABAMA

N

MILES

10

0

Chattanooga and Environs

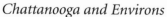

Chattanooga. Troops from Chattanooga would capture Brown's Ferry while Maj. Gen. Joseph H. Hooker marched from Bridgeport, Alabama, to secure Lookout Valley. After minor skirmishing at the ferry and an intense night-fight at Wauhatchie, by October 29, Union troops had achieved their goals. With these objectives secured, supply boats could unload at Brown's Ferry, only a short distance by wagon to Chattanooga. The "cracker line" was now open.

With his logistical problems abating, Grant turned to resuming the offensive. Geography presented one the more significant obstacles. Situated on the south bank of the Tennessee where the river curves toward the south, Chattanooga was dominated by several significant terrain features. To the southwest, Lookout Mountain, rising eighteen hundred feet above a sharp bend in the river, not only commanded the Tennessee but also Moccasin Point on the north bank and Lookout Valley to the west. Union lines lay within range of the Confederate guns posted along its steep, craggy heights. To the west stood Raccoon Mountain, which guarded other important approaches to the city. Four miles east of Lookout Mountain lay Missionary Ridge, with its countless wooded ravines, steep slopes, and heights that commanded Chattanooga. The ridge ran unbroken to the southeast until punctured by a gap at Rossville. On the northern end of Missionary Ridge, the key feature was Tunnel Hill, located just north of the Chattanooga and Cleveland Railroad tunnel and one of the highest elevations in the area. Unfortunately for the Federals, the Confederates held all of this high ground.[5]

Not only did the terrain and lack of knowledge about the enemy haunt Grant, other concerns plagued him as well. The situation in East Tennessee had become troublesome. Before Grant's arrival in Chattanooga, Maj. Gen. Ambrose Burnside had fulfilled the wishes of the Lincoln administration by driving Confederate forces out of predominantly Unionist East Tennessee and occupying Knoxville. But only time would tell whether Burnside's presence in the region would be an asset or a liability for Federal operations around Chattanooga. On October 26 it appeared as if Burnside might indeed become a burden. Reports indicated that troops from the Army of Northern Virginia were en route to Knoxville. Though Burnside discounted this report, he warned that Bragg had detached a sizable force to operate against Knoxville. When Grant learned of this development, he had received no intelligence indicating that enemy units had departed the Chattanooga area, even though Bragg had indeed sent Carter L. Stevenson's division and another under Frank Cheatham toward Knoxville (these were recalled soon after). Unable to determine whether enemy troops were moving from Chattanooga and Knoxville, the prospect was troubling. If true, then Bragg had the ability to transfer substantial forces to East Tennessee undetected by Union intelligence. On top of this, Lincoln was also pressing Grant to aid Burnside and help ensure that Unionists in East Tennessee remained under Federal protection. But the Army of the Cumberland remained unfit for offensive operations, limiting his ability to meet this requests. The whole situation, he later recalled, caused him "much uneasiness."[6]

Concerned that Bragg might advance on Knoxville and drive a wedge between the two Union armies, Grant anxiously awaited the chance to prevent it. Due to the condition of Thomas's army, and with Hooker maintaining the "cracker line," Grant waited eagerly for Sherman's forces, still on their way from Mississippi. By early November, however, nature and human error had combined to slow Sherman's progress. Until his trusted subordinate reached Chattanooga, Grant had little choice but to delay active operations. Despite hearing more reports of large forces being sent to threaten Knoxville, Grant hoped that, once Sherman arrived, "I will be able to make [Bragg] take a respectful distance South of us." Until that time, he planned to launch demonstrations both in Lookout Valley and against Missionary Ridge to force his adversary into recalling the troops sent to East Tennessee. By November 5, "Baldy" Smith had again formulated a plan to accomplish this end. He proposed that Thomas extend his picket lines on the left flank toward Citico Creek and then "threaten the seizure of the northwest extremity of Missionary Ridge." However, Grant leaned toward a cavalry raid on Bragg's communications in East Tennessee in conjunction with a demonstration up Lookout Valley. He was still convinced that Sherman's arrival was the key to future success and remained reluctant to use the Army of the Cumberland's exhausted troops unless absolutely necessary. "Whether Thomas makes any demonstration before [Sherman's] arrival," Grant advised Burnside, "will depend on the advices of the enemys movements."[7]

That "advice" was not long in coming. On November 6 Burnside's outposts came under attack. In addition, an officer who had deserted from a Georgia regiment brought Grant some potentially valuable information. According to Charles A. Dana, who was still attached to Grant's headquarters, the deserter disclosed that Stevenson's and Cheatham's divisions were already in East Tennessee and, more importantly, that Longstreet's corps had departed Bragg's lines on November 4–5 to join the operations against Burnside. Although incorrect in that those two divisions had already been recalled to Chattanooga, the information regarding Longstreet was accurate. When another deserter corroborated the Georgian's story, Grant decided to act. Believing the enemy had "moved a great part of their force from this front" to assail Burnside, he determined to "make an immediate move from here toward their lines of communication to bring [their detachments] back." On November 7 Grant ordered Thomas to attack the northern end of Missionary Ridge and, if successful, threaten or sever Bragg's communications between Dalton, Georgia, and Cleveland, Tennessee.[8]

Convinced his army was in no shape to carry out these instructions, Thomas appealed to "Baldy" Smith to "get that order for an advance countermanded." If the attack proceeded, Thomas warned, "I shall lose my army." After reconnoitering the area, Smith and Thomas found that Bragg's lines extended farther north than anyone realized, and they advised Grant that an attack was unwise. Reluctantly, he canceled the assault, noting later that this turn of events left him feeling "restless beyond any thing I had before experienced in this War." Once again, he was forced into a defensive posture because of problems beyond his control. As his past campaigns had revealed, Grant grew increasingly anxious when not possessing the initiative, reacting to what Horace Porter had called an "inborn dislike" for the defensive. Waiting for the enemy to act went against his nature. Experience had shown him that ceding the initiative placed the burden of uncertainty—and therefore the need for intelligence—squarely on his shoulders. And given the unreliability of intelligence gathering revealed during his tenure in Mississippi as well as the absence of Dodge, the additional weight could prove costly. With continuing pleas from Washington and Knoxville to relieve the pressure on East Tennessee, Grant wanted to do something—anything—rather than remain passive. The recent orders to Thomas demonstrated that he could make hasty decisions based upon very little information. He had sent Thomas against a position without reconnoitering the area or knowing how far north Bragg's right flank extended. In his official report and later in his memoirs, Grant placed the onus on Thomas for delaying this offensive operation but neglected to acknowledge that he had ordered the assault based primarily upon the word of two deserters against a position he knew little about.[9]

Frustrated, Grant anxiously awaited Sherman, who by November 15 had reached Chattanooga ahead of his troops. The next day, Grant, Sherman, Thomas, and Smith surveyed the ground and positions of both armies. Among other things, their reconnaissance revealed that the northern end of Missionary Ridge was "imperfectly guarded." That afternoon, the officers formulated a plan. It called upon Sherman to assail the northernmost end of Missionary Ridge and Thomas to engage the center of the line once the attack was underway. Hooker would threaten the enemy's left at Lookout Mountain and hopefully confuse Bragg. Like the plan of November 7, he hoped to dislodge the Confederates and drive a wedge between Bragg and Longstreet. To assure success, deception would play a key role. Grant had already sensed that Bragg "seem[ed] to be looking for an attack on his left flank." On the day of the reconnaissance, Elisha Breedlove, a scout for Thomas who had just returned from Lookout Mountain, seemed to confirm this when he noted, "They are expecting you every minute." Sensing an opportunity, Grant sent one of Sherman's divisions, led by Brig. Gen. Hugh Ewing, up Lookout Valley to reinforce Bragg's expectations. On November 18 Ewing advanced to Trenton and began gathering forage and building fake campfires, all to give the impression that his men were but "the head of a strong column, waiting for the rear to close up." Two days later his men withdrew. By confirming the conclusion Grant *believed* Bragg had reached, he hoped to force the Confederate's to weaken the Missionary Ridge line to meet the perceived threat on their left.[10]

By this time, Grant had shifted his purpose from merely forcing Bragg to recall troops to striking an Army of Tennessee weakened by substantial detachments to East Tennessee. He now believed Bragg had only thirty thousand men in the siege lines, an estimate over sixteen thousand too low. With the addition of Sherman, however, Grant would have over seventy thousand men. If the plan worked, he reasoned, he would send Bragg reeling into Georgia and force Longstreet to abandon his position around Knoxville. As was characteristic of his generalship, Grant saw an opportunity to do more than force Bragg to shift troops between fronts. Here was a chance to drive the Confederates out of Tennessee entirely. With the attack slated for November 21, all that remained was for Sherman's column to assume their positions. Once they did, Grant informed Halleck, "A battle or a falling back of the enemy is inevitable."[11]

But muddy roads slowed Sherman's progress and forced Grant to postpone the attack until November 23. More heavy rains and repairs to a broken pontoon bridge at Brown's Ferry caused further delays and forced Grant to suspend the assault another day. The enemy has "been able to send Longstreet off, before my eyes," he wrote in frustration, "and I have not been able to move a foot to stop his advance." Moreover, Grant had also concluded (erroneously) that Bragg had not been fooled by Ewing's diversion in Lookout Valley. This only added to his aggravation, making him even more anxious to get the attack underway.[12]

Early on November 23, two deserters wandered into Union lines, and what they said accelerated his plans. The men claimed that Bragg was retreating and that by evening all of the Confederates would be gone, save for a few pickets. Not only did they seemingly corroborate the testimony gleaned earlier from a captured enemy officer, their story appeared to make sense of the increased activity reported along the railroad in Bragg's rear and possibly also the heavy columns Union signalmen observed marching along Missionary Ridge toward the Confederate right. Adding weight to this interpretation, Brig. Gen. Jefferson C. Davis observed that the enemy camps nearest the Federal right flank appeared deserted. From these reports it appeared as if Bragg was indeed marching to join Longstreet. In fact, a note sent by Bragg under flag of truce three days earlier now took on new cast. Bragg had advised Grant to clear Chattanooga of all noncombatants. At the time this indicated a possible enemy attack. But after hearing the deserters' stories, Grant concluded that the Confederate commander wanted him to believe an attack was imminent to cover the withdrawal of his army toward Knoxville. Ever since Grant had arrived in Chattanooga, his chief fear was that idleness would allow Bragg to send enough reinforcements to enable Longstreet to defeat Burnside and reclaim East Tennessee. When the deserters brought news that seemed to substantiate this fear, therefore, he had little trouble believing it. Unwilling to stand by, Grant ordered the Army of the Cumberland to launch a reconnaissance in force against the center of Missionary Ridge to ascertain the "truth or falsity" of the deserters' reports.[13]

Thomas's demonstration on the afternoon of November 23 accomplished that and more. Long lines of Union troops advanced across the open plain east of Chattanooga in full view of the Confederates manning entrenchments at the base and along the crest of Missionary Ridge; Braxton Bragg even watched the martial display from his headquarters. Before long it was clear that the Army of Tennessee had not retreated. Nevertheless, Thomas's men pressed on and captured Orchard Knob, a small eminence over two thousand yards closer to the enemy lines. The ease with which the Federals overcame the defenses at Orchard Knob buoyed Grant's spirits and led him to conclude that, if Bragg was not retreating before, he surely would now. As Dana noted later that evening: "Nothing shows decisively whether [the] enemy will fight or fly. Grant thinks the latter."[14]

Before losing Orchard Knob, no withdrawal was in progress, a fact confirmed after the fighting by Confederate prisoners. The large body of troops observed by Union signalmen heading toward the Confederate right, a movement Grant believed indicated a general retreat, turned out to be only the divisions of Patrick Cleburne and Simon B. Buckner shifting to protect communications with Longstreet. In fact, Bragg sent them in response to the sudden appearance of Sherman's columns moving toward the Federal left.

As it turned out, the Confederate deserters who brought the news on November 23 had reported only camp rumors, a common occurrence during interrogations. Whether to impress their captors or in hope that their information might earn better treatment, deserters often conveyed rumors rather than remain silent. As Grant later noted, these men had not intentionally misinformed him but had only "mistaken Braggs movements."[15] The Federal commander often shied away from placing much stock in information from deserters because they rarely knew what was happening at the corps or army level. In this case, however, their stories fit with other pieces of intelligence indicating a general withdrawal. And given Grant's concern that Bragg might get away, the evidence meshed with his own perceptions of what the enemy would likely do given the current situation.

Contrary to Grant's hopes, the loss of Orchard Knob had not persuaded Bragg to retreat. His fortifications at the base and particularly along the crest of Missionary Ridge were formidable and would, the Southern commander believed, cost the Federals dearly if they attempted a direct assault. Ironically, the capture of Orchard Knob would have an adverse effect on later Union efforts to turn the Confederate right.

Thomas's victory convinced Bragg that the Missionary Ridge line was the main Union target and led him to transfer a division from Lookout Mountain to his right and recall Cleburne's command, which he placed in reserve behind the ridge. This would not be good news for Sherman. During his attack against the Confederate right on November 25, he found himself confronting Cleburne, one of the Confederacy's best soldiers leading one of its toughest divisions.[16]

Despite Thomas's gains and Grant's optimism that the enemy would probably retreat, the Southerners remained in their trenches on November 24. But recent Union movements befuddled Bragg. Two days earlier he had discovered what were believed to be Sherman's troops crossing the Tennessee into Chattanooga. In response, he shifted troops from his left flank to meet what he believed was a growing threat on his right. This left only two divisions for the defense of Lookout Mountain. Carter Stevenson, who commanded this force, complained that his position was "exceedingly weak" as a result and warned Bragg that, in his view, the Union activity on the Confederate right was merely a ruse to weaken the Lookout Mountain sector, the true Federal objective. On the evening of November 23, Stevenson sent Bragg a message transmitted by a signal detachment atop the mountain. "I observed closely the movements of the enemy until dark. [The] object seemed to be to attract our attention. . . . If they intend to attack, my opinion is it will be upon our left [i.e., Lookout Mountain]." Bragg, however, believed the Federals were focused upon Missionary Ridge and paid little attention to Stevenson's observations.[17]

Thomas, on the other hand, was greatly interested in what Stevenson had to say. Union signalmen had cracked the enemy's signal cipher, allowing them to read his message. When the deciphered message reached Grant, he misinterpreted it to mean that Bragg expected the main Federal attack to fall on Lookout Mountain. Earlier, Ewing's division in Lookout Valley had tried to foster this perception, but Grant concluded that Bragg had not taken the bait. Based on Stevenson's message, it now appeared that the Confederate commander indeed believed that his left was the primary target. To cultivate this mistaken belief in Bragg's mind, Grant sent Hooker to demonstrate against the Lookout Mountain defenses. At roughly the same time, Sherman's divisions, now in position, would cross the Tennessee below the mouth of South Chickamauga Creek and seize the north end of Missionary Ridge. Although Hooker's operation was designed to deceive Bragg into concentrating on his left while the main Union thrust fell upon his right, Grant wisely gave "Fighting Joe" permission to "take the point of Lookout if your demonstration develops its practicability."[18]

Unknown to the Federal commander, Thomas's advance the previous day had led the enemy to *weaken* his left flank, a move based upon Bragg's conviction that Lookout Mountain was not a primary Union objective despite Stevenson's warnings to the contrary. In the end, Bragg was right and Grant was wrong. But when Hooker's men seized Lookout Mountain on November 24, it no longer mattered. Similar to the unexpected success of the reconnaissance on November 23, Hooker's demonstration the following day, designed primarily to deceive Bragg, achieved a stunning success despite the flawed interpretation of intelligence and the misperceptions upon which it was based. On November 24 luck *and* Braxton Bragg worked in Grant's favor.[19]

While Hooker advanced on Lookout Mountain, Sherman's divisions crossed the Tennessee and seized what he thought was Tunnel Hill, the key to turning Bragg's right along Missionary Ridge. Due to Sherman's absence at the front, poor reconnaissance work, and faulty maps, by nightfall of November 24, his men had only reached Billy Goat Hill, another elevation just north of the true objective. This mistake, in conjunction with other problems, not the least of which was the fact that Cleburne's division soon moved to defend Tunnel Hill, would dramatically reduce Sherman's chances of seizing the northern end of Missionary Ridge.

The following day, as Sherman attempted to capture the correct height, Thomas's men sat idle, listening to the events unfolding northeast of their position. After Hooker's success and fearing that Bragg might have retreated during the night, Grant considered sending Thomas's men to probe the Confederate works at the base of Missionary Ridge to determine if they were still occupied. But by the morning of November 25, closer observation revealed that the enemy still manned the rifle pits, obviating the need for a demonstration. When Sherman resumed his assault on Bragg's right, Thomas maintained a threatening position in front of Missionary Ridge to prevent him from shifting troops from that sector to face Sherman. Grant also instructed Hooker to cross Chattanooga Valley, "carry the pass at Rossville, and operate against Bragg's left and rear."

Overall, he hoped to keep the Confederates occupied on all fronts until they were crushed between the forces on both flanks.[20]

On the morning of November 25, Grant observed Sherman's attack from his command post on Orchard Knob. Much to his chagrin, by mid-afternoon it appeared as if Bragg had successfully parried Sherman's attempt to envelop the Confederate right. More alarming was the apparent movement of enemy troops from the center toward Tunnel Hill. Grant saw this redeployment as disturbing evidence that Thomas's presence alone had failed to prevent Bragg from reinforcing his right. In reality, however, the troops seen heading toward the right had not come from the center of Missionary Ridge but from Lookout Mountain. After the loss of that prominent height, Bragg ordered Stevenson's command to help defend the right flank. Grant believed Bragg had weakened his center when, in reality, it remained as strong as ever.[21]

In response to this, Grant sent the Army of the Cumberland to demonstrate against Missionary Ridge to halt Confederate redeployments to their right. With orders to seize and hold the rifle pits at the base of the ridge with the sole purpose of relieving pressure on Sherman, Thomas's men embarked upon what would become a legendary assault in the annals of the Civil War. By this time, Sherman had already broken off his attack, and Hooker remained too far away to assist Thomas, whose men would be advancing against the strongest point of the Confederate defensive line, unsupported on either flank. It appeared to be a recipe for disaster. At that moment, as historian Wiley Sword has observed, it appeared as if "Grant had already been soundly beaten." Once again, luck—combined with the bravery and determination of the much-maligned Army of the Cumberland—saved the day.[22]

Thomas's men advanced toward the rifle pits, captured them, and then, on their own initiative, continued upward toward the crest of Missionary Ridge and into the teeth of the Confederate defenses. Although this spectacle caused Grant much distress because they were disobeying his orders to merely demonstrate against the lower rifle pits, the Midwesterners eventually breached the enemy's works, dislodged the defenders, and crushed the Confederate position, forcing the Army of Tennessee to fall back into Georgia. Bragg's decisive defeat and Grant's swift action in sending a portion of his victorious army toward East Tennessee also helped persuade Longstreet to abandon the siege of Knoxville. Except for the pounding Cleburne gave Hooker's pursuing troops during a rearguard action at Ringgold, Georgia, on November 27, Grant emerged victorious from Chattanooga in what would be his last western campaign.[23]

Several times during the Chattanooga operations, Grant had acted upon faulty information, misperceptions, and misinterpretations of evidence. But fortune had favored the Union commander. Perhaps John Rawlins reflected Grant's own philosophy regarding the role of chance in warfare. "Whether it be called luck or military ability to which is attributed General Grant's successes, I have but little care," he wrote. All that mattered was the end result.[24] In the final analysis, the key to Grant's victory remained his steadfast belief in the initiative and his willingness to risk defeat in order to achieve victory. Although intelligence certainly played a significant role, Grant demonstrated how even faulty information could be turned to advantage if one maintained the initiative and forced the enemy into making mistakes. If anything, Grant's conduct of the Chattanooga campaign revealed just how sweet the fruits of intelligence and luck could be if one was unafraid of taking risks.

The astounding victory at Chattanooga not only added luster to Grant's ascending star but it also earned him another one for his epaulettes. Congress rewarded him with the rank of lieutenant general in the regular army and gave him command of all Union armies. Opting to campaign in Virginia with the Army of the Potomac in the spring of 1864, he left the western theater with a three-year education in how to wage war successfully. He had also learned a tremendous amount about gathering and using intelligence. Although Chattanooga had not been his finest hour in this regard, Grant had learned through experience that it was indeed an essential—but not the only—element in warfare. Reliable intelligence was fleeting, and the search for "perfect" information could lead to the worst of all military sins: paralysis and the forfeiture of the initiative. As the Chattanooga campaign had demonstrated, as long as he retained the critical advantage of initiative, possessing imperfect intelligence could still lead to victory. Now it remained for Grant to apply what he had learned against his next and most formidable adversary—Robert E. Lee and the Army of Northern Virginia.

Chapter 8

"That Gives Just the Information I Wanted"

Echoing the sentiments of many in the North, on March 23, 1864, John A. Rawlins expressed hope that "our former success in the West will be with us here." The next day he accompanied Grant from Washington to his new headquarters at Culpeper Court House, Virginia, to plan the 1864 campaign. As general in chief, Grant could have remained in the West or stayed in Washington. But sensing that Lee deserved his undivided attention, he left Sherman to handle affairs in Georgia while he established headquarters with the Army of the Potomac, camped north of the Rapidan River in northern Virginia. Although he retained Maj. Gen. George G. Meade in direct command of the army, it was clear that Grant would oversee its future operations. On the south bank of the Rapidan, Gen. Robert E. Lee's Army of Northern Virginia—minus Longstreet's corps, which was still in northeastern Tennessee—prepared to give the new Union commander an introduction to the war in the East.[1]

Unconcerned with the past disasters in Virginia and shrugging off the aura of invincibility surrounding Lee's veterans, Grant approached the next campaign convinced that maintaining the initiative was a key to success, even though this meant taking risks against a seasoned and audacious opponent. According to his basic plan, all Federal armies would advance simultaneously to prevent the Confederacy from shifting troops from inactive to active fronts on interior lines as they had done with impunity in the past. "[T]he conquering of the organized armies of the enemy" was the primary goal, he stressed, not the acquisition of territory or strategic points. Two main thrusts comprised the centerpiece of the campaign. Sherman would advance toward Atlanta while Meade moved on Richmond, both aimed at smashing the opposing armies and preventing them from reinforcing each other. To support these major campaigns, Grant ordered Maj. Gen. Nathaniel Banks to capture Mobile and then move upon Montgomery, Alabama, and Maj. Gen. Franz Sigel to control the Shenandoah Valley and prevent Confederate forces in that region from reinforcing Lee.[2]

But the most important of these secondary campaigns was Maj. Gen. Benjamin F. Butler's advance up the James River to threaten Richmond from the east. Grant hoped Butler would seize the Confederate capital quickly since "that would tend more than anything else to break the

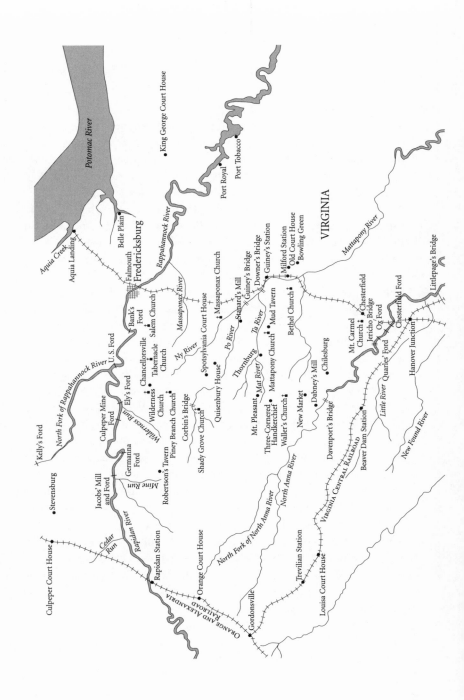

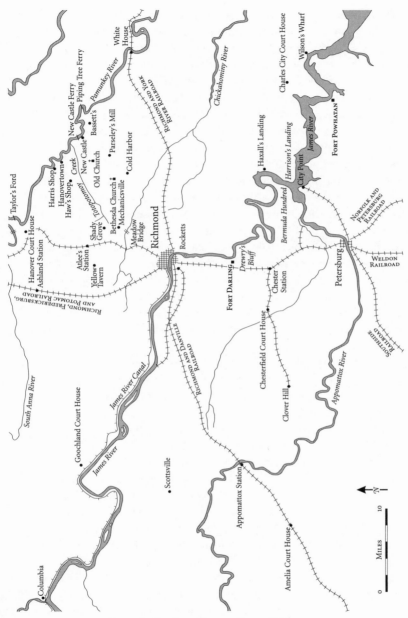

Grant's Spring Campaign of 1864

military power of the rebellion." By capturing the city or at least threatening the Army of Northern Virginia's railroad supply lines running through it, Butler's Army of the James would perform a valuable service. With Richmond in danger, Lee would have the choice of either reducing his own forces to defend the capital or transferring his entire army to save the city. If he chose that latter option, Grant planned to join Butler on the James and lay siege to the Confederate capital.[3]

After establishing these roles and objectives, Grant turned his attention to the Army of the Potomac. Burnside's Ninth Corps, fresh from the Knoxville campaign in East Tennessee, had arrived and came under Grant's personal direction. Though hoping Butler would accomplish great things on the Virginia Peninsula, the general in chief also anticipated his failure. Should Butler's advance proved ineffectual, "it was my determination, by hard fighting, either to compel Lee to retreat or to so cripple him that he could not detach a large force to go north and still retain enough for the defense of Richmond." Moving overland, Grant hoped to engage Lee in the open, avoiding entrenched positions, and maximize the numerical superiority of the Union army while still shielding Washington. To Meade he stressed that Lee's army—not Richmond—constituted the primary objective: "Wherever Lee goes there you will go also."[4]

The Army of the Potomac's future success depended in part upon Grant's ability to track the movements of Lee's army, something previous commanders had found exceedingly difficult. In the beginning, he too struggled with this task. Shortly after arriving in Culpeper, Rawlins complained: "No information comes from the enemy's lines," which was "greatly different . . . from what it was out West." Back there, "we were always getting some information that kept up an excitement and made it seem that we were doing something."[5] Before long, however, Meade was making frequent visits to Grant's headquarters armed with the latest information provided by an organization devoted solely to that mission.

In early 1863, Maj. Gen. Joseph Hooker, then commander of the Army of the Potomac, had created the "Bureau of Military Information" (BMI) within the army's Provost Marshal General's Department. Under the guidance of Col. George H. Sharpe, deputy provost marshal and former attorney from New York, the bureau blossomed into an "all source" intelligence service that procured information from a wide array of sources and then provided timely analyses of it. Sharpe's chief subordinate, civil-

ian John C. Babcock, had served in Allan Pinkerton's "detective" service
under McClellan's command and brought valuable experience to the
BMI. An accomplished architect from Chicago, Babcock reveled in "the
business," telling his aunt in 1862, "There is probably nothing for which
I am in every way so well qualified to perform, as the duties that have
devolved upon me during my connection with the Secret Service." Babcock sketched information maps, kept BMI records, and prepared reports. More importantly, he became Sharpe's chief interrogator, a position of critical importance for the bureau's mission, and used his vast
knowledge of the organization and composition of the Army of Northern Virginia—known today as "order of battle" intelligence—to elicit
information from captives and find the truth amidst lies and attempts at
deception.[6] Babcock also compiled order-of-battle charts, which he updated periodically, and distributed them to corps commanders. From
this chart Babcock fashioned estimates of enemy strength that, on occasion, proved unbelievably accurate. For example, before the battle of
Chancellorsville in May 1863, Babcock estimated Lee's strength at 55,300
men, a figure within 2 percent of the official number.[7]

As the activities of the BMI (also called the "secret service") increased,
Sharpe alleviated Babcock's workload by adding Capt. John McEntee
to the staff. Formerly an officer in the Twentieth New York Infantry,
McEntee joined the BMI in April 1863 and undertook multiple tasks, including organizing scouting operations, writing reports, and conducting
interrogations. Sharpe also tasked him with establishing BMI "branch offices" in other sectors of the Virginia theater. By April 1864, Sharpe had
personnel at Harpers Ferry and with the Army of the James. McEntee
would become an integral part of BMI operations and play a key role in
one of Grant's most serious intelligence failures.[8]

Compared to Grenville Dodge's network, Sharpe's organization focused on a much smaller theater of operations and primarily upon one
enemy army. Not an ad hoc organization overseen by a single individual
operating many miles from the front, the BMI had a permanent staff that
traveled with Army of the Potomac headquarters and, though officially
part of Brig. Gen. Marsena R. Patrick's provost marshal's department,
Sharpe reported directly to Meade. This meant the commander had immediate access to information collected by the BMI staff, could personally
question personnel about assessments, and even make special requests.
Like Dodge, Sharpe would cultivate contacts behind enemy lines and em-

ployed Virginia Unionists as spies, including many who worked for underground organizations operating within Richmond. BMI scouts, most of them noncommissioned officers and enlisted men such as veterans Philip Carney of the Fifth New York Cavalry and Milton Cline of the Third Indiana Cavalry, also ventured into the no man's land between enemy lines in search of information and to meet with messengers coming out of Richmond.[9]

Though the BMI employed numerous scouts and spies and gained valuable information from these informants, the staff spent more time gleaning information from predominantly passive sources, something Dodge did not pursue as avidly. Significant news emerged from systematic interrogations of refugees, "contrabands" (former slaves), and especially from enemy deserters and prisoners. At a minimum, every captive in uniform was asked to identify his regiment, brigade, division, and corps; when and where he entered the lines; the location of his corps and when it arrived on the front; how he was captured or why he deserted; and other questions depending upon the kind of information needed.[10] From this the bureau assembled an impressive order of battle for the Army of Northern Virginia, allowing them to monitor enemy movements and, given Lee's penchant for splitting his army, determine the size of detachments. "We are entirely familiar with the organization of the rebel forces in Virginia and North Carolina," Sharpe boasted in late 1863. From the accumulation of reports from prisoners and deserters, the BMI became acquainted "with each regiment, brigade, and division, with the changes therein, and [with] their officers and locations." By early 1864, therefore, Sharpe felt "the state of our information has been such as to form a standard of credibility by which these men were gauged, while each was adding to the general sum."[11]

Deserters were often more forthcoming than prisoners captured in action because they had voluntarily abandoned their comrades and had little reluctance to tell all they knew. Even if reticent to impart information, few suspected that a mere regimental or brigade designation could prove valuable to their captors. Union authorities tried hard to lure Southerners to desert their posts and pledge fealty to the Union with offers of employment and, if their homes were within Union lines, passes to travel the military railroads. By February 1864 these inducements had become official policy aimed at slowly eroding Confederate manpower from within. Given the efforts made to lure his soldiers away, Lee recognized that deserters and prisoners could become a serious information hemorrhage. In a circular issued a month before the 1864 campaign began, he advised those men who might fall into enemy hands to "preserve entire silence with regard to everything connected with the army, the positions, movements, organizations, or probable strength of any portion of it." Knowing the importance of order-of-battle intelligence, Lee also urged his commanders to instruct their men "not to disclose the brigade, division, or corps to which they belong." He implored that "[p]roper prudence on the part of all will be of great assistance in preserving that secrecy so essential to success." Judging by the number of captives interrogated by the BMI and the amount of detailed information extracted from them, Lee's exhortation did little to plug this critical leak.[12]

Deserters could also provide a barometer of enemy morale, especially if they left the ranks in droves. Even so, interrogators had to handle the information they provided with care. Given his means of escaping service, a deserter was likely one of the most disheartened soldiers in the Southern ranks, meaning that his story of rampant privation and universal low morale might not be a true reflection of reality. He might claim that everyone in his unit would also desert if given the chance in order to assuage his guilt over abandoning his comrades. Some deserters remained silent. Many knew little more than current camp gossip and rumors, while others embellished their responses in the hopes of receiving special treatment. A story that caused a stir might win extra food, a blanket, or even new shoes from an appreciative captor. Seasoned interrogators, however, could detect such deception. Sharpe dismissed one such tale as merely "one of those devices, which I have so often detected in deserters, to add to their consequences, and the supposed value of their information."[13]

Frightened and disoriented, prisoners captured in action might also be cooperative to obtain better treatment. They might also strut about boastful and defiant. In either case, the BMI interrogators treated their testimony with care so as not to mistake bluster or embellishment for the truth. Sometimes they refused to cooperate. In those cases, Sharpe was not above resorting to torture to loosen tongues. When McEntee suspected one prisoner of giving suspicious information, he tied him up by the thumbs. This method not only failed to convince the man of his transgression but it also unhinged him. "I think it useless to abuse this man [further]," he wrote, since we "had him tortured here and it made a perfect lunatic of him for twenty-four hours."[14] However they extracted information, both interrogator and commander had to remain wary of believing what they wanted to hear from captives. Though Grant often complained that prisoners and deserters could only "tell of their own Brigades and Divisions at furthest," on occasion he failed to heed his own warning and readily swallowed stories that harmonized with his own preconceptions.

Along with information derived from these sources, the BMI collected information from cavalry reconnaissances, visual observations, signal intercepts, and captured correspondence. Due to their value at shedding light on military, economic, and political matters in the Confederacy, as well as for highlighting living conditions in Richmond and elsewhere in the South, enemy newspapers became an important source, and the BMI placed a premium on acquiring them. The bureau staff then collated, analyzed, and condensed this mass of information from a variety of sources, presenting the product in a daily written summary to the army commander.[15] These summaries provided not raw information but the product of careful analysis. Sharpe based the worth of information on both its own merits and an evaluation of the source. Sprinkled throughout his reports are phrases such as "they are honest looking, intelligent men," "he is honest but not intelligent," "informant is certain of this and has opportunities of knowing it," and "they are bad men ... and are not to be trusted." Using the BMI's accumulated knowledge of Lee's army, Sharpe felt confident his men could separate truth from fiction during interrogations. To determine the credibility of a captive and his story, his staff assessed: "the truth of the general story told by the prisoners and deserters; the circumstances of their capture; the locations in which their commands were raised; the corroborative statements of other prisoners from the same commands, sometimes made before and sometimes after capture; [and] their conduct and declarations at the time of coming in or capture compared with their present frame of mind." This intensive examination also uncovered Union soldiers who disguised themselves as Confederate deserters to avoid further service. As a result of the BMI's all-source capability, constant search for corroboration, and intensive source assessment, Meade and Grant received not an assemblage of undigested bits of news seemingly of equal weight but true intelligence, the finished product of systematic information analysis. Though the BMI would become more sophisticated and efficient than Dodge's network, Grant would not fully utilize its services during the campaign from the Rapidan to Petersburg. By midsummer, however, as the war in Virginia lapsed into a protracted siege, Sharpe and his men would play a key role in Grant's eventual success.[16]

As the spring campaign season approached, Grant faced two key intelligence problems. First, he had to watch for the movement of Southern troops toward the Rapidan front, especially Longstreet's corps rumored to be returning to Virginia from East Tennessee. Second, he had to decide upon the direction of Meade's advance. Wishing to avoid Lee's formidable entrenchments along Mine Run south of the Rapidan, Grant chose to outflank his opponent and force him to either fight or retreat. But whether to target Lee's left (west) or his right (east) flank remained unanswered as the weather warmed and the roads dried.[17]

The BMI proved instrumental in solving the first intelligence puzzle. The future plans of Longstreet's First Corps, which had wintered in East Tennessee after abandoning the siege of Knoxville, caused concern at army headquarters. Not only would the return of Longstreet's men significantly augment Confederate numbers along the Rapidan, but their return to the Army of Northern Virginia would also bring back Lee's "Old War Horse," whose presence would be invaluable to him. In early April 1864, the War Department informed Grant that Longstreet planned to invade Kentucky. Although he warned Sherman of this possibility, before long it appeared as if Longstreet would return to Virginia. Whether he would rejoin Lee below the Rapidan or head somewhere else remained a mystery.

By April 25 the BMI knew that Longstreet had reached Charlottesville. This information came from deserters and prisoners who heard it mentioned in camp and from others who witnessed firsthand the arrival of the columns. It soon emerged, however, that these troops were not destined for the Rapidan. Instead, Sharpe reported that the "old man," the sobriquet of Isaac Silver, a farmer from the Fredericksburg area and longtime spy for the BMI, predicted that Longstreet would march north down the Shenandoah Valley and outflank Grant at Culpeper. According to the agent, when Longstreet advanced, Lee would "open on the Union army" across the Rapidan.[18] The following day a Confederate deserter corroborated this news, adding that troops under Gen. P. G. T. Beauregard, lately in Charleston, South Carolina, were slated to join the First

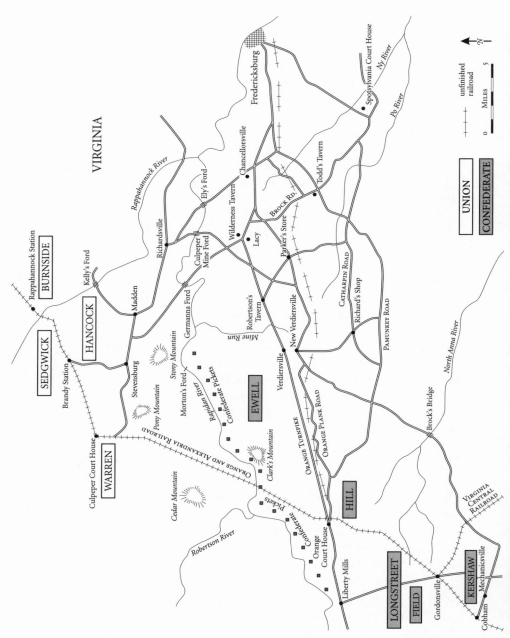

The Rapidan Front

Corps in its flanking maneuver. These reports squared with earlier news of Confederate forces concentrating in the valley to screen what Grant believed must be "a formidable movement of the enemy by that route, northward." The general in chief had not yet decided upon a date to launch his first Virginia offensive but now worried that Lee might move first. "Dont know exactly the day when I will start," he wrote on April 27, "or whether Lee will come here before I am ready to move." Fearful of losing the initiative and jolted by this recent intelligence, Grant promptly set a firm date for the commencement of the campaign. The next day he announced that the Army of the Potomac would cross the Rapidan on May 4.[19]

By April 29 the BMI had a better fix on Lee's "Old War Horse." McEntee, on assignment with Franz Sigel's valley command, telegraphed Sharpe that Longstreet's corps was camped "in the neighborhood of Gordonsville in easy supporting distance of Lee." That very day, in fact, Lee had traveled to Gordonsville to review the First Corps and welcome home his trusted subordinate.[20] After McEntee's telegram, Grant's concern for Longstreet dissipated. He now knew that Lee had reunited his army; all that remained was to discern what he planned to do with it. On April 30 a report crossed his desk that seemingly addressed that issue. A Confederate captain captured in Baltimore had provided the War Department a detailed description of Lee's organization and plans. According to this officer, Lee intended to send two of his corps against the Union right at Culpeper Court House. Other explicit details, including that Lee planned to invade Pennsylvania again, prompted Secretary of War Edwin Stanton to forward the captain's statement to army headquarters with an offer to send the prisoner if the general in chief needed to question him in person. Though promising to be vigilant, Grant placed little stock in the report and told Stanton to keep the captain in Washington. Always one to keep his cards close to his vest, he expected an opponent of Lee's caliber to do likewise. "I do not place great reliance on the information," he told Stanton, "because I do not see how an officer of that ran[k] comes to know so much of future plans."[21] Now, Grant's focus shifted more toward solving his second intelligence problem.

By the time he located Longstreet, barely five days remained before the scheduled opening of his own campaign. But Grant had yet to decide whether to move by Lee's right or left flank. The main objective was to flush Lee out of his works and force him into battle on open ground in order to maximize the numerical advantage held by the Army of the Potomac. But each route posed significant disadvantages along with its advantages. Though the left flank option promised an abundance of open expanses more suitable for combined arms and large-scale maneuvers, pursuing that alternative meant relying upon tenuous overland supply lines. The right flank, however, offered easy access to supplies brought up the navigable rivers off Chesapeake Bay. Perhaps remembering the disaster at Holly Springs in 1862, Grant hoped to avoid dependence upon vulnerable lines of communication that, if cut, could sink yet another campaign. Moving around Lee's right flank would also enable Grant to maintain contact with Butler and expedite the junction of the two armies outside Richmond.[22] At last, he decided upon the right flank option. His plan was simple: cross the Rapidan at Germanna and Ely's Fords, march south into a dense area of tangled second-growth forest known as "the Wilderness," turn Lee's eastern flank, and force him to fight in the open. But timing was critical; the army had to plow through the dense thickets of the Wilderness quickly, not only to flank the Confederates but also to reach more open, maneuverable ground farther south. To get caught in that nearly impenetrable expanse using a very limited road network would neutralize Grant's numerical advantage and lead to a blind fight. Logistical concerns and the desire to link with Butler's forces advancing up the James, however, were the key factors behind this choice.

But information from the BMI and past experience also informed Grant's decision. In February a Union force crossed the Rapidan and assaulted the Confederate position at Morton's Ford, a key crossing on Lee's extreme right. Though the attack met disaster, the affair revealed to Lee the need to strengthen his defenses at the fords. Intelligence received in April began to confirm this buildup but also revealed other promising developments. On April 14 a BMI scout reported that the only fords protected by significant fortifications were Raccoon, Somerville, and Morton's. Eight days later another scout confirmed this, stating, "work has recently been done about Morton's Ford and the fords above." But, he added, "nothing is believed to have been done at Culpeper or Germanna Fords, or the fords upon the Rapidan below [including Ely's Ford]." Added to this was the location of Longstreet's corps, which by April 25 was known to be at Gordonsville. The First Corps occupied a perfect position from which to support Lee's left. To reinforce the right would take more time. The vulnerability of the lower fords, the location of Longstreet behind the opposite flank, and the experience from November's Mine Run campaign, where Lee took over thirty hours to assemble a defense of his right, all supported the decision to move around the enemy's eastern flank.

Planning the movement fell to Meade's chief of staff, Maj. Gen. Andrew A. Humphreys. His plan rested in part upon Lee's response to the Federal advance across the Rapidan the previous November. At that time, Meade had crossed the river and moved west toward the Confederate defenses along Mine Run. Lee reacted slowly and cautiously, taking over a day to develop the strength of the Union advance. Deciding against an attack in the Wilderness, he instead retreated behind prepared defenses at Mine Run and dared Meade to come after him. The Federal commander, however, withdrew rather than smash his army needlessly against strong fortifications. Using Lee's earlier reactions as a guide, Humphreys developed a plan whose success hinged upon the ability of the Army of the Potomac to cross the Rapidan undetected, drive rapidly through the Wilderness to the south, and turn the right flank of Lee's Rapidan defenses. The Federals would then turn westward and get below the Confederate's Mine Run fortifications, forcing Lee into the open and, due to his smaller size, to either retreat or fight at a disadvantage. The key was to steal a march on Lee and get through the Wilderness before the Confederate commander could intercept the Federal columns in the thickets.[23]

Although Humphreys relied upon past enemy behavior and knowledge of the disposition of Lee's individual corps to formulate the plan, it seems that Grant had made the momentous decision to advance against Lee's right without such knowledge. Concerned mostly with logistics, maintaining contact with Butler, and gaining the initiative, Grant himself gave little thought to his opponent's intentions or possible responses, even though fully aware of Lee's capacity for celerity and boldness. In addition, his maps of the region were simply inadequate. During the winter, Meade's engineers had created and distributed updated maps based on old surveys and reconnaissances made by topographers. The chief engineer complained that these provided "little of that detailed information so necessary" for planning a campaign and "were too decidedly deficient in accuracy and detail to enable a general to maneuver with certainty his troops in the face of a brave and watchful enemy." (So troublesome were these maps that one of Meade's staff later wrote an article about them entitled "Uselessness of the Maps Furnished to Staff of the Army of the Potomac Previous to the Campaign of May, 1864.") To make matters worse, Union officers had trouble finding trustworthy guides familiar with the south bank and the Wilderness. In addition, probably neither Grant nor Meade sent cavalry to reconnoiter the area of operations. The absence of sufficient cavalry to perform these reconnaissance missions likely factored into this oversight. During the crossing on May 4, two-thirds of Sheridan's cavalry corps remained behind guarding the army's long supply train instead of probing for the enemy ahead of the infantry. The remaining division screened the army's movement but performed poorly when called upon for reconnaissance duty. The nature of the terrain only compounded these difficulties. Thus, when Meade discovered Confederate troops advancing toward the Union column on May 5, this warning came from his infantry, not his mounted arm. Before the campaign, a few of the BMI scouts and spies provided intelligence pertaining to the area south of the Rapidan. But these operatives rarely went beyond assessments of fortifications protecting certain fords, the strength of the Mine Run defenses, and Longstreet's latest whereabouts. Given the limits of Grant's knowledge regarding the future area of operations, it appeared as if he intended to plunge blindly into the Wilderness, hoping to win a footrace with Lee to more maneuverable ground. Beyond this, he planned to wait and see what happened. "My own notions about our line of march are entirely made up," Grant told Chief of Staff Henry Halleck, because "circumstances beyond my controll may change them."[24]

This does not mean, however, that he forged ahead without thinking through the possible problems and choices he might face. "[B]eing within a few miles of the enemy we had to condend [sic] against," he wrote later, "no orders were necessary further than for the first movement" across the river.[25] This statement illuminated a key element driving Grant's plan. He was aware that Lee's army—including Longstreet— lay just across the river. What more did he need to know? No amount of detailed intelligence would change that basic fact. Simply put, if the Army of the Potomac advanced first, Lee would have little choice but to respond and perhaps fight at a serious disadvantage. To make George B. McClellan's mistake of delaying action until possessing "perfect" intelligence on the enemy would not only lose time but also the initiative, and Grant was already fearful that Lee might beat him to the punch. Moreover, it would be unlike his adversary to wait for the Federals, for he too understood the importance of striking first. In any event, the endgame for Grant was not the capture of strategic points but the destruction of Lee's army, and he could achieve this in one of two ways. He could fight him on open ground or in the Wilderness, or perhaps force him to retreat. Even if Lee withdrew, Grant understood that it would only delay the inevitable. To prevail in this war, the military might of the Confederacy had to be destroyed. At some point, therefore, Grant would have to stand toe to toe with Lee and beat him, regardless of the circumstances. Nothing short of this would guarantee the death of the rebellion. And after the Federal army descended into the Wilderness, Grant revealed this was precisely what he had in mind.

On the morning of May 4, Union signal-corps personnel on Stony Mountain intercepted and successfully deciphered several Confederate messages. One in particular indicated that instead of retreating, Lee was rushing troops toward the Federal columns lapping around his flank. A staff officer noted that Grant "manifested considerable satisfaction" upon receiving this news. "That gives just the information I wanted," he was heard to exclaim. "It shows that Lee is drawing out from his position, and is pushing across to meet us." But whether he would retreat, attack the Federals in the Wilderness, or like the previous November wait behind his Mine Run fortifications remained unknown. Lack of cavalry and unfamiliarity with the area only exacerbated this mystery. But the Army of the Potomac pressed on, its soldiers unaware that to the west Lee's veterans were on a collision course. "Forty-eight hours," Grant predicted confidently, "will demonstrate whether the enemy intends giving battle this side of Richmond." [26]

The following day, Lee delivered his answer. Meade notified Grant at 7:30 A.M. that enemy infantry had appeared in battle lines on the Orange Turnpike, one of the major east-west roads between Lee's camps and the Wilderness. Even though fighting in the tangled thickets would negate Union superiority in men and artillery, not to mention interrupt Humphreys precious timetable to envelop Lee's flank, the ever-flexible Grant recognized that "circumstances beyond his controll" had forced a revision. He turned to meet the enemy. "If any opportunity presents [it]self for pitching into a part of Lee's Army," he told Meade, "do so." If Lee wanted a fight, Grant was more than willing to oblige.[27]

Years later, Grant summarized the guiding rationale behind this perspective. "[T]he armies now confronting each other had already been in deadly conflict for . . . three years," he wrote, "and neither had made any real progress toward accomplishing the final end." By 1864 the war had become a standoff, and neither army "knew which could whip." He saw the 1864 campaign as the only way to break the stalemate and win the war. But, he noted soberly, "We had to have hard fighting to achieve this." Sherman also understood why Grant had to engage Lee's veterans. Only in combat could his friend "impress the Virginians with the knowledge that the Yankees can and will fight." The strategy's psychological impact on both armies, he concluded, would "do more good than to capture Richmond."[28]

Plenty of hard fighting awaited Grant's men as they descended into the dark Wilderness. During May 5–6, the Army of the Potomac battled Lee's army, resulting in over twenty-five thousand casualties. But when the firing ceased the stalemate remained. Still sanguine in the inevitability of Union success, Grant informed Halleck that "all things are progressing favorably." Instead of retreating, he resolved to maintain the initiative and deny Lee any chance to gain the upper hand as he had at Second Bull Run and Chancellorsville.[29] In Grant's mind, as long as the Army of the Potomac kept advancing, any battle was a victory.

Early on May 7, Grant knew very little about the enemy's position, movements, or intentions. His aide Adam Badeau recalled that during this critical time the general experienced "anxiety in regard to the enemy's movements." One of Meade's staff officers also sensed the uncertainty hanging like a cloud over the Union command as a result of this information shortage. "[I]t would be hard to say what opinion was most held in regard to the enemy," he wrote, "whether they would attack, or stand still; whether they were on our flanks, or trying to get in our rear, or simply in our front." This situation frayed nerves and tested resolve. Grant listened to a panicky officer predict that Lee's boldness and unpredictability would surely result in another humiliating defeat for the Army of the Potomac. Bristling at this suggestion, the general in chief snapped: "Oh, I am heartily tired of hearing about what Lee is going to do. Some of you always seem to think he is suddenly going to turn a double somersault, and land in our rear and on both flanks at the same time. Go back to your command, and try to think what we are going to do ourselves, instead of what Lee is going to do." This terse rebuttal reveals both his commitment to the initiative as a substitute for intelligence and his dogged determination to prevent uncertainty from causing panic or paralysis. Refusing to let the unknown overwhelm him, Grant abandoned his Wilderness positions and moved southeastward toward the tiny crossroads hamlet of Spotsylvania Court House. The reason for this maneuver was the same as those that had guided him across the Rapidan three days earlier. He hoped to outflank the Confederates, interpose his army between Lee and Richmond, and "draw him into the open field" by threatening his access to the city. Grant had reached a critical crossroads. "Now was the time to strike," observed historian Gordon C. Rhea. "The question was not whether to continue fighting, but where." By proceeding with only minimal knowledge of the enemy's movements, Grant again revealed that the initiative not only fit the situation and his character but it was also a handy substitute for intelligence, especially in the chaotic environment spawned by the recent fighting and maneuvering.[30]

After dark on May 7, the Army of the Potomac and Burnside's corps began moving toward Spotsylvania Court House hoping to reach the crossroads before Lee. Early the next morning, Gouverneur Warren's Fifth Corps approached the village and met only slight resistance from Confederate cavalry. Believing that Lee's infantry had not yet arrived, Warren informed Meade at 8 A.M. that the "opposition to us amounts to nothing as yet." Charles A. Dana, once again at Grant's headquarters as Stanton's field correspondent, noted two hours later that the Federals had stolen a march on the enemy and captured Spotsylvania Court House. "There are no indications that Lee has moved in any direction," he announced. More importantly, he added, "General Grant is decidedly of the opinion that he remains in the old place [his Wilderness line]."[31]

At 10:15 A.M. Warren wrote another optimistic report but also noted an ominous development: he had captured prisoners from Longstreet's corps. If this were so, then Lee had actually beaten the Federals to the town. But Meade and Grant still believed that the Confederates remained ignorant of the Federal movements. The army commander brushed off Warren's report, remarking, "I hardly think Longstreet is yet at Spotsylvania." At 11 A.M. Grant reflected Meade's optimism. "It is not yet demonstrated what the enemy will do," he told Halleck, but he felt "no apprehension for the result." In fact, his mind had already turned toward the future and establishing a linkage with Butler. So confident was Grant that he dispatched most of Sheridan's cavalry on an extended raid to disrupt Confederate communications and defeat Maj. Gen. "Jeb" Stuart's legendary Confederate horsemen. For the next sixteen days the Union army operated without much of its chief reconnaissance instrument. But with Spotsylvania ostensibly in his grasp on May 8, the campaign hatched on the Rapidan seemed to be proceeding on course.[32]

Robert E. Lee, however, had other ideas. Shortly after noon on May 8, Warren sent another dispatch to headquarters, this time announcing his failure to capture Spotsylvania. Southern infantry now held the town, and Warren felt too weak to dislodge them. The Fifth Corps had not only encountered enemy cavalry but also had collided with two divisions of Longstreet's corps that had marched all night to reach the crossroads, successfully eluding Union intelligence patrols in the process. These troops repulsed Warren's advance and managed to hold the crossroads while the rest of Lee's army rushed to join them. The following day both sides began digging in and before long had erected extensive and formidable entrenchments. This turn of events dampened Grant's earlier enthusiasm. "Enemy hold our front in very strong force," he wrote on May 10, "and evince strong determination to interpose between us and Richmond to the last." Unwilling to retreat and with Lee blocking his way, to fight at Spotsylvania or attempt another flanking movement became Grant's only options.[33]

On the afternoon of May 9, he received news that the troops manning the Confederates' left flank had apparently "disappeared." In addition, Burnside reported that his probes against the Confederate right had met with heavy opposition. Concluding that Lee had weakened his left flank to reinforce the opposite wing, Grant prepared to attack the weak point. He slated the move against Lee's left for the evening of May 9, but delays and nightfall forced Maj. Gen. Winfield S. Hancock, the commander of the assault force, to postpone the strike. This delay gave Lee time to shore up his left, and the next morning Hancock discovered that the previous day's thinly held lines had been strongly reinforced. Frustrated, Grant called off the attack.[34]

Despite the missed opportunity, Grant determined to drive the Confederates from their Spotsylvania defenses and, if necessary, "fight it out on this line if it takes all summer." On May 10 Grant launched a massive assault against Lee's entrenchments, resulting in savage fighting, severe losses, and minimal Union success. In part, the belief that Lee's lines had to be weak somewhere drove Grant to attack. Rawlins also revealed another reason why the general in chief believed his men could overcome Lee, even if behind stout fortifications. "The feeling of our army is that of great confidence," he wrote on May 9, "and with the superiority of numbers on our side, I think we can beat them notwithstanding their advantage of position."[35]

News of Butler's problems on the Peninsula also impelled him to assail Lee. Reports indicated that the campaign to capture Richmond from the east had stalled and that Butler was strengthening his lines at Bermuda Hundred rather than forcing Lee to detach troops to defend the capital. As of May 11, Grant noted that there was "no indication of any portion of Lee's army being detached for the defence of Richmond." With Butler's strike against the city a failure and his own campaign grinding to a halt, Grant concluded that the best option remained to "compel Lee to retreat or to . . . cripple him." Given the circumstances, he chose to attack Lee's army in its Spotsylvania works, for only "hard fighting" could achieve either of those outcomes.[36]

The Union commander's perception of enemy morale also fed his aggressiveness. After the carnage of May 10, Grant received summaries of BMI interrogations of prisoners and deserters. "[T]he enemy are very shaky," he concluded from these reports, "and are only kept up to the mark by the greatest exertion on the part of their officers." This assessment echoed descriptions of his earlier opponents in the West. The previous fall at Chattanooga, Grant believed that Braxton Bragg's men were demoralized and the Army of Tennessee was on the verge of collapse. The apparent ease with which the western Federals drove those Southerners from seemingly impregnable entrenchments along Missionary Ridge seemed to validate his appraisal. Lee's men, he believed, had reached a similar state of despair and diminished combat effectiveness. Moreover, the Confederate defenses at Spotsylvania, though formidable, seemed much less imposing than Bragg's Missionary Ridge position. News from Sheridan on May 12 also supported Grant's view. According to local citizens, reported the cavalry commander, "Lee is beaten."[37]

Though the fighting in the Wilderness and at Spotsylvania had provided little evidence to support the prediction of Lee's impending collapse, Grant remained wedded to the belief that the Army of Northern

Virginia would crumble against a frontal assault. But the Confederates surprised him with their tenacity, though he interpreted it as their last gasp. "The enemy are obstinate and seem to have found the last ditch," he wrote following the unsuccessful assaults on May 12. Amazed, Meade hoped his superior would soon understand that "Virginia and Lee's army is not Tennessee and Bragg's army." But Grant's rhetoric showed no evidence that he had experienced this epiphany. Two days later he still believed the casualties suffered by the enemy had crushed their morale, making their situation "desperate beyond anything heretofore known."[38] But despite Grant's wishful thinking, Lee refused to budge. The battle of Spotsylvania ended where it began—in a stalemate. Once again, the general in chief pondered his options.

On the night of May 20–21, the Army of the Potomac abandoned Spotsylvania and moved southeast in another flanking maneuver. The next day BMI scouts reported that Maj. Gen. George E. Pickett's division, lately in Richmond, had recently joined Lee. Prisoners captured from that division confirmed his arrival. This discovery indicated that Butler, who was now "bottled up" behind his works at Bermuda Hundred, had failed to distract Lee and prevent reinforcements from the capital from augmenting the Army of Northern Virginia. Worse yet, Grant also discovered that Shenandoah Valley forces under John C. Breckinridge had also reached the front, a sure indication that Sigel's offensive had failed to cut off and isolate the enemy's valley army. In fact, Sigel's campaign had ended in defeat at New Market on May 15, and his subsequent retreat down the valley freed Breckinridge to support Lee. With the Army of Northern Virginia receiving reinforcements and little hope of significant diversions from other fronts, Grant approached the North Anna hoping again to catch his opponent in the open and maximize the Federals' numerical superiority. But the Confederates reached the river ahead of him. When Grant arrived at the North Anna on May 23, he discovered Lee firmly entrenched in an inverted V-shaped position on the south bank. Over the next few days, the Confederates blunted Federal advances along the North Anna line. Seeing little benefit in continuing operations against Lee's present position, on May 26 Grant once more shifted his army to the southeast.[39]

Despite the lackluster results of the North Anna encounter, Grant still felt that he held the psychological, not to mention physical, advantage over the enemy. "Lee's Army is really whipped," he informed Halleck on

May 26, adding, "The prisoners we now take show it." In support, Dana observed that these captured Southerners appeared "more discouraged than any considerable number of prisoners ever captured before" and, echoing Grant's assessment, told Stanton that the "Rebels have lost all confidence, and are already morally defeated." The enemy evinced this defeatism "not only by their not attacking," observed Dana, "but by the unanimous statements of prisoners." Grant also reacted to Lee's defensive preparations in a predictable way. During the western campaigns, when the enemy resorted to fighting behind prepared defenses, he often interpreted this act to mean they were beaten and preparing for a last stand. That assumption had not changed by 1864. At every encounter since the Wilderness, Lee fought from behind strong entrenchments. Instead of seeing this as a prudent move made by an outnumbered adversary, Grant interpreted it as a sign of weakness and shattered morale. The only way Lee could keep his army in the field, Grant believed, was through "the greatest exertion on the part of their officers, and by keeping them entrenched in every position they take." As a result, he complained, "a battle with them outside of intrenchments cannot be had." Given this prevailing sentiment at headquarters, Grant undoubtedly smelled victory. The Union general in chief again sidled east and south toward a new position closer to Richmond, hoping to lure the Army of Northern Virginia into a fight on *his* terms, confident the Army of the Potomac would prevail in the contest.[40]

After four days of maneuvering, Grant's army emerged near Cold Harbor, an obscure crossroads northeast of Richmond. To continue shielding the capital, Lee also hastened to that vicinity and quickly entrenched. On June 1 the Sixth Corps nearly cracked Lee's lines, but nightfall and a lack of support negated the Union gains. Grant lengthened his lines, forcing Lee to compensate, and planned another major assault on June 2, hoping to strike before the Confederates could strengthen their works. Although the attack never materialized, Union corps commanders were instructed to assess the strength of the enemy fortifications opposite their positions. Tired and exhausted from the march in the Virginia heat, many officers neglected to perform this duty. Across no man's land, the Confederates used the lull to dig in. When Grant ordered a general assault the following day, he knew little about the actual strength of Lee's defenses.[41]

Instead of showing concern, prisoner testimony and estimates of recent Confederate losses had convinced Grant that Lee's thinning ranks would crumble in the face of an all-out frontal assault. The near success on June 1 and Lee's apparent reluctance to leave his works and counter-attack encouraged his already aggressive nature. "The rebels are making a desperate fight," he wrote on June 1, "and I presume will continue to do so as long as they can get a respectable number of men to stand." The ghosts of past campaigns also affected his decision. "He had succeeded in breaking the enemy's line at Chattanooga, Spottsylvania, and other places under circumstances which were not more favorable," explained one of his staff officers, Horace Porter. At Cold Harbor, Porter continued, the potential for success was "so great that it seemed wise to make the attempt." As on other battlefields, Grant based his decision more on faith in the initiative and an optimistic reading of the enemy's condition than on hard intelligence. His men would pay dearly for it. Lee's veterans repulsed the frontal assaults on June 3, inflicting over seven thousand casualties in less than an hour.[42]

"Without a greater sacrifice of human life than I am willing to make," Grant wrote two days after this disastrous attack, "all cannot be accomplished that I had designed outside of the City." Abandoning the goal of defeating Lee's army north of Richmond, Grant decided to slide to the left again, this time crossing the James River and joining Butler's army. Once on the south bank, he planned to cut the city's logistical connections with the rest of the Confederacy, including seizing the important rail hub at Petersburg. In conjunction with Grant's maneuver, Maj. Gen. David Hunter, Sigel's successor in the Shenandoah, would ascend the valley toward the Confederate supply depots at Lynchburg and Charlottesville. Meanwhile, Sheridan and two-thirds of the Army of the Potomac's cavalry would tear up the railroads between the capital and the valley, denying Lee access to the region's bountiful resources.

Although Grant foresaw that the move south of the James might end in a siege, he hoped for one more opportunity to defeat Lee in battle and avoid protracting the campaign into the summer, especially since the war-weary Northern populace might interpret it as another costly failure and take out their frustration on the Lincoln administration in the fall elections. Despite the most recent carnage, the general in chief remained committed to his post-Spotsylvania strategy of striking Lee when the opportunity arose. As before, an optimistic reading of Confederate morale—based on examinations of prisoners and deserters—helped fuel this desire. "All the fight, except defensive and behind breast works, is taken out of Lee's army," he proclaimed just three days after the bloodletting at Cold Harbor.[43]

Forcing the Army of Northern Virginia to fight outside its fortifications depended upon Grant's ability to get to the south side of the James without Lee's knowledge. The longer the Army of Northern Virginia remained on the north of the river while the Federals slid to the south, the better chance Grant had of seizing Petersburg and forcing Lee to fight or face starvation. But to evacuate the Cold Harbor entrenchments, some within forty yards of enemy lines, march nearly fifty miles, cross two rivers (the Chickahominy and the James), and reach Petersburg without being detected posed a significant challenge. If Lee discovered the move early, he could easily utilize his interior lines and either beat Grant to Petersburg or, worse yet, decimate the vulnerable Federal army as it crossed the James. To this, Grant had a simple solution. "I relied," he later claimed, "upon Lee's not seeing my danger as I saw it." To complicate matters further, on June 11, Sharpe reported that "a large number of [enemy] scouts are employed to continually approach and reconnoiter our lines in front, as it is their momentary expectation to find our lines withdrawn . . . to the James River." Given that Lee evidently expected such a movement, secrecy became paramount. Aware of the risks, Grant slated the "deep turning movement" for the night of June 12.[44]

That evening, Grant sent James H. Wilson's troopers, the only remaining cavalry division in the Army of the Potomac due to Sheridan's absence, across the Chickahominy River to clear the roads toward Richmond. Warren's Fifth Corps moved out next to secure the route the rest of the army would follow between the Chickahominy and the James. Both of these forces, however, remained north of the latter river, screening the other corps as they marched. Even though Confederate pickets reported only empty Union trenches at Cold Harbor the next morning, the presence of Union cavalry and an infantry corps north of the river astride the roads leading to Richmond gave Lee pause. The movement appeared strikingly similar to Grant's patented flanking maneuvers and, combined with the presence of Wilson and Warren, convinced the Confederate leader to keep his army in place and await further developments. He dared not march for Petersburg until certain the Army of the Potomac had not stopped short of the James to attack Richmond from the southeast. Since a sizable portion of his mounted arm still pursued Sheridan, the lack of cavalry and the inability to pierce Wilson's screen directly contributed to Lee's lingering uncertainty.[45]

By June 15, half of Grant's army had crossed south, but Lee remained in the dark. He knew the Federals were on the move, possibly across the James, but certainty eluded him. To protect Richmond from that direction, he cautiously moved his army south of the Chickahominy but advanced no farther. Over the next two days, vigorous demonstrations by Wilson's troopers against Lee's new lines added to the uncertainty at Confederate headquarters. "I do not know the position of Grant's army," and therefore "[I] cannot strip [the] north bank of the James River," Lee wrote on June 16. As the Confederate commander cast about for information on the Army of the Potomac's whereabouts, the gathering Union forces south of the river attacked and nearly captured Petersburg. Concluding that Grant had indeed crossed the James and aware of the acute danger to his valuable rail hub, on June 17 Lee finally ordered the Army of Northern Virginia to Petersburg. Soon both sides had constructed massive fortifications stretching from below Petersburg north across the James toward Richmond. The siege had commenced.[46]

During the crossing of the James, Grant had hoped to deceive his opponent. Similar to the opening of the Vicksburg campaign, however, he also struggled to find information regarding the enemy's reaction. The BMI's intelligence operations ceased while the army changed base. In addition, although Butler had cultivated some important contacts with the Union underground in Richmond, Sharpe had not yet established direct communication with them and, therefore, had no information from behind enemy lines.[47] Wilson's cavalry, the only Federals in contact with the enemy after June 13, spent much of its time fending off enemy troopers, screening the army's movements, and demonstrating against Lee's lines south of the Chickahominy, leaving little energy for reconnaissance missions. With reliable information scarce, Grant and his staff could only guess at Lee's possible response. On June 13 Rawlins believed the race to Petersburg might be close. "I have no doubt," he wrote, "the enemy is also moving to the south side of the James." On the first day of the maneuver, Dana saw "strong indications that Lee is moving troops to Petersburg." The following day, however, Wilson brought more accurate news, reporting that two of Lee's three infantry corps had crossed the Chickahominy but had stopped short of the James to "resist the farther approach of the [Union] army toward Richmond" from the southeast. Perhaps summarizing Grant's own interpretation of events, Dana wrote: "Lee appears to have had no idea of our crossing the James River."[48]

By June 16, substantive intelligence had evaporated and Grant remained as uninformed as his adversary. But he forged ahead, gambling that uncertainty about his ultimate destination might temper Lee's boldness and permit the Federals to seize Petersburg. To prevent exposing the capital north of the James, the Confederates had to be certain that all of Grant's army had crossed before committing the Army of Northern Virginia to Petersburg. Aware that the burden of uncertainty was on his adversary, Grant pressed on, hoping, as the authors of one study concluded, "to catch Lee in a mistake."[49] In Lee, however, he had found an opponent capable of turning the tables. When it came to taking risks, the Confederate commander had few equals. The Federals would learn soon enough that, despite the attrition suffered over the past month, the Army of Northern Virginia—and Robert E. Lee—remained as dangerous and defiant as ever.

From the Wilderness to the James River, Grant relied upon the initiative as the key to defeating Lee. Not only did moving first force Lee into a reactionary posture but it also shifted the burden of uncertainty to the Confederates, which enhanced Grant's willingness to take risks and make decisions with little foreknowledge of his foe. But the cost for taking these risks could be heavy, as he discovered at Cold Harbor. Grant also stubbornly adhered to the notion that the Confederates teetered on the brink of collapse. This steadfast belief was perhaps the most dangerous of all because it allowed wishful thinking to color his view of the enemy's will, even when Lee's stubborn resistance demonstrated otherwise. In short, when Lee retreated behind earthworks, Grant saw not determination and sound generalship but desperation and loss of control. Information gleaned from prisoners and deserters formed the foundation of this perception. But accepting as truth the tales of woe spun by deserters and prisoners had become one of Grant's weaknesses. Ironically, this was the same general who had earlier commented that these men could shed little light on the larger situation. Now he believed their stories of hardship and shattered Confederate morale because they confirmed what he *wanted* to believe. Perceptions and the drive to maintain the initiative, not analyzed intelligence, composed the major guideposts for his decision-making during the Virginia campaign. Perhaps the observation of one historian captures the essence of Grant's generalship during this period. The Union general in chief, he concluded, "relied on chance and improvisation to an extraordinary degree." [50]

"Is It Not Certain That Early Has Returned?"

In the late afternoon of July 3, 1864, Grant received an alarming dispatch from Chief of Staff Henry Halleck claiming that a Confederate corps under Lt. Gen. Jubal A. Early was marching down the Shenandoah Valley toward the Potomac River, perhaps with the goal of threatening Washington. "Early's Corps is now here," Grant responded calmly, assuring "Old Brains" that no significant enemy forces remained in the valley. The general in chief based his reply on earlier intelligence reports showing Early's command still manning the trenches outside Richmond and Petersburg alongside the rest of the Army of Northern Virginia. As Grant telegraphed Washington, however, twelve thousand Confederates in "Old Jube" Early's Second Corps were marching northward from Winchester in the Shenandoah toward the Potomac and Maryland, over one hundred miles from the siege lines. Not until July 5, twenty-two days after Early's men had departed Cold Harbor for the valley, did Grant finally conclude, "[Early's] Corps is away from here." Before this realization, however, Early had expelled Union forces from the valley and marched to Harpers Ferry, a key post at the confluence of the Shenandoah and Potomac Rivers. On the same day as Grant's revelation about his absence, Early stood on the banks of the Potomac. The Federal capital lay barely fifty miles away.[1] How Early slipped away unnoticed and eluded detection until his corps reached the gates of Washington haunted Grant, especially since this near-disaster stemmed directly from the failure of his intelligence system.

After crossing the James River in June, reports of valley troops reinforcing Robert E. Lee convinced Grant that few Confederates remained in the Shenandoah. By this time, moreover, the Army of the Potomac had Lee's army pinned in trenches outside Richmond and Petersburg. Given his current predicament, Grant reasoned his opponent would have no choice but to concentrate forces to save the capital rather than detach precious manpower to a secondary theater. Due to its bountiful resources, however, the Shenandoah had become the Confederacy's "breadbasket," a distinction that made it a valuable asset worthy of protecting. The valley also provided Lee with a natural invasion corridor into the North, which he had utilized in 1862 and 1863. Running southwest to northeast, the Shenandoah's northern reaches opened on the

Potomac River and Maryland farmland within two or three days' march of Washington. As Northerners had learned over the years, any Confederate troops in the valley posed a threat to Maryland, Pennsylvania, and Washington.

Though aware of its importance, Grant failed to see the valley in the same light as his foe. As a result, he committed minimal resources to securing the Shenandoah. Maj. Gen. David Hunter had the task of destroying the resources in the region. Once underway, his men won a sharp battle at Piedmont on June 5; seized Staunton; joined forces with George Crook and William Averell, boosting his force to eighteen thousand men; and headed toward Lee's supply depot at Lynchburg. Meanwhile, Maj. Gen. Philip Sheridan was instructed to tear up the Virginia Central Railroad and the James River Canal, both vital links between Richmond and the Shenandoah, before joining Hunter. If successful, these expeditions would smash any remaining Confederate forces and remove the valley from the strategic picture. Leaving that formerly troublesome region to Hunter and Sheridan, Grant focused on Richmond.[2]

Seeing what his opponent had in mind for the valley, Lee rushed Wade Hampton's cavalry westward to intercept Sheridan. Hampton's troopers turned back the Sheridan's column at Trevilian Station on June 11, forcing that general to abort his mission, thus leaving Hunter on his own. The following day, Lee informed Jefferson Davis that stopping Hunter was critical, but "the only difficulty with me is the means" because it "would [take] one corps of this army." Although this would further weaken the capital's defenses, he also understood that the Federals might gain control of the valley and prevent its rich harvests from reaching his hungry army in Richmond. Reluctantly, he detached an infantry corps and rushed it toward Lynchburg.[3]

For this mission Lee selected Richard Ewell's old Second Corps, about eight thousand strong, now commanded by Early. Many of its veterans had participated in Stonewall Jackson's 1862 campaign and were eager to teach the Federals another lesson in valley warfare. Lee ordered his subordinate to depart for Lynchburg at 2:00 A.M. on June 13, defeat Hunter, and reclaim the valley. After that, instructed Lee, circumstances would dictate future plans. If needed back in Richmond, Early was to return quickly. If not, he had permission to advance down the valley, securing supplies as he went, cross the Potomac, and threaten Washington. All forces currently in the region would participate, including John C. Breckinridge's troops, who had returned to the valley on June 7, providing Early a total of around twelve thousand men. The goal was to distract Grant. A Confederate force outside the gates of Washington just might force him to break his grip on Richmond. With politicians and Northern civilians screaming for protection, the Union commander would have to detach forces for Washington's defense. Perhaps then the Army of Northern Virginia could attack the weakened Union lines and break the siege. And even if Grant attempted to force Early's recall by attacking Lee's lines, he risked repeating the slaughter of Cold Harbor. In Lee's mind, it appeared to be a gamble worth taking.[4]

The Second Corps, bivouacked in reserve behind A. P. Hill's Third Corps on Lee's left flank, departed at the appointed hour and cleared its camp at Gaines' Mill by daylight of June 13. Since the mission's success depended upon secrecy, Lee hoped the departure would go unnoticed by Union pickets and cavalry. But the first potential leak came from behind his own lines. A Richmond newspaper correspondent had uncovered the plan and prepared to expose it. Knowing that Grant read Southern newspapers regularly, the Confederate general asked President Davis to tell "all newspapers not to allude to any movement by insinuation or otherwise." Amazingly, the city's editors complied and buried the story. Of course, even media censorship could not guarantee the concealment of the move from an alert adversary. Early's departure would go undetected by Union intelligence, though not because of measures taken by Lee. On this occasion, the secrecy shrouding the mission was assured in part by Grant himself.[5]

As dusk fell on June 12 and Early's men began their trek westward, the Army of the Potomac initiated its change of base maneuver across the James River. The Union Fifth Corps abandoned its Cold Harbor trenches on the left flank behind James H. Wilson's cavalry, crossed the Chickahominy River, and screened the movement of the rest of the army. That same evening, the Union Second Corps slipped behind the screen and reached the James with the two remaining corps, from the center and right at Cold Harbor, following shortly thereafter. William F. "Baldy" Smith's Eighteenth Corps from the Army of the James had departed earlier that day on transports up the James to join Maj. Gen. Benjamin Butler at Bermuda Hundred. By June 16, the Army of the Potomac had successfully crossed the river.[6] After finally confirming that Grant had indeed moved south of the James, the Army of Northern Virginia followed.

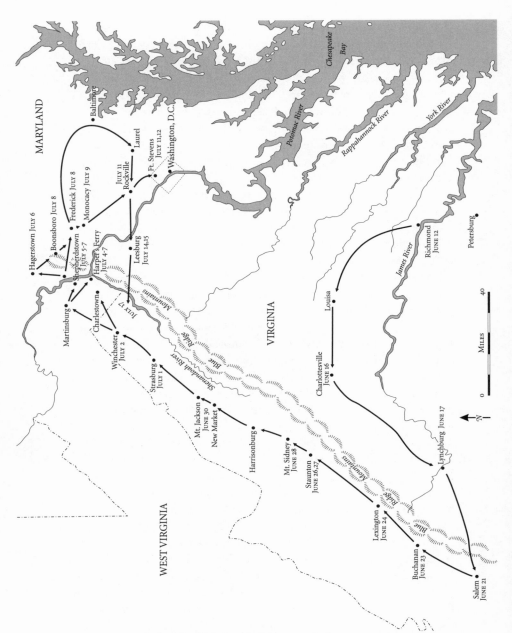

Jubal Early's Raid, June 12–July 18, 1864

As Lee rushed his army to Petersburg on June 17, Early had already reached Lynchburg in time to meet Hunter. Grant, however, still had no idea that Early was gone. In fact, he thought Early's corps was south of the Chickahominy between White Oak Swamp and Malvern Hill as late as June 14. His ignorance was due in part to bad timing. As it turned out, the movement to the James occurred at roughly the same time as Early's departure from the Cold Harbor vicinity. The first Federals pulled out at dusk on June 12; Early's command marched at 2 A.M. the following morning. By the time the Confederate Second Corps departed, the Union troops opposite its position were marching in the other direction. After the last pickets were withdrawn, no Federals remained to detect the move. Moreover, Wilson's busy troopers were occupied south of the Chickahominy screening the army, leaving no time for reconnaissance north of the river.[7] Grant had unknowingly opened a window of opportunity for Lee, an opening Early quickly slipped through and vanished.

The army's intelligence service had also encountered difficulties during and after the move across the James. As the army marched, the Bureau of Military Intelligence's (BMI) operations were disrupted by the increased activity concomitant with a change of base. With John McEntee in the valley and George H. Sharpe occupied with provost marshal duties—sweeping up stragglers and prisoners, preventing destruction of private property, and arresting looters—only John C. Babcock remained to shoulder the bureau's intelligence business. As a result, BMI operations ground to a halt during the army's move. Not until June 17 would Sharpe issue his first summary of information to Maj. Gen. George Meade since leaving Cold Harbor. But that report focused primarily on whether Lee had detected the Federal move. Five more BMI summaries reached Meade the following day, but only one mentioned Early. In that report, Sharpe noted only that the Second Corps had not yet arrived in Petersburg. The colonel assumed that Early's men—sighted only four days earlier south of the Chickahominy—remained in the vicinity of Richmond.[8]

The same day Sharpe filed his first report, Grant received hints that a Confederate force, reportedly a division and two brigades, had embarked toward Lynchburg on June 13. But this news failed to elicit concern at headquarters. Believing that Hunter could handle a force of that size, Grant's only concern was that Hunter might exhaust his ammunition supply. And given the new danger to Richmond, he also believed firmly that Lee would undoubtedly recall these troops to shore up the capital's defenses. Confident in his assessment, Grant failed to acknowledge the possibility that he faced an opponent known for doing the unexpected. By this time, a strong sense that Army of Northern Virginia was beaten colored his perspective. During the Wilderness campaign, Grant had blasted a subordinate for fixating too much on "what Lee is going to do." This mindset led to paralysis and the general in chief would have none of it. But he would learn the hard way that Lee was not finished and that prudence dictated a healthy respect for his adversary's legendary audacity.[9]

The simultaneous movements of the Army of the Potomac and the Second Corps caused intelligence problems for both commanders, but in the end Lee profited more from the confused circumstances. Grant's crossing of the James helped cloak Early's departure better than Lee himself could have accomplished. Now, the burden of finding Early and determining his intentions fell to a lone Union intelligence officer in the Shenandoah Valley.

Capt. John McEntee of the BMI traveled to the Shenandoah in early April to establish a branch office with Maj. Gen. Franz Sigel's command. He corresponded regularly with Sharpe and provided detailed accounts of the conditions in the area and his efforts to construct an effective intelligence system at Harpers Ferry. But he faced a very difficult task from the outset. On his second day of duty, he learned that Brig. Gen. Max Weber, in command of the garrison at Harpers Ferry, employed no scouts and rarely received reports from Union cavalry in the area, leaving him virtually blind to enemy activity. Few deserters or refugees came in, and the provost marshal apparently knew little about extracting information from those who did. With limited access to traditional sources and burdened by incompetent or uncaring personnel, the young captain faced a formidable challenge.[10]

McEntee attempted to establish a scouting force by adopting some existing organizations in the area, including members of the Union League of Loudon County, to patrol areas beyond the reach of Union cavalry. These arrangements failed, however, since most residents of the vicinity were far more concerned with protecting themselves from Confederate guerrillas than with providing information. In any event, the indigenous population was generally hostile toward the Federals anyway. "The cavalrymen say that there is no safety in a party of four or five

men," he complained, since "the citizens bushwhack and rob them."
This situation seriously limited the activities of McEntee's men. He complained to Sharpe that Henry W. Dodd and Benjamin F. McCord, veteran BMI operatives who had accompanied McEntee to Harpers Ferry,
found the countryside "so infested with guerrillas they can do very little
scouting." Unable to penetrate any great distance up the Shenandoah,
McEntee had to rely upon the trickle of refugees and deserters for
information.[11]

Despite these setbacks, he worked diligently to create an effective secret service in the valley command. But other obstacles stood in his way.
When he arrived in Harpers Ferry, McEntee examined the files relating
to the existing intelligence system and was shocked to discover that Sigel
remained ignorant of the order of battle or the current dispositions of
the Confederate valley forces. After a thorough examination of the files,
the captain lamented that he could "make very little of them, [as] the
thing is so mixed." Further complications arose when Hunter succeeded
Sigel in command after the New Market disaster in mid-May 1864.
McEntee regretted this change, complaining that Hunter cared little
about intelligence operations. "General Sigel gave me every facility and
seemed to feel an interest in organizing a good [scouting] party," he
stated. "But Gen H. feels little interested in it." By early June, the prospects for creating an efficient BMI valley branch appeared bleak.[12]

Communications between McEntee and Sharpe also created difficulties for the transmission of timely intelligence. In early June, Hunter's
army moved up the valley toward Lynchburg and away from the telegraph station at Harpers Ferry, the only rapid means of communication
with the Army of the Potomac. To compensate for the lack of telegraphic
access as the army advanced, McEntee sent messengers back to Harpers
Ferry. But these couriers were in constant danger of being captured by
guerrillas, making the captain's communication links with Sharpe all the
more tenuous. "[T]here is so much difficulty in communicating what I
do get to you as our lines are so long & unguarded," he observed. He
also complained that, as the army progressed, fewer deserters and refugees materialized. When Hunter reached Cedar Creek south of Winchester, none came in at all.[13]

McEntee also wrestled with a severe bout of "homesickness" and continually prodded the colonel to arrange his transfer back to the Army of
the Potomac. Being snubbed by Hunter's staff only fueled his desire to

leave. When he attempted to aid the army's provost marshal with constructing an intelligence system, he received a cold shoulder. "I would render him much assistance if he would permit me," fumed McEntee, "but he thinks I am interfering with his business." In the same letter, he begged Sharpe to write often, "as I am again among strangers and feel mighty seasick." As his efforts foundered, Early and Hunter raced toward a confrontation at Lynchburg. Though no one knew it at the time, the stage had been set for Early's disappearance.[14]

Early reached Charlottesville on June 16 and learned that Hunter was only twenty miles from Lynchburg. Nearly three times that distance away, the Confederate commander had to act fast. The Second Corps boarded trains on the Orange and Alexandria Railroad, hoping to save Lynchburg from the fate that had befallen Lexington and other places torched by "Black Dave's" army. The next day Early arrived in time to reinforce the small Confederate garrison and, after a brief engagement on June 18, forced Hunter to withdraw. "[U]p to the morning of the 18th," the Federal commander wrote later, "I had no positive information as to whether General Lee had detached any considerable force for the relief of Lynchburg." Believing that retracing his steps down the valley would mean starvation for his army and exposure to guerrillas, Hunter chose another route. Since ample supplies waited in West Virginia, he headed westward toward the Kanawha River. Early pursued until June 22, then turned toward Staunton, letting Hunter take himself out of the Shenandoah theater and knowing that the Federal withdrawal would continue until they reached the Kanawha, over one hundred miles distant, as good roads and the lure of provisions left little choice.[15]

Hunter's departure from the Shenandoah not only presented Early with an open road north but also removed the valley's only intelligence service from action as well. McEntee's hasty departure with Hunter's command meant that Sharpe—and Grant—would have little means of monitoring events in the valley. His continued absence increased the likelihood that the Union garrisons in the lower valley would remain ignorant of Early's future movements. Without McEntee, moreover, Grant would know even less about enemy activity in the region, a dangerous situation since the general in chief had already drained away most of the available manpower from Washington's defenses for his campaign against Richmond.[16]

Back at Grant's City Point headquarters, rumors indicating an increased Confederate presence in the valley began to trickle in. On June 20 Sharpe reported a prisoner had claimed that "Ewell's [Early's] corps left General Lee at Cold Harbor . . . toward Lynchburg" and that he had "not seen any part of it since, and is quite certain that no part . . . is in our front." The following morning five prisoners from Hill's corps corroborated this information. On June 24 the BMI chief remained "satisfied . . . that no part of Ewell's [Early's] corps has returned or is in this vicinity." By this time, most of the evidence suggested that Early had left the Richmond-Petersburg area, rescued Lynchburg, and forced Hunter to retreat. But nothing indicated that the Second Corps had turned toward the Potomac River.[17]

On June 28, the same day Early reached Mount Sidney on his way down the valley, Grant finally received reports from Hunter and McEntee describing the engagement at Lynchburg. Hunter's account failed to provide substantive information about the forces that defeated him, mentioning only that he withdrew in the face of a numerically superior foe "constantly receiving re-enforcements from Richmond." McEntee's report contained more details. He claimed that Hunter had "engaged part of Ewell's corps commanded by Early" and estimated its size at twenty thousand men. More importantly, McEntee provided the first significant information concerning the Second Corps' whereabouts in ten days with his remark that Early's command was "probably at Richmond again by this [time]." Grant agreed with this assessment, perhaps based upon the conviction that Lee needed every man to defend Richmond and Early had departed before the danger posed by the movement across the James had become clear. Given the circumstances, Lee would have little choice but to recall the detachment, making McEntee's conclusion probable. And before long, more intelligence emerged to support the captain's assessment.[18]

Maj. Gen. Winfield S. Hancock notified Meade on July 1 that three deserters from Mississippi regiments reported that "Ewell's [Early's] corps arrived yesterday and that part of it was marching to [the Confederate] right." Later that day, Halleck informed Grant of "conflicting reports about rebel forces in the Shenandoah Valley," warning that it "would be good policy for them while Hunter's army is on the Kanawha . . . [to] make a raid in Maryland & Penn." Despite this warning, Grant felt certain that "Ewell's [Early's] corps has returned here." The statements of the Mississippi deserters and McEntee's report of June 28 provided enough evidence of Early's return to satisfy him. As the Confederates in the valley neared Strasburg, less than forty-five miles from the Potomac, Grant felt confident he could account for all of Lee's army as being in the Richmond-Petersburg defenses.[19]

While Grant remained blissfully unaware of Early's true location, the small Union garrisons at Martinsburg, Harpers Ferry, and other posts in the lower valley began hearing rumors of a large Confederate force heading their way. John W. Garrett, president of the Baltimore and Ohio Railroad, sensed early on that a formidable enemy expedition edged northward. Knowing that raiders would intercept his trains and destroy miles of his track and rolling stock, Garrett was especially sensitive to these ominous reports. On June 29 he wired Secretary of War Edwin Stanton that "Breckinridge and Ewell [Early] are reported moving up" and warned "the operations and designs of the enemy in the Valley demand the greatest vigilance and attention." But Lincoln and Stanton dismissed his warnings after Grant allayed their fears with his telegram of July 1.[20]

By July 2, though, the trickle of rumors reaching the valley garrisons had become a steady stream of frightening reports. Sigel, now in command of the Martinsburg post, warned the War Department that a large, unidentified Confederate force approached Strasburg. The next day, reports of skirmishing and sightings of enemy troops escalated. The Martinsburg telegraph operator wired that a large body of the enemy, "supposed to be the same that fought Hunter," lurked nearby and was now less than a dozen miles from Harpers Ferry. Shortly after this transmission, the Martinsburg telegraph fell silent. Reports of more assaults against Union posts filtered in to Washington. As tension mounted in the capital city, Garrett chided Stanton for ignoring his earlier warning, predicting "the information recently sent you of heavy forces in the Valley is about to prove correct." Disturbed by this growing clamor, Lincoln, Stanton, and Halleck turned to City Point for answers.[21]

Halleck informed Grant on July 3 that Early and Breckinridge were reportedly moving down the Shenandoah. Once again, the general in chief assured the secretary of war that "Early's corps is now here," adding, "There are no troops that can now be threatening Hunter's Dept." except the remnants of smaller commands. Garrett, however, did not agree that insignificant forces menaced the Union outposts. "It is clear," he wrote with palpable sarcasm, "that if there is not a large rebel force they are being handled with great vigor and skill to make such numerous attacks at points so distant." To ease their concerns, Grant reevaluated his previous intelligence. "Is it not certain that Early has returned to your front?" he asked Meade. The general replied that his only information concerning Early had come from deserters—the three Mississippians in Hancock's dispatch of July 1—who claimed the Second Corps had returned from Lynchburg. Meade added, however, that "[n]o prisoners have been taken from any of the divisions of that corps," and "[i]t was never reported as in our front but only that it had returned." Later that evening, Grant repeated Meade's response to Halleck, stressing that, despite having no prisoners from Early, "Deserters . . . from other Commands state [Early's corps] returned five or six days ago."[22]

Independence Day brought more news. Sharpe learned from another deserter the current rumors circulating through Southern camps claimed that Early "had taken Arlington Heights and was about to capture the city of Washington." In a telegram summarizing the colonel's information, Grant noted skeptically: "This report of Ewell's [Early's] Corps being north is only the report of a deserter and we have similar authority for it being here and on the right of Lee's army." Reflecting his growing uncertainty, he then added, "We know however that it does not occupy this position." He now faced the dilemma of which deserters to believe.[23]

After July 4, Grant launched a concentrated search for intelligence on the missing Confederates. Sharpe and Babcock queried all prisoners and deserters on their knowledge of Early's whereabouts. Since his report on June 17, Sharpe had issued twenty intelligence assessments; of those, four contained information intimating—but not explicitly stating—that Early's corps remained in the valley. The BMI's intensified search failed to clarify the situation beyond what was known in these earlier reports. Some sources placed Early in Maryland, while others were convinced that he occupied the trenches outside Richmond. "Very little is known in their army of the whereabouts of Ewell's [Early's] corps," concluded a frustrated Sharpe. By July 6, the BMI chief's uncertainty had yet to fade.[24]

In dispatches to Halleck, Grant revealed the confusion at his headquarters as a result of these contradictory reports. "Except for despatches forwarded from Washington in the last two days," he bemoaned, "I have learned nothing which indicates an intention on the part of the rebels to attempt any northern movement." Later on, however, he seemed more certain that Early was indeed absent from Richmond but still had no idea where he was. Feeling pressure from Washington, as a precaution Grant sent a division of the Sixth Corps to the capital with the remainder of the corps to follow shortly thereafter. Finally, on July 6, the general in chief acknowledged that Early was probably near the Potomac River, but no one at his headquarters knew for sure "how large a force the rebs have up there, nor . . . to what extent Lee has diminished his forces in our immediate front."[25]

As Grant scrambled to get the Sixth Corps to Washington and Hunter, returning to the valley, tried to overtake Early from behind, the responsibility for stopping the Confederates fell upon Grant's former division commander Lew Wallace. Upon hearing the news of the enemy's approach, Wallace positioned a small scraped-together force along the Monocacy River near Frederick, Maryland, astride the roads to Baltimore and Washington. At first ignorant of the size and the leader of the forces bearing down on him, he soon discovered that Early commanded the invasion and had already driven Sigel and Weber out of Harpers Ferry. When Brig. Gen. James B. Ricketts arrived on July 9 with part of the Sixth Corps, the division commander was shocked to find out that Early, who at last report was supposedly in Richmond, lurked beyond the mountains. By the time Early's Confederates overwhelmed Wallace later that day and sent the Federals limping toward Baltimore, daylight had faded and the Southerners were forced to halt for the night. Wallace's delaying action cost Early precious time, allowing the remaining Sixth Corps divisions to reach the capital ahead of the Confederate advance.[26]

The Sixth Corps, soon joined by the Nineteenth Corps, arrived in time to prevent the capture of the Federal capital. The Confederates had reached the outskirts of the city by July 11 and probed its defenses the next day. Early realized he could not attack such strong fortifications, now manned by Grant's veterans, without risking serious loss. Had he been a day earlier, he might have taken Washington. The time lost on the Monocacy had cost him dearly. During the night of July 12, almost a month after departing Lee's army, Early's command withdrew toward Leesburg, Virginia. Two days later, the last substantial threat to the Federal capital crossed the Potomac and reentered the Old Dominion. Grant had barely escaped the disastrous consequences of a monumental intelligence failure. The whole affair, wrote staff officer Ely S. Parker, "gives our Genl considerable anxiety and uneasiness."[27]

Meade revealed the depth of the uncertainty and frustration at headquarters when, at one point during the raid, he reported that not only had Early's corps disappeared, but the location of Lee's two remaining corps also seemed in doubt. Prisoners and deserters, he complained, had placed one particular Confederate division "in our front—on our left & rear & on its way to P[ennsylvania]." Lt. Col. Cyrus B. Comstock, one of Grant's aides, reflected in his diary the confusion caused by these rumors. On July 11 a deserter reported that Hill's corps had departed for Pennsylvania and other evidence seemed to corroborate it. "Today it is contradicted," Comstock wrote the next afternoon, but not before the "General had almost decided on an attack [based] on the first information." Though plagued by these erroneous reports, including some indicating that Lee's entire army was marching on the Federal capital, Grant struggled to maintain a grasp on the true situation. Finally, on July 13, he wrote, "Summary of evidence gathered from deserters, scouts & Cavalry reconnoissance show that none of Hills or Longstreets Corps have left our front." Rawlins noted on the same day that, despite rumors of Longstreet's troops joining Early's assault on Washington, the evidence indicated otherwise. "We have deserters from it daily and also make captures of prisoners from it," he wrote. He also revealed that perhaps a lesson had been learned about verification. "This latter evidence never has failed us."[28]

Grant understood the dangerous precedent set by Early's raid. But Halleck was quick to remind him that as long as Union forces remained concentrated outside Richmond and Petersburg, the Confederates could make large detachments "unknown to us for a week or ten days." They had already moved an entire corps from under Grant's nose, shielded it behind the Blue Ridge, and marched it to the gates of Washington with little warning. What would prevent them from repeating this feat? This question had great importance since another raid like the last one might jeopardize both Grant's Virginia campaign and Lincoln's November reelection bid. Incessant grumbling from political opponents, government officials, and Northern citizens, some believing that Grant's stalemated campaign had already failed, plagued the Union commander and forced a reevaluation of the strategic situation in Virginia and of his intelligence system.[29]

But Early refused to cooperate. Instead of returning to Richmond, the newly christened Army of the Valley remained in the Shenandoah to gather the fall harvest and continue threatening Baltimore and Washington. Lee hoped Early's presence there would force the Federals to either detach troops to deal with him or attack Confederate lines at Richmond and Petersburg in an attempt to force his recall. With two lines of operation in Virginia, Grant now faced a complex problem: how to keep Early at bay and sever Lee from his supply source in the Shenandoah without jeopardizing his main operations against the Confederate capital. To isolate and defeat Early, secure Washington, and deny access to the valley's resources would irreparably damage Lee, forcing him to face Grant's growing multitudes with a hungry army and time running out. The realization of this plan hinged on the Federal commander's ability to obtain accurate intelligence on enemy troop movements between Richmond and the Shenandoah. If Early's raid was any indication, achieving this objective would be extremely difficult. With access to this sort of information, however, Grant could coordinate Union movements in both regions to isolate Lee from Early and make it difficult for them to support one another. Once accomplished, interior lines would no longer provide an advantage because Lee would be denied strategic mobility, which had been one of his most potent weapons. The BMI would take the lead in this effort, but until Sharpe and Grant corrected the inadequacies revealed by Early's invasion, the present campaign would continue, as one War Department official lamented, "in the deplorable and fatal way in which it has." [30]

Grant moved quickly to address the Shenandoah situation. First, he resolved the divided Union command structure in the region, which had severely hampered coordination during the raid. By consolidating the departments in northern Virginia, Washington, West Virginia, Maryland, and Pennsylvania into the Middle Military Division, he ensured that operations in the area would be coordinated under one commander. The Union Army of the Shenandoah, consisting of the Sixth and the Nineteenth Corps and Hunter's Army of West Virginia, comprised the force of the new command. To oversee this important region and direct operations against Early, Grant appointed Maj. Gen. Philip H. Sheridan and ordered him to find Early and "follow him to the death," destroying the valley's resources along the way. After completing the consolidation and sending Sheridan to his new post, Grant made changes in the BMI designed to increase his access to intelligence on troop movements between Lee and Early. [31]

Prior to the raid on Washington, the BMI operated out of the Army of the Potomac's Provost Marshal General Department and, as a result, intelligence reports reached Grant indirectly through Meade, who jealously guarded his authority from usurpation by his superior. Hoping to address the problem of locating various segments of Lee's army and detecting their movements, Grant saw the BMI as the solution and maneuvered to gain more control over its operations. On July 11 Ely S. Parker wrote that the general in chief "directed such steps to be taken as to ascertain positively [the enemy's] present position and strength in our front." He first elevated Marsena R. Patrick to the post of provost marshal of the newly designated "Armies Operating Against Richmond" (AOAR), the umbrella organization over the Armies of the Potomac and the James based at City Point. With this appointment, Patrick commanded all provost marshal departments, including the BMI and its branch offices. Patrick immediately requested that Sharpe and the bureau accompany him to Grant's headquarters, claiming that Meade "refused to let us do what was desired" for efficient intelligence operations. Grant acquiesced and, in so doing, ignited a small war over control of the BMI. Believing the move infringed upon his authority, Meade bitterly opposed it, declaring he wanted "no partnership with Grant." Due to its poor showing during Early's raid, he also lashed out at the BMI, calling it "good for nothing" and threatening to disband it. This war of words ended in late July when Meade and Grant reached a compromise. To ensure Meade had continued access to intelligence, McEntee, Babcock, and most of the scouts would remain with the Army of the Potomac to interview deserters, prisoners, and refugees and continue collecting order-of-battle intelligence. Assigned to Grant's City Point headquarters as the AOAR's assistant provost marshal, Sharpe would coordinate all BMI operations, maintain contact with spies in Richmond, and serve as the central information clearinghouse. For the first time, Grant had his own intelligence officer at headquarters.[32]

From the moment he arrived at City Point, Sharpe worked to develop a systematic method for detecting Confederate movements between Richmond and the valley. His transfer came at a critical time. In late July, Early once again occupied the lower valley and made threatening overtures, including a raid that left Chambersburg, Pennsylvania, a smoldering ruin. Lee also appeared determined to reinforce the valley army whenever possible to maintain a constant threat against Washington. Once Grant and Sharpe realized what the Rebels were up to, the detection of Confederate detachments from the Richmond-Petersburg front grew in importance. Not only could this intelligence improve their ability to protect the capital but it might also help isolate the two fronts and prevent the armies from supporting each other. To meet the demands of this important mission, Sharpe would need more than Babcock, McEntee, and the small cadre of BMI scouts. These secret operations demanded the employment of more scouts and spies prowling around the enemy's camps and transportation facilities so that no enemy detachment would escape undetected.

On July 21 Patrick ordered Sharpe to first "arrange matters [at City Point], and at Bermuda Hundred with Butler, about sending off Scouts etc in the direction of Orange Court House to watch Early." He also instructed his subordinate to "get into Richmond," which meant obtaining information from within the Rebel capital. To fulfill the first component of this mission, Sharpe sent Babcock to Washington in early August to establish an organization to monitor Early's main rail links with Richmond. This operation depended upon three Virginia Unionists who lived in the vicinity of the depots of the Orange and Alexandria; the Richmond, Fredericksburg, and Potomac; and the Virginia Central Railroads. Isaac Silver (alias "the old man), James W. Cammack, and Ebenezer McGee, all of whom lived west of Fredericksburg, would visit the depots regularly, question passengers and railroad employees about the composition and direction of recent traffic, and watch specifically for troop trains heading for the valley. Using a similar method of communication devised to contact Richmond agents, six bureau scouts based in Fredericksburg—Benjamin McCord, Henry Dodd, Sanford McGee, Phil Carney, and two others identified only as Rose and O'Bryan—would meet the Unionists several times a week at prearranged locations, collect their observations, and pay them according to the value of their information. This communication system allowed the agents to remain close to home, thereby preventing neighbors from becoming suspicious of their activities. After each visit, the scouts would report their findings to Babcock and Capt. George K. Leet, a liaison officer from Grant's headquarters on special duty with Halleck's Washington staff. Leet or Babcock would then wire the news to Sharpe and Lt. Col. Theodore S. Bowers, an aide on Grant's staff. Bowers and Sharpe collated and analyzed these reports, meshed them with information from other sources, and issued a summary to Grant. By early September 1864, Babcock announced that information came in from his sources "as often as five times in two weeks."[33]

While placing the railroads under surveillance, Sharpe also addressed the second part of his mission: to procure information from inside Richmond. He still relied heavily upon daily interrogations of deserters, prisoners, refugees, and contrabands, his knowledge of Lee's order of battle, and enemy newspapers to track enemy movements. But in order to acquire the kind of sensitive information available only from within the Confederate capital, Sharpe strengthened ties with Unionists in Richmond, whom he referred to in correspondence as "our friends." Three major groups supplied information to the Federals: a "spy ring" headed by Elizabeth Van Lew; another led by the superintendent of the Richmond, Fredericksburg, and Potomac railroad, Samuel Ruth, and his principal agents, Charles M. Carter and F. W. E. Lohman; and a third established by Thomas McNiven, an abolitionist baker with contacts throughout the city, including within the municipal government. To transmit their intelligence without raising suspicion, Sharpe established five "depots" outside the city where BMI scouts met with Richmond agents or their messengers to collect both oral and written reports (some were encoded using bureau-supplied ciphers) and relay specific information requests from Sharpe or Grant. Scouts met with agents two to three times a week using the "upper" (along the James) or "lower" (along the Chickahominy) routes to reach the depots. Traveling these routes was dangerous, and the scouts were always aware that enemy operatives might discover the nature of their sojourns and thus worked to prevent detection. For example, when BMI operatives discovered that Southern scouts had also established a secret route along the James, the initial response at headquarters was to neutralize the enemy's line to preserve the secrecy of the upper route. But the BMI protested, arguing that this heavy-handed solution would have negative consequences for their own operations. The scouts, Sharpe reported, "do not desire to interfere with it, as thereby their own business would be apparent."[34]

After submitting their reports, Richmond agents often received money and food as payment. Though preferring Union "greenbacks" to worthless Confederate script, agents nevertheless requested the latter and for good reason. In January 1865, Confederate authorities arrested a Richmond operative "on suspicion founded upon the use of greenbacks." To avoid raising eyebrows and risking the lives of informants, Sharpe sent in Confederate dollars and Southern state notes as well as United States currency. A month after the agent's arrest, Grant asked the War Department to provide fifty thousand dollars in Confederate currency for Sharpe's use.[35] Sometimes Richmond agents requested more than money for their services. For example, McEntee forwarded an appeal from Van Lew for a pair of shoes, some gunpowder tea, and a "muff of the latest style." Though the last item seemed a bit extravagant, McEntee urged Sharpe to "[p]lease get [it] as the people are worth it."[36]

Sharpe cultivated the strongest ties with Van Lew's organization, crediting her with establishing a vital communication network between City Point and Richmond. A wealthy spinster, Van Lew pretended to be mentally unbalanced to divert suspicion, earning her the nickname "Crazy Bet." In addition to bringing food to Union prisoners languishing in Libby Prison and sheltering escapees, she smuggled any information she could find to Union officials. Her first official contact with a Federal commander came in late 1863 when she volunteered her services to Benjamin Butler. In February 1864 her pleas to rescue Union prisoners in Richmond and observation that the city was vulnerable to attack triggered an ill-fated cavalry raid, the results of which would spark a bitter controversy.[37]

Led by Brig. Gen. Judson Kilpatrick and Col. Ulric Dahlgren, the objective of the two-pronged raid was ostensibly to liberate Union soldiers from Richmond's military prisons. But Confederate resistance forced Kilpatrick to retreat and intercepted Dahlgren's column outside the city. In a sharp skirmish, local home guards killed Dahlgren and dispersed his command, including three BMI scouts who had accompanied the expedition.[38] Papers supposedly found on Dahlgren's body, however, indicated he planned more than a massive jailbreak. According to the documents, Dahlgren had apparently instructed his men to "burn the hateful city" and proclaimed that "Jeff. Davis and his Cabinet must be killed on the spot." A firestorm of angry protest erupted across the South once the content of the documents became public. The Confederate government charged the North with barbarism and violation of the laws of war by authorizing Dahlgren's mission, a charge vehemently denied by Union officials. Though some believed that Dahlgren issued such orders, others contended the Confederates forged the documents for propaganda purposes. That the young colonel actually ordered the assassination of Davis and other officials or that the Union high command endorsed such action remains in dispute. But Meade later hinted that the papers were authentic, as did Babcock and McEntee.[39]

An extract of a report submitted during this time from the Richmond underground, probably from either Van Lew or McNiven, may shed some light on the origination of Dahlgren's plan. "[N]ow is the time to capture Richmond," the document stated, and it "can be done either by forcing Lee to retreat there to winter, or by the capture of Davis, which would not be a feat hard to accomplish." The author went on to explain that, since "Davis is the head and front of the rebellion," his capture would cause the fall of Richmond and the Confederacy. "He has many enemies (all Union men) who, with his fall, would be glad to welcome again the stars and stripes." Though not calling for Davis's assassination, this information from inside the enemy's capital, coupled with the news about the vulnerability of Richmond, may have influenced the thinking of Union officials planning the raid.[40]

Van Lew's association with Dahlgren, however, did not end with his death. Concerned that the colonel's father, Union admiral John A. Dahlgren, might never know the fate of his son's remains, she spearheaded a covert operation, using individuals from the three major underground networks, to find Dahlgren's body, which the Confederates had buried in a secret location, and smuggle it out of Richmond. They located the grave, spirited the body out of the city, and reburied it on a nearby farm owned by Isaac Silver's brother-in-law. Thanks to Van Lew's efforts, after the war a grateful Admiral Dahlgren reclaimed his son's body. Though the operation's success demonstrated the resourcefulness and daring of the Richmond underground, had Confederate officials discovered the plot and arrested the operatives, they might have unraveled all three major networks, thereby denying Grant future access to important intelligence from behind enemy lines.[41]

After the Army of the Potomac's arrival before Richmond, Sharpe and his scouts established contact with Van Lew, who in secret correspondence went by the names of "Babcock" and later "Romona." Her reports, sometimes encoded using her own homemade cipher, commented upon current rumors circulating among the residents, the actions and proclamations of the Confederate government, and movements of troops through the city. But many more focused on the living conditions within Richmond and the morale of its citizens. On occasion, she sent Grant a copy of the *Richmond Dispatch*. Her "Occassional Journal," a diary she kept despite fears that its discovery might end her life, not only contains a record of some of her activities and observations but also provides a chilling glimpse into the harsh existence of a Unionist living among the enemy, many of whom were neighbors and friends. Though Grant said little about Van Lew after the war, he did appoint her postmaster of Richmond in reward for her services, a post she held until 1877. Sharpe wrote later that the general in chief was well acquainted with "the regular information obtained by our Bureau from the City of Richmond, the greater proportion of which in its collection, and in good measure in its transmission we owed to the intelligence and devotion of Miss E. L. Van Lew." [42]

Samuel Ruth, Charles Carter, and F. W. E. Lohman provided valuable intelligence to the Union cause despite the brief incarceration of some on suspicion of espionage. In October 1864, Sharpe asked Van Lew to find someone who could "open communication from Richmond by way of the R. F. & P railroad." Van Lew turned to Ruth, who answered the summons. From that day on he provided information about Confederate rail traffic at least once a week, sending messages to Sharpe via secret courier. Using his position as superintendent of a major railroad, he deliberately delayed the delivery of supplies to Lee's army. In January 1865, however, Confederate authorities arrested Ruth and charged him with treason. While awaiting disposition of his case, the *Richmond Whig* reported, "Mr. Ruth's friends, among whom are many gentlemen of influence, believe Mr. Ruth to be innocent." When a court exonerated him a month later, the *Whig* declared: "It is outrageous that a respectable citizen should be seized . . . upon no better ground than a malicious whisper. The charge against Ruth was trumped up." Having fooled both the authorities and Richmond society, Ruth quickly returned to the railroad and to spying for the BMI. When Sharpe learned that Ruth had "removed the suspicion leading to his late arrest, and been returned to duty," he immediately assigned him another mission. Carter served as Sharpe's "special messenger" to Richmond, while Lohman, an employee of Ruth's railroad who had helped Van Lew find and move Dahlgren's body, also collected and relayed intelligence. After the war, all three men requested compensation from the government for their wartime services, attaching a list of nine significant examples of the information they provided. Sharpe verified their claims, as did Grant, who endorsed their petition with the following: "Much of the information [claimed by the petition-ers] was reported by [Sharpe] to me, and proved of great value to the service."⁴³

An abolitionist and baker, Thomas McNiven (alias "Quaker") also performed secret service for the Union, though some of his claims remain somewhat suspect. After the war, for example, he undoubtedly exaggerated when he stated that at least three hundred informants fed him information, including prostitutes who shared beds with both low- and high-ranking Confederate officials. McNiven also spun a tale that a prostitute named Clara "got the plans for [Confederate] Genl. [A. P.] Hill's movements out of Petersburg [on April 2], and Miss Van Lew's courier got them to Grant just in time to ambush and kill him [Hill]." Though the Rebel general was indeed killed that day, his death came at the hands of two Union soldiers who had accidentally stumbled upon Hill as he rode with a staff officer, not as a result of an organized ambush. Also questionable is his assertion that he recruited Van Lew and that she worked for him. According to McNiven, his bakery became a "major central exchange point for intelligence, and his daily deliveries became a convenient cover to collect information and reports, some coming from individuals in the Richmond municipal government. Like Van Lew, "Quaker" established contact with Butler in February 1864, sending him detailed information on enemy activity in the capital. With Van Lew, Ruth, McNiven, and the railroad scouts on duty by mid-August, Sharpe provided Grant with a system to gather information on enemy troop movements between Richmond and the valley and much more. All that remained was to incorporate Sheridan's command into this system so that both he and Grant could work together to deny Lee unimpeded mobility between the two fronts.⁴⁴

After Sheridan arrived at Harpers Ferry on August 6, he quickly established an intelligence unit within his army to operate in conjunction with the BMI. The new valley commander possessed a great appreciation for good intelligence, as evidenced by his conduct in northern Mississippi in 1862. However, his predecessor had done little to construct an effective intelligence service, a revelation that alarmed Sheridan. "I felt the need of an efficient body of scouts," he observed, "for the defective intelligence-establishment with which I started out from Harper's Ferry . . . had not proved satisfactory." In early September, Sheridan, convinced of the "absolute necessity of more reliable information of the enemy's numbers and movements," created "a system of espionage that would give me a more accurate knowledge of him than I had as yet been able to obtain." He recruited between fifty and sixty volunteers, all from the ranks, and organized them into a special battalion of scouts commanded by Maj. Henry K. Young of the First Rhode Island Infantry. Known as "Sheridan's Scouts," these men, often disguised in Confederate attire, reconnoitered enemy positions, watched for movements and reinforcements, and frequently operated behind enemy lines. They soon became an integral part of an intelligence system that kept one eye on Early and the other trained on Richmond. With both Sharpe's and Young's men working in concert through their respective commanders, Grant could now monitor and direct operations in the Shenandoah and use the information the intelligence organizations produced to keep Lee and Early in check.[45]

Grant's new network was still in its infancy when Early once again advanced toward the lower valley and the Potomac. To counter this threat, Grant sent Sheridan two cavalry divisions. Lee responded by detaching Maj. Gen. Joseph B. Kershaw's division of Longstreet's First Corps, Maj. Gen. Fitzhugh Lee's cavalry division, and an artillery battalion commanded by Maj. Wilfred E. Cutshaw. Fearful of losing the valley despite his own tenuous situation, Lee believed it wiser to "detach these troops than to hazard [Early's] destruction and that of our railroads north of Richmond." With Lt. Gen. Richard H. Anderson in overall command of the detachment, the troops departed for the valley on August 6.[46]

Rumors concerning this reinforcement surfaced at Grant's headquarters on August 8 when Babcock reported that a "considerable" force of infantry—identified as Kershaw's division—had gone to Early. The following day Sharpe learned from a Richmond refugee that on August 6 a large infantry detachment had boarded the Virginia Central trains bound for the valley. The bureau chief put great stock in this particular report since the source was a friend of a "Richmond man in our employ." Bowers forwarded this information to Leet in Washington and instructed that the "attention of the men sent by Col Sharpe" should be directed toward the Virginia Central.[47]

On August 10 the BMI office at Butler's headquarters discovered from a deserter that a large cavalry force had been sent to Early four days earlier. Babcock reported the following day that another deserter had witnessed Kershaw's division passing through Orange Court House en route to the valley, and on August 11 Isaac Silver, one of the spies recruited by Babcock to watch the railroads, warned that the enemy's entire First Corps had passed over the rails toward the Shenandoah. Later that evening, Grant informed Meade that all evidence confirmed Lee had detached sizable reinforcements—at least two divisions—to bolster Early. With no direct telegraphic link between City Point and Sheridan's headquarters, he advised Halleck to alert the valley command.[48]

Before this news reached him, Sheridan had forced Early to retreat to Fisher's Hill south of Winchester. When Grant's relayed message arrived on August 13, the valley commander replied that his intelligence had also discovered the approaching Confederate reinforcements. Fearful that the advancing column might emerge from the mountain gaps and pounce upon his flank and rear, Sheridan canceled an assault on Early's position and, on August 15, retreated toward Halltown, heeding Grant's advice to "act now on the defensive until movement here force[s] them to detach to send this way."[49]

As promised, Grant unleashed an offensive designed to prevent Lee from providing any further reinforcements and to "create a tendency to draw from [Sheridan's] front." To accomplish this and to determine the composition and size of the enemy force already en route to Early, Grant ordered an attack against the Richmond defenses to remind Lee that sending troops away would be costly. Although the August 14–16 offensive failed to break the enemy's lines or force Kershaw's recall, the Federals captured prisoners from various enemy units that helped ascertain the correct identity of the recent detachment. After reviewing the evidence from prisoners, Grant wired Sheridan on August 14, "It is now positive that Kershaw's Division has gone." Between August 18 and 19, the general in chief once again tried to force Lee to call back Kershaw, sending Gouverneur K. Warren's corps to cut the Weldon Railroad, an important logistical line between Petersburg and supplies in North Carolina. Although severing this vital rail link was one objective, the operation's principal goal was to "force Lee to withdraw a portion of his troops from the Valley so that Sheridan can strike a blow against the balance." After hard fighting, Warren not only cut the railroad but also held it against vicious counterattacks. Jubilant, Grant believed Warren had inflicted "a blow to the enemy he cannot stand" and predicted Lee would now abandon the valley in order to reopen the rail line. "Watch closely," he advised Sheridan. "If you find Early sending off any of his troops strike suddenly and hard." From the brigades represented in the latest crop of prisoners and deserters, Grant also possessed solid evidence that no more troops had gone west.[50]

By late August, rumors of Kershaw's probable return to help recapture the Weldon reached City Point. Sharpe reported that "general talk among the southern soldiers," along with a Richmond spy's report, indicated that Early's entire command would return to Lee. But spy Isaac Silver had found no evidence to support this claim, and BMI officers with Butler reported that most deserters believed Lee had no intention of abandoning the valley. Though most of the evidence pointed toward the conclusion that Early would remain in the Shenandoah, Sharpe still warned Babcock in Washington that Lee might yet recall troops from the valley. If that proved true, he told his subordinate, "we shall expect to hear the first information from you."[51]

Rumors continued to spread purporting that Lee planned to use Early's troops to reclaim the Weldon. "From reports of deserters coming in," Grant advised Sheridan on September 6, "we learn that Kershaw's Division arrived in Petersburg last night." The next day, however, Sharpe dismissed this news by using information from a Richmond spy who reported confidently that Kershaw had not returned. McEntee also corroborated Sharpe's version and explained the origin of the earlier rumor of Kershaw's arrival. From recent interrogations, he noted that several deserters witnessed some brigades from other First Corps divisions pass through Petersburg at about the same time the rumors about Kershaw surfaced. This simple redeployment, McEntee surmised, "gave rise to the rumor" of Kershaw's return. Finally, Sheridan confirmed Kershaw's continued presence in the valley when recent skirmishes netted prisoners from that division. "I am able to say positively that no troops have left," Sheridan wrote on September 8, and he promised to "press hard" should Early move toward Richmond.[52]

Sheridan's plan to "press" the Confederates was the result of a month of constant moves and countermoves that drove Early from the lower valley. Despite the continuous sparring, "Old Jube" had frustrated Sheridan's plans to destroy the Confederate valley army and transform the Shenandoah into a wasteland. Determining the size of the enemy's forces had become a key obstacle for the Union command. Erring on the side of caution, Sheridan believed (erroneously) that Early's army equaled his own and remained on the defensive until the odds shifted in the Federals' favor. Political concerns also fueled his caution. "The Presidential campaign in the north was now fairly opened," he explained after the war, and "under no circumstances, could we afford to risk defeat." Nor could he chance opening the valley to another raid into Maryland so close to the November elections. As a result, Sheridan awaited the recall of a portion or all of Early's forces to Richmond before making any decisive moves. In the meantime, he resolved to "take all the time necessary to equip myself with the fullest information and then seize an opportunity under such conditions that I could not . . . fail." As he searched for intelligence on the next Confederate move, Sheridan sought Grant's advice on future plans. The general in chief traveled to West Virginia on September 14 to confer with his subordinate. While en route, however, Young's men informed Sheridan that the long-awaited opportunity was at hand.[53]

By this time, Early had concluded that, due to his reluctance to engage the Southerners, Sheridan "possessed an excessive caution which amounted to timidity." On the basis of that perception, and knowing how desperately Richmond needed troops, he returned Kershaw's division and Cutshaw's artillery to Lee. On September 15 these forces departed Winchester for Richmond and three days later reached Culpeper Court House, far from supporting distance of Early. On the day Kershaw left, Young's scouts located a former slave named Tom Laws who possessed a permit to travel through Confederate lines to Winchester. Their resulting plan was simple: Laws would enter the town to sell vegetables and secretly pass a message to Rebecca Wright, a local schoolteacher and known Unionist. In the note, Sheridan requested that she provide any news concerning the movements of Early's troops. The messenger delivered it the day after Kershaw's departure. Wright replied that although she knew little specific information, she heard from a Confederate officer boarding with neighbors that Kershaw and Cutshaw had returned to Lee, that Early's strength was far less than Sheridan supposed, and that "no more [reinforcements] are expected, as they cannot be spared from Richmond."[54]

As it turned out, Wright provided Sheridan with a key bit of information that corroborated other reports of the recall of troops and "was most important in showing positively that Kershaw was gone." In addition, her last sentence indicated that Grant's relentless pressure would prevent Lee from sending any more troops to Early. Seeing Kershaw's departure as evening the odds, Sheridan felt confident that he could "strike the balance" with success. Armed with this information, the Union valley commander met Grant with a plan to assault Early's weakened command. Impressed with his subordinate's enthusiasm, Grant gave him but one simple order: "Go in!" [55]

Sheridan followed this brief command to the letter. On September 19, while Kershaw continued on toward Richmond, the Federals attacked and defeated Early at Winchester, forcing him south across Cedar Creek. Three days later Grant ordered a one-hundred-gun salute when Sheridan again crushed Early at Fisher's Hill. This last victory brought the entire lower valley, from the Potomac to Strasburg, under Union control. The twin triumphs, Grant told Sheridan, had "wipe[d] out much of the stain upon our arms by previous disasters in that locality." And in a statement revealing the intimate connection between events in the two fronts, Grant proclaimed that if Sheridan continued on the present course, his "good work [would] cause the fall of Richmond." [56]

After Fisher's Hill, the retreating Confederates found refuge at Rock-fish Gap on the western edge of the Blue Ridge, giving the Federals the opportunity to reduce the Shenandoah's resources to ashes. As they moved up the valley, Sheridan's men burned crops, barns, mills, and anything of military value as far south as Harrisonburg and Port Republic. The Union commander believed that this pyrotechnic display had closed the final chapter of his 1864 campaign. After recommending that portions of his army be sent elsewhere, Sheridan marched back down the valley and bivouacked along Cedar Creek south of Middletown. Early, however, had other ideas. Trailing Sheridan's columns back north, he prepared one last surprise.[57]

With Early on the ropes, Grant pressed Lee once again to make him think twice about helping his beleaguered subordinate. From September 29 to October 2, he battered Confederate lines north and south of the James, resulting in the capture of Fort Harrison, a formidable redoubt outside Richmond. The engagements south of the river forced Lee to extend his already thin lines another three miles southwest of Petersburg. Although no breakthroughs resulted from these offensives, Grant prevented Lee from ever again sending substantial reinforcements to the Shenandoah. Isolated and alone, Early had one last chance to redeem the situation.[58]

Sheridan's twin victories had not only punished the Confederates but they also forced Lee to send Kershaw, who had not yet reached the capital, *back* to the valley. Kershaw's return to Early denied the Confederates at Richmond and Petersburg much-needed reinforcements when Grant launched his simultaneous offensive on September 29. "Kershaw's absence," claimed an authority on the subject, "nearly resulted in disaster on both sides of the James." Utilizing quality intelligence, Grant and Sheridan had effectively isolated Kershaw in transit between the two theaters, denying both Early and Lee the services of a veteran division at a critical time. The intelligence provided by Sharpe's and Young's scouts succeeded in isolating Early's army from Richmond and precluded Lee from again using the valley as a diversion.[59]

As the war entered its final October, events foreshadowed a grim future for Confederate valley operations. On October 9 Sheridan's cavalry defeated Early's troopers at Tom's Brook and sent them fleeing up the valley. Certain that his adversary possessed no more offensive punch, Sheridan departed for Washington on October 15 to meet with War Department officials and decide on a future course in the Shenandoah. Only one day into his journey, however, he received startling news from his Cedar Creek headquarters. A message arrived informing him that a Union signal station had intercepted a message transmitted to Early at Fisher's Hill. Federal signal operators, in possession of the Confederate signal code, quickly deciphered the intercept, which read, "Be ready to advance on Sheridan as soon as my forces get up, and we can crush him before he finds out I have joined you." The message was signed "J. Longstreet." Since this news ran contrary to his own intelligence, Sheridan asked Halleck to wire City Point for corroboration. Halleck replied that Grant believed Longstreet was indeed in the valley but that he "brought with him no troops from Richmond." Recalling Grant's intelligence blunders during Early's raid, Halleck cautioned Sheridan to remain vigilant: "I have very little confidence in the information collected at his headquarters." Sheridan canceled a scheduled cavalry raid and placed his army on alert. But feeling "confident of good results" even if the intercepted message proved true, the valley commander hastened to Washington to keep his appointment.[60]

Longstreet had not joined Early nor had Lee reinforced the valley army. The signal dispatch was a ruse perpetrated by Early to prevent Sheridan from sending forces back to Grant. Knowing the Federals could read his signal traffic, Early planted the information to fool his opponent. While Sheridan failed to rise to the bait, he did leave his army at a critical moment. Though on alert, few in Sheridan's ranks were prepared for what happened on the banks of Cedar Creek soon afterward. On October 19 the Army of the Valley steamrolled through the supposedly vigilant Union camps, seemingly winning a major victory until Sheridan appeared, rallied his army, and drove the Confederates from the field, sending the remnants fleeing up the Valley Pike.[61]

Despite losing several engagements and a substantial portion of his army, Early somehow kept his battered command together and made a final stand in early March 1865. After learning of Sheridan's advance toward Lynchburg in late February, the Confederates constructed defenses at Waynesboro. Unfortunately for Early, Sheridan had learned all about Confederate deployments and their strength from a female spy in his employ. Guided by this information, on March 2 the Federals easily swept aside the tattered remnants of the Second Corps. The once-feared Army of the Valley ceased to exist after that day, effectively ending operations in the Shenandoah. Sheridan had finally destroyed Early's army and the valley they defended, leaving only a trail of smoke, the charred remains of barns and mills, and the searing memory of "The Burning" in the minds of the region's inhabitants.[62]

Attempting to exorcise the ghosts of his failure to detect the movement of the Second Corps west, Grant improved his intelligence system to prevent a repeat of the debacle of June and July. Eventually, he and Sheridan reaped the rewards of their improved network and isolated the valley, making it difficult—and costly—for Lee to shuttle troops between Richmond and Shenandoah. In early August, the BMI's timely discovery of Kershaw's departure from Richmond and Young's even timelier discovery of its recall had a profound impact on the war in the valley. News of Kershaw's departure on September 15 presented Sheridan with an opportunity to attack a weakened foe, resulting in two major Confederate defeats. In both engagements, Kershaw's presence might have tipped the balance in the Confederates' favor. In fact, one historian of the campaign contends, "had Joseph Kershaw's division been with the army, Early would have won at Winchester." Similarly, Early's troubles forced Lee to return Kershaw's command to the valley, leaving him without a veteran division at a time when he desperately needed all the men he could muster to blunt Grant's offensives of September 29–October 2.

The dual Union intelligence system developed by Grant and Sheridan provided quality information that led to Kershaw's absence from both theaters at critical times. Lee's "misuse" of his division, argues historian Richard Sommers, "was one of the worst miscalculations he ever made." Stated another way, Grant and Sheridan's "use" of Kershaw's division by keeping it away from where it was needed most—a situation made possible by the intelligence organizations created in both commands— was an important factor that doomed Jubal Early and the Army of the Valley.[63]

"He Could Not Send Off Any Large Body without My Knowing It"

Although the Shenandoah Valley had become a key concern for Grant after crossing the James River, his most pressing problem remained the siege of Richmond and Petersburg. He had vowed to "fight it out" all summer, but the coming elections and the perception in the North that the recent campaign had failed made him anxious to defeat Lee. Before the summer of 1864 ended, he hoped to keep the Army of Northern Virginia pinned in its trenches, prevent the detachment of troops to the valley or to Georgia, continue the destruction of Richmond's communication lines, and force Lee to stretch his thinning manpower. To accomplish these goals, intelligence on troop deployments and detachments would be critical. Until the war ended, the Bureau of Military Information focused primarily on examining the growing number of deserters and prisoners—supplemented by news from their "friends" inside the Confederate capital—to formulate an order of battle for use in tracking elements of Lee's army. Systematic interrogations provided information on the whereabouts and movements of brigades and divisions, which were then plotted on "information maps" distributed to field commanders. Captives also told of brigade consolidations and changes in command and offered insights on morale within the ranks.[1] Working feverishly behind the scenes, the BMI would become an invaluable asset in Grant's campaign to capture Richmond, destroy Lee's army, and end the war.

After the siege commenced in mid-June 1864, Grant focused on severing Lee's logistical lines south of Petersburg and forcing his opponent to weaken other sections to defend them. If the BMI could detect these resulting soft spots, Grant might be able to end the siege quickly. He started this process on June 22 by sending forces south and west of Petersburg to threaten the Weldon and Southside Railroads, both key links to the rest of the Confederacy. Although the offensive fell short of the railroads, Lee had to extend his right flank and tax his manpower even further. After Jubal Early's withdrawal to Virginia after menacing Washington in mid-July, Grant continued this extension south while the BMI watched for redeployments using Southern deserters, who were daily entering Union lines by the dozen, as a key source for information. In fact, this information hemorrhage caused the Confederates considerable headaches. For example, numerous deserters had alerted George Sharpe that Lee planned to attack on July 18. Union troops braced for the assault but none occurred. As Grant scratched his head, another deserter arrived and solved the mystery. According to his testimony, Confederate troops were indeed ready to advance on that day, but Lee suspended the order because, as Grant wrote, "so many deserters had come into our lines and exposed their plans." [2]

During the siege, information from inside Richmond also helped in planning future operations. On July 25 Grant proposed sending Philip H. Sheridan's cavalry north of the James to destroy the rail connections north of Richmond, specifically the Virginia Central and the Richmond, Fredericksburg, and Potomac Railroads. The focus on these two rail lines resulted in part from Samuel Ruth's observations that tearing them up would lead to food shortages in the capital, for "the people of Richmond were fed mostly from the North side of the James River and the Army to a limited extent also." At the same time as Sheridan's raid, Maj. Gen. Winfield S. Hancock's corps would demonstrate against the Richmond defenses. Having heard from three refugees that there were "no troops in Richmond save the second class militia," Grant hoped Hancock would "surprise the little garrison of Citizen soldiery now in Richmond and get in." If that failed, however, he believed the demonstration would at least "force them to weaken Petersburg so that we can take it" with Union forces south of the river. Once underway, Grant advised commanders in the rest of the Army of the Potomac opposite Petersburg to be ready "to take advantage of any movement of the enemy" away from his front. To ensure success, he also authorized a daring plan to literally blast a hole in the enemy's works guarding Petersburg. In early July, Maj. Gen. Ambrose Burnside had proposed digging a tunnel beneath the Confederate lines, filling it with explosives, and setting it off. The resulting explosion, in theory, would create a gap in the enemy's defenses large enough for Union troops to flood through, overcome their dazed opponents, and seize Petersburg. But this scheme depended heavily upon Lee depleting the Petersburg lines to meet Hancock's supposed attack on Richmond. Determining whether the Virginian had risen to the bait fell to Sharpe, John C. Babcock, and the BMI. [3]

On July 26 Grant revealed that Sharpe's bureau was performing this duty well. "Deserters come in every day," he wrote Chief of Staff Henry Halleck, "enabling us to keep track of every change the enemy makes."

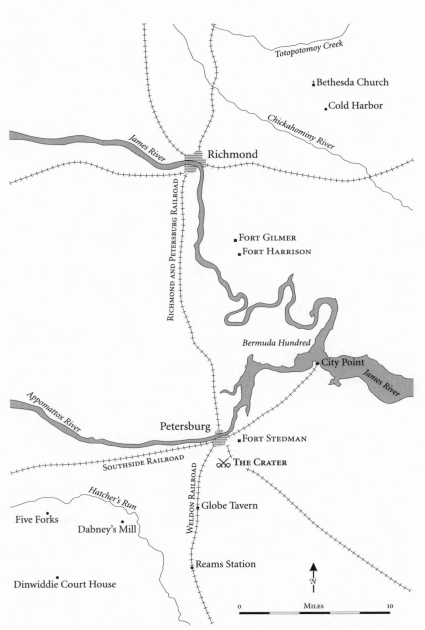

The Richmond and Petersburg Theater, 1864–1865

At the same time, Babcock forwarded information on the layout of the Petersburg defenses. During an interrogation, one deserter noted that "there is no second line of works to the rear . . . between their present line and Petersburg." In fact, Babcock added, "This is the repeated statement of all deserters." Burnside's engineers had feared that a second line of works would jeopardize the whole operation, but this intelligence revealed that after breaching the front line, the attackers would have a clear path to Petersburg. From this and other reports, Grant concluded that the assault had an excellent chance of success. "[T]he enemy," he wrote, appeared to be "looking for a formidable attack either from Bermuda [Butler] or north of the James and . . . will detach from Petersburg heavily to prevent its success." The key to success, however, lay in the BMI's ability to uncover this movement. As Hancock and Sheridan moved into position on the night of July 26, the general in chief waited for Lee's reaction.[4]

Meeting heavy opposition the following day, Hancock's demonstration and Sheridan's raid fell short of their objectives. But Lee had swallowed the bait. "The enemy evidently became very sensitive over our move to the North bank," Grant wrote late on July 28, "and have been moving to meet it ever since they discovered it." That same day, Babcock and Sharpe questioned deserters who claimed that brigades from different Confederate divisions had departed Petersburg and moved north. Hancock concurred with their reports, citing information from an "intelligent prisoner" who claimed that most of Longstreet's and Hill's corps had rushed to meet the threat. From Richmond agents came news that at least two divisions went north from Petersburg and that most citizens believed an attack on the capital was imminent. Based upon this information, by July 29, Maj. Gen. George Meade and Grant had concluded that most of Lee's infantry was now north of the James, leaving only three divisions to defend Petersburg.[5]

With the enemy "evidently piling up everything" to defend the capital, the Federals moved on Petersburg. A little before 5 A.M. on July 30, Burnside's mine exploded, annihilating a large section of the Confederate line and the men who manned it, creating an enormous crater 170 feet long, 50 feet wide, and 30 feet deep. Shocked Confederates farther down the lines abandoned their positions to seek safety, leaving a gap nearly a quarter-mile wide for the attacking Federals to exploit. Despite this rare opportunity, Burnside's assault sputtered due to poor leadership, lack of coordination, and the dogged determination of those Confederates who eventually turned the crater into a death trap for the Union soldiers plunging through the gap. By midmorning, Grant called off the attack and the Southerners regained control of their lines. The so-called battle of the Crater was a disastrous failure for the Federals. All the good intelligence, planning, and destruction caused by the mine had amounted to nothing. "Such an opportunity for carrying fortifications I have never seen and do not expect to have again," wrote an embittered Grant. The siege continued.[6]

Between July 30 and October 2, the BMI tracked the movements of Southern troops while Grant again forced Lee to stretch his lines farther and prevented him from detaching forces to the valley. Although failing to crack Lee's defenses, by October Grant had extended his lines across the Weldon, edged closer to the Southside Railroad, and captured Fort Harrison, a key Confederate stronghold north of the James. After another attempt to sever the Southside failed at Burgess' Mill later that month, major operations around Richmond and Petersburg ground to a halt until spring. But the BMI kept busy during the winter, especially since Sheridan's victory at Cedar Creek and Lee's need for troops meant Early's valley command would probably return to Richmond. In early November, evidence surfaced indicating that Lee had indeed recalled the Second Corps. On November 18 Sharpe learned from the Richmond underground that all rolling stock on the Virginia Central had been sent west to retrieve Early's men. Two days later the BMI chief noted that Kershaw's division had returned. "The fact of it's return," commented John A. Rawlins, "is undoubted" because some of Kershaw's men had visited the Petersburg market and "one of our agents . . . had his stall robbed by them." In early December the remainder of the valley army returned. Two of the three Second Corps divisions, commanded by Maj. Gen. John B. Gordon and Brig. Gen. John Pegram, departed the Shenandoah for Richmond on December 7. Four days later—at the same time these two units trudged into Richmond—Grant wired Sheridan: "there is no doubt but that all of Gordon's and Pegram's divisions are here." The general in chief now knew that Early had but one division left. On December 19 a Richmond spy sent news that this last division, under Brig. Gen. Bryan Grimes, had also returned from the valley, leaving Early with only scattered remnants of assorted commands. The same Confederate corps that had befuddled Grant for nearly a month the previous

summer had finally returned, this time under the watchful eyes of the
BMI. Advised of these reductions, Sheridan dealt Early a final blow at
Waynesboro the following March.[7]

Besides tracking the return of the Second Corps, the BMI, aided by the
Richmond underground, also sought intelligence on the living conditions and morale of Confederate soldiers and civilians behind the siege
lines. For example, on March 19, 1865, Sharpe reported news from Richmond agents that Southern resolve had crumbled. A week earlier, a sharp
skirmish north of Richmond had apparently caused great consternation
in the city. But the agents claimed, "When the alarm-bells were rung . . .
for citizens to turn out only some 20 appeared with guns." This lackluster response, Sharpe noted, was viewed by many as a sign "of the general
abandonment of the cause."[8]

The Richmond agents, in particular Van Lew and Ruth, passed along
newspapers and other correspondence, keeping Grant apprised of Confederate government activities and proclamations; the price of gold, flour,
bacon, and tobacco (all indicators of Southern fortunes); the amount of
food in the markets; and the latest rumors circulating in the capital. For
example, Van Lew revealed the dire circumstances in the city during the
winter when she wrote: "May God bless and bring you soon to deliver us.
We are all in an awful situation here. There is great want of food." When
an explosion ripped apart sections of City Point in August, she was the
first to discover that the Confederate Secret Service had planted the explosives. Another agent claimed the failure of the Hampton Roads Peace
Conference on February 3 "is having a very depressing effect generally."
As evidence, he noted that food and gold prices, which had been falling,
were now on the rise. Another message told of Jefferson Davis's preparations for leaving the city after it fell and provided as evidence a catalog
of "some portions of his household effect[s] . . . sold at private auction"
in preparation for his move. As for the determination of the soldiers
defending Richmond, another spy informed Grant not to worry about
them since the local defense forces guarding the city "are prepared to
run." Sharpe's summaries also showed that the underground monitored
Confederate recruitment efforts, the movements of troops and supplies,
the types of ordnance in short supply, the affects of news from other
fronts, the activities of Confederate gunboats on the James, and the
placement of "torpedoes" (mines) along the roads and in the river. At
times, however, agents unknowingly reported wild rumors as truth,

which proved to be the case in December when an operative announced that a deeply depressed Jefferson Davis had "made a second attempt to poison himself and came near succeeding in his attempt."[9]

During the winter of 1865, two concerns led Sharpe to extend BMI operations beyond City Point. First, Union officials were worried about a potential increase in Union desertion as a result of Grant's Special Orders Number Eighty-two, which updated an earlier policy designed to induce Confederates to defect. Under the new orders, copies of which were spirited into Southern lines, Southern deserters who took an oath to the Union would receive subsistence and, if their homes were within Union lines, free transportation back to their families. If their homes were behind enemy lines, the Federal government would transport them without charge to "any point in the Northern States." Anxious to get home, some enterprising Union soldiers sensed an opportunity and left their regiments (usually while on picket duty) and disguised themselves as Southern deserters. With any luck, they might convince their "captors" that their "home" was in enemy territory, which meant free transportation anywhere in the North. The policy was designed to shrink Southern armies through desertion, but the prospect of Federal runaways slipping through the cracks and being sent not to the stockade but home at government expense forced the army to act. Capt. John McEntee's primary mission at Norfolk, a concentration point for processing Confederate prisoners, was to be the official "examining officer" tasked with using his familiarity with the enemy's organization (which few enlisted men knew anything about) to trip up Union deserters and close this avenue for escaping service.

Sharpe also had McEntee procure information on William T. Sherman's progress through the Carolinas and on the enemy forces confronting him. Southern papers had provided most of Grant's news on Sherman's progress, but he now needed more reliable knowledge. Seeing Norfolk as "a proper base from which to send scouts southward" into North Carolina, Sharpe instructed McEntee to recruit personnel for this mission and to direct their operations.[10]

Another concern of the BMI in early 1865 was the possible Confederate withdrawal from Richmond. To uncover such a movement, Grant had the BMI watch Lee's movements for warning signs so that the Federals could "pitch into him" before he escaped. Rumors to this effect had been circulating since January, and as a result, Sharpe directed Samuel Ruth to question employees of the Richmond and Danville Railroad to discover the truth. Although Ruth's investigation revealed that the Confederates were indeed preparing for an evacuation, Sharpe remained skeptical. Based on information from "the best informed of our friends in Richmond," and aware of the political ramifications for Davis if he relinquished the city, the BMI chief concluded that Richmond "will not be evacuated because it is the capital of the Confederacy, and so long as they retain their capital, they are as much of a country as they have ever been." Nevertheless, rumors of a possible abandonment haunted Grant until April.[11]

Perhaps the most interesting concern for the BMI that winter was the Confederacy's decision to arm blacks to fight for Southern independence. Davis had advocated the recruitment of blacks for service in the Confederate armies since November 1864, and the following March the Confederate Congress, after much argument, authorized the use of these men in combat roles. Three days after the House passed the bill, Sharpe wrote a fascinating analysis on how black Confederates, which he estimated would total as many as two hundred thousand, might be employed by the enemy and what the North could do to undermine this potential advantage. If Lee placed fifty thousand black troops in the Richmond-Petersburg lines, Sharpe reasoned, he could defend these key points while freeing "a moveable column" of white troops to "throw upon any threatened point, or for unexpected and diverting attacks." Black troops deployed similarly at Danville, Gordonsville, and Lynchburg might be decisive. "[W]ill not negro troops . . . be able to hold these points," he asked, "and will not the white forces still under the control of the Confederacy be substantially free for supporting and aggressive movements?" This troubling scenario led Sharpe to consider ways of ending this experiment "before, by habit, discipline and experience with arms, they shall have grown to that aptitude of a soldier which will bring them to obey orders under any circumstances." Obviously, Sharpe placed great stock in the ability of military discipline to overcome black animosity toward their white masters and produce soldiers willing to die in the ranks with those who enslaved them. In any event, he wished to avoid testing his hypothesis. Sharpe proposed a covert operation using blacks from Union ranks to slip into Richmond and sow discontent among the new recruits and foment mass desertion. This plan could work, he concluded, because "Negroes are an eminently secret people;

they have a system of understanding amounting almost to free masonry among them; they will trust each other when they will not trust white men." Though the Confederacy's bold experiment never really developed, the BMI carefully monitored these efforts until the war's end.[12]

New threats to Washington also became a concern as spring approached. But Grant replied calmly to concerns from the Lincoln administration that Lee no longer enjoyed the luxury of being able to detach forces for such a mission. First, the Virginian could not afford to deplete his ranks further without endangering Richmond and Petersburg. Deserters interrogated by the BMI had also indicated that the Army of Northern Virginia remained paralyzed by fears of mass desertions. "A retrograde movement would cost him thousands of men even if we did not follow," predicted Grant. More importantly, he boasted, "The great number of deserters and refugees coming in daily enables us to learn if any considerable force starts off almost . . . as soon as it starts." Revealing his faith in Sharpe's men, Grant believed Lee "could not send off any large body without my knowing it." With the help of the BMI, Grant had finally exorcised the ghost of Jubal Early.[13]

Indeed, Lee had no plans to dispatch forces to save what was left of the valley forces. But he was planning a bold stroke to punch through Union lines. On March 25, 1865, Confederate forces launched a surprise assault against Fort Stedman, a key Federal fortification outside Petersburg. Lee hoped this action would force Grant to withdraw troops from other parts of the line to meet the threat, thereby relieving pressure on his right below Petersburg. The Confederates captured the fort, but Federal counterattacks eventually drove them out with serious loss. Lee's final gamble had failed miserably. Ruth had informed Grant of an impending attack on the fort but could not pinpoint a date. All he knew was the assault would come "as soon as the ground was dry enough to move artillery." He also told the general in chief that Lee felt confident "he could whip Genl. Grant and that he would do it or die in the ditch." Since the BMI failed to detect the concentration of over eighteen thousand troops in the vicinity of Colquitt's Salient, the origination point of the attack, the date of the attack remained a mystery until too late. Ruth's ambiguous message and the BMI's mistake, however, meshed with Grant's perception of the enemy. He believed Lee had nothing left and that his men were "demoralized and deserting very fast," a statement founded upon the large number of deserters arriving every day bearing tales of misery and despair in the ranks. Though surprised by Lee's un-expected move, Grant focused on the results. At Fort Stedman, the Army of Northern Virginia had drawn its final breath. But Lee was still a dangerous adversary and could prolong the war if he escaped Richmond. In fact, during the preceding months, Richmond agents had filed numerous reports indicating that Lee planned to abandon the capital and join Joseph E. Johnston's army in North Carolina. On March 29 one informant stated that Jefferson Davis "had his things all packed up and was ready to leave." The testimony of several agents that carloads of machinery, boxes of government records, and the wounded were being sent out of the city heightened Grant's anxiety. In his memoirs he noted that his greatest fear was that "Lee should get away some night before I was aware of it." [14]

Instead of waiting for Lee to act, Grant seized the initiative, hoping to crush Lee before he joined Johnston and avoid a "long, tedious and expensive campaign" to defeat their combined armies. In order to prevent "the rapid concentration of Lee's and Johnston's Armies," Sheridan moved south and west of Petersburg to cut the railroad connections with North Carolina. On April 1 he punched through Confederate lines at Five Forks and raced toward the enemy's rear. The next day Grant attacked along the entire front and finally overwhelmed the defenders. Facing disaster, Lee evacuated Richmond and Petersburg that night. With the roads illuminated by the fires raging in the capital, the Army of Northern Virginia marched westward. [15]

In the early evening of April 2, officers at AOAR headquarters received the first news of the evacuation. The next morning Grant began his pursuit. Lee's objective remained unclear, but the general in chief surmised that he would probably head toward Danville, Virginia, via Burkeville, a major depot on the Richmond and Danville Railroad. If Lee reached Danville, he would be that much closer to Johnston. In fact, Grant warned Sherman about that possibility, noting, "It is reported here that Johnston has evacuated Raleigh and is moving up to join Lee." From an earlier intelligence report, however, Grant knew that the enemy had constructed fortifications along the Richmond and Danville at Amelia Court House, leading him to conclude that Lee would "make a stand" there to protect his escape route as well as his connections with Lynchburg. Information acquired the following day altered this assessment somewhat. A railroad engineer reported that Jefferson Davis and his cabinet had passed through Burkeville a day earlier bound for Danville. More importantly, the informant saw two trainloads of supplies heading for Farmville, which he claimed was Lee's immediate destination before turning south to Danville. Armed with this knowledge, Grant ordered Sheridan's cavalry to intercept them.[16]

Although Grant believed on April 4 that Farmville was Lee's objective, his evaluation proved premature. Not until the following day did the Confederate commander reach that decision. His army had arrived at Amelia Court House on April 4 expecting to find trains loaded with rations. Finding the tracks empty, the army remained in the vicinity to forage until the following day. During this time, Lee received bad news. Federal troops had reached Jetersville, halfway between Burkeville and Amelia Court House, and blocked his path to Danville. Changing course, Lee marched for Farmville later that evening, hoping to cross the Appomattox River, burn the bridges, and reach Lynchburg, where ample supplies awaited his army.[17]

But Sheridan's scouts had followed his every step. They knew Lee was at Amelia Court House and had captured orders from his commissary general directing that supplies be sent along the Richmond and Danville Railroad to Burkeville. Sheridan moved to cut him off. On April 4, Union cavalry and three infantry corps cut the railroad at Jetersville, forcing Lee to redirect his march toward Farmville. The following morning one of Sheridan's reconnaissance patrols confirmed that the enemy was indeed headed toward that hamlet. On April 6, several miles east of Farmville, Sheridan's cavalry and elements of the Sixth Corps intercepted and overwhelmed an enemy column at Sayler's Creek, capturing around six thousand prisoners and several high-ranking Confederate officers. Although the rest of Lee's army reached the Appomattox River safely, Sheridan's scouts, effective cavalry reconnaissance, and a spirited pursuit had provided a stunning victory that helped seal the fate of the Army of Northern Virginia.[18]

Despite the losses at Sayler's Creek and those resulting from rampant straggling, Lee pressed on toward Lynchburg while Sheridan moved into position at Appomattox Station to block his escape. The Federal general chose that location based on the report of Sgt. James White, one of Young's scouts, who saw four trainloads of supplies waiting for Lee at the depot. On April 7 Sheridan's cavalry descended on the station and captured the trains, burning one and sending the remainder out of Lee's reach. Soon, Union infantry arrived, and by the following day, Grant had Lee boxed in near Appomattox Court House. Seeing the road to Lynchburg closed and without enough strength to punch through Grant's encircling troops, Lee surrendered on April 9.[19]

Though jubilant about the victory and anxious to go home, George Sharpe had one last duty to complete. To ensure an accurate accounting of Lee's army, Grant tasked the BMI chief with issuing paroles to the officers and men of the Army of Northern Virginia. For nearly a week, Sharpe processed Lee's veterans as they filed by, complaining that the task quickly became "difficult and laborious" due to the "very considerable disorganization" of the Southern army. Despite this grumble, however, he undoubtedly relished informing stunned Confederate officers, many of whom "did not clearly understand their own organization," which brigade and division they belonged to.[20]

"The Difference in War Is
Full Twenty Five Per Cent"

Reflecting upon Grant's triumphs during the war, William Tecumseh Sherman hinted that his friend's success stemmed in part from his disdain for military intelligence. "He don't care a damn for what the enemy does out of his sight he proclaimed.[1] Given Grant's ill-informed status before Fort Donelson, Shiloh, the Wilderness, and during Jubal Early's raid, Sherman's description certainly has merit. But his suggestion that the eventual general in chief placed little emphasis on intelligence fails to appreciate the complex nature of Grant's true views on the subject. In reality, he cared a great deal about what the enemy did on the "other side of the hill," but unlike Henry Halleck, George McClellan, or William Rosecrans, he refused to allow that concern to become an obsession in which the search for "perfect" information became an end in itself, effectively stifling intuitive risk taking.

Though Grant considered intelligence indispensable and pursued it when possible, experience had also taught him that no amount of information could vanquish all doubts. On this point he would have agreed with Napoleon, who once stated, "Uncertainty is the essence of war." Not even Grenville Dodge and George Sharpe, whose intelligence networks became incredibly sophisticated and productive, completely cleared the fog. But while some officers saw this persistent, nagging uncertainty as an obstacle, Grant viewed it as fertile ground for opportunity. To him, military intelligence was neither a panacea nor the only means of determining future plans. Instead of being enervated by the lack of information or by the search for the unchallenged truth, he compensated by using the initiative to shift the burden of uncertainty to the enemy, who undoubtedly experienced similar problems finding reliable and timely intelligence on him. Keeping the Confederates off balance by relentless offensive activity forced them to react and perhaps provide opportunities to exploit. Sherman understood Grant's faith in the initiative as a substitute for accurate intelligence. "[I]nstead of guessing at what [the enemy] means to do," Sherman explained, "he would have to guess at my plans." Though not guaranteed to bring victory, he concluded, "The difference in war is full twenty five per cent."[2]

At times Grant also relied upon his *coup d'oeil*, or what Clausewitz called an "inward eye," to guide him. But Shiloh, Holly Springs, and

Early's raid were harsh reminders that substituting the initiative and intuition for intelligence entailed risks. Even at the best of times, these could not provide an ironclad assurance against surprise. Being human, moreover, meant his "inward eye" was not immune to blindness or myopia. Wishful thinking and fixed perceptions, especially with regard to the enemy's supposedly shattered morale, often guided Grant even in the face of powerful contradictory evidence. Nevertheless, this fixed belief that the enemy would crack in the next battle also drove him to maintain the initiative and to keep pushing on, a strategy that eventually led to success. At times, however, only sheer luck distinguished a good decision from a bad one.

As the war progressed, Grant's respect for intelligence as an indispensable yet flawed tool increased, particularly after Early's raid. Rejecting George Meade's advice to scuttle the Bureau of Military Information, the general in chief instead embraced the organization and trusted Sharpe to provide his information needs. As a result, the BMI became an integral part of Grant's successful campaign to neutralize the Shenandoah Valley and to stretch Lee's manpower to the brink of collapse. In the final analysis, Sherman's postwar observation described the Grant who forged ahead through the fog of uncertainty, trusting in his *coup d'oeil* and the initiative to tip the balance in his favor. Left unsung in this description, however, was the Grant of 1864–65 who realized that neither his judgment nor the initiative were infallible. The result was a more pronounced reliance upon intelligence supplied by the BMI. By the fall of 1864, Grant's intuition, the initiative, and Sharpe's intelligence network had fused to create a potent weapon. Contrary to Sherman's view, therefore, a key element of Grant's success was *not* his lack of concern for what the enemy did out of his sight, but rather his ability to *prevent* that concern—and the paralyzing uncertainty it fostered—from becoming an insurmountable impediment on the road to victory. Perhaps no other statement captures this merger better than Grant's own formula for success. "The art of war is simple enough," he observed. "Find out where your enemy is. Get at him as soon as you can. Strike him as hard as you can and as often as you can, and keep moving on."[3]

NOTES

ABBREVIATIONS

B&L   C. C. Buel and R. U. Johnson, eds. *Battles and Leaders of the Civil War.* 4 vols. New York: Thomas Yoseloff, 1887–88.

DP   Grenville M. Dodge Papers, State Historical Society of Iowa, Des Moines

GP   John Y. Simon, ed. *The Papers of Ulysses S. Grant.* 24 vols. to date. Carbondale: Southern Illinois University Press, 1967–.

ISHS   Indiana State Historical Society, Indianapolis

ISHL   Illinois State Historical Library, Springfield

ISL   Indiana State Library, Indianapolis

LC   Library of Congress, Washington DC

NARA   National Archives and Records Administration, Washington DC

NYPL   New York Public Library, New York City

OR   U.S. War Department. *The War of the Rebellion: Official Records of the Union and Confederate Armies.* 128 vols. Washington DC: Government Printing Office, 1880–1901. (Unless otherwise noted, all cited volumes are from series 1).

ORN   U.S. War Department. *Official Records of the Union and Confederate Navies in the War of the Rebellion.* 30 vols. Washington DC: Government Printing Office, 1894–1922.

PMUSG   Ulysses S. Grant, *Personal Memoirs of U. S. Grant.* 2 vols. New York: Charles L. Webster and Sons, 1885.

RG   Record Group

USG   Ulysses S. Grant

UVL   University of Virginia Library, Charlottesville

Introduction: "He Don't Care a Damn for What the Enemy Does Out of His Sight"

1. Mahan, *An Elementary Treatise*, 73; Jomini, *The Art of War*, 268.
2. Fishel, "Mythology of Civil War Intelligence," 344–67. In addition to HU-MINT, signals intelligence, or SIGINT, which was the interception of enemy signal traffic (telegraph and visual signaling), also became an important source during the war.
3. Clausewitz, *On War*, 117; Fishel, *Secret War*, 294; Peter Maslowski, "Military Intelligence Sources during the Civil War: A Case Study," in Hitchcock, *Intelligence Revolution*, 41. Maslowski's article is the best discussion of Civil War intelligence sources to date.
4. Statement of Levi Cecil, October 20, 1909, Benjamin Wilson Smith Papers, ISL. For Davis, see Hirshson, *Grenville M. Dodge*, 81–84. For Webster, see Fishel, *Secret War*, 148–49, 598–99.
5. Clausewitz, *On War*, 102, 112; Michael I. Handel, *War, Strategy, and Intelligence*, 70.
6. By far the best biography of Grant to date is Simpson, *Ulysses S. Grant*.
7. Lewis, *Captain Sam Grant*, 100–102, 114–15; Traas, *Golden Gate to Mexico City*, 124–25, 132–36; Bauer, *Mexican War*, 34; Caruso, *Mexican Spy Company*, 89; Meade, *Life and Letters*, 1:101; Hitchcock, *Fifty Years in Camp and Field*, 199.
8. *PMUSG*, 1:138–39; McWhiney, "Ulysses S. Grant's Pre–Civil War Education," in *Southerners and Other Americans*, 69.
9. Caruso, *Mexican Spy Company*, 152; Bauer, *Mexican War*, 261–68; *GP*, 1:131–37; *PMUSG*, 1:131–34.
10. Bauer, *Mexican War*, 270–72, 274; *PMUSG*, 1:136–37; Caruso, *Mexican Spy Company*, 152.
11. Caruso, *Mexican Spy Company*, 152–58; Hitchcock, *Fifty Years in Camp and Field*, 263.
12. Bauer, *Mexican War*, 288, 290–91; Traas, *Golden Gate to Mexico City*, 193.
13. USG to [unknown], September 12, 1847, *GP*, 1:145; Lewis, *Captain Sam Grant*, 217, 223; *PMUSG*, 1:165.
14. Quoted in Wilson, *Under the Old Flag*, 2:17.

1. "My Means of Information Are Certainly Better Than Most"

1. *PMUSG*, 1:248.
2. Catton, *Grant Moves South*, 12; USG to Stephen Hurlbut, July 16, 1862, *GP*, 2:71; USG to Julia Grant, July 19, 1861, *GP*, 2:72.

3. USG to Hurlbut, July 16, 1861, 2:71; *PMUSG*, 1:249–50.

4. USG to Hurlbut, July 16, 1861, 2:71.

5. John C. Kelton to USG, August 8, 1861, *GP*, 86–87; J. P. Sanderson to J. B. Devoe, n.d., RG 393 (Records of the United States Army Continental Commands), entry 2778 (Letters Sent Relating to Secret Service), NARA; C. Carroll Marsh to Fremont, August 12, 1861, RG 393, entry 5502 (Western Department, Letters Received), box 14; Hurlbut to John Pope, August 12, 1861, *OR*, 3:133–34. For the "Jessie Scouts" and Edward M. Kern, see Rolle, *John Charles Fremont*, 13–15; Hine, *Shadow of Fremont*, 149; RG 110 (Records of the Provost Marshal Generals Bureau) entry 36 (Correspondence, Reports, Appointments, and Other Records Relating to Individual Scouts, Spies, and Detectives), NARA; RG 393, entry 5500 (Western Department, Letters Sent). Unless otherwise noted, all RG 393 citations are from part 1.

6. Lew Wallace to Susan Wallace, October 13, 1861, box 1, Lew Wallace Collection, ISHS; Hurlbut to Pope, August 21, 1861, *OR*, 3:133–34; USG to W. E. McMackin, August 12, 1861, *GP*, 2:104.

7. USG to Kelton, August 11, 1861, *GP*, 2:98; "Special Orders," August 13, 1861, *GP*, 2:111; USG to Kelton, August 15, 1861, *GP*, 2:114; *Illinois State Journal*, August 24, 1861.

8. USG to Kelton, August 9, 1861, *GP*, 2:89; USG to Kelton, August 10, 1861, *GP*, 94.

9. William J. Hardee to Leonidas Polk, July 29, 1861, *OR*, 3:619; Gideon Pillow to Polk, July 30, 1861, *OR*, 3:621; Hughes and Stonesifer, *Gideon J. Pillow*, 180–82; Hughes, *General William J. Hardee*, 78–79.

10. Hardee to Polk, August 20, 1861, *OR*, 3:664; Hughes and Stonesifer, *Gideon J. Pillow*, 183–88; USG to Kelton, August 13, 1861, *GP*, 2:106–7; Hardee to Polk, August 20, 1861, *OR*, 3:664.

11. Castel, *Sterling Price*, 25–50; Ben McCulloch to Hardee, August 24, 1861, *OR*, 3:672; Catton, *Grant Moves South*, 28–36; *PMUSG*, 1:258–59; USG to Speed Butler, August 27, 1861, *GP*, 2:142; USG to Jesse Grant, August 27, 1861, *GP*, 2:145–46; USG to Butler, August 26, 1861, *GP*, 2:138–39; USG to Julia, August 26, 1861, *GP*, 2:141; USG to Jesse Grant, August 27, 1861, *GP*, 2:146. See also McCulloch to Jefferson Davis, August 24, 1861, *OR*, 3:671; and USG to Pope, August 26, 1861, *GP*, 2:139.

12. USG to Julia, August 26, 1861, *GP*, 2:141.

13. Welcher, *Union Army*, 2:155.

14. *PMUSG*, 1:261; Monaghan, *Swamp Fox*, 32–36; Conger, *Rise of U. S. Grant*, 37–38; Thompson to Pillow, August 16, 1861, *OR*, 3:657; Fremont to USG, August 28, 1861, *GP*, 2:151. For Fremont's plans, see Fremont to Abraham Lincoln, September 8, 1861, *OR*, 3:478–79.

15. Pillow to Polk, August 28, 1861, *OR*, 3:686; Polk to Jefferson Davis, Sep-

tember 4, 1861, *OR*, 4:181; Woodworth, *Davis and His Generals*, 34–39; Woodworth, "'Indeterminate Quantities,'" 289–97.

16. Hillyer to Kelton, September 1, 1861, *GP*, 2:165; USG to Kelton, September 1, 1861, *GP*, 2:164; USG to John A. McClernand, September 1, 1861, *GP*, 2:166; USG to Kelton, September 1, 1861, 2:165–66.

17. Gustav Waagner to USG, September 3, 1861, *GP*, 2:178–79; John Rodgers to USG, September 4, 1861, *GP*, 2:187; USG to Speaker of the Kentucky House of Representatives, September 5, 1861, *GP*, 2:189; USG to Fremont, September 4, 1861, *GP*, 2:186.

18. Deposition of Charles De Arnaud, March 28, 1889, Charles De Arnaud pension record, RG 15, NARA. See also RG 110, entry 95 (Accounts of Secret Service Agents, 1861–70), box 1; and John C. Fremont, "In Command in Missouri," *B&L*, 1:281–85.

19. De Arnaud deposition, De Arnaud pension record; De Arnaud to Fremont, September 5, 1861, *GP*, 2:193.

20. USG to Fremont, September 5, 1861, *GP*, 2:190, 193; *PMUSG*, 1:264–65; Catton, *Grant Moves South*, 48–49; De Arnaud deposition, De Arnaud pension record; USG to Fremont, September 6, 1861, *GP*, 2:196–97; Fremont to USG, September 5, 1861, *GP*, 2:191–92; *PMUSG*, 1:265–66.

21. USG to De Arnaud, November 30, 1861, *GP*, 3:243.

22. Polk to Jefferson Davis, September 4, 1861, *OR*, 4:191.

23. Clausewitz, *On War*, 191.

24. Luvaas, "Napoleon on the Art of Command," 31; Chandler, *Military Maxims of Napoleon*, 80.

25. Clausewitz, *On War*, 102; Sherman quoted in Simpson, *Ulysses S. Grant*, 462. See also William B. Feis, "'He Don't Care a Damn'," 68–72, 74–81.

2. "I Always Try to Keep Myself Posted"

1. USG to Fremont, September 4, 1861, *GP*, 2:186.

2. Woodworth, *Davis and His Generals*, 52–53, 57–58; Mullen, "Turning of Columbus," 217–18; Hughes, *Belmont*, 36–38.

3. Hughes, *Belmont*, 82–83; Mullen, "Turning of Columbus," 218.

4. Fremont to USG, August 28, 1861, *OR*, 3:141–42; USG to Fremont, September 10, 1861, *GP*, 2:224–25; *PMUSG*, 1:269; Catton, *Grant Moves South*, 39–40; Fremont to USG, September 8, 1861, *OR*, 3:478.

5. Fremont to USG, August 28, 1861, *GP*, 2:151.

6. Castel, *Sterling Price*, 48–50; Catton, *Grant Moves South*, 59; Fremont to USG, September 10, 1861, *OR*, 3:484.

7. Richard J. Oglesby to Fremont, August 30, 1861, RG 393, entry 5502, box 14. For a list of his scouts and spies, see the report of Oglesby's assistant adjutant general, August 18, 1861, RG 393, entry 5502, box 13.

8. USG to Oglesby, September 13, 1861, *GP*, 2:252; USG to Fremont, September 21, 1861, *GP*, 2:292; USG to Oglesby, September 21, 1861, *GP*, 2:294; *ORN*, 22:307; Rodgers to USG, September 4, 1861, *GP*, 2:187; Hughes, *Belmont*, 5; Stanton et al., *Reminiscences of General M. Jeff Thompson*, 89. See also James B. Eads, "Recollections of Foote and the Gunboats," *B&L*, 1:342, 346; Rear Adm. Henry Walke, "The Gunboats at Belmont and Fort Henry," *B&L*, 1:359–60.

9. S. Ledyard Phelps to Andrew H. Foote, *ORN*, 22:324–25; USG to Fremont, September 10, 1861, 2:225; General Orders No. 19, September 7, 1861, *OR*, 3:699; USG to Fremont, September 8, 1861, *GP*, 2:210; USG to Charles F. Smith, September 10, 1861, *GP*, 2:227–28.

10. USG to Fremont, September 10, 1861, 2:225.

11. Woodworth, "'Indeterminate Quantities,'" 289–97; Parks, *General Leonidas Polk*, 181–85; W. H. L. Wallace to Anne Wallace, box 2, Wallace-Dickey Papers, ISHL; Woodworth, *Davis and His Generals*, 30–31; anonymous officer quoted in Smith and Judah, *Chronicles of the Gringos*, 440; USG to Jesse Grant, May 6, 1861, *GP*, 2:22; USG to Butler, August 23, 1861, *GP*, 2:131; USG to Julia Grant, October 1, 1861, *GP*, 3:10; Simon, "Grant at Belmont," 164.

12. USG to Fremont, September 11, 1861, *GP*, 2:231–32; Oglesby to USG, September 11, 1861, *GP*, 2:235–36; USG to Oglesby, September 13, 1861, *GP*, 2:252; Oglesby to USG, September 16, 1861, *GP*, 2:252–53; USG to Fremont, September 14, 1861, *GP*, 2:258.

13. USG to Fremont, September 12, 1861, *GP*, 2:242.

14. USG to Fremont, September 15, 1861, *GP*, 2:262; USG to Fremont, September 6, 1861, *GP*, 2:216; USG to Fremont, September 15, 1861, 2:262–63; USG to Parmenas Turnley, September 18, 1861, *GP*, 2:282–83.

15. USG to Fremont, September 16, 1861, *GP*, 2:269–70; USG to Fremont, September 20, 1861, *GP*, 286–87. Lellyett spied mostly for Maj. Gen. Don Carlos Buell from 1861 to 1862. See Graf and Haskins, *Papers of Andrew Johnson*, 4:63. See also "Concerning John Lellyett," January 11, 1862, *GP*, 4:34–35.

16. Polk to Davis, September 14, 1861, *OR*, 4:191; Hughes and Stonesifer, *Gideon J. Pillow*, 195; Losson, *Tennessee's Forgotten Warriors*, 33; F. R. R. Smith to A. Heiman, September 25, 1861, *OR*, 4:428; Woodworth, *Davis and His Generals*, 52–53; Parks, *General Leonidas Polk*, 187–88.

17. USG to Fremont, September 23, 1861, *GP*, 2:300–301; USG to Oglesby, September 23, 1861, *GP*, 2:304; Oglesby to USG, September 24, 1861, *GP*, 2:304; Oglesby to USG, September 26, 1861, *GP*, 2:315–16; USG to Chauncey McKeever, September 26, 1861, *GP*, 2:314.

18. Castel, *Sterling Price*, 48–56; Catton, *Grant Moves South*, 70; John C. Fremont, "In Command in Missouri," *B&L*, 1:286–87; *PMUSG*, 1:269–70; Fremont to USG, September 26, 1861, *OR*, 3:507; Simon, "Grant at Belmont,"

162–63. See also the sympathetic Turkoly-Joczik, "Fremont and the Western Department," 359–67.

19. USG to Julia Grant, September 25, 1861, *GP*, 2:311; Simon, "Grant at Belmont," 162–63.

20. Fremont to USG, September 28, 1861, *OR*, 2:507–8; USG to McKeever, September 29, 1861, *GP*, 2:321; USG to McKeever, October 1, 1861, *GP*, 3:4; USG to Joseph B. Plummer, October 3, 1861, *GP*, 3:14.

21. USG to McKeever, September 30, 1861, *GP*, 2:329; USG to John A. McClernand, September 30, 1861, *GP*, 2:330; Smith to McKeever, October 1, 1861, *OR*, 3:510; USG to McKeever, October 1, 1861, 3:4; USG to McKeever, October 4, 1861, *GP*, 3:17.

22. McKeever to USG, October 6, 1861, *GP*, 3:18, 19; USG to Julia Grant, October 6, 1861, *GP*, 3:23. Johnston Brown passed through W. H. L. Wallace's command at Bird's Point. See "pass" from Grant for Brown, October 6, 1861, box 2, Wallace-Dickey Papers. See also Fremont to B. Gratz Brown, July 31, 1861; and pass for "J. E. Brown," July 31, 1861, RG 393, entry 5500; and USG to McKeever, October 6, 1861, *GP*, 3:19.

23. Smith to USG, October 6, 1861, 3:25; Wallace to Susan Wallace, October 27, 1861, box 1, Lew Wallace Collection, ISHS; USG to McKeever, October 7, 1861, *GP*, 3:24.

24. Conger, *Rise of U. S. Grant*, 79; M. Jeff Thompson to Aden Lowe, September 30, 1861, *OR*, 3:712; Wills, *Army Life*, 36; USG to McKeever, October 2, 1861, *GP*, 3:11, 12; USG to McKeever, October 4, 1861, 3:16.

25. Thompson to Lowe, October 3, 1861, *OR*, 3:713; Thompson to James A. Walker, October 7, 1861, *OR*, 3:714; Thompson to Albert Sidney Johnston, October 8, 1861, *OR*, 53:748; USG to McKeever, October 11, 1861, *GP*, 3:33.

26. Thompson to Johnston, October 11, 1861, *OR*, 3:22; Thompson to Johnston, October 18, 1861, *OR*, 3:225–26; USG to McKeever, October 18, 1861, *GP*, 3:54; USG to Plummer, October 18, 1861, *GP*, 3:56–57; Stanton, et al., *Reminiscences of General M. Jeff Thompson*, 106–17; USG to Marsh, November 5, 1861, *GP*, 3:116.

27. Hardee to Johnston, September 18, 1861, *OR*, 3:703; Simon B. Buckner to W. W. Mackall, October 11, 1861, *OR*, 4:444; Johnston to Samuel Cooper, October 13, 1861, *OR*, 4:445; Hughes, *General William J. Hardee*, 81–82.

28. McKeever to USG, September 28, 1861, *OR*, 3:508; Marsh to Rawlins, September 29, 1861, *GP*, 2:322; William T. Sherman to USG, October 16, 1861, *GP*, 3:43; USG to McKeever, October 17, 1861, *GP*, 3:47; USG to McKeever, October 18, 1861, 3:54–55; USG to Plummer, October 18, 1861, *GP*, 3:56–57; Marszalek, *Sherman*, 157–63.

29. USG to McKeever, October 16, 1861, *GP*, 3:42; USG to Smith, October 16, 1861, *GP*, 3:43; USG to Julia Grant, October 20, 1861, *GP*, 3:63–64. Grant dismissed

another report of Confederates crossing to Belmont, claiming that they were only harvesting corn for Polk's commissary. See USG to McKeever, October 17, 1861, *GP*, 3:47.

30. Smith to USG, October 25, 1861, *GP*, 3:72; returns for First Division, Western Department, for October 1861, *OR*, 3:730; USG to McKeever, October 27, 1861, *GP*, 3:78; Catton, *Grant Moves South*, 60.

31. USG to McKeever, October 7, 1861, *GP*, 3:25; USG to McKeever, October 9, 1861, *GP*, 3:30; USG to McKeever, October 6, 1861, *GP*, 3:18, 19; Luvaas, "Napoleon on the Art of Command," 35; Polk to Johnston, November 4, 1861, *OR*, 4:513.

32. McKeever to USG, November 1, 1861, *GP*, 3:143–44; McKeever to Smith, November 1, 1861, *OR*, 3:300–301.

33. McKeever to USG, November 2, 1861, *GP*, 3:144; USG to Oglesby, November 3, 1861, *GP*, 3:108–9; USG to Plummer, November 4, 1861, *GP*, 3:111–12. See also Hughes, *Belmont*, 4.

34. USG to Smith, November 5, 1861, *GP*, 3:114; Hughes, *Belmont*, 48–55, 78–84.

35. Polk to Mackall, November 10, 1861, *OR*, 3:306–8; Hughes, *Belmont*, 67–68, 71–77, 91–188.

36. Quoted in Andrews, *The North Reports*, 119; Wills, *Army Life*, 43.

37. Augustus W. Alexander, *Grant as a Soldier*, 41; Simon, "Grant at Belmont," 165–66; Williams, *Lincoln Finds a General*, 3:86; Hughes, *Belmont*, 207.

38. USG to Seth Williams, November 10, 1861, *GP*, 3:141; USG to Williams, November 17, 1861, *GP*, 3:143–49.

39. McKeever to Fremont, November 9, 1861, *OR*, 53:507. See also McKeever's testimony before the Committee on the Conduct of the War in U.S. Congress, *House Reports of Committees*, 251–52; USG to Smith, November 5, 1861, *GP*, 3:114.

40. USG to McKeever, November 8, 1861, *GP*, 3:133.

41. USG to Jesse Grant, November 8, 1861, *GP*, 3:136–38.

42. USG to Williams, November 17, 1861, *GP*, 3:146; Hughes, *Belmont*, 51; Simon, "Grant at Belmont," 165. Brooks Simpson argued that Grant's explicit memory of the 2 A.M. intelligence report and his never having "specified that he received a *written* message" lend credibility to the story. But this interpretation fails to explain why Grant neglected to mention this crucial report in his immediate afteraction reports or why its existence remained hidden until 1864. Did Grant's memory of the event *improve* with age? Moreover, not to include such information was unusual for him. Throughout his official correspondence—both before and after Belmont—Grant was meticulous about including references to intelligence he received, especially if it dramatically influenced his actions. Simpson, *Ulysses S. Grant*, 478.

43. W. H. L. Wallace to Anne Wallace, November 14, 1861, box 2, Wallace-Dickey

Papers; Wallace, *Life and Letters of General W. H. L. Wallace*, 141; William S. McFeely argued that Grant had "set out to fight . . . not to demonstrate." McFeely, *Grant*, 92.

44. On April 27, 1864, Rawlins wrote "Colonel Bowers and myself finished yesterday General Grant's report of the battle of Belmont" and commented that "it places that engagement in its true light for transmittal to posterity, so far as could be known on our side." Wilson, *Rawlins*, 425.

45. Simon, "Grant at Belmont," 165. See also Simon's analysis of Grant's official report in *GP*, 3:152.

46. USG to Smith, November 5, 1861, *GP*, 3:114.

47. USG to Oglesby, November 6, 1861, *GP*, 3:123; Oglesby to USG, November 7, 1861, *GP*, 3:124; W. H. L. Wallace to Anne Wallace, November 6, 1861, box 2, Wallace-Dickey Papers.

48. Oglesby to USG, November 7, 1861, *GP*, 3:124; Simon, "Grant at Belmont," 163−64; Conger, *Rise of U. S. Grant*, 372; Wills, *Army Life*, 42−43; Williams, *Lincoln Finds a General*, 3:74.

49. Fremont to USG, September 5, 1861, *GP*, 2:191; Fremont to Lincoln, September 8, 1861, *OR*, 3:478−79; Fremont to USG, September 9, 1861, *GP*, 2:216; Fremont to USG, September 10, 1861, *OR*, 3:484; Fremont, "In Command in Missouri," 1:287.

50. See Fremont's testimony before the Committee on the Conduct of the War, January 30, 1862, in U.S. Congress, *House Reports of Committees*, 74−75.

51. Wilson, *Rawlins*, 39. Foote and Porter also pressured Grant to advance on Columbus. See report of William D. Porter, November 15, 1861, *ORN*, 22:430; and Foote to Gideon Welles, November 7, 1861, *ORN*, 22:396−97.

52. Simon, "Grant at Belmont," 165; Hughes, *Belmont*, 53, 83.

53. McGhee, "Neophyte General," 471; Catton, *Grant Moves South*, 74.

3. "You Will Soon Hear if My Presentiment is Realized"

1. USG to Elihu B. Washburne, November 20, 1861, *GP*, 3:205; USG to John C. Kelton, November 21, 1861, *GP*, 3:208.

2. USG to Kelton, December 29, 1861, *GP*, 3:353; Leonard Ross to USG, December 11, 27, 1861, *GP*, 3:280−81, 353; E. W. Gantt to Polk, December 21, 1861, *OR*, 8:717; USG to Oglesby, December 13, 1861, *GP*, 3:283−84; Oglesby to Rawlins, December 15, 1861, *GP*, 3:290; Thirteenth Wisconsin soldier quoted in Cooling, *Forts Henry and Donelson*, 91−92.

3. This conclusion is derived from various items in Hillyer's correspondence, box 1, William S. Hillyer Papers, UVL.

4. USG to Henry W. Halleck, December 21, 1861, *GP*, 3:278. For reports received from these various sources, see dispatches from USG to Kelton, *GP*, 3:263, 293−94, 304−5, 324, 353.

5. Charles C. Carpenter file and map, RG 110, entry 36, box 1, NARA; USG to Kelton, December 29, 1861, GP, 3:353; USG to Kelton, December 8, 1861, GP, 3:263.

6. USG to Samuel R. Curtis, November 16, 1861, GP, 3:177; Special Orders, November 20, 1861, GP, 3:285.

7. USG to William McMichael, November 25, 1861, GP, 3:220; General Orders No. 3, November 20, 1861, OR, 7:370; General Orders No. 20, December 6, 1861, GP, 3:285; USG to John Cook, December 23, 1861, GP, 3:334.

8. Pillow to Johnston, November 28, 1861, OR, 7:708; Mason Brayman to Rawlins, December 11, 1861, GP, 3:414–15; Johnston to Judah P. Benjamin, December 30, 1861, OR, 7:809–11.

9. General Orders No. 1, November 19, 1861, OR, 7:439; Davis to W. P. Harris, December 3, 1861, OR, 8:701; Halleck to Abraham Lincoln, January 6, 1862, OR, 7:532. See also Ambrose, *Halleck*.

10. Carpenter to Halleck, December 24, 1861, RG 110, entry 36, box 3; Carpenter to Halleck, January 1862, RG 110, box 1. See also USG to Leonard Ross, January 8, 1862; and McMichael to USG, January 10, 1862, GP, 4:16.

11. General Orders No. 22, December 23, 1861, GP, 3:330; Special Orders No. 90, December 24, 1861, in U.S. General Service Schools, *Fort Henry and Fort Donelson*, 46; Welcher, *Union Army*, 2:127–28; Ambrose, "Union Command System," 78–79; Ambrose, *Halleck*, 18; Cooling, *Forts Henry and Donelson*, 63, 65, 67; USG endorsement of Lellyett, January 11, 1862, GP, 4:34; Lellyett's reports to Grant, January 7, 11, 1862, GP, 4:34–35. See also Lellyett to Andrew Johnson, January 14, 1862, in Graf and Haskins, *Papers of Andrew Johnson*, 5: 97–98; and Lellyett Correspondence in the Don Carlos Buell Papers, Rice University, Houston TX.

12. USG to Kelton, November 21, 1861, GP, 3:208; USG to Kelton, November 29, 1861, GP, 3:234–35; USG to Williams, November 20, 1861, GP, 3:192; Grant to Kelton, December 8, 1861, GP, 3:263.

13. USG to Kelton, December 16, 1861, GP, 3:293–94; USG to Kelton, December 18, 1861, GP, 3:304–5; USG to Mary Grant, December 18, 1861, GP, 3:308; USG to Kelton, December 22, 1861, GP, 3:324.

14. Polk to Johnston, December 24, 1861, OR, 7:790; Grant to Kelton, December 29, 1861, GP, 3:353; Johnston to Polk, December 18, 1861, OR, 7:773; Polk to Johnston, December 18, 1861, OR, 7:773–74; Polk to Johnston, January 11, 1862, OR, 7:826; Connelly, *Army of the Heartland*, 105–6.

15. Smith to USG, January 3, 1862, GP, 3:429–30; Grant to Kelton, January 6, 1862, GP, 3:375; USG to Kelton, January 6, 1862, GP, 3:376; Cooling, *Forts Henry and Donelson*, 91; PMUSG, 1:286–87.

16. McClellan to Halleck, January 3, 1862, OR, 7:527–28; Halleck to Buell, January 6, 1862, OR, 7:533; Halleck to Lincoln, January 6, 1862, OR, 7:532; Halleck to USG, January 6, 1862, OR, 7:533–34; McClernand to Halleck,

January 24, 1862, *OR*, 7:70. For the Kentucky reconnaissance, see Ripley, "Prelude to Donelson," 311–18.

17. USG to Halleck, January 12, 1862, *GP*, 4:37; McClernand to Halleck, January 24, 1862, *OR*, 7:69, 71.

18. USG to Julia Grant, January 23, 1862, *GP*, 4:96; USG to Kelton, January 17, 1862, *GP*, 4:62–63; USG to McClernand, January 18, 1862, *GP*, 4:67–68; USG to Kelton, January 20, 1862, *GP*, 4:74; Smith to USG, January 27, 1862, *GP*, 4:100–101.

19. USG to Kelton, January 20, 1862, 4:74; *PMUSG*, 1:286–87; Smith to USG, January 21, 1862, *GP*, 4:90; McClernand to Halleck, January 24, 1862, *OR*, 7:69; Smith to Rawlins, January 22, 1862, *OR*, 7:561; Phelps to Foote, January 212, 1862, *ORN*, 22:512–13. Smith also noted the absence of Confederate ironclads. In fact, the Southern brownwater navy was still virtually nonexistent, save for the converted steamer *Eastport.* See Still, *Iron Afloat,* 41–42.

20. Cooling, *Forts Henry and Donelson,* 44–46.

21. *PMUSG*, 1:287; USG to Halleck, January 28, 1862, *GP*, 4:99; USG to Halleck, January 29, 1862, *GP*, 4:103–4.

22. Halleck to USG, January 30, 1862, *GP*, 4:121–22; McClellan to Halleck, January 29, 1862, *OR*, 7:571.

23. Smith to Rawlins, January 30, 1862, *GP*, 4:123; USG to Halleck, February 1, 1862, *GP*, 4:131; Cooling, *Forts Henry and Donelson,* 88, 66; D. K. Boswell to Aaron Harding, n.d.; and John Lellyett to Andrew Johnson, March 5, 1862, Abraham Lincoln Papers, LC.

24. General Orders No. 5, February 1, 1862, *GP*, 4:129; Field Orders No. 1, February 5, 1862, *GP*, 4:151; USG to Halleck, February 4, 1862, *GP*, 4:147; Cooling, *Forts Henry and Donelson,* 92; Smith to Rawlins, January 22, 1862, *OR*, 7:561. McClernand's command had already disembarked once, at Itra Landing, and then had to reload the boats after Grant returned with his intelligence. See Cooling, *Forts Henry and Donelson,* 92.

25. McClernand to USG, February 10, 1862, *OR*, 7:126–27; McClernand's endorsement of Carpenter's services, February 9, 1862, RG 110, entry 36, box 1; McClernand to USG, February 4, 1862, *GP*, 4:148–49; McClernand to USG, February 5, 1862, *GP*, 4:152.

26. USG to Julia Grant, February 5, 1862, *GP*, 4:153. The actual Confederate strength in Fort Henry was only around 3,033 men present for duty. See "Abstract Report of the Fourth Division," January 31, 1862, *OR*, 7:855.

27. Buell to Halleck, February 5, 1862, *OR*, 7:580; Alexander McD. McCook to Buell, January 23, 1862, *OR*, 7:563; Halleck to McClellan, February 5, 1862, *OR*, 7:583–84; Halleck to McClellan, February 6, 1862, *OR*, 7:586–87; USG to Kelton, February 6, 1862, *GP*, 4:157; Connelly, *Autumn of Glory,* 84–85, 106–7.

28. Cooling, *Forts Henry and Donelson*, 101–21; "Abstract Report of Fourth Division," January 31, 1862, 7:855; USG to Mary Grant, February 9, 1862, *GP*, 4: 179.

29. Cooling, *Forts Henry and Donelson*, 116; *PMUSG*, 1:291, 297–98.

30. Phelps to Foote, December 10, 13, 1861, *ORN*, 22:457–58, 461; Phelps to Foote, January 7, 1862, *ORN*, 22:485–86; Phelps to Foote, January 21, 1862, *ORN*, 22: 512–13.

31. USG to Kelton, February 6, 1862, *GP*, 4:155; USG to Cullum, February 8, 1862, *GP*, 4:171–72; Cooling, *Forts Henry and Donelson*, 140.

32. McPherson to USG, February 22, 1862, *OR*, 7:161–62; Webster to USG, February 22, 1862, *OR*, 7:165. See also McPherson to USG, February 22, 1862, *OR*, 7:162.

33. Wallace to Susan Wallace, February 11, 1862, box 1, Lew Wallace Collection, ISHS; USG to Cullum, February 8, 1862, *GP*, 4:171–72; General Field Orders No. 12, February 11, 1862, *GP*, 4:191–92; Cooling, *Forts Henry and Donelson*, 115. See also Williams, *Lincoln Finds a General*, 3:228.

34. McPherson to USG, February 22, 1862, *OR*, 7:162; Cooling, *Forts Henry and Donelson*, 139, 148; USG to Halleck, February 12, 1862, *GP*, 4:195.

35. *PMUSG*, 1:294–95; USG to Mary Grant, February 9, 1862, *GP*, 4:179–80; "Fort Donelson," 43; *PMUSG*, 1:294–95, 313; USG to Mary Grant, February 9, 1862, *GP*, 4:179–80. USG to Julia Grant, February 22, 1862, *GP*, 4:271.

36. Cooling, *Forts Henry and Donelson*, 122–46; USG to Halleck, February 13, 1862, *GP*, 4:200; USG to Cullum, February 14, 1862, *GP*, 4:209; USG to Julia Grant, February 13, 1862, *GP*, 4:203–4.

37. Halleck to Buell, February 12, 1862, *OR*, 7:607; Halleck to McClellan, February 15, 1862, *OR*, 7:616; Halleck to McClellan, February 17, 1862, *OR*, 7: 627–28; Halleck to Cullum, February 17, 1862, *OR*, 7:628; Ambrose, "Union Command System," 84, 82; Scott to Halleck, February 11, 1862, *OR*, 7:604; McClellan to Buell, February 13, 1862, *OR*, 7:609; Sherman to USG, February 15, 1862, *GP*, 4:215.

38. Cooling, *Forts Henry and Donelson*, 147–65; *PMUSG*, 1:305; Martin van Creveld, *Command in War*, 8.

39. Cooling, *Forts Henry and Donelson*, 209–13.

40. Clausewitz, *On War*, 201; Ferris and Handel, "Clausewitz, Intelligence, Uncertainty," 6.

41. USG to Julia, February 22, 1862, *GP*, 4:271.

4. "There Will Be No Fight at Pittsburg Landing"

1. USG to Julia Grant, March 1, 1862, *GP*, 4:305; USG to Julia Grant, February 16, 1862, *GP*, 4:229–30; USG to Washburne, February 21, 1862, *GP*, 4:264; USG to

Cullum, February 19, 1862, *GP*, 4:245; USG to Julia Grant, February 24, 1862, *GP*, 4:284.

2. Halleck to USG, March 16, 1862, *GP*, 4:367; Clausewitz, *On War*, 357.

3. USG to Cullum, February 24, 1862, *GP*, 4:279; USG to Julia, February 24, 1862, 4:284; USG to Cullum, February 25, 1862, *GP*, 4:286–87.

4. USG to Buell, February 27, 1862, *GP*, 4:293–94; USG to Kelton, February 28, 1862, *GP*, 4:299; Buell to McClellan, February 28, 1862, *OR*, 7:671; Catton, *Grant Moves South*, 191–93; Connelly, *Army of the Heartland*, 138–39; Roland, *Albert Sidney Johnston*, 301–5.

5. USG to Cullum, February 25, 1862, *GP*, 4:286–87. See also USG to Sherman, February 25, 1862, *GP*, 4:288–89.

6. Halleck to USG, March 1, 1862, *OR*, 7:674.

7. Sword, *Shiloh*, 6–11; Halleck to McClellan, March 10, 1862, *OR*, 10(2):24–25; Halleck to Buell, March 14, 1862, *OR*, 10(2):38.

8. USG to Julia, March 11, 1862, *GP*, 4:348–49; Sword, *Shiloh*, 123–30; USG to Halleck, March 5, 1862, *GP*, 4:317–18; USG to Sherman, March 5, 1862, *GP*, 4:325; Sherman to Halleck, March 6, 1862, *GP*, 4:12; Smith to Rawlins, March 14, 1862, *GP*, 4:369–70; USG to Halleck, March 15, 1862, *GP*, 4:366; Sherman to William McMichael, March 16, 1862, RG 393, entry 2593 (Department of the Missouri, Letters Received), box 5, NARA.

9. Sword, *Shiloh*, 24, 27–30, 35–37; Sherman to Rawlins, March 17, 1862, *GP*, 4:379; Sherman, *Memoirs*, 229; *PMUSG*, 1:332–33. According to Rawlins, however, even Smith believed fortifications were unnecessary and ultimately detrimental to morale. See Rawlins to Henry Coppee, November 25, 1865, box 2, William S. Hillyer Papers, UVL. For an excellent discussion of Grant and Sherman's decision in light of contemporary regulations and military engineering, see Hagerman, *Civil War and the Origins of Modern Warfare*, 169.

10. Simpson and Berlin, *Sherman's Civil War*, 207; *PMUSG*, 1:333.

11. USG to McLean, March 17, 1862, *GP*, 4:378; USG to Halleck, March 18, 1862, *GP*, 4:386–87; USG to McLean, March 19, 1862, *GP*, 4:393–93; Lew Wallace to Susan Wallace, March 15, 1862, box 1, Lew Wallace Collection, ISHS.

12. USG to McLean, March 19, 1862, 4:392–93; USG to Buell, March 19, 1862, *GP*, 4:393–94. The trip to find Buell would be Carson's last mission. He was killed during the battle of Shiloh less than a month later. See *Chicago Tribune*, May 4, 1862.

13. Halleck to USG, March 18, 1862, *OR*, 10(2):46; USG to Halleck, March 19, 1862, *GP*, 4:400–401; Halleck to USG, March 20, 1862, *OR*, 10(2):50–51.

14. USG to Halleck, March 21, 1862, *GP*, 4:400–401; USG to Halleck, March 20, 1862, *GP*, 4:396–97 Lew Wallace to Susan Wallace, March 21, 1862, box 1, Lew Wallace Collection.

15. USG to Halleck, March 23, 1862, *GP*, 4:410; Smith to USG, March 23, 1862, *GP*,

4:411; USG to Smith, March 23, 1862, *GP*, 4:411; Sherman to McMichael, March 20, 1862, *OR*, 10(2):53; Sword, *Shiloh*, 33.

16. Smith to USG, March 23, 1862, 4:411; USG to Smith, March 23, 1862, 4:411. Ruggles assumed command of the Corinth forces on February 17 and remained in charge until Bragg arrived in mid-March. Why Grant viewed Ruggles with such disdain is not clear. Sword, *Shiloh*, 64–65, 74, 82.

17. Buell to Halleck, March 23, 1862, *OR*, 10(2):59; Sword, *Shiloh*, 44–47; USG to Halleck, March 26, 1862, *GP*, 4:424.

18. Johnston to Davis, March 25, 1862, *OR*, 10(2):303; Johnston to Davis, March 7, 1862, *OR*, 10(2): 302; Sword, *Shiloh*, 63–68, 84–85, 91–92, 109.

19. Buell to Halleck, March 24, 1862, *OR*, 10(2):64–65; Halleck to Buell, March 26, 1862, *OR*, 10(2):66; USG to McLean, March 31, 1862, *GP*, 4:451–52.

20. William W. Lowe to Rawlins, March 28, 1862, *GP*, 4:435–36; William Rowley to Washburne, March 29, 1862, *GP*, 4:446; Halleck to Buell, March 29, 1862, *OR*, 10(2):77.

21. USG to McLean, March 30, 1862, *GP*, 4:447–48; Halleck to Stanton, April 8, 1862, *OR*, 10(2):98; Halleck to USG, March 31, 1862, *OR*, 10(2):82.

22. General Orders No. 33, April 2, 1862, *OR*, 10(2):87; Jay A. Jorgensen, "Scouting for Ulysses S. Grant," 53.

23. Spencer Kellogg Brown, a spy employed by Commodore William D. Porter, traveled from Corinth to Pittsburg Landing during the battle of Shiloh, but his information was cold by the time he reported to Grant. Brown's original mission, however, was not to aid Grant but to gather intelligence on Confederate fortifications along the Mississippi River for the navy. He was in Corinth only by happenstance and headed toward Shiloh not to report his findings but to end his harrowing journey in the South, during which he narrowly escaped the hangman's noose. Brown's father later claimed that his son told Grant on the morning of April 7 that the Confederates had exhausted their reinforcements, leading the general to counterattack that day with renewed vigor. The general, however, did not meet Brown until April 9. In addition, the intelligence Grant attributed to him does not corroborate the elder Brown's version. See Smith, *Spencer Kellogg Brown*, 231–54; Porter to Foote, April 20, 1862, *OR*, 10(2):121; "Report of Fourth Master [S.] Kellogg, regarding the Confederate fortifications on the Mississippi River, April 8, 1862," *ORN*, 22:767–68; USG to Halleck, April 9, 1862, *GP*, 5:31.

24. McMichael to Grenville M. Dodge, December 16, 1861, box 2, DP.

25. John J. Riggin Jr. to McClernand, March 25, 1862, *GP*, 4:422; McClernand to USG, March 25, 1862, *GP*, 4:442; USG to McClernand, March 25, 1862, *GP*, 4:421–22; USG to McLean, March 29, 1862, *GP*, 4:440.

26. Sherman to Halleck, February 25, 1862, *OR*, 7:666; Sherman to Grenville M.

Dodge, October 8, 1862, box 4, DP; Sword, *Shiloh*, 136, 117–18; James Marshall-Cornwall, *Grant as Military Commander*, 72.

27. Sword, *Shiloh*, 116–17; USG to McLean, March 15, 1862, GP, 4:368; USG to Julia, March 18, 1862, GP, 4:389.

28. Sherman, *Memoirs*, 229.

29. Sword, *Shiloh*, 81.

30. PMUSG, 1:333; Simpson and Berlin, *Sherman's Civil War*, 219.

31. Sherman to Taylor, April 2, 1862, OR, 10(2):87; Sherman to David Stuart, April 2, 1862, OR, 10(2):87; USG to Smith, March 26, 1862, GP, 4:425; Sherman to Rawlins, April 3, 1862, OR, 10(2):90; Taylor to Sherman, April 3, 1862, OR, 10(1):86. See also Sword, *Shiloh*, 119.

32. Taylor to Sherman, April 3, 1862, OR, 10(1):86; Sherman to Ellen Sherman, April 3, 1862, GP, 5:5; Sherman to Thomas Ewing, April 4, 1862, GP, 5:5.

33. The First Alabama Cavalry had arrived at Pea Ridge on March 31 with orders to scout the Union position. Yet Johnston's marching orders were not disseminated until late on April 2. Thus, when captured the following day, the Alabama trooper probably knew very little about the upcoming offensive. See Bragg to James R. Chalmers, March 31, 1862, OR, 10(2):375–76; and Sword, *Shiloh*, 92.

34. USG to McLean, April 3, 1862, GP, 5:3.

35. Sword, *Shiloh*, 97–114; Roland, *Albert Sidney Johnston*, 317–25.

36. Sword, *Shiloh*, 94–97; Wallace, *Autobiography*, 1:449–50; PMUSG, 1:334.

37. Horace Bell enlisted in the Sixth Indiana Volunteer Infantry for three months' service and later became a scout for Wallace. For some reason, Grant had him incarcerated briefly after Shiloh. He went on to scout for James C. Veatch and ended the war working for Edward R. S. Canby in the Military Division of West Mississippi. See Horace Bell pension record, RG 15, NARA; and E. A. McLaflin to James Bowen, February 3, 1863, RG 393, entry 2637 (Two or More Citizens File), box 1. John C. Carpenter enlisted in the Fifth Ohio Cavalry in February and was detailed on secret service at Crump's Landing on March 19, 1862. See Wallace to Rawlins, April 11, 1862, RG 393, entry 2593, box 5; and Wallace, *Autobiography*, 1:450. Specific information on Sanders remains scarce, but Confederate authorities detained him on March 31 along the road to Purdy. Preston Smith to C. G. Rogers, March 31, 1862, OR, 10(2):374–75.

38. Wallace, *Autobiography*, 1:450–58.

39. Horace Bell to Wallace, November 29, 1901, Lew Wallace Collection; Wallace, *Autobiography*, 1:458; Sword, *Shiloh*, 118.

40. Lew Wallace to W. H. L. Wallace, April 5, 1862, Wallace-Dickey Papers, box 2, ISHL.

41. Wallace to Rawlins, April 12, 1862, OR, 10(1):169–174; Wallace, *Autobiography*, 1:458. On the Grant-Wallace controversy, see the reports of Wallace and

Grant's staff in *OR*, 10(1):174 – 90; Sword, *Shiloh*, 439 – 40; and Wallace, "Lew Wallace's March," 19 – 30.

42. Sword, *Shiloh*, 122 – 25.

43. Simpson and Berlin, *Sherman's Civil War*, 202. See also Sherman to Ewing, April 4, 1862, *GP*, 5:5; and Frank and Reaves, *Seeing the Elephant*, 77.

44. On Sherman's jubilant mood, see W. H. L. Wallace to Ann Wallace, April 5, 1862; Special Orders No. 18, April 4, 1862, *OR*, 10(2):92 – 93; and Sword, *Shiloh*, 125 – 30.

45. Sword, *Shiloh*, 125.

46. Sherman to *USG*, April 5, 1862, *GP*, 5:14, 16; Sherman to Rawlins, April 5, 1862, *GP*, 5:14, 16; Sherman to *USG*, April 10, 1862, *OR*, 10(1):248; *USG* to Jesse Grant, April 26, 1862, *GP*, 5:78; *PMUSG*, 1:332, 334.

47. Sherman to Rawlins, April 5, 1862, 5:16; Sword, *Shiloh*, 133; *USG* to Halleck, April 5, 1862, *GP*, 5:13; "Diary of General Jacob Ammen," April 5, 1862, *OR*, 10(1):330 – 31; Frank and Reaves, *Seeing the Elephant*, 143.

48. Halleck also believed Beauregard and "part of the Manassas army" confronted Grant. Halleck to Stanton, April 5, 1862, *OR*, 10(2):93.

49. *USG* to Halleck, April 5, 1862, *GP*, 5:13; *USG* to Julia, April 8, 1862, *GP*, 5:27; *USG* to Buell, April 5, 1862, *GP*, 5:16.

50. Sword, *Shiloh*, 189; Sherman's official report, April 10, 1862, *OR*, 10(1):249.

51. Sword, *Shiloh*, 213, 215 – 16; *USG* to Buell, April 6, 1862, *GP*, 5:17 *PMUSG*, 1:336; Buell to McLean, April 15, 1862, *OR*, 10(1):292.

52. Sword, *Shiloh*, 191 – 368; *PMUSG*, 1:348.

53. Sword, *Shiloh*, 369 – 422; Richard Betts, "Analysis, War, and Decision: Why Intelligence Failures Are Inevitable," in Dearth, *Strategic Intelligence*, 395. The Confederates suffered over 23,000 casualties. See Sword, *Shiloh*, Appendix C, 460 – 61.

54. Frank and Reaves, *Seeing the Elephant*, 142 – 43; Wilson, *Rawlins*, 448.

55. Roland, *Albert Sidney Johnston*, 329.

56. See Marszalek, *Sherman*, 176; and Fellman, *Citizen Sherman*, 91 – 109, 114; Sherman to *USG*, April 5, 1862, *OR*, 10(2):94.

57. Marszalek, *Sherman*, 175; Fellman, *Citizen Sherman*, 114.

58. Wohlstetter, *Pearl Harbor*, 3, 392. Handel, *War, Strategy, and Intelligence*, 70.

59. Wohlstetter, *Pearl Harbor*, 392; Frank and Reaves, *Seeing the Elephant*, 77.

60. Allied intelligence officers made the same mistake just prior to the surprise German counteroffensive in the Ardennes in December 1944. See Dupuy et al., *Hitler's Last Gamble*, 40.

61. Cohen and Gooch, *Military Misfortunes*, 42 – 43.

62. Dupuy et al., *Hitler's Last Gamble*, 40, 44; Luvaas, "Napoleon on the Art of Command," 31.

63. *PMUSG*, 1:249 – 50.

5. "With All the Vigilance I Can Bring to Bear"

1. General Field Order No. 62, July 17, 1862, *GP*, 5:210; Welcher, *Union Army*, 2:376–77; Catton, *Grant Moves South*, 263–77; Cozzens, *Darkest Days of the War*, 35; *PMUSG*, 1:304–5; Porter, *Campaigning with Grant*, 5.

2. *PMUSG*, 1:395–96.

3. For a discussion of this ad hoc approach, see Fishel, "Mythology of Civil War Intelligence," 345.

4. Halleck to Rosecrans, June 22, 1862, *OR*, 17(1):24.

5. General Order No. 65, July 28, 1862, *GP*, 5:247.

6. USG to Halleck, June 29, 1862, *GP*, 5:167; Halleck to USG, June 29, 1862, *GP*, 5:168, 169.

7. Connelly, *Army of the Heartland*, 197–204, 207; Price to Earl Van Dorn, September 4, 1862, *OR*, 17(2):692; Bearss, *Decision in Mississippi*, 2–3.

8. McClernand to USG, July 19, 1862, *GP*, 5:228; William S. Rosecrans to USG, July 20, 1862, *GP*, 5:221–22; Rosecrans to USG, July 23, 1862, *GP*, 5:229; USG to Halleck, July 23, 1862, *GP*, 5:227–28.

9. "Rosecrans's Campaigns," in U.S. Congress, *Report of the Joint Committee*, 3:17; Shiman, "Engineering Sherman's March," 128–29; *PMUSG*, 1:408. The process of making copies of information maps is described in Stephenson, *Civil War Maps*, 6–7.

10. Philip H. Sheridan to Rawlins, July 16, 1865, *OR*, 46(1):481; Sheridan, *Personal Memoirs*, 1:167–71; USG to Halleck, July 29, 1862, *GP*, 5:250; USG to Halleck, July 30, 1862, *GP*, 5:254; Rosecrans to USG, July 30, 1862, *GP*, 5:255; Sherman to Rawlins, July 31, 1862, *GP*, 5:269.

11. USG to Halleck, August 1, 1862, *GP*, 5:257; USG to Lorenzo Thomas, August 7, 1862, *GP*, 5:269; USG to Halleck, August 9, 1862, *GP*, 5:278; Buell to USG, August 13, 1862, *GP*, 5:291; USG to Halleck, August 25, 1862, *GP*, 5:329.

12. USG to Buell, August, 12, 1862, *GP*, 5:289; Special Orders No. 163, August 14, 1862, *GP*, 5:293; *PMUSG*, 1:394–98; USG to Mary Grant, August 19, 1862, *GP*, 5:310.

13. USG to Halleck, August 14, 1862, *GP*, 5:292; Rosecrans to USG, August 19, 1862, *GP*, 5:304; Gordon Granger to USG, August 23, 1862, *GP*, 5:330; Halleck to USG, August 28, 1862, *GP*, 5:334.

14. USG to Halleck, September 1, 1862, *GP*, 6:5; Halleck to USG, September 2, *GP*, 6:7; Catton, *Grant Moves South*, 309; *PMUSG*, 1:404–5, 395; Rosecrans to USG, September 9, 1862, *GP*, 6:27; USG to Halleck, September 9, 1862, *GP*, 6:26; USG to Halleck, September 9, 1862, *GP*, 6:31; Catton, *Grant Moves South*, 306–307; *PMUSG*, 1:395.

15. Report of Sterling Price, September 26, 1862, *OR*, 17(1):119–24; Samuel Jones to Price, September 6, 1862, *OR*, 17(2):694; Cozzens, *Darkest Days of the War*, 50–52; Price to Van Dorn, September 14, 1862, *OR*, 17(2):702.

16. Hamilton to USG, September 7, 1862, *GP*, 6:26–27; Rosecrans to USG, September 8, 1862, *GP*, 6:27; Rosecrans to USG, September 9, *GP*, 6:27, 28.

17. USG to Halleck, September 9, 1862, *GP*, 6:31; USG to Halleck, September 9, 1862, *GP*, 6:26; USG to Halleck, September 9, 1862, *GP*, 6:28.

18. Rosecrans to USG, September 11, 1862, *GP*, 6:34; Hamilton to USG, September 11, 1862, *GP*, 6:35–36; USG to Halleck, September 11, 1862, *GP*, 6:39.

19. Castel, *Sterling Price*, 97; Report of Sterling Price, September 26, 1862, *OR*, 17(1):121; Sherman to Rawlins, September 12, 1862, *OR*, 17(2):216; Rosecrans to USG, September 13, 1862, *GP*, 6:39; Rosecrans to USG, September 13, 1862, *GP*, 6:42; Hamilton to Grant and Rosecrans, September 14, 1862, *GP*, 6:42; John V. D. Du Bois to USG, September 15, 1862, *GP*, 6:47.

20. USG to Halleck, September 15, 1862, *GP*, 6:46; Price to Van Dorn, September 14, 1862, *OR*, 17(2):702; USG to Kelton, October 22, 1862, *OR*, 17(1):65; Castel, *Sterling Price*, 100.

21. Rosecrans to USG, September 16, 1862, *OR*, 17(2):220; Rosecrans to USG, September 17, 1862, *OR*, 17(2):224, 223; Rosecrans to USG, September 17, 1862, *GP*, 6:58; Rosecrans to USG, September 18, 1862, *GP*, 6:65; USG to Rosecrans, September 18, 1862, *GP*, 6:64; USG to Halleck, September 19, 1862, *GP*, 6:67.

22. Halleck to USG, September 17, 1862, *OR*, 17(2):222; USG to Kelton, October 22, 1862, *OR*, 17(1):68; Bearss, *Decision in Mississippi*, 32–62; Castel, *Sterling Price*, 99–100; Catton, *Grant Moves South*, 312.

23. Naron began his scouting career with Pope and continued working for Rosecrans. After Rosecrans' transfer to the Army of the Cumberland in October 1862, both Hamilton and Dodge retained "Chickasaw" despite the scout's desire to remain with his old commander. See report of L. H. Naron, ca. July 1862, RG 110, entry 36, box 4, NARA; Levi H. Naron pension record, RG 15, NARA; and Rosecrans to USG, September 22, 1862, *GP*, 6:76–77.

24. USG to Kelton, October 30, 1862, *OR*, 17(1):157.

25. Van Dorn to [unknown], October 20, 1862, *OR*, 17(1):377–78; George W. Randolph to Van Dorn, September 29, 1862, *OR*, 17(2):715; Castel, *Sterling Price*, 104–7, 108–11; Van Dorn to Price, September 18, 1862, *OR*, 17(2):706; Woodworth, *Davis and His Generals*, 154–55; Catton, *Grant Moves South*, 313–17.

26. Castel, *Sterling Price*, 109; Rosecrans to USG, September 30, 1862, *GP*, 6:96; Van Dorn to [unknown], October 20, 1862, *OR*, 17(1):377; USG to Halleck, September 25, 1862, *GP*, 6:87; Stephen A. Hurlbut to USG, September 25, 1862, *GP*, 6:88; Rosecrans to USG, September 27, 1862, *GP*, 6:92; USG to Halleck, September 30, 1862, *GP*, 6:95; Rosecrans to USG, October 1, 1862, *GP*, 6:97; Hurlbut to Rawlins, October 2, 1862, *GP*, 6:100; USG to Halleck, October 1, 1862, *GP*, 6:96–97; USG to Hurlbut, October 1, 1862, *GP*, 6:98.

27. USG to Halleck, October 1, 1862, 96–97; Rosecrans to USG, October 1, 1862, *OR*, 17(2): 252; William S. Rosecrans, "The Battle of Corinth," in *B&L*, 2:743;

Rosecrans to USG, October 3, 1862, *GP*, 6:107; Rosecrans to Rawlins, October 25, 1862, *OR*, 17(1):166; "Rosecrans's Campaigns," 3:20–21; Rosecrans, "Battle of Corinth, 745.

28. Rosecrans to USG, October 2, 1862, *GP*, 6:99–100; USG to Rosecrans, October 2, 1862, *GP*, 6:99; Castel, *Sterling Price*, 111.

29. Catton, *Grant Moves South*, 316–17; Lamers, *Edge of Glory*, 159–80.

30. *PMUSG*, 1:420. For examples of these intelligence reports, see Rosecrans to USG, October 13, 1862, *GP*, 6:150; Rosecrans to USG, October 22, 1862, *GP*, 6: 179; and USG to Halleck, October 23, 1862, *GP*, 6:178–79.

31. General Orders No. 1, October 25, 1862, *GP*, 6:186; Welcher, *Union Army*, 2: 143–22, 251.

32. Hattaway and Jones, *How the North Won*, 300; USG to Halleck, October 26, 1862, *GP*, 6:199–200.

33. Ballard, *Pemberton*, 114–15; USG to Halleck, October 29, 1862, *GP*, 6:210; Sherman to Rawlins, November 1, 1862, *OR*, 17(2):857; Hamilton to USG, November 1, 1862, *GP*, 6:238; USG to Hamilton, November 1, 1862, *GP*, 6:238; USG to Halleck, November 2, 1862, *GP*, 6:243; "Organization of Troops in the Department of the Tennessee," November 10, 1862, *OR*, 17(2):338–40; USG to Halleck, November 4, 1862, *GP*, 6:256.

34. USG to Sherman, November 6, 1862, *GP*, 6:263; Bearss, *Vicksburg Campaign*, 1:36; Hamilton to USG, November 7, 1862, *GP*, 6:270; McPherson to USG, November 8, 1862, *GP*, 6:277; McPherson to USG, November 9, 1862, *GP*, 6: 284; USG to Halleck, November 9, 1862, *GP*, 6:278; Sherman to USG, November 8, 1862, *OR*, 17(2):861; USG to Hamilton, November 9, 1862, *GP*, 6:285–86; USG to McPherson, November 8, 1862, *GP*, 6:276.

35. McPherson to USG, November 9, 1862, *OR*, 17(2):331; USG to Sherman, November 10, 1862, *GP*, 6:290–91; Bearss, *Vicksburg Campaign*, 1:50–51; Pemberton to P. B. Starke, November 9, 1862, *OR*, 17(2):745; USG to Halleck, November 13, 1862, *GP*, 6:305.

36. Bearss, *Vicksburg Campaign*, 1:70–72; Special Field Orders No. 7, November 27, 1862, *OR*, 17(2):364; USG to Sherman, November 14, 1862, *GP*, 6:310–12.

37. Dodge to Anne Dodge, November 14, 1862, 3:912; and Dodge to Anne Dodge, November 4, 1862, Dodge Records, 3:897, DP.

38. Special Orders No. 320, October 30, 1862, *OR*, 17(2):308; USG to Dodge, November 8, 1862, *GP*, 6:287; Halleck to USG, November 10, 1862, *GP*, 6:286; Dodge to USG, November 12, 1862, *GP*, 6:313; USG to Halleck, November 14, 1862, *GP*, 6:310–12; USG to Dodge, November 18, 1862, *GP*, 6:373–74; Rawlins to Dodge, November 22, 1862, *GP*, 6:374; Rosecrans to USG, November 21, 1862, *GP*, 6:374; Grenville M. Dodge, "The Secret Service in the Civil War," Dodge Records, 5:1–47, DP.

39. Dodge, "Secret Service," 5:1–2; Samuel R. Curtis to N. H. McLean, April 1,

1862, *OR*, 8:197. For Fremont's orders to use "special spies or scouts," see J. H. Eaton to Dodge, September 24, 1861, box 2, DP; Hirshson, *Grenville M. Dodge*, 67. See also Curtis's report, April 1, 1862, *OR*, 8:197.

40. Grenville M. Dodge, "Personal Biography," 4 vols., Dodge Records, 1:93, 101, DP.

41. Dodge to Hurlbut, October 30, 1863, RG 110 (Records of the Provost Marshal Generals Bureau), entry 31 (Records of Two or More Scouts, Guides, Spies, and Detectives), box 2; Dodge, "Secret Service," 5:14–15, 5; inventory of Dodge's Scouts and Dodge Secret Service Vouchers, box 148, DP; Hirshson, *Grenville M. Dodge*, 73–74. See also Hoole, *Alabama Tories*.

42. Dodge to Rawlins, May 5, 1863, RG 393, entry 6159, NARA; Dodge, "Secret Service," 5:5; John Craig Stewart, *The Governors*, 116–18; Walter L. Fleming, *Civil War and Reconstruction*, 510; Dodge "Secret Service Vouchers," box 148; and "Vouchers Not Filled Out," box 149, DP. See also Dodge, "Secret Service," 5:14; and Perkins, *Trails, Rails, and War*, 119–20. Perkins's biography must be used with care since it was based primarily upon Dodge's "Personal Biography" and is rather biased.

43. Dodge to Rawlins, January 30, 1863, *GP*, 7:523; General Order No. 5, January 16, 1863, *OR*, 17(2):569; Dodge, "Secret Service," 5:29–30; Jeremiah Sullivan to USG, January 16, 1863, *GP*, 6:349; "Final Report of Receipts and Expenditures of Col. Wm. S. Hillyer, Provost Marshal General, Department of the Tennessee," box 1, William S. Hillyer Papers, UVL; Dodge, "Secret Service Vouchers," box 148, DP. See also Rawlins to Dodge, February 26, 1863, *GP*, 7:523.

44. Dodge, "Secret Service," 5:29–30; Hirshson, *Grenville M. Dodge*, 68.

45. Hillyer to USG, June 30, 1863, *GP*, 8:220; Dodge Secret Service Vouchers, box 148, DP; USG to Dodge, December 11, 1862, *OR*, 17(2):399. This kind of blind faith in subordinates would of course become a serious flaw during Grant's later political life.

46. USG to Halleck, November 24, 1862, *OR*, 17(2):345–46; Catton, *Grant Moves South*, 331–32; USG to Sherman, November 29, 1862, *GP*, 6:361; Hamilton to USG, November 30, 1862, *GP*, 6:366.

47. Bearss, *Vicksburg Campaign*, 1:75–76; USG to Halleck, December 2, 1862, *GP*, 6:368; Special Order, November 30, 1862, *OR*, 17(2):772; Pemberton to Bragg, December 4, 1862, *OR*, 17(2):778. Grant had arranged earlier for Maj. Gen. Samuel R. Curtis in Arkansas to send an expedition across the Yazoo Delta toward the Confederate rear. Bearss, *Vicksburg Campaign*, 1:77–94.

48. USG to Halleck, December 3, 1862, *GP*, 6:373; "Inventory of Dodge's Scouts," box 148, DP; USG to David D. Porter, December 3, 1862, *GP*, 6:385.

49. Dodge to Rawlins, December 7, 1862, *GP*, 7:10–11; USG to Halleck, December 10, 1862, *GP*, 7:9–10; USG to Halleck, December 14, 1862, *GP*, 7:26; Bragg

to Davis, November 24, 1862, *OR*, 20(2):423; Special Orders No. 7, December 17, 1862, *OR*, 17(2):799; Bearss, *Vicksburg Campaign*, 1:143.

50. USG to Sherman, December 8, 1862, *GP*, 6:406–7; Catton, *Grant Moves South*, 332; *PMUSG*, 1:431.

51. Bearss, *Vicksburg Campaign*, 1:275–76; USG to Halleck, December 16, 1862, *GP*, 7:46; USG to Rosecrans, December 16, 1862, *GP*, 7:46.

52. Rosecrans to USG, December 17, 1862, *GP*, 7:59; Bragg to Cooper, November 21, 1862, *OR*, 17(2):755; Bragg to Pemberton, November 21, 1862, *OR*, 17(2):755. See also Wills, *Battle from the Start*, 84–85.

53. Rosecrans to USG, December 10, 1862, *GP*, 7:15; Dodge to USG, December 12, 1862, *GP*, 7:15. Forrest's brigade numbered only 2,100 men. Bearss, *Vicksburg Campaign*, 1:232.

54. Bearss, *Vicksburg Campaign*, 1:245–46, 275–318.

55. USG to Dodge, December 19, 1862, *GP*, 7:71; USG to Murphy, December 19, 1862, *GP*, 7:76; USG to Murphy, December 19, 1862, *GP*, 7:76; C. C. Marsh to USG, December 20, 1862, *OR*, 17(2):443; Bearss, *Vicksburg Campaign*, 1:307, 319; *PMUSG*, 1:434.

56. Bearss, *Vicksburg Campaign*, 1:299; Dickey to Rawlins, December 20, 1862, *OR*, 17(1):498–99; Williams, *Lincoln Finds a General*, 4:190.

57. Dickey to Rawlins, December 20, 1862, *OR*, 17(1):499; Dickey to [wife], December 28, 1862, *GP*, 7:75. Col. John K. Mizner at Water Valley had also informed Grant on December 19 that a sizeable enemy cavalry force lurked about Pontotoc a day earlier and that it may have even advanced farther north. See Mizner to USG, December 19, 1862, *OR*, 17(2):437; and Mizner to USG, December 19, 1862, *OR*, 17(2):439.

58. USG to commanders at Holly Springs, Davis' Mill, Grand Junction, La Grange, and Bolivar, December 19, 1862, *GP*, 7:71; USG to Murphy, December 19, 1862, *GP*, 7:76; Murphy to Rawlins, December 20, 1862, *GP*, 7:76. For Grant's indictment of Murphy, see *PMUSG*, 1:433–34; and USG to Kelton, December 25, 1862, *GP*, 7:105.

59. Bearss, *Vicksburg Campaign*, 1:321; USG to Kelton, December 25, 1862, 7:105.

60. Ballard, *Pemberton*, 128–29; Bearss, *Vicksburg Campaign*, 1:154, 113–224, 347.

61. Special Orders No. 66, December 18, 1862, *OR*, 17(2):800; Symonds, *Joseph E. Johnston*, 194; Connelly, *Autumn of Glory*, 40–41; Bearss, *Vicksburg Campaign*, 1:208–9, 346–47.

62. USG to Hamilton, January 1, 1863, *GP*, 7:156; Rosecrans to Horatio Wright, December 24, 1862, *OR*, 20(2):234; Julius P. Garesche to George H. Thomas, December 28, 1862, *OR*, 20(2):258; Connelly, *Autumn of Glory*, 31–32, 41; Dodge to USG, December 23, 1862, *GP*, 7:93; Dodge to USG, December 26, 1862, *GP*, 7:25; Dodge to USG, December 27, 1862, *GP*, 7:129; Dodge to USG,

December 29, 1862, *GP*, 7:129–30; Dodge to USG, December 31, 1862, *GP*, 7: 149.

6. "I Have Reliable Information from the Entire Interior of the South"

1. Halleck to Stanton, November 15, 1863, *OR*, 24(1):5; USG to Halleck, January 20, 1863, *GP*, 7:233; Symonds, *Joseph E. Johnston*, 204–5; Bearss, *Vicksburg Campaign*, 2:xiii–xiv, 60–64; "Return of the Department of Mississippi and Eastern Louisiana," January 31, 1863, *OR*, 24(3):611.

2. *PMUSG*, 1:442, 431–595;*OR*, 24(2):19–51; Catton, *Grant Moves South*, 409–10; USG to Julia, March 27, 1863, *GP*, 7:479.

3. John A. McClernand to USG, January 22, 1863, *GP*, 7:240; Jeremiah C. Sullivan to Rawlins, January 26, 1863, *OR*, 24(3):17; Hamilton to USG, February 2, 1863, *GP*, 7:292–93; Hamilton to Rawlins, February 25, 1863, *GP*, 7:362; USG to Hurlbut, February 27, 1863, *GP*, 7:361; USG to Halleck, March 17, 1863, *GP*, 7: 428; Charles A. Dana to Stanton, March 23, 1863, *OR*, 24(1):64.

4. Bearss, *Vicksburg Campaign*, 1:428–29; Welcher, *Union Army*, 2:293–94. Hamilton wrote Grant, "I do not know whether Hurlbut has furnished you with the information received from time to time through Dodge's and my own spies from the south." Hamilton to USG, March 15, 1863, *OR*, 24(3):138. See also Dodge to USG, February 23, 1863, RG 393, entry 4719 (Department of the Tennessee, Register of Letters Received), NARA.

5. Grenville M. Dodge, "The Secret Service in the Civil War," 5:14, Dodge Records, DP; Dodge to USG, February 27, 1863, *GP*, 7:363; Dodge, "Personal Recollections of General Grant," 360–61; Hamilton to USG, February 9, 1863, *OR*, 24(3):41; Hamilton to Rawlins, February 26, 1863, *GP*, 7:363–64. For examples of the Dodge-Rosecrans correspondence, see Dodge to Rosecrans, March 3, 1863, *OR*, 23(2):100; and Dodge to Rosecrans, April 1, 1863, *OR*, 23(2):200.

6. Dana to Stanton, April 10, 1863, *OR*, 24(1):72–73; Dana, *Recollections*, 20–22; Bearss, *Vicksburg Campaign*, 2:107–26; Pemberton to Cooper, August 2, 1863, *OR*, 24(1):251–52; Pemberton to Gen. Joseph E. Johnston, April 12, 1863, *OR*, 24(3):738; Pemberton to Cooper, April 11, 1863, *OR*, 24(3):733; Pemberton to Cooper, *OR*, 24(3):751.

7. For Morris's report, see Dodge's "Report of Spys 1863 to Feb. 1864" [henceforth Dodge, Secret Service diary], April 13, 1863, box 149, DP; and Richard Oglesby to Henry Binmore, April 13, 1863, *OR*, 24(3):191. See also "Final Report of Receipts and Expenditures of Col. Wm. S. Hillyer, Provost Marshal General, Department of the Tennessee, February–May, 1863" [henceforth Hillyer Report], William S. Hillyer Papers, box 1, UVL; and Dodge, "Secret Service Vouchers," box 148, DP.

8. USG to Col. J. C. Kelton, July 6, 1863, *GP*, 8:485; Bearss, *Vicksburg Campaign*, 2:19–21.

9. Dana to Stanton, April 14, 1863, *OR*, 24(1):75; USG to Jesse Grant, April 21, 1863, *GP*, 8:109.

10. Bearss, *Vicksburg Campaign*, 2:53–82, 129–236; USG to Jesse Grant, April 21, 1863, 8:109; Starr, *Union Cavalry*, 3:185–97; Catton, *Grant Moves South*, 422. See also USG to Kelton, July 6, 1863, 8:506–7.

11. James W. Denver to McPherson, February 27, 1863, *OR*, 24(3):71–72; Hillyer Report. See also Lorain Ruggles pension record, RG 15, NARA; [Ruggles], *Great American Scout and Spy*, 228–41; Woolworth, *The Mississippi Scout*, 5–9. Grant recalled that Ruggles's reports were "always reliable, and were held in high estimation by me." USG to Edward C. Downs, July 9, 1866, *GP*, 12:458.

12. Oglesby to Binmore, April 21, 1863, *OR*, 24(3):218; Oglesby to Hurlbut, April 18, 1863, box 2, Richard J. Oglesby Papers, ISHS. The absence of entries in Dodge's Secret Service diary between April 13 and May 8 confirms Oglesby's observations. See Dodge, Secret Service diary.

13. Special Orders No. 110, April 20, 1862, *OR*, 24(3):212–13; USG to McClernand, April 18, 1863, *GP*, 8:88; USG to Sherman, April 27, 1863, *GP*, 8:130; Bearss, *Vicksburg Campaign*, 2:253–68; Bowen to Pemberton, April 28, 1863, *OR*, 24(3):797.

14. Porter to USG, April 23, 1863, *GP*, 8:114–15; USG to Sherman, April 24, 1863, *GP*, 8:117. Grant also sent Lt. Col. James H. Wilson on a reconnaissance north of Grand Gulf to find a suitable landing and roads ascending the bluffs between Warrenton and the Big Black River. Wilson found the region and the roads under water. Wilson to Frederick E. Prime, May 30, 1863, *OR*, 24(1):127–28.

15. USG to Halleck, April 29, 1863, *GP*, 8:133; *PMUSG*, 1:476–77; USG to Kelton, July 6, 1863, *GP*, 8:494; Bearss, *Vicksburg Campaign*, 2:317.

16. USG to Kelton, July 6, 1863, 8:491; Catton, *Grant Moves South*, 424–25; *PMUSG*, 1:477–78, 481.

17. Bearss, *Vicksburg Campaign*, 2:317–46; USG to Halleck, May 3, 1863, *GP*, 8:143; McClernand to Rawlins, June 17, 1863, *OR*, 24(1):143 (emphasis added); USG to Halleck, May 3, 1863, *GP*, 8:147; Catton, *Grant Moves South*, 428.

18. Bearss, *Vicksburg Campaign*, 2:351, 417; Pemberton to Davis, May 1, 1863, *OR*, 24(3):807.

19. USG to Kelton, July 6, 1863, 8:494–95; *PMUSG*, 1:493–96; Bearss, *Vicksburg Campaign*, 2:431–57, 480; USG to Hurlbut, May 6, 1863, *GP*, 8:170; USG to Halleck, May 6, 1863, *GP*, 8:169.

20. With Grierson's command retained by Banks, Grant possessed only one

complete cavalry regiment in addition to a mix of companies from other regiments. Starr, *Union Cavalry*, 3:182–83.

21. Report of Ocran H. Howard, chief signal officer, June 6, 1863, *OR*, 24(1):130; Wilson, "Staff Officer's Journal," 93–109, 261–75.

22. USG to McClernand, May 13, 1863, *GP*, 8:208. See also McClernand to USG, May 7, 1863, *GP*, 8:173; McClernand to USG, May 8, 1863, *GP*, 8:177; Ballard, *Pemberton*, 147; and Wilson, "Staff Officer's Journal," 95, 97–99. Pemberton had about 23,000 men in the field and another 8,000 manning the Vicksburg defenses. Symonds, *Joseph E. Johnston*, 207.

23. USG to McClernand, May 13, 1863, 8:208; USG to Kelton, July 6, 1863, 8:494; Wilson, "Staff Officer's Journal," 100. President Davis had indeed urged Pemberton to hold Vicksburg and Port Hudson. See Davis to Pemberton, May 4, 1863, *OR*, 24(3):842; McPherson to USG, May 9, 1863, *GP*, 8:183. Beauregard sent two brigades (5,000 men) from South Carolina but did not accompany them to Mississippi. Bearss, *Vicksburg Campaign*, 2:525; Wilson, "Staff Officer's Journal," 99.

24. USG to Kelton, July 6, 1863, 8:495–96; USG to Maj. Gen. Francis P. Blair Jr., May 14, 1863, *GP*, 8:213; Wilson, "Staff Officer's Journal," 105; *PMUSG*, 1:499–500; Pemberton to Davis and Johnston, May 12, 1863, *OR*, 24(3):859; Ballard, *Pemberton*, 153–54.

25. Symonds, *Joseph E. Johnston*, 208–9. Though the identity of the courier has been a mystery ever since, Hurlbut's favorite scout, Charles S. Bell, is the most likely nominee. Both Adam Badeau and Grant recalled that a few months earlier Hurlbut had publicly expelled Johnston's messenger from Memphis for disloyalty. Unknown to the Confederate commander, however, the man was actually a Union operative, and his expulsion was merely a cover orchestrated to secure his pro-Confederate credentials and thus increase his effectiveness as a spy. Though different in details, Badeau's account of this man's ruse to gain the trust of Southerners appears similar to Bell's method of winning the enemy's trust. According to a *New York Ledger* article from 1869, several months before the Vicksburg campaign, Bell, with Hurlbut's acquiescence, arranged to be "captured" by Union authorities and then "escape," making sure his daring jailbreak made all the papers. And War Department files indicate that Bell was the only scout in Hurlbut's employ to use this innovative technique. In addition, provost marshal pay records reveal that the Memphis commander had no other operatives in the Jackson area at that time. Disguised as a volunteer on a Confederate general's staff, moreover, Bell would have been a natural choice for a courier. Though the scout never claimed credit for being the double agent, he is clearly the most likely candidate. Badeau, *Military History of General Ulysses S. Grant*, 1:252; *PMUSG*, 1:508. See also Hurlbut to Provost Marshal, St. Louis, July 28, 1863,

RG 110, entry 36, box 2, NARA; Hurlbut to Rawlins, June 7, 1863, RG 393, entry 4720 (Department of the Tennessee, Letters Received), box 1; *New York Ledger*, March 27, 1869; Charles S. Bell pension record, RG 15, NARA. For Bell's interesting career, see Feis, "Charles S. Bell."

26. USG to Blair, May 14, 1863, GP, 8:213–14; USG to Halleck, May 15, 1863, GP, 8:220; USG to McClernand, May 14, 1863, GP, 8:215; Wilson, "Staff Officer's Journal," 106; USG to Halleck, May 15, GP, 8:220. Edwin Bearss argued that, upon receipt of the captured dispatch, Grant "began to marshal his army to counter Pemberton's efforts to comply with Johnston's instructions." From the orders given after reading the intercept, however, Grant clearly hoped to prevent Johnston from reaching Pemberton on the west bank and to defeat their combined forces before they could slip into the Vicksburg works. See Bearss, *Vicksburg Campaign*, 2:568.

27. McClernand to USG, May 15, 1863, OR, 24(3):313; report of Peter J. Osterhaus, May 26, 1863, OR, 24(2):13; Wilson, "Vicksburg Journal," 106–7; PMUSG, 1:511; Bearss, *Vicksburg Campaign*, 2:579; Frederick D. Grant, "A Boy's Experience at Vicksburg," 93; USG to McPherson, May 16, 1863, GP, 8:226.

28. Johnston to Davis, December 24, 1863, OR, 24(1):240; Pemberton to Cooper, August 25, 1863, OR, 24(1):261–63; Johnston to Pemberton, May 15, 1863, OR, 24(3):882; Symonds, *Joseph E. Johnston*, 207–9.

29. Dodge, "Secret Service," 5:14; Bearss, *Vicksburg Campaign*, 2:559–651, 653–89. See also Frederick D. Grant, "Address," 200. Frederick Grant's rendition of Sanburn's contribution differs from Dodge's version, but he notes that the "plan of battle . . . was made on information conveyed from General Dodge." Sanburn never returned to Corinth, nor was he heard from again. See Grenville M. Dodge, "Personal Biography," 4 vols., Dodge Records, 1:106, DP.

30. USG to Sherman, May 17, 1863, GP, 8:233; Bearss, *Vicksburg Campaign*, 3:731–873.

31. USG to Porter, May 23, 1863, GP, 8:257; USG to Jacob G. Lauman, May 23, 1863, GP, 8:259–60; Wilson, "Staff Officer's Diary," 264; Porter to USG, May 23, 1863, GP, 8:258. USG to Halleck, May 24, 1863, GP, 8:261.

32. Rawlins to Hurlbut, May 25, 1863, GP, 8:273; USG to Banks, May 25, 1863, GP, 8:268–69; USG to Prentiss, May 25, 1863, GP, 8:272; Starr, *Union Cavalry*, 3:180–85.

33. Special Orders No. 141, May 26, 1863, GP, 8:288; USG to Porter, May 29, 1863, GP, 8:285–86; Blair to USG, May 29, 1863, GP, 8:285–86; USG to Halleck, May 29, 1863, GP, 8:283; Blair to USG, May 31, 1863, GP, 8:290; Dana to Stanton, May 30, 1863, OR, 24(1):90; USG to Porter, June 2, 1863, GP, 8:299; Wilson, "Staff Officer's Journal," 270.

34. See Dodge, "Secret Service Vouchers," box 148, DP; and Dodge, Secret Service diary. See also Dodge, "Secret Service," 5:16.

35. Dodge, "Secret Service," 5:14.

36. Voucher for J. T. Evans, June 31, 1863, box 148, DP. For examples of Dodge's protective behavior, see vouchers of Mary Malone and Jane Featherstone, box 148, and "List of Secret Service Men & Expenses," box 149, DP; Dodge to Oglesby, May 30, 1863, box 2, Oglesby Papers; and Johns, *Philip Henson*, 38.

37. Dodge to Oglesby, May 9, 12, 1863, Oglesby Papers; Dodge to "Capt. Farrand," December 30, 1862, RG 393, entry 6159 (Sixteenth Corps, Letters Sent), pt. 2.

38. Wilson, "Staff Officer's Journal," 270; Hurlbut to USG, May 30, 1863, GP, 8:274; Dana to Stanton, May 31, 1863, OR, 24(1):90–91; A. K. Johnson to Francis P. Blair, May 28, 1863, OR, 24(3):355; Blair to USG, May 28, 1963, OR, 24(3):354–55; USG to Banks, May 31, 1863, GP, 8:295; USG to Hurlbut, May 31, 1863, GP, 8:297. For Pemberton's strength, see "Inspection Report of Army at Vicksburg," May 26, 1863, OR, 24(3):923.

39. USG to Kelton, May 21, 1863, GP, 8:293; George Thom to USG, June 16, 1863, GP, 8:294. For the enciphered message and two slightly different translations, see OR, 24(1):39–40.

40. The spies were most likely Jane Featherstone, Mary Malone, and John Coleman. See Dodge, Secret Service diary, May 31, 1863; and "Secret Service Vouchers," box 148, DP. See also Dodge to Oglesby, May 31, 1863, box 3, Oglesby Papers; and Oglesby to Hurlbut, May 31, 1863, OR, 24(3):369.

41. Clark Wright to Rawlins, May 30, 1863, GP, 8:292; USG to Halleck, May 30, 1863, GP, 8:326; USG to Banks, May 31, 1863, GP, 8:294–95; USG to Hurlbut, May 31, 1862, GP, 8:297; USG to Halleck, May 29, 1863, GP, 8:283.

42. USG to Kimball, June 3, 1863, GP, 8:308–9; USG to Kimball, June 4, 1863, GP, 8:315; Kimball to USG, June 5, 1863, GP, 8:316–17; Kimball to Rawlins, June 6, 1863, GP, 8:317; Bearss, *Vicksburg Campaign*, 3:1021–30; Dana to Stanton, June 7, 1863, OR, 24(1):94; Dana to Stanton, June 8, 1863, OR, 24(1):94; USG to Halleck, June 8, 1863, GP, 8:325.

43. Dodge, Secret Service diary, May 21, 1863; T. B. Roy to John C. Breckinridge, May 23, 1863, OR, 24(3):912; Benjamin Ewell to Johnston, June 1, 1863, OR, 24(3):942; Dodge to Oglesby, May 30, 1863, box 2, Oglesby Papers; Dodge, "Secret Service Vouchers," box 148, DP; W. H. Thurston to Hurlbut, May 31, 1863, OR, 24(3):370; USG to Halleck, June 8, 1863, GP, 8:325; USG to Halleck, June 11, 1863, GP, 8:345–36; Ewell to Johnston, June 1, 1863, OR, 24(3):942; "Return of the Army in Mississippi," June 25, 1863, OR, 24(3):978. For the estimates of Dodge's spies, see Hurlbut to Halleck, June 3, 1863, OR, 24(3):381; and Hurlbut to Rawlins, June 10, 1863, OR, 24(3):397. See also Dodge, Secret Service diary, May 31, June 9, 1863.

44. USG to Hurlbut, June 11, 1863, GP, 8:348; USG to Halleck, June 11, 1863, GP, 8:

345; Osterhaus to Rawlins, June 7, 1863, *OR*, 24(2):215–16; McClernand to USG, June 12, 1863, *GP*, 8:358; Washburn to USG, June 11, 1863, *GP*, 8:353; Osterhaus to Rawlins, June 12, 1863, *GP*, 8:339–40; Wright to Rawlins, June 12, 1863, *GP*, 8:340; McClernand to USG, June 12, 1863, *GP*, 8:358; Capt. J. B. Gorsuch to USG, June 13, 1863, *OR*, 24(3):407; USG to Washburn, June 13, 1863, *GP*, 8:359–60.

45. Washburn to USG, June 14, 1863, RG 393, entry 4720, box 2; USG to Washburn, June 15, 1863, *GP*, 8:373; Dana to Stanton, June 15, 1863, *OR*, 24(1):100; USG to McClernand, June 15, 1863, *GP*, 8:368–69; Dana to Stanton, June 20, 1863, *OR*, 24(1):104–5; Bearss, *Vicksburg Campaign*, 3:1083–87; Johnston to Pemberton, June 16, 1863, *OR*, 24(3):965.

46. On June 8 Hurlbut had sent Bell south to provide Grant with "all the information he can gather." See Hurlbut to USG, June 7, 1863, RG 393, entry 4720, box 1. During the 1864 Virginia campaign, Bell visited Grant's headquarters with a letter from Hurlbut introducing him as the spy "who penetrated through Johnson's army in rear of Vicksburg and reported to you." Hurlbut to USG, October 4, 1864, *GP*, 10:387. See also William Sooy Smith to USG, January 17, 1864, RG 393, entry 2521 (Military Division of the Mississippi, Records of the Provost Marshal), box 2.

47. USG to Ord, June 22, 1863, *GP*, 8:404; USG to McPherson, June 22, 1863, *GP*, 8:403; USG to Maj. Gen. E. O. C. Ord, June 22, 1863, *GP*, 8:404; Dana to Stanton, June 22, 1863, *OR*, 24(1):106–7; USG to Sherman, June 22, 1863, *GP*, 8:408; USG to Halleck, June 26, 1863, *GP*, 8:432.

48. Sherman to Rawlins, June 27, 1863, *OR*, 24(2):247; Dana to Stanton, June 24, 1863, *OR*, 24(1):107.

49. Dana to Stanton, June 27, 1863, *OR*, 24(1):110; USG to Hurlbut, June 27, 1863, *GP*, 8:435; USG to Banks, June 30, 1863, *GP*, 8:446; Dana to Stanton, July 2, 1863, *OR*, 24(1):113–14; Sherman to USG, July 1, 1863, *GP*, 8:453; USG to Ord, July 1, 1863, *GP*, 8:452.

50. Johnston to Davis, December 24, 1863, *OR*, 24(1):244–45.

51. For examples, see Dana to Stanton, June 11, 1863, *OR*, 24(1):96; Dana to Stanton, June 14, 1863, *OR*, 24(1):98; USG to Julia, June 15, 1863, *GP*, 8:376–77; and Wilson, "Staff Officer's Journal," 266–67, 271, 273. Porter's operative was probably named Trussel, the same man who had accompanied Spencer Kellogg Brown on his first mission in January 1862. In a footnote, Brown's chronicler noted that during the Vicksburg campaign, Trussel "reported to General Grant with very important information." See Smith, *Spencer Kellogg Brown*, 239.

52. Wilson, "Staff Officer's Journal," 273; USG to Sherman, June 25, 1863, *GP*, 8:423.

53. USG to Sherman, July 3, 1863, *GP*, 8:460, 461; USG to Julia Grant, June 29, 1863, *GP*, 8:444.

7. "What Force the Enemy Have . . . I Have No Means of Judging Accurately"

1. USG to Halleck, September 22, 1863, *GP*, 9:229; USG to Halleck, September 30, 1863, *GP*, 9:253; Sword, *Mountains Touched with Fire*, 50–53.

2. *PMUSG*, 2:28; USG to Halleck, October 26, 1863, *GP*, 9:321. For Rosecrans' intelligence network, see RG 393, entry 986 (Summaries of the News Reaching Headquarters of Gen. W. S. Rosecrans), NARA. For Truesdail and the Army of the Cumberland Police, see Fitch, *Annals*, 346–56. For examples of Rosecrans' collection and use of intelligence during the Tullahoma campaign, see Feis, "Deception of Braxton Bragg," 10–21, 46–53.

3. USG to Halleck, October 26, 1863, 9:321. Apparently, Grant was unaware of the intelligence network operating out of Army of the Cumberland headquarters, now under Thomas's direction. Even before replacing Rosecrans, Thomas had diligently pursued information on the enemy. When Dana visited the general in early October, he noted that during his stay, "[s]couts were coming in constantly." See Dana, *Recollections*, 109. For examples of information reaching Thomas, see RG 393, entry 958 (Intelligence Reports Received by Gen. Thomas, 1863–1865).

4. USG to Halleck, October 26, 1863, 9:320; Sword, *Mountains Touched with Fire*, 86, 114; USG to Julia, November 14, 1863, *GP*, 9:396–97.

5. Sword, *Mountains Touched with Fire*, 85–86, 112–22.

6. Cozzens, *Shipwreck of Their Hopes*, 106; USG to Ambrose Burnside, October 26, 1863, *GP*, 9:325; Burnside to USG, October 27, 1863, *GP*, 9:325–26; Connelly, *Autumn of Glory*, 263; USG to Kelton, December 23, 1863, *GP*, 9:558–59; *PMUSG*, 2:49. No reinforcements were coming from Virginia. Only Confederate general Samuel Jones's 6,000 men occupied the southwestern tip of Virginia. Catton, *Grant Takes Command*, 58–59.

7. Sword, *Mountains Touched with Fire*, 150–51, 154–56; USG to Halleck, October 28, 1863, *GP*, 9:337; USG to Burnside, October 31, 1863, *GP*, 9:343; USG to Halleck, November 2, 1863, *GP*, 9:349; Dana to Stanton, November 4, 1863, *OR*, 31(2):56; USG to Burnside, November 5, 1863, *GP*, 9:359; William F. Smith, "An Historical Sketch of the Military Operations around Chattanooga, Tennessee, September 22 to November 27, 1863," in *Papers of the Military Historical Society of Massachusetts*, 8:192; Cozzens, *Shipwreck of Their Hopes*, 106–7; USG to Halleck, November 6, 1863, *GP*, 9:264; USG to Burnside, November 5, 1863, *GP*, 9:359.

8. Burnside to USG, November 6, 1863, *GP*, 9:369; Dana to Stanton, November 7, 1863, *OR*, 31(2):57–58; USG to Sherman, November 7, 1863, *GP*, 9:370; USG to George H. Thomas, November 7, 1863, *GP*, 9:370–71.

9. Catton, *Grant Takes Command*, 60–61; Smith, "Military Operations around Chattanooga," 193–94; Dana to Stanton, November 58, 1863, *OR*, 31(2):58; Cozzens, *Shipwreck of Their Hopes*, 107–8 (Thomas quoted on 108); USG to Kelton, December 23, 1863, *GP*, 9:559; Porter, *Campaigning with Grant*, 5. Grant admitted that Thomas "had a better opportunity of studying [the terrain] than myself." USG to Thomas, November 7, 1863, *GP*, 9:371; USG to Kelton, December 23, 1863, 9:559; *PMUSG*, 2:50.

10. USG to Kelton, December 23, 1863, 9:559; USG to Burnside, November 14, 1863, *GP*, 9:391; USG to Halleck, November 15, 1863, *GP*, 9:399–400; Sherman to Ewing, November 18, 1863, *OR*, 31(2):584; Sword, *Mountains Touched with Fire*, 157–58. See "Statement of Elisha Breedlove," November 16, 1863, *OR*, 31(3):164. Bragg apparently expected an attack upon his left as late as November. See Cozzens, *Shipwreck of Their Hopes*, 124–25; USG to Sherman, November 22, 1863, *GP*, 9:430.

11. Dana to Stanton, November 8, 1863, *OR*, 31(2):59; USG to Burnside, November 14, 1863, 9:393; USG to Halleck, November 15, 1863, 9:400; USG to Burnside, November 17, 1863, *GP*, 9:404–5; Sword, *Mountains Touched with Fire*, 188–89; USG to Halleck, November 18, 1863, *GP*, 9:409.

12. USG to John Riggin Jr., November 18, 1863, *GP*, 9:413; USG to Sherman, November 20, 1863, *GP*, 9:421; USG to Sherman, November 22, 1863, *GP*, 9:430.

13. Thomas J. Wood to Joseph S. Fullerton, November 23, *OR*, 31(2):40; Dana to Stanton, November 23, 1863, *OR*, 31(2):64; Luther M. De Motte to Jesse Merrill, November 22, 1863, *OR*, 31(2):100–101; Jefferson C. Davis to Joseph J. Reynolds, November 22, 1863, *OR*, 31(2):102; Dana to Stanton, November 20, 1863, *OR*, 31(2):63; USG to Kelton, December 23, 1863, *GP*, 9:560, 568; *PMUSG*, 2:331; Sword, *Mountains Touched with Fire*, 176; USG to Thomas, November 23, 1863, *OR*, 31(2):41.

14. Sword, *Mountains Touched with Fire*, 175–85; Dana to Stanton, November 23, 1863, *OR*, 31(2):66.

15. USG to Kelton, December 23, 1863, 9:560; USG to Halleck, October 26, 1863, *GP*, 9:321.

16. Sword, *Mountains Touched with Fire*, 186, 202.

17. Carter L. Stevenson to Hardee and Bragg, November 23, 1863, *OR*, 31(2):674; Bragg actually saw the corps under Oliver O. Howard entering the city. Sword, *Mountains Touched with Fire*, 186–87.

18. Brown, *Signal Corps*, 481; Merrill to Reynolds, November 23, 1863, *OR*, 31(2):103; Sword, *Mountains Touched with Fire*, 205; Reynolds to Hooker, November 23, 1863, *OR*, 31(2):105; Reynolds to Hooker, November 24, 1863, *OR*, 31(2):106.

19. Cozzens, *Shipwreck of Their Hopes*, 126; Sword, *Mountains Touched with Fire*, 231; Dana to Stanton, November 24, *OR*, 31(2):67.

20. Sword, *Mountains Touched with Fire*, 199–201, 232.
21. Dana to Stanton, November 25, 1863, *OR*, 31(2):67; USG to Kelton, December 23, 1863, 9:562; Montgomery C. Meigs, to Stanton, November 26, 1863, *OR*, 31(2):78; Sword, *Mountains Touched with Fire*, 238, 264.
22. Gordon Granger to William D. Whipple, February 11, 1864, *OR*, 31(2):132; Sword, *Mountains Touched with Fire*, 263–65.
23. Cozzens, *Shipwreck of Their Hopes*, 387–88.
24. Wilson, *Rawlins*, 171.

8. "That Gives Just the Information I Wanted"

1. Wilson, *Rawlins*, 404; Catton, *Grant Takes Command*, 121–22.
2. Hattaway and Jones, *How the North Won*, 516–33; USG to Sherman, April 4, 1864, *GP*, 10:251–53; USG to Maj. Gen. Franz Sigel, April 15, 1864, *GP*, 10:286–87; USG to Banks, March 15, 1864, *GP*, 10:200–201.
3. Hattaway and Jones, *How the North Won*, 528–29; USG to Stanton, July 22, 1865, *OR*, 36(1):17; USG to Benjamin F. Butler, April 2, 1864, *GP*, 10:245–47.
4. USG to Stanton, July 22, 1864, *OR*, 36(1):17; USG to George G. Meade, April 9, 1864, *GP*, 10:273–75.
5. Wilson, *Rawlins*, 405.
6. John C. Babcock to "Dear Aunt," June 6, 1862, John C. Babcock Papers, LC. See also "Record of Service of John C. Babcock during Civil War of 1861–65," [henceforth "Babcock's Service Record"], Babcock Papers. Babcock is often mistaken for Lemuel E. Babcock, a BMI scout captured in February 1865 while infiltrating Richmond with another operative named Pole. Once in the city, Pole betrayed Babcock, which led to his arrest and confinement in Castle Thunder until Richmond fell that April. John C. Babcock never went into Richmond to spy because he was much too valuable at headquarters. See Lemuel E. Babcock, "Statement to Southern Claims Commission," RG 217 (Records of the General Accounting Office), NARA.
7. For a thorough discussion of the origins, personnel, and activities of the BMI prior to 1864, see Fishel, *Secret War*, 275–537. For Babcock's order-of-battle chart, see "Organization and strength of force comprising the present Army of Northern Virga., Corrected to Apr. 28, 1863," Joseph Hooker Papers, Huntington Library, San Marino CA. See also Babcock's "Organization of the Rebel Army of N. Va.," Miscellaneous Civil War Papers, Southern Historical Collection, University of North Carolina, Chapel Hill; Army of the Potomac, "Intelligence Diary," RG 393, entry 3988 (Daily Diary of Intelligence Information, Aug.–Dec. 1863), NARA; and "Index of the Army of Northern Virginia," Babcock Papers.
8. Fishel, *Secret War*, 493. For the creation of BMI "branch offices," see Marsena M. Patrick to Edward R. S. Canby, March 16, 1864, RG 107 (Records

of the Office of the Secretary of War, Letters Received, December 1863–
March 1864), NARA.

9. For Patrick's duties, see David S. Sparks, "General Patrick's Progress: Intelligence and Security in the Army of the Potomac," 371–84. See also Sparks,
Inside Lincoln's Army; and "List of BMI Scouts," compiled by Edwin C. Fishel
from payroll records, in author's collection.

10. Officers in charge of pickets were instructed to bring all deserters to the
rear where they "must be examined respecting the movements, &c., of
the enemy." U.S. War Department, *Instructions for Officers and Noncommissioned Officers on Outpost and Patrol Duty* (1861; Ellicott City MD:
Courtney B. Wilson and Associates, n.d.), 12. For an example of Grant inter-
rogating a prisoner, see Porter, *Campaigning with Grant*, 157–60.

11. George H. Sharpe to "General Martindale," December 12, 1863, RG 393, entry
3980 (Miscellaneous Letters, Reports, and Lists Received). See also Army of
the Potomac, "Intelligence Diary."

12. General Orders No. 64, February 18, 1864, *OR*, ser. 3, 4:118; Dowdey and
Manarin, *Wartime Papers of Robert E. Lee*, 693. For a general discussion of
deserter information, see Ella Lonn, *Desertion during the Civil War*.

13. Sharpe to Ely S. Parker, July 31, 1864, RG 108 (Headquarters of the Army,
Headquarters in the Field), entry 112 (Reports Containing Military Intelligence Received By Gen. Grant), NARA.

14. USG to Halleck, October 26, 1863, *GP*, 9:321.

15. See BMI reports from March 1864 to March 1865 in RG 108, entry 112.

16. Evidence of Grant's interest in Southern newspapers is sprinkled throughout
his correspondence. By March 1865 he received the Richmond papers on a
daily basis. USG to Halleck, March 2, 1865, *GP*, 14:80; Sharpe to Martindale,
December 12, 1863, RG 393, entry 3980.

17. Fishel, *Secret War*, 544; USG to Halleck, April 29, 1864, *GP*, 10:370–71.

18. USG to Sherman, April 8, 1864, *GP*, 10:271. For BMI reports on Longstreet's
return to Virginia, see George H. Sharpe to Andrew A. Humphreys, April 13,
17, 23, 25, 1864, RG 108, entry 112. For Isaac Silver's previous services, see
Fishel, *Secret War*, 272–73, 315–18. See also Stuart, "Colonel Ulric Dahlgren,"
196–204.

19. Sharpe to Humphreys, April 26, 1864, RG 108, entry 112; USG to Sigel, April 15,
1864, *GP*, 10:287; USG to Julia Grant, April 27, 1864, *GP*, 10:363; USG to Butler,
April 28, 1864, *GP*, 10:364.

20. John McEntee to Sharpe, April 29, 1864, RG 393, entry 3980, box 11; Rhea,
Battle of the Wilderness, 21. The First Corps remained in that vicinity along
the rail connections with Richmond to shield the capital and act as a mobile
reserve until Grant's intentions became evident. Lee to Davis, April 29, 1864,
OR, 33:1326.

21. Stanton to USG, April 30, 1864, *OR*, 33:1022–23; USG to Stanton, May 1, 1864, *GP*, 10:381.

22. USG to Halleck, April 29, 1864, *GP*, 10:370–71; USG to Meade, April 9, 1864, *GP*, 10:274–75; Rhea, *Battle of the Wilderness*, 49–52; Steere, *Wilderness Campaign*, 26–29.

23. Rhea, *Battle of the Wilderness*, 52–56. See also Humphreys, *Virginia Campaign*, 9–11.

24. Nathaniel Michler to Seth Williams, October 20, 1864, *OR*, 36(1):292–93; Theodore Lyman, "Uselessness of the Maps Furnished to Staff of the Army of the Potomac Previous to the Campaign of May, 1864," in *Papers of the Military Historical Society of Massachusetts*, 4:77–80; Hattaway and Jones, *How the North Won*, 560; Porter, *Campaigning with Grant*, 40; Rhea, *Battle of the Wilderness*, 64, 69, 102; Matter, *If It Takes All Summer*, 2; USG to Halleck, April 29, 1864, *GP*, 10:371.

25. USG to Stanton, June 20, 1865, *GP*, 15:168.

26. "Intercepted Signal Messages," May 4, 1864, *OR*, 36(2):371–72; Porter, *Campaigning with Grant*, 44; Rhea, *Battle of the Wilderness*, 70–78; USG to Halleck, May 4, 1864, *GP*, 10:397.

27. Meade to USG, May 5, 1864, *GP*, 10:399; USG to Meade, May 5, 1864, *GP*, 10:399.

28. *PMUSG*, 2:177–78; Sherman to Stanton, May 23, 1864, *OR*, 38(4):294.

29. Rhea, *Battle of the Wilderness*, 435, 440, 437; USG to Halleck, May 6, 1864, *GP*, 10:400.

30. Badeau, *Military History of General Ulysses S. Grant*, 2:133; Agassiz, *Meade's Headquarters*, 101; Porter, *Campaigning with Grant*, 69–70; Wilson, *Rawlins*, 218; USG to Stanton, July 22, 1865, *OR*, 36(1):18–19; *PMUSG*, 2:211.

31. USG to Meade, May 7, 1864, *GP*, 10:408; Matter, *If It Takes All Summer*, 44–70; G. K. Warren to Meade, May 8, 1864, *OR*, 36(2):539; Dana to Stanton, May 8, 1864, *OR*, 36(1):63.

32. Warren to Meade, May 8, 1864, *OR*, 36(2):540; Meade's endorsement of Warren's dispatch, May 8, 1864, *OR*, 36(2):540; USG to Halleck, May 8, 1864, *GP*, 10:411; Matter, *If It Takes All Summer*, 111–112; Hattaway and Jones, *How the North Won*, 554.

33. Warren to Meade, May 8, 1864, *OR*, 36(2):540–41; Catton, *Grant Takes Command*, 213–17; USG to Halleck, May 10, 1864, *GP*, 10:418.

34. USG to Burnside, May 9, 1864, *GP*, 10:415; Matter, *If It Takes All Summer*, 110–11; USG to Halleck, May 9, 1864, *GP*, 10:414; Catton, *Grant Takes Command*, 218–19; USG to Burnside, May 9, 1864, *GP*, 10:415–16.

35. USG to Stanton, May 11, 1864, *GP*, 10:422; Catton, *Grant Takes Command*, 219; Wilson, *Rawlins*, 218.

36. Hattaway and Jones, *How the North Won*, 555–58; Dana to Stanton, May 10,

1864, *OR*, 36(1):66; USG to Halleck, May 11, 1864, *GP*, 10:423; USG to Stanton, July 22, 1864, *OR*, 36(1):17.

37. Meade to USG, May 10, 1864, *OR*, 36(2):596; USG to Halleck, May 11, 1864, 10:423; Sheridan to Meade, May 10, 1864, *GP*, 10:426; Hattaway and Jones, *How the North Won*, 559.

38. USG to Halleck, May 12, 1864, *GP*, 10:428; USG to Julia Grant, May 13, 1864, *GP*, 10:443; Meade, *Life and Letters*, 2:201. On May 17 Sharpe reported that one enemy deserter indicated that the "spirit of the men has somewhat failed." Sharpe to Humphreys, May 17, 1864, *OR*, 36(2):842.

39. USG to Halleck, May 22, 1864, *GP*, 10:477; Sharpe to Humphreys, May 22, 1864, *OR*, 36(3):80; Catton, *Grant Takes Command*, 250–53; USG to Halleck, May 26, 1864, *GP*, 10:490–91. For an excellent account of the North Anna campaign, see Rhea, *To the North Anna River*.

40. USG to Halleck, May 26, 1864, *GP*, 10:491; Dana to Stanton, May 24, 1864, *OR*, 36(1):78; Dana to Stanton, May 26, *OR*, 36(1):70; USG to Halleck, May 11, 1864, *GP*, 10:423.

41. Catton, *Grant Takes Command*, 259–262; circular from Meade's headquarters, June 2, 1864, *OR*, 36(3):479; Hattaway and Jones, *How the North Won*, 580.

42. USG to Julia Grant, June 1, 1864, *GP*, 11:5; Porter, *Campaigning with Grant*, 172; Hattaway and Jones, *How the North Won*, 579–80. For Grant's opinion of Lee's reluctance to fight in the open, see USG to Halleck, May 26, 1864, 10:491.

43. USG to Halleck, June 5, 1864, *GP*, 11:19; Catton, *Grant Takes Command*, 274–79, 294–95;USG to Washburne, June 9, 1864, *GP*, 11:32.

44. Catton, *Grant Takes Command*, 280–81; Reid, "Grant's Crossing of the James," 299–300; *PMUSG*, 2:281; Sharpe to Humphreys, June 11, 1864, *OR*, 36(3):747.

45. Reid, "Grant's Crossing of the James," 302; Catton, *Grant Takes Command*, 281–82.

46. USG to Julia Grant, June 15, 1864, *GP*, 11:55; Dowdey and Manarin, *Wartime Papers of Robert E. Lee*, 778–79, 780–81, 784; Wilson to James W. Forsyth, February 18, 1865, *OR*, 36(1):883–84.

47. John Van Lew, brother of Elizabeth Van Lew, who headed a spy ring in Richmond, visited Grant on June 11 perhaps to update the commander on his sister's operation. Humphreys to Rawlins, June 11, 1864, *OR*, 36(3):746; Fishel, *Secret War*, 552.

48. Wilson to Forsyth, February 18, 1865, *OR*, 36(1):883–84; Wilson, *Rawlins*, 231; Dana to Stanton, June 13, 1864, *OR*, 40(1):19; Wilson to Humphreys, June 14, 1864, *OR*, 40(2):34–35; Dana to Stanton, June 15, 1864, *OR*, 40(1):20.

49. USG to Butler, June 14, 1864, *GP*, 11:45; *PMUSG*, 2:281; Hattaway and Jones, *How the North Won*, 588.

50. Reid, "Grant's Crossing of the James," 314.

9. "Is It Not Certain That Early Has Returned?"

1. Halleck to USG, July 3, 1864, *GP*, 11:166; USG to Halleck, July 3, 1864, *GP*, 11:166; USG to Halleck, July 5, 1864, *GP*, 11:170.

2. Vandiver, *Jubal's Raid*, 6–10, 20; Cooling, *Jubal Early's Raid*, 10; Hattaway and Jones, *How the North Won*, 600.

3. USG to Meade, June 5, 1864, *GP*, 11:21; USG to Hunter, June 6, 1864, *GP*, 11:24; Dowdey and Manarin, *Wartime Papers of Robert E. Lee*, 767, 774–75; Catton, *Grant Takes Command*, 297.

4. Special Order No. 139, June 4, 1864, *OR*, 34(3):873–74; Early, *War Memoirs*, 371–72, 331; Catton, *Grant Takes Command*, 309–10.

5. Freeman, *Lee's Dispatches*, 240–41; Dowdey and Manarin, *Wartime Papers of Robert E. Lee*, 772; Early, *War Memoirs*, 371.

6. *PMUSG*, 2:288; Catton, *Grant Takes Command*, 280–83; "Itineraries of the Army of the Potomac and Army of the James," *OR*, 40(1):178–218.

7. Cooling, *Early's Raid*, 10–12; USG to Butler, June 14, 1864, *GP*, 11:45; Dowdey and Manarin, *Wartime Papers of Robert E. Lee*, 791; Early, *War Memoirs*, 372; Catton, *Grant Takes Command*, 281.

8. Sharpe to Humphreys, June 17, 1864, *OR*, 40(2):119; Sharpe to Humphreys, June 18, 1864, *OR*, 40(2):158–60.

9. USG to Halleck, June 17, 1864, *GP*, 11:67; USG to Halleck, June 19, 1864, *GP*, 11:130; Porter, *Campaigning with Grant*, 70.

10. McEntee to Sharpe, April 17, 1864, RG 393, entry 3980, NARA.

11. McEntee to Sharpe, April 18, 1864; and McEntee to Sharpe, May 3, 1864, RG 393, entry 3980.

12. McEntee to Sharpe, May 20, 1864; and McEntee to Sharpe, May 24, 1864, RG 393, entry 3980.

13. McEntee to Sharpe, May 7, 1864; and McEntee to Sharpe, May 20, 1864, RG 393, entry 3980.

14. McEntee to Sharpe, May 24, 1864.

15. Vandiver, *Jubal's Raid*, 43; Hunter to Adjutant General, U.S. Army, August 8, 1864, *OR*, 37(1):99; Hunter to Adjutant General, U.S. Army, August 8, 1864, *OR*, 37(1):101–2.

16. Diary of Capt. W. W. Old, Jubal Anderson Early Papers, Rice University, Houston TX; Vandiver, *Jubal's Raid*, 57–58, 142–47.

17. Sharpe to Humphreys, June 20, 1864, *OR*, 40(2):235; Sharpe to Humphreys, June 21, 1864, *OR*, 40(2):271; Meade to USG, June 21, 1864, *GP*, 11:102; Butler to

USG, June 23, 1864, *GP*, 11:113; Sharpe to Humphreys, June 24, 1864, *OR*, 40(2): 375–76.

18. Hunter to Adjutant General, U.S. Army, June 28, 1864, *OR*, 37(1):683–84; McEntee to Sharpe, June 28, 1864, RG 393, entry 3980.

19. Hancock to Williams, July 1, 1864, *OR*, 40(2):566; Halleck to USG, July 1, 1864, *GP*, 11:154; USG to Halleck, July 1, 1864, *GP*, 11:153.

20. John W. Garrett to Stanton, June 29, 1864, *OR*, 37(1):694–95.

21. Sigel to Adjutant General, U.S. Army, July 2, 1864, *OR*, 37(1):174–75; Garrett to Stanton, July 3, 1864, *OR*, 37(2):17; Sigel to Adjutant General, U.S. Army, July 3, 1864, *OR*, 37(1):175–76; Garrett to Stanton, July 3, 1864, *OR*, 37(2):16.

22. USG to Meade, July 3, 1864, *GP*, 11:167; Meade to USG, July 3, 1864, *GP*, 11:167; USG to Halleck, July 3, 1864, *GP*, 11:167.

23. Sharpe to Humphreys, July 4, 1864, *OR*, 40(2):620; USG to Halleck, July 4, 1864, *GP*, 11:169.

24. Sharpe to Humphreys, June 20, 1864, *OR*, 40(2):235; Sharpe to Humphreys, June 21, 1864, *OR*, 40(2):271; Sharpe to Humphreys, June 24, 1864, *OR*, 40(2): 375–76; Sharpe to Humphreys, July 4, 1864, *OR*, 40(2):620; Sharpe to Humphreys, July 6, 1864, *OR*, 40(3):37–38.

25. USG to Halleck, July 5, 1864, *GP*, 11:169, 170; USG to Halleck, July 6, 1864, *GP*, 11:178; Ely S. Parker to Leet, July 9, 1864, William R. Rowley Papers, ISHL.

26. Cooling, *Symbol, Sword, and Shield*, 192; Wallace to E. D. Townsend, [n.d.], *OR*, 37(1):195; Vandiver, *Jubal's Raid*, 112, 161–64; USG to Halleck, July 9, 1864, *GP*, 11:197–98.

27. USG to Lincoln, July 10, 1864, *GP*, 11:201; Vandiver, *Jubal's Raid*, 172; Parker to Leet, July 11, 1864, Rowley Papers.

28. Meade to USG, July 12, 1864, *GP*, 11:225; Cyrus B. Comstock, diary, July 12, 1864, Cyrus B. Comstock Papers, LC; USG to Halleck, July 13, 1864, *GP*, 11:233; Wilson, *Rawlins*, 244; USG to Hurlbut, February 27, 1863, *GP*, 7:361.

29. Halleck to USG, July 19, 1864, *GP*, 11:286–87; Hattaway and Jones, *How the North Won*, 603.

30. Gallagher, *Struggle for the Shenandoah*, 11; Wert, *Winchester to Cedar Creek*, 8; Lee to Davis, June 29, 1864, *OR*, 37(1):769–70; Lee to Davis, July 11, 1864, *OR*, 37(2):594–95; Dana to USG, July 12, 1864, *GP*, 11:252–53.

31. USG to Sherman, August 7, 1864, *GP*, 11:381; USG to Meade, August 1, 1864, *GP*, 11:368; Special Orders No. 68, August 2, 1864, *GP*, 11:369; USG to Halleck, August 1, 1864, *GP*, 11:358; Wert, *Winchester to Cedar Creek*, 29.

32. Parker to Leet, July 11, 1864, Rowley Papers; Sparks, *Inside Lincoln's Army*, 392–93, 382. For details on Sharpe's move to City Point, see BMI scout Judson Knight's article in *The National Tribune*, May 4, 1893.

33. Gallagher, *Struggle for the Shenandoah*, 11; Dowdey and Manarin, *Wartime Papers of Robert E. Lee*, 818–20; USG to Sheridan, September 2, 1864, *GP*, 11:

12:181; USG to Meade, July 30, 1864, *GP*, 11:352; Sparks, *Inside Lincoln's Army*, 400–401; Babcock to Sharpe, August 21, 1864; Babcock to Sharpe, August 27, 1864; and Babcock to Sharpe, September 5, 1864, RG 393, entry 3980; Porter, *Campaigning with Grant*, 34; Sharpe to Andrew A. Humphreys, September 15, 1864, *OR*, 42(2):382–83. For more on Silver, Cammack, and McGee, see Fishel, *Secret War*. See also Stuart, "Dahlgren," 197–98.

34. Postwar lecture by George H. Sharpe, Harlem Congregational Church, Kingston NY, Elizabeth Van Lew Papers, NYPL; McEntee to Bowers, November 10, 1864, RG 108, entry 112, NARA; Sharpe to Meade, January 18, 1865, *OR*, 46(2): 171.

35. Sharpe to Bowers, January 21, 1865; and "Descriptions of Confederate Bonds, Monies, etc. in the hands of Col. George H. Sharpe, January 1864," RG 393, entry 3980; USG to Stanton, February 4, 1865, *GP*, 13:361. Scout Judson Knight met regularly with Richmond agents between December 1864 and April 1865. Pay records show that, during this time, Sharpe gave him over $9,700, which far exceeded his pay of $4 a day. Undoubtedly, the money went to Van Lew, Ruth, McNiven, and others. See payroll record of Judson Knight, RG 110, entry 36, NARA.

36. Van Lew Report, December 1864; and McEntee to Sharpe, December 19, 1864, RG 393, entry 3980. For the frequency of trips, see USG to Stanton, February 4, 1865, *GP*, 13:361.

37. Butler to Stanton, February 5, 1864, *OR*, 33:519–21. See also Fishel, *Secret War*, 551–55; and Butler to "Col. Hardie," April 5, 1865, Van Lew Papers. Examples of her messages and those of other Richmond agents are found in RG 393, entry 3980; and in RG 108, entry 112.

38. At least eight BMI employees accompanied the raiders as guides and to collect information. McEntee, Milton Cline, and Joseph Humphries traveled with Kilpatrick, while Anson Carney, Martin Hogan, J. R. Dykes, Jake Swisher, and another named Chase rode with Dahlgren's column. Confederate authorities captured Carney, Hogan, Dykes, and Swisher. Carney escaped in June and returned to work for the BMI, Hogan remained "in irons" in Richmond, and Dykes and Swisher were "sent to Georgia" for incarceration. See McEntee to Sharpe, March 4, 1864; and Joseph Humphries to Sharpe, March 14, 1864, RG 393, entry 3980; and Sharpe to Humphreys, June 25, 1864, *OR*, 40(2):403.

39. Meade, *Life and Letters*, 190–91; "Babcock Service Record," John C. Babcock Papers, LC. For an in-depth study of the raid, see Virgil Carrington Jones, *Eight Hours before Richmond* (New York: Henry Holt, 1957).

40. The contents of the extract, filed with other reports from the Union underground, indicate it was written during the winter of 1863–64. Van Lew's correspondence of February 5, 1864, with Butler, in which McNiven (alias

"Quaker") also provides information, resembles information contained in the abstract. See "Extract," RG 393, entry 3980.

41. For a detailed description of the operation and the individuals involved, see Stuart, "Colonel Ulric Dahlgren," 153–204. See also Furgurson, *Ashes of Glory*, 256–58.

42. Elizabeth Van Lew, "Occasional Journal," Van Lew Papers, NYPL. For an edited version, consult Ryan, *Yankee Spy in Richmond*. Sharpe lecture, Harlem Congregational Church; and Sharpe to Cyrus B. Comstock, January 1867, Van Lew Papers, NYPL.

43. Castel, "Samuel Ruth," 41–42; Sharpe to Bower, February 23, 1865, RG 108, entry 112. For Ruth's description of his service, see Ruth to Stanton, December 21, 1865, Samuel Ruth File, box 2, William S. Hillyer Papers, UVL. For further discussion of Ruth's activities, see Stuart, "Samuel Ruth and General R. E. Lee," 90–101; Johnston, "Disloyalty on Confederate Railroads in Virginia," 418–22. For examples of information Ruth, Lohman, and Carter claimed they provided Grant, see U.S. Congress, *Samuel Ruth, W. F. E. Lohman, and Charles M. Carter*; and U.S. Congress, *F. W. E. Lohman, Samuel Ruth, Deceased, and Charles M. Carter*. Examples of Ruth's messages can be found in RG 393, entry 3980.

44. "Recollections of Thomas McNiven," Thomas McNiven Papers, Library of Virginia, Richmond. See also Ryan, "Thomas McNiven," 34–37; and Butler to Stanton, Feb 5, 1864, *OR*, 33:519–21.

45. Sheridan to USG, August 6, 1864, *GP*, 11:380; Sheridan, *Personal Memoirs*, 2:1; *PMUSG*, 2:317–18; "Sheridan's Report of Activities in the Shenandoah Valley, 1864–65," RG 108, entry 32 (Correspondence on Various Subjects of Special Concern to Army Headquarters, 1863–99), box 9. The number of scouts is found in RG 393, entry 2420 (List of Men of Sheridan's Scouts Furnished Clothing and Equipment). For Young, see Richard P. Weinert, "The South Had Mosby: The Union Had Maj. Henry Young," *Civil War Times Illustrated* (April 1964): 38–42; Beymer, *On Hazardous Service*, 100–132; and Tremain, *Last Hours of Sheridan's Cavalry*, 97–101.

46. Sheridan, *Personal Memoirs*, 2:1–2; Wert, *Winchester to Cedar Creek*, 33–40; *PMUSG*, 2:216–17; Lee to Davis, August 4, 1864, *OR*, 42(2):1161.

47. Babcock to Humphreys, August 8, 1864, *OR*, 40(2):86; Sharpe to Theodore S. Bowers, August 9, 1864, RG 108, entry 112; Bowers to Leet, August 10, 1864, *GP*, 11:395.

48. Butler to USG, August 10, 1864, *OR*, 40(2):106–7; Babcock to Sharpe, August 11, 1864, RG 393, entry 3980, box 11; Leet to Bowers, August 11, 1864, *GP*, 11:402; USG to Meade, August 11, 1864, *OR*, 40(3):115; USG to Halleck, August 11, 1864, *GP*, 11:401.

49. "Sheridan's Activities in the Shenandoah," RG 108, entry 32, box 9; Sheridan,

Personal Memoirs, 2:478–81; Wert, *Winchester to Cedar Creek*, 34–35; USG to Halleck, August 12, 1864, *GP*, 11:403.

50. USG to Sheridan, August 9, 1864, *GP*, 11:388; *PMUSG*, 2:321–22, 23–26; Sharpe to Babcock, August 12, 1864; and John I. Davenport to Sharpe, August 12, 1864, RG 393, entry 3980, box 11; USG to Halleck, August 14, 1864, *GP*, 11:415–16; USG to Sheridan, August 14, 1864, *GP*, 11:420; USG to Meade, August 17, 1864, *GP*, 12:21–22; USG to Sheridan, August 26, 1864, *GP*, 12:96–97; USG to Sheridan, August 20, 1864, *GP*, 12:54.

51. Sharpe to Bowers, September 1, 1864, RG 108, entry 112; USG to Sheridan, September 1, 1864, *GP*, 12:118; Frederick L. Manning to Sharpe, September 1, 1864, RG 108, entry 112; Babcock to Sharpe, September 1, 1864, RG 393, entry 3980.

52. Manning to Sharpe, September 6, 1864, RG 108, entry 112, box 1; Sharpe to Babcock, August 25, 1864, Babcock Papers; USG to Sheridan, September 6, 1864, *GP*, 12:133; Sharpe to Bowers, September 7, 1864, RG 108, entry 112, box 1; McEntee to Sharpe, *GP*, 12:133; Sheridan to USG, September 8, 1864, RG 393, entry 3980.

53. Early had nearly 14,000 men compared to Sheridan's 40,000. Gallagher, *Struggle for the Shenandoah*, 47; Wert, *Winchester to Cedar Creek*, 26, 30–31, 38–40; Sheridan, *Personal Memoirs*, 2:499–500; *PMUSG*, 2:327–28.

54. Rebecca Wright affidavit, Philip H. Sheridan Papers, LC; Wert, *Winchester to Cedar Creek*, 40–42; Sheridan, *Personal Memoirs*, 2:2–6.

55. Sheridan, *Personal Memoirs*, 5, 9; *PMUSG*, 2:328; Wert, *Winchester to Cedar Creek*, 43.

56. Report of James P. Simms, Kershaw's Division, December, 1864, *OR*, 43(1):589–90; Sheridan, *Personal Memoirs*, 2:11–32; Wert, *Winchester to Cedar Creek*, 47–116; USG to Sheridan, September 22, 1864, *GP*, 12:191; USG to Sheridan, September 23, 1864, *OR*, 43(2):152.

57. USG to Sheridan, August 26, 1864, *GP*, 12:96–97; Sheridan to USG, October 7, 1864, *OR*, 43(1):30–31; Sheridan to USG, November 27, 1864, *OR*, 43(1):37–38; Wert, *Winchester to Cedar Creek*, 167–72.

58. For a detailed examination of Grant's "Fifth Offensive," see Sommers, *Richmond Redeemed*.

59. Wert, *Winchester to Cedar Creek*, 134; Dowdey and Manarin, *Wartime Papers of Robert E. Lee*, 847–50; Babcock to Sharpe, September 30, 1864, RG 393, entry 3980; Leet to USG, October 2, 1864, RG 108, entry 112; Early, *War Memoirs*, 435; USG to Halleck, September 30, 1864, *GP*, 12:242; Sommers, *Richmond Redeemed*, 421.

60. Wert, *Winchester to Cedar Creek*, 161–66; Sheridan to Halleck, October 16, 1864, *OR*, 43(2):386. For the intercepted dispatch, see Brown, *The Signal Corps*, 213; *PMUSG*, 2:338; and Sheridan, *Personal Memoirs*, 62–65.

61. Wert, *Winchester to Cedar Creek*, 177–238; Gallagher, *Struggle for the Shenandoah*, 33–39, 67–74.

62. Early, *War Memoirs*, 462–63; Sheridan, *Personal Memoirs*, 2:115–16; Sheridan, "Activities in the Shenandoah," RG 108, entry 32, box 9; Wert, *Winchester to Cedar Creek*, 250–51.

63. Wert, *Winchester to Cedar Creek*, 10. Kershaw's subsequent battlefield performance lends credence to Wert's view. See Dowdey and Manarin, *Wartime Papers of Robert E. Lee*, 847–50, 853–63; and Sommers, *Richmond Redeemed*, 421–22.

10. "He Could Not Send Off Any Large Body without My Knowing It"

1. For an example, see Sharpe to Bowers, February 6, 1865, RG 393, entry 3980, NARA; and Babcock to Meade, January 15, 1865, OR, 46(2):134–35.

2. Catton, *Grant Takes Command*, 296; PMUSG, 2:308; USG to Butler, July 18, 1864, GP, 11:275.

3. Catton, *Grant Takes Command*, 318–20; Ruth to Stanton, December 21, 1865, box 2, William S. Hillyer Papers, UVL; USG to Meade, July 25, 1864, GP, 11:313–14.

4. USG to Halleck, July 26, 1864, GP, 11:317; Babcock to Humphreys, July 26, 1864, OR, 40(3):459; USG to Meade, July 26, 1864, GP, 11:322.

5. USG to Halleck, July 28, 1864, GP, 11:332–31; Babcock to Humphreys, July 28, 1864, OR, 40(3):556; Winfield S. Hancock to Meade, July 28, 1864, OR, 40(3):561–62; Sharpe to Rawlins, July 29, 1864, RG 108, entry 112, NARA; Humphreys to Warren, July 29, 1864, OR, 40(3):605. See also USG to Halleck, July 30, 1864, GP, 11:345.

6. USG to Halleck, August 1, 1864, GP, 11:361.

7. Catton, *Grant Takes Command*, 351, 366–67; Sheridan, *Personal Memoirs*, 2:98; Dowdey and Manarin, *Wartime Papers of Robert E. Lee*, 868; Sharpe to Bowers, November 18, 1864, RG 108, entry 112; Rawlins to USG, November 20, 1864, GP, 13:13–14; Rawlins to Sheridan, November 18, 1864, John A. Rawlins Papers, Chicago Historical Society; Sharpe to Babcock, November 20, 1864, RG 393, entry 3980; USG to Sheridan, December 9, 1864, GP, 13:95; USG to Sheridan, December 10, 1864, GP, 13:110.

8. Sharpe to Bowers, March 19, 1865, RG 108, entry 112.

9. Van Lew message, March 15, [1865,] RG 393, entry 3980; Van Lew message, n.d.; and Sharpe to Bowers, February 8, 1865, RG 108, entry 112; message of unidentified Richmond agent, n.d., RG 393, entry 3980; Sharpe to Bowers, March 31, 1865; Sharpe to Bowers, September 7, 1864; and McEntee to Bowers, December 19, 1864, RG 108, entry 112.

10. Special Orders No. 82, August 28, 1864, GP, 13:435; Sharpe to Bowers, February 27, 1865, RG 393, entry 3980.

11. USG to Sherman, March 16, 1865, *GP*, 14:174; Sharpe to Bowers, February 23, 1864, RG 108, entry 112, box 1.

12. Sharpe to Bowers, February 23, 1864, RG 108, entry 112, box 1.

13. USG to Stanton, March 2, 1865, *GP*, 14:83, 82; USG to Sherman, March 16, 1865, *GP*, 14:175.

14. Trudeau, *Last Citadel*, 330–54; Ruth to Stanton, December 21, 1865, box 2, Hillyer Papers;USG to Sherman, March 16, 1865, *GP*, 14:175; USG to Sherman, March 22, 1865, *GP*, 14:203; USG to Meade, March 24, 1865, *GP*, 14:211–14; USG to Sheridan, March 21, 1865, *GP*, 14:196; Dana to USG, March 21, 1865, *OR*, 46(3):62; Sharpe to Bowers, March 24, 1865; and Sharpe to Bowers, March 26, 1865, RG 108, entry 112; *PMUSG*, 2:430.

15. USG to Stanton, June 20, 1865, *GP*, 15:198–99; Catton, *Grant Takes Command*, 444–45.

16. USG to Meade, April 2, 1865, *GP*, 14:315–16; Catton, *Grant Takes Command*, 449–50; USG to Sherman, April 3, 1865, *GP*, 14:339; USG to Sheridan, April 3, 1865, *GP*, 14:336; USG to Sheridan, April 4, 1865, *GP*, 14:344.

17. Catton, *Grant Takes Command*, 450–53.

18. Starr, *Union Cavalry*, 2:463–73; Catton, *Grant Takes Command*, 453–54.

19. Starr, *Union Cavalry*, 2:477–82.

20. Sharpe to Bowers, April 20, 1865, *OR*, 46(3):852.

Epilogue: "The Difference in War Is Full Twenty Five Per Cent"

1. Quoted in Wilson, *Under the Old Flag*, 2:17.

2. Napoleon quoted in Michael I. Handel, "Strategic Surprise: The Politics of Intelligence and the Management of Uncertainty," in Maurer et al., *Intelligence*, 265; Simpson and Berlin, *Sherman's Civil War*, 733.

3. Quoted in Simpson, *Ulysses S. Grant*, 458.

BIBLIOGRAPHY

MANUSCRIPT COLLECTIONS

Chicago Historical Society (Chicago IL)
    John A. Rawlins Papers
    Army of the Potomac File
Huntington Library (San Marino CA)
    Joseph Hooker Papers
Illinois State Historical Library (Springfield)
    Richard J. Oglesby Papers
    William S. Rowley Papers
    Wallace-Dickey Papers
Indiana State Historical Society (Indianapolis)
    Lew Wallace Collection
Indiana State Library (Indianapolis)
    Benjamin Wilson Smith Papers
Library of Congress (Washington DC)
    John C. Babcock Papers
    Cyrus B. Comstock Papers
    Abraham Lincoln Papers
    Philip H. Sheridan Papers
Library of Virginia (Richmond)
    William Fay Papers
    Thomas McNiven Papers
National Archives and Records Administration (Washington DC)
    RG 15, Records of the Veterans Administration (Pension Office)
        Charles S. Bell Pension Record
        Horace Bell Pension Record
        Charles De Arnaud Pension Record
        Levi H. Naron Pension Record
        Lorain Ruggles Pension Record
    RG 107, Records of the Office of the Secretary of War, Letters Received
    RG 108, Headquarters of the Army
    RG 110, Records of the Provost Marshal General's Bureau
    RG 217, Records of the General Accounting Office
    RG 393, Records of the U.S. Army Continental Commands, Part 1
New York Public Library (New York)
    Elizabeth Van Lew Papers

Rice University (Houston TX)
  Don Carlos Buell Papers
  Jubal Anderson Early Papers
Southern Historical Collection (Chapel Hill NC)
  Bureau of Information File, Miscellaneous Civil War Papers
State Historical Society of Iowa (Des Moines)
  Grenville M. Dodge Papers
University of Virginia Library (Charlottesville)
  William S. Hillyer Papers
Virginia State Historical Society (Richmond)
  Elizabeth Van Lew Papers

PUBLISHED PRIMARY SOURCES

Agassiz, George R., ed. *Meade's Headquarters, 1863–1865: Letters of Colonel Theodore Lyman from the Wilderness to Appomattox.* Boston: Atlantic Monthly Press, 1922.

Badeau, Adam. *Military History of General Ulysses S. Grant, from April, 1861 to April, 1865.* New York: D. Appleton, 1881.

Brown, J. Willard. *The Signal Corps, U.S.A., in the War of the Rebellion.* 1896. Reprint, New York: Arno Press, 1974.

Buel, C. C., and R. U. Johnson, eds. *Battles and Leaders of the Civil War.* 4 vols. New York: Thomas Yoseloff, 1887–88.

Chandler, David G., ed. *The Military Maxims of Napoleon.* New York: Macmillan, 1987.

Clausewitz, Carl von. *On War.* Edited and translated by Michael Howard and Peter Paret. Princeton: Princeton University Press, 1976.

Dana, Charles A. *Recollections of the Civil War.* New York: D. Appleton, 1898.

Dodge, Grenville M. "Personal Recollections of General Grant, and His Campaigns in the West." In Military Order of the Loyal Legion of the United States, New York Commandery, *Personal Recollections of the War of the Rebellion.* 3d series. Garden City NY: Doubleday, 1907.

Dowdey, Clifford, and Louis H. Manarin, eds. *The Wartime Papers of Robert E. Lee.* 1961. Reprint, New York: DaCapo, 1987.

Downs, E. C. *Four Years a Scout and Spy.* Zanesville OH: Hugh Dunne, 1866.

Early, Jubal A. *War Memoirs: Autobiographical Sketch and Narrative of the War between the States.* Edited by Frank E. Vandiver. Bloomington: Indiana University Press, 1960.

Fitch, John. *Annals of the Army of the Cumberland.* Philadelphia: J. B. Lippincott, 1864.

Freeman, Douglas S. *Lee's Dispatches: Unpublished Letters of General Robert E. Lee, C.S.A., to Jefferson Davis.* New York: G. P. Putnam's Sons, 1915.

Graf, Leroy, and Ralph W. Haskins, eds. *The Papers of Andrew Johnson.* 11 vols. to date. Knoxville: University of Tennessee Press, 1976–.

Grant, Frederick D. "A Boy's Experience at Vicksburg." In *Personal Recollections of the War of the Rebellion,* edited by A. Noel Blakeman. New York: G. P. Putnam's Sons, 1907.

———. "Address by Gen. Frederick D. Grant." *Report of the Proceedings of the Society of the Army of the Tennessee, 1909–1911.* Cincinnati: Charles O. Ebel, 1913.

Grant, Ulysses S. *Personal Memoirs of U. S. Grant.* 2 vols. New York: Charles L. Webster and Sons, 1885.

Hitchcock, Ethan Allen. *Fifty Years in Camp and Field: Diary of Major-General Ethan Allen Hitchcock, U.S.A.* Edited by W. A. Croffut. Freeport NY: Books for Library Press, 1909.

Humphreys, Andrew A. *The Virginia Campaign of '64 and '65.* New York: Charles Scribner's Sons, 1883.

Johns, George S. *Philip Henson: The Southern Union Spy.* St. Louis: Nixon-Jones Printing, 1887.

Jomini, Antoine Henri. *The Art of War.* Translated by G. H. Mendell and W. P. Craighill. 1862. Reprint, Westport CT: Greenwood Press, 1971.

Mahan, Dennis Hart. *An Elementary Treatise on Advanced Guard, Outpost, and Detachment Service of Troops.* New York: Wiley and Putnam, 1847.

Meade, George G., ed. *The Life and Letters of George Gordon Meade.* 2 vols. New York: Charles Scribner's Sons, 1913.

Papers of the Military Historical Society of Massachusetts 15 vols. 1881–1918. Reprint, Wilmington NC: Broadfoot, 1990.

Porter, Horace. *Campaigning with Grant.* Edited by Wayne C. Temple. New York: Bonanza Books, 1961.

[Ruggles, C. Lorain]. *The Great American Scout and Spy, "General Bunker."* New York: Olmsted, 1870.

Ryan, David D., ed. *A Yankee Spy in Richmond: The Civil War Diary of "Crazy Bet" Van Lew.* Mechanicsburg PA: Stackpole Books, 1996.

Sheridan, Philip H. *Personal Memoirs of P. H. Sheridan.* 2 vols. New York: Charles L. Webster, 1888.

Sherman, William T. *Memoirs of General William T. Sherman.* 1875. Reprint, New York: DaCapo Press, 1984.

Simon, John Y., ed. *The Papers of Ulysses S. Grant.* 24 vols. to date. Carbondale IL: Southern Illinois University Press, 1967–.

Stanton, Donal J.; Goodwin F. Berquist; and Paul C. Bowers, eds. *The Civil War Reminiscences of General M. Jeff Thompson.* Dayton OH: Morningside, 1988.

U.S. Congress. *House Reports of Committees.* 37th Cong., 2d sess., 1861. H. Doc. 108, part 3.

————. *Report of the Joint Committee on the Conduct of the War.* 3 vols. Washington DC: Government Printing Office, 1865.

————. House of Representatives. *Samuel Ruth, W. F. E. Lohman, and Charles Carter.* H. Rept. 792, 43d Cong., 1st sess., 1874. Serial 1627.

————. *F. W. E. Lohman, Samuel Ruth, Deceased, and Charles M. Carter.* H. Rept. 823, 44th Cong., 1st sess., 1876. Serial 1716.

U.S. General Service Schools. *Fort Henry and Fort Donelson Campaigns, February 1862: Source Book.* Ft. Leavenworth KS: General Service School, 1923.

U.S. War Department. *Official Records of the Union and Confederate Navies in the War of the Rebellion.* 30 vols. Washington DC: Government Printing Office, 1894–1922.

————. *The War of the Rebellion: Official Records of the Union and Confederate Armies.* 128 vols. Washington DC: Government Printing Office, 1880–1901.

Wallace, Isabel. *Life and Letters of W. H. L. Wallace.* Chicago: R. R. Donnelley and Sons, 1909.

Wallace, Lew. *Lew Wallace: An Autobiography.* 2 vols. New York: Harper and Brothers, 1906.

Wills, Charles W. *Army Life of an Illinois Soldier.* Edited by Mary E. Kellogg. Washington DC: Globe Printing, 1906.

Wilson, James H. *The Life of John A. Rawlins.* New York: Neale, 1916.

————. "A Staff Officer's Journal of the Vicksburg Campaign, April 30 to July 4, 1863." *Journal of the Military Service Institution of the United States* 43 (July 1908): 93–109, 261–75.

————. *Under the Old Flag.* 2 vols. New York: D. Appleton, 1912.

Woolworth, Solomon. *The Mississippi Scout.* Chicago: [n.p.], 1868.

NEWSPAPERS

Chicago Tribune
Illinois State Journal
National Tribune
New York Ledger

SECONDARY SOURCES

Alexander, Augustus W. *Grant as a Soldier.* St. Louis: published by author, 1887.

Ambrose, Stephen. *Halleck: Lincoln's Chief of Staff.* Baton Rouge: Louisiana State University Press, 1962.

————. "The Union Command System and the Donelson Campaign." *Military Affairs* 24 (summer 1960): 78–86.

Andrews, J. Cutler. *The North Reports the Civil War.* Pittsburg: University of Pittsburg Press, 1955.

Ballard, Michael B. *Pemberton: A Biography.* Jackson: University Press of Mississippi, 1991.

Bauer, K. Jack. *The Mexican War, 1846–1848.* 1974. Reprint, Lincoln: University of Nebraska Press, 1992.

———. *Zachary Taylor: Soldier, Planter, Statesman of the Old Southwest.* Baton Rouge: Louisiana State University Press, 1985.

Bearss, Edwin C. *Decision in Mississippi: Mississippi's Important Role in the War between the States.* Jackson: Commission on the War between the States, 1962.

———. *The Vicksburg Campaign.* 3 vols. Dayton OH: Morningside, 1985–86.

Beymer, William Gilmore. *On Hazardous Service: Scouts and Spies of the North and South.* New York: Harper and Brothers, 1912.

Bradford, James C., ed. *Captains of the Old Steam Navy.* Annapolis MD: U.S. Naval Institute Press, 1986.

Caruso, A. Brooke. *The Mexican Spy Company: United States Covert Operations in Mexico, 1845–1848.* Jefferson NC: McFarland, 1991.

Castel, Albert. *General Sterling Price and the Civil War in the West.* Baton Rouge: Louisiana State University Press, 1968.

———. "Samuel Ruth: Union Spy." *Civil War Times Illustrated* (February 1976): 36–44.

Catton, Bruce. *Grant Moves South.* Boston: Little, Brown, 1960.

———. *Grant Takes Command.* Boston: Little, Brown, 1968.

Cohen, Eliot, and John Gooch. *Military Misfortunes: The Anatomy of Failure in War.* New York: Free Press, 1990.

Conger, Arthur. L. "Fort Donelson." *Military Historian and Economist* 1 (January 1916): 33–62.

———. *The Rise of U. S. Grant.* New York: Century, 1931.

Connelly, Thomas L. *Army of the Heartland: The Army of Tennessee, 1861–1862.* Baton Rouge: Louisiana State University Press, 1967.

———. *Autumn of Glory: The Army of Tennessee, 1862–1865.* Baton Rouge: Louisiana State University Press, 1971.

Cooling, Benjamin Franklin. *Forts Henry and Donelson: The Keys to the Confederate Heartland.* Knoxville: University of Tennessee Press, 1987.

———. *Jubal Early's Raid on Washington, 1864.* Baltimore: Nautical and Aviation Publishing, 1989.

———. *Symbol, Sword, and Shield: Defending Washington during the Civil War.* Hamden CT: Archon Books, 1975.

Cozzens, Peter. *The Darkest Days of the War: The Battles of Iuka and Corinth.* Chapel Hill: University of North Carolina Press, 1997.

———. *The Shipwreck of Their Hopes: The Battles for Chattanooga.* Urbana: University of Illinois Press, 1994.

Dearth, Douglas H., ed. *Strategic Intelligence: Theory and Application.* Carlisle Barracks PA: U.S. Army War College, 1991.

Dupuy, Trevor N.; David L. Bongard; and Richard C. Anderson Jr. *Hitler's Last Gamble: The Battle of the Bulge, December 1944–January 1945.* New York: HarperCollins, 1994.

Feis, William B. "Charles S. Bell, Union Scout." *North & South* 4 (June 2001) 26–37.

————. "The Deception of Braxton Bragg: The Tullahoma Campaign, June 23–July 4, 1863." *Blue & Gray* 10 (October 1992): 10–21, 46–53.

————. "Finding the Enemy: The Role of Military Intelligence in the Campaigns of Ulysses S. Grant, 1861–1865." Ph.D. diss., Ohio State University, 1997.

————. "Grant and the Belmont Campaign: A Study in Intelligence and Command." In *The Art of Command in the Civil War,* edited by Steven E. Woodworth. Lincoln: University of Nebraska Press, 1998.

————. "'He Don't Care a Damn for What the Enemy Does Out of His Sight': A Perspective on U. S. Grant and Military Intelligence," *North & South* 1 (January 1998): 68–72, 74–81.

————. "A Military Intelligence Failure: Jubal Early's Raid, June12–July 14, 1864." *Civil War History* 36 (September 1990): 209–25.

————. "Neutralizing the Valley: The Role of Military Intelligence in the Defeat of Jubal Early's Army of the Valley, 1864–1865." *Civil War History* 39 (September 1993): 199–215.

Fellman, Michael. *Citizen Sherman: A Life of William Tecumseh Sherman.* New York: Random House, 1995.

Ferris, John, and Michael I. Handel. "Clausewitz, Intelligence, Uncertainty, and the Art of Command." *Intelligence and National Security* 10 (January 1995): 1–58.

Fishel, Edwin C. "The Mythology of Civil War Intelligence." *Civil War History* 10 (December 1964): 344–67.

————. *The Secret War for the Union: The Untold Story of Military Intelligence in the Civil War.* New York: Houghton Mifflin, 1996.

Fleming, Walter L. *Civil War and Reconstruction in Alabama.* New York: Columbia University Press, 1905.

Frank, Joseph Allen, and George A. Reaves, *Seeing the Elephant: Raw Recruits at the Battle of Shiloh.* Westport CT: Greenwood Press, 1989.

Fuller, J. F. C. *The Generalship of Ulysses S. Grant.* 1929. Reprint, New York: DaCapo Press, 1991.

Furgurson, Ernest. *Ashes of Glory: Richmond at War.* New York: Alfred A. Knopf, 1996.

Gallagher, Gary W., ed. *Struggle for the Shenandoah: Essays on the 1864 Valley Campaign.* Kent OH: Kent State University Press, 1991.

Granger, J. T. *A Brief Biographical Sketch of the Life of Major-General Grenville M. Dodge*. New York: Ayer, 1893.

Hagerman, Edward. *The American Civil War and the Origins of Modern Warfare: Ideas, Organization, and Field Command*. Bloomington: Indiana University Press, 1988.

Handel, Michael I. *War, Strategy, and Intelligence*. London: Frank Cass, 1989.

Hartje, Robert G. *Van Dorn: The Life and Times of a Confederate General*. Nashville: Vanderbilt University Press, 1967.

Hattaway, Herman, and Archer Jones. *How the North Won: A Military History of the Civil War*. Urbana: University of Illinois Press, 1983.

Hine, Robert V. *In the Shadow of Fremont: Edward Kern and the Art of Exploration, 1845–1860*. Norman: University of Oklahoma Press, 1981.

Hirshson, Stanley P. *Grenville M. Dodge: Soldier, Politician, Railroad Pioneer*. Bloomington: Indiana University Press, 1967.

Hitchcock, Lt. Col. Walter T., ed. *The Intelligence Revolution: A Historical Perspective*. Washington DC: Office of Air Force History, 1991.

Hoole, William Stanley. *Alabama Tories: The First Alabama Cavalry, U.S.A., 1862–1865*. Tuscaloosa AL: Confederate Publishing, 1960.

Hughes, Nathaniel Cheairs, Jr. *The Battle of Belmont: Grant Strikes South*. Chapel Hill: University of North Carolina Press, 1991.

———. *General William J. Hardee, Old Reliable*. Baton Rouge: Louisiana State University Press, 1965.

Hughes, Nathaniel Cheairs, Jr., and Roy P. Stonesifer Jr. *The Life and Wars of Gideon J. Pillow*. Chapel Hill: University of North Carolina Press, 1993.

Johnston, Angus J. "Disloyalty on Confederate Railroads in Virginia." *Virginia Magazine of History and Biography* 63 (October 1955): 418–22.

Jones, Archer. *Civil War Command and Strategy: The Process of Victory and Defeat*. New York: Free Press, 1992.

Jorgensen, Jay A. "Scouting for Ulysses S. Grant: The 5th Ohio Cavalry in the Shiloh Campaign." *Civil War Regiments* 4 (1995): 44–77.

Kurtz, Henry I. "The Battle of Belmont." *Civil War Times Illustrated* 3 (June 1963): 18–24.

Lamers, William M. *Edge of Glory: A Biography of General William S. Rosecrans*. New York: Harcourt, Brace, 1961.

Lewis, Lloyd. *Captain Sam Grant*. Boston: Little, Brown, 1950.

Long, E. B. "The Paducah Affair: Bloodless Action That Altered the War in the Mississippi Valley." *Register of the Kentucky Historical Society* (October 1972): 253–76.

Lonn, Ella. *Desertion during the Civil War*. New York: Century, 1928.

Losson, Christopher. *Tennessee's Forgotten Warriors: Frank Cheatham and His Confederate Division*. Knoxville: University of Tennessee Press, 1989.

Luvaas, Jay. "Napoleon on the Art of Command." *Parameters* 15 (summer 1985): 30–36.

Marshall-Cornwall, James. *Grant as Military Commander.* New York: Van Nostrand Reinhold, 1970.

Marszalek, John F. *Sherman: A Soldier's Passion for Order.* New York: Free Press, 1993.

Matter, William D. *If It Takes All Summer: The Battle of Spotsylvania.* Chapel Hill: University of North Carolina Press, 1988.

Maurer, Alfred; Marion Tunstall; and James Keagle, eds. *Intelligence: Policy and Process.* Boulder CO: Westview, 1985.

McDonough, James Lee. *Shiloh: In Hell before Night.* Knoxville: University of Tennessee Press, 1977.

McFeely, William S. *Grant: A Biography.* New York: W. W. Norton, 1981.

McGhee, James E. "The Neophyte General: U. S. Grant and the Belmont Campaign." *Missouri Historical Review* 67 (July 1973): 465–83.

McWhiney, Grady. *Southerners and Other Americans.* New York: Basic Books, 1973.

Miller, J. Michael. "Strike Them a Blow: Lee vs. Grant on the North Anna." *Blue & Gray* 10 (April 1993): 13–22, 44–55.

Milligan, John D. *Gunboats down the Mississippi.* Annapolis MD: U.S. Naval Institute Press, 1965.

Monaghan, Jay. *Swamp Fox of the Confederacy: The Life and Military Services of M. Jeff Thompson.* Tuscaloosa AL: Confederate Publishing, 1956.

Moore, Wilton P. "Union Army Provost Marshals in the Eastern Theater." *Military Affairs* 26 (fall 1962): 120–26.

Mullen, Jay Carlton. "The Turning of Columbus." *Register of the Kentucky Historical Society* 64 (July 1966): 209–25.

Nettesheim, Maj. Daniel D. "Topographical Intelligence and the American Civil War." Master's thesis, U.S. Army Command and General Staff College, 1978.

Parks, Joseph H. *General Leonidas Polk, C.S.A.: The Fighting Bishop.* Baton Rouge: Louisiana State University Press, 1962.

Peavey, James Dudley, ed. *Confederate Scout: Virginia's Frank Stringfellow.* Onancock VA: Eastern Shore, 1956.

Perkins, J. R. *Trails, Rails, and War: The Life of General G. M. Dodge.* Indianapolis: Bobbs-Merrill, 1929.

Randall, James G. "The Newspaper Problem in Its Bearing upon Military Secrecy during the Civil War." *American Historical Review* 23 (January 1918): 303–23.

Reid, Brian Holden. "Another Look at Grant's Crossing of the James, 1864." *Civil War History* 39 (December 1993): 291–316.

Rhea, Gordon C. *The Battle of the Wilderness, May 5–6, 1864.* Baton Rouge: Louisiana State University Press, 1994.

————. *The Battles for Spotsylvania Court House and the Road to Yellow Tavern, May 7–12, 1864.* Baton Rouge: Louisiana State University Press, 1997.

————. *To the North Anna River: Grant and Lee, May 13–25, 1864.* Baton Rouge: Louisiana State University Press, 2000.

Ripley, C. Peter. "Prelude to Donelson: Grant's January 1862 March into Kentucky." *Register of the Kentucky Historical Society* 68 (October 1970): 311–18.

Roland, Charles P. *Albert Sidney Johnston: Soldier of Three Republics.* Austin: University of Texas Press, 1964.

Rolle, Andrew. *John Charles Fremont: Character as Destiny.* Norman: University of Oklahoma Press, 1991.

Ryan, David D. "Thomas McNiven: Scotsman, Baker, Union Spy." *Civil War* 62 (June 1997): 34–37.

Schmidt, Lt. Col. C. T. "G-2, Army of the Potomac." *Military Review* 28 (July 1948): 45–56.

Shiman, Philip Lewis. "Engineering Sherman's March: Army Engineers and the Management of Modern War." Ph.D. diss., Duke University, 1991.

Simon, John Y. "Grant at Belmont." *Military Affairs* 45 (December 1981): 161–66.

Simon, John Y., and David L. Wilson, eds. *Ulysses S. Grant: Essays and Documents.* Carbondale: Southern Illinois University Press, 1981.

Simpson, Brooks D. *Ulysses S. Grant: Triumph over Adversity, 1822–1865.* New York: Houghton Mifflin, 2000.

Simpson, Brooks D., and Jean V. Berlin, eds. *Sherman's Civil War: Selected Correspondence of William T. Sherman, 1860–1865.* Chapel Hill: University of North Carolina Press, 1999.

Smith, George Gardner, ed. *Spencer Kellogg Brown: His Life in Kansas and His Death as a Spy, 1842–1863.* New York: D. Appleton, 1903.

Smith, George Winston, and Charles Judah, eds. *Chronicles of the Gringos: The U.S. Army in the Mexican War, 1846–1848.* Albuquerque: University of New Mexico Press, 1968.

Sommers, Richard. *Richmond Redeemed: The Siege at Petersburg.* New York: Doubleday, 1981.

Sparks, David S. "General Patrick's Progress: Intelligence and Security in the Army of the Potomac." *Civil War History* 10 (December 1964): 371–84.

————, ed. *Inside Lincoln's Army: The Diary of Marsena Rudolph Patrick, Provost Marshal General, Army of the Potomac.* New York: Thomas Yoseloff, 1964.

Starr, Stephen V. *The Union Cavalry in the Civil War.* 3 vols. Baton Rouge: Louisiana State University Press, 1979–85.

Steere, Edward. *The Wilderness Campaign: The Meeting of Grant and Lee.* 1960. Reprint, Mechanicsburg PA: Stackpole, 1994.

Stephenson, Richard W., comp. *Civil War Maps: An Annotated List of Maps and Atlases in the Library of Congress.* Washington DC: Library of Congress, 1989.

Stewart, John Craig. *The Governors of Alabama*. Gretna LA: Pelican, 1975.

Still, William N., Jr. *Iron Afloat: The Story of Confederate Armorclads*. Columbia: University of South Carolina Press, 1971.

Stuart, Meriwether. "Colonel Ulric Dahlgren and Richmond's Union Underground." *Virginia Magazine of History and Biography* 72 (April 1964): 152–204.

———. "Samuel Ruth and General R. E. Lee: Disloyalty and the Line of Supply to Fredericksburg, 1862–1863." *Virginia Magazine of History and Biography* 71 (January 1963): 35–109.

Sword, Wiley. *Mountains Touched with Fire: Chattanooga Besieged*. New York: St. Martin's Press, 1995.

———. *Shiloh: Bloody April*. New York: William Morrow, 1974.

Symonds, Craig L. "General Patrick's Progress: Intelligence and Security in the Army of the Potomac." *Civil War History* 10 (December 1964): 371–84.

———. *Joseph E. Johnston: A Civil War Biography*. New York: W. W. Norton, 1992.

Traas, Adrian G. *From the Golden Gate to Mexico City: The U.S. Army Topographical Engineers in the Mexican War, 1846–1848*. Washington DC: Government Printing Office, 1993.

Tremain, Henry Edwin. *Last Hours of Sheridan's Cavalry*. New York: Bonnell, Silver, and Bowers, 1904.

Trudeau, Noah Andre. *The Last Citadel: Petersburg, Virginia, June 1864–April 1865*. Boston: Little, Brown, 1991.

Turkoly-Joczik, Robert L. "Fremont and the Western Department." *Missouri Historical Review* 82 (July 1988): 359–67.

Van Creveld, Martin. *Command in War*. Cambridge MA: Harvard University Press, 1985.

Vandiver, Frank E. *Jubal's Raid: General Early's Famous Attack on Washington in 1864*. New York: McGraw-Hill, 1960.

Wallace, Harold Lew. "Lew Wallace's March to Shiloh Revisited." *Indiana Magazine of History* 59 (March 1963): 19–30.

Welcher, Frank J. *The Union Army, 1861–1865: Organization and Operations*. 2 vols. Bloomington: Indiana University Press, 1989–93.

Wert, Jeffry D. *From Winchester to Cedar Creek: The Shenandoah Campaign of 1864*. Carlisle PA: South Mountain Press, 1987.

Williams, Kenneth P. *Lincoln Finds A General: A Military Study of the Civil War*. 5 vols. New York: Macmillan, 1949–58.

Wills, Brian Steel. *A Battle from the Start: The Life of Nathan Bedford Forrest*. New York: HarperCollins, 1992.

Wohlstetter, Roberta. *Pearl Harbor: Warning and Decision*. Stanford CA: Stanford University Press, 1962.

Woodworth, Steven E. "'The Indeterminate Quantities': Jefferson Davis, Leonidas Polk, and the End of Kentucky Neutrality, September 1861." *Civil War History* 38 (December 1992): 289–97.

———. *Jefferson Davis and His Generals: The Failure of Confederate Command in the West.* Lawrence: University Press of Kansas, 1990.

———. *Six Armies in Tennessee: The Chickamauga and Chattanooga Campaigns.* Lincoln: University of Nebraska Press, 1998.

Woolfolk, Sarah V. "George E. Spencer: A Carpetbagger in Alabama." *Alabama Review* 19 (January 1966): 41–52.

INDEX

Page references in italic type refer to photographs.

Valley, 221, 229, 230, 231, 243; intelligence viewed by, 267; and Pittsburg Landing, 102, 109, 111; and Rosecrans' intelligence operations, 110

Hamilton, Charles S., 126; and Dodge, 142, 290 n.4; at Grand Junction TN, 124; and Grant's offensive against Vicksburg, 125; intelligence work of, 112, 118–19, 123, 131; Naron retained by, 286 n.23

Hampton, Wade, 222

Hampton Roads Peace Conference, 258

Hancock, Winfield S., 210, 229, 231, 254, 256

Handel, Michael I., 6

Hardee, William J., in Columbus KY, 40; at Corinth, 87; Grant's intelligence on, 16–17, 19, 24, 39, 40, 41; Ironton attack planned by, 16–17; in northern Arkansas, 30

Harris, Thomas, 13, 14, 24

Hennessey, William, 162–63, 164

Hickman KY, 19, 21, 23, 30, 32

Hill, A. P., 223, 229, 233, 241, 256

Hillyer, William S., 19, 55, 129–30

Hitchcock, Ethan Allen, 7, 8–9

Hogan, Martin, 304 n.38

Holly Springs: 132, 204; evacuation of, 124–25; Grant's intelligence on, 119, 134–35, 289 n.57; initiative substituted for intelligence at, 137, 267–68; Van Dorn at, 134

Hooker, Joseph H., 188; and the BMI, 196; and the "cracker line," 180, 181; at Lookout Mountain, 183, 186–87

Houts, Henry, 16

Howard, Oliver O., 297 n.17

HUMINT (human intelligence), 4

Humphreys, Andrew A., 205, 207

Humphries, Joseph, 304 n.38

Hunter, David, 214, 230; in the Shenandoah Valley, 222, 225, 227, 228, 232; and views on intelligence, 227

Hurlbut, Stephen: 89, 121; and Charles S. Bell, 161, 292–93 n.25, 295 n.46; and the financing of Dodge's secret service, 129–30; intelligence forwarded by, 142, 144, 166, 290 n.4; intelligence on Vicksburg provided by, 167–68; at Pittsburg Landing, 90, 94, 100

information, defined, 3–4

"information maps," 112

intelligence: and accuracy, 4–5; analysis of, 4; in Civil War, 3–4, 13; Grant's views on, 267, 268; military, defined, 3; reliability of, 15–16; signals and noise in, 102; sources of, 4–5, 271 n.2; and strategic calculation, 104; three responses to, 6; and timeliness, 5

Ironton MO, 16–17

Iuka MS, 119, 120, 137

Jackson, Thomas J. "Stonewall," 222

Jefferson City MO, 17–18

Jessie Scouts, 15, 56, 57–58, 89

Johnson, Andrew, 34

Johnson, Bushrod Rust, 70, 73

Johnston, Albert Sidney, 57; Buell's intelligence on, 86, 87; at Corinth, 84, 87, 91, 99, 283 n.33; in Decatur AL, 80; and Forts Henry and Donelson, 71, 72, 73, 74, 79; Grant's intelligence on, 38, 41, 42, 80–81, 84; and Kentucky, 34, 35, 40, 58; Pillow ordered to northern Tennessee by, 43; at Pittsburgh Landing, 79, 93–94, 95, 99–100, 101–2, 104

Johnston, Joseph E.: at Big Black River, 172–73, 174; Dodge's intelligence on, 167; and Grant's campaign on Vicksburg, 163, 164; Grant's intelligence on, 124, 161, 162, 164–66, 168–69, 170–72, 173, 293 n.26, 295 n.46; Lee's plans to join, 262; Pemberton abandoned by, 171; pursued by Sherman, 173; and Vicksburg, 161, 162, 165

Jomini, Antoine Henri, 3

Jones, Samuel, 296 n.6

Kentucky, 19–20, 23, 29, 33

Kern, Edward M., 15

Kershaw, Joseph B., 249; Grant's intelligence on, 243, 244, 245, 247, 248; recalled to Richmond, 246, 257; returns to Lee, 245; and the Shenandoah Valley, 242–43, 247

Kilpatrick, Judson, 238, 304 n.38

Kimball, Nathan, 169

Knight, Judson, 304 n.35
Knoxville TN, 180, 188

Laws, Tom, 245
Lee, Fitzhugh, 242
Lee, Robert E., 151, 189, 249; Babcock's in-
telligence on, 197; deserters viewed as information problem by, 198–99; and
Early, 233–34, 245, 246; and Grant's
crossing the James River, 215–16; and
Grant's 1864 campaign plan, 193, 196;
Grant's intelligence on, 198, 201–2, 203,
206, 207, 208–9, 216–17, 225, 229, 230,
233, 243, 256, 261–63; interpreted by
Grant, 211–15, 217, 221, 226, 261, 301 n.38;
legendary audacity of, 217, 226; and
Meade's Mine Run campaign, 205; in the
Mexican War, 8; and Petersburg, 216,
217, 262; and Richmond, 196, 213, 216,
222–23, 225, 229, 262; and the Shenandoah Valley, 221, 222, 242, 243–44, 246–
47; at Spotsylvania, 210–11, 211–12;
surprise attack on Fort Stedman, 261;
surrender of, 264
Leet, George K., 236, 242
Lellyett, John, 34, 58, 66
Lexington, 21, 31, 66
Libby Prison (Richmond), 238
Lincoln, Abraham, 30, 214; Grant pressured by, 181; and reelection bid, 233;
Rosecrans described by, 177; warned
about Early, 230
Lohman, F. W. E., 237, 240–41
Longstreet, James, 193; at Chattanooga, 177,
183, 184, 185; and Early's planted infor-
mation, 247; Grant's intelligence on, 182,
201, 203, 204–5, 206, 209, 233, 247, 256;
and Knoxville, 188; and the Shenandoah
Valley, 242
Loring, William W., 164, 168
Lynchburg VA, 228–29

Mahan, Dennis Hart, 3
Mainard, Mary, 167
Malone, Mary, 167, 294 n.40
Marsh, C. Carroll, 15–16

Marszalek, John, 102
Mayfield KY, 34, 35
"McBirney, Mr." (Union Scout), 170–71
McCardle, Peter, 163, 164
McClellan, George B., 197; Buell's friend-
ship with, 58; and Columbus KY, 60, 61;
and Forts Henry and Donelson, 65, 68,
71, 72; intelligence viewed by, 206–7,
267
McClernand, John, 46, 58; and the assault
on Fort Henry, 66–67, 68, 279 n. 24; and
Columbus KY, 61, 62, 63, 73; and Ed-
ward's Depot, 161, 162; and Grant's attack
on Fort Donelson, 70, 71; and Grant's
Vicksburg campaign, 144, 145, 146, 158,
160, 161; intelligence work at Pittsburg
Landing, 89, 90; and Port Gibson, 159
McCord, Benjamin F., 227, 236
McCown, John P., 111, 170
McCulloch, Ben, 17, 18
McEntee, John, 152, 154, 203, 236; and
Army of the Potomac, 235; and the BMI,
153, 197, 199–200; and intelligence in the
Shenandoah Valley, 226–28, 229–30;
and intelligence on Kershaw, 244; and
intelligence on Sherman, 259; and the
move across the James, 225; at Norfolk
VA, 259; and payment for Richmond
agents, 238; and the raid on Richmond
prisons, 239, 304 n.38; and Union desert-
ers, 259
McGee, Ebenezer, 236
McGee, Sanford, 236
McKeever, Chauncey, 45
McNiven, Thomas ("Quaker"), 237, 237–
38, 239, 241, 304 n.35, 304–5 n.40
McPherson, James B., 98, 161, 162; at Grand
Junction TN, 124; and Grant's campaign
on Vicksburg, 125, 160, 163; intelligence
work of, 124–25; and Port Gibson, 159
McWhiney, Grady, 7
Meade, George G., 150, 256; and Army of
the Potomac, 193; and the BMI, 150, 197,
225, 235, 268; and Grant's 1864 campaign
plan, 193, 196; and intelligence in the
Shenandoah Valley, 229; and intelligence

man, 259; Lee's veterans processed by, 264; and the move across the James, 225; payment to Richmond agents, 237–38, 304 n.35

Shenandoah Valley: Grant's intelligence on, 228–30, 242, 243–44, 268; and Lee, 221, 222, 243; as natural invasion corridor, 221–22; under Union control, 246; viewed by Grant, 222

Sheridan, Philip H., 206, 210, 215, 257; and Early, 234, 243, 244–45, 246–48, 258, 306 n.53; and Grant's 1864 campaign plan, 214; and intelligence on Kershaw, 244; intelligence system created by, 241–42, 248–49; intelligence viewed by, 113; and Lee, 211, 216, 262, 263; raid on railroads north of Richmond, 254, 256; and the Shenandoah Valley, 222, 242

"Sheridan's Scouts," 242

Sherman, William Tecumseh, 259; and the Army of the Tennessee, 177; in central Kentucky, 40; and Chattanooga, 145, 181, 183, 185, 186, 187, 188; at Chickasaw Bluffs, 135–36, 145; on Corinth, 91–92; entrenchments viewed by, 82, 91; on Grant, 10, 25, 267, 268; and Grant's 1864 campaign plan, 193; and Grant's campaign on Vicksburg, 125, 132, 141, 146, 158, 160, 163, 165, 172; and Grant's plan to take Fort Donelson, 72; intelligence work of, 40, 81, 82, 86, 90, 110, 113, 119, 124, 125; Johnston pursued by, 173; and Missionary Ridge, 187, 188; at Pittsburg Landing, 81, 82–83, 89, 90, 92, 94, 96, 97–98, 100, 102

Shiloh, Battle of. See Corinth MS; Pittsburg Landing TN

Sigel, Franz, 203, 214, 230; driven out of Harpers Ferry by Early, 232; and the Shenandoah Valley, 193, 212, 227; and views on intelligence, 227

"signals" (in intelligence analysis), 102

Silver, Isaac, 201, 236, 239, 243, 244

Simon, John Y., 48

Smith, Charles F.: and the Belmont attack, 44, 45–46, 49, 52; and Corinth, 85; and Grant's attack on Fort Donelson, 70, 71,

72; intelligence work of, 62–63, 73, 81–82, 84, 86, 279 n. 19; in Kentucky, 30, 33, 37, 38, 41, 42–43, 61

Smith, Edmund Kirby, 111

Smith, William F., 177, 181, 182, 183, 223

Smith, William Hugh, 128–29

Sommers, Richard, 249

Southside Railroad, 253, 257

Special Orders Number Eighty-two, 259

spies: defined, 4; fate of, 5, 16; payment of, 166–67; recruited by Grant, 15; women among, 167

Spotsylvania VA, 209; Battle of, 212

St. Louis MO, 30

Stanton, Edwin M., 169, 177, 203, 209, 213, 230

Starr, Stephen Z., 89

Steele, Frederick, 144

Stevenson, Carter L., 145, 181; at Chattanooga, 186, 187, 188; Grant's intelligence on, 137, 182; in Vicksburg, 136–37

Streight, Abel D., 146

Stuart, "Jeb," 210

Swisher, Jake, 304 n.38

Sword, Wiley, 188

Tappan, James C., 43

Taylor, W. H. H., 92, 93

Taylor, Zachary, 7, 8, 10

Thomas, George H., 177, 296 n.3; and Chattanooga, 181, 182–83, 184–86, 187, 188, 297 n.9

Thompson, M. Jeff: decreasing threat posed by, 55; at Fredericktown, 39–40, 41; Grant's intelligence on, 35, 37–38, 51; and Grant's motivations for attacking Belmont, 45, 47, 49, 50, 276 n.42; in Missouri, 18–19, 30, 43

Truesdail, William, 178

Trussel (Union Scout), 295 n.51

Tyler, 21, 31

Union City TN, 33–34

Unionists, Southern: in Missouri, 15–16; in Tennessee, 166

Union League, 226

U.S. Army Topographical Engineers, 112